Mastering Stress 2001

A LifeStyle Approach

David H. Barlow, Ph.D.
Boston University

Ronald M. Rapee, Ph.D.
Macquarie University, Australia

Leslie C. Reisner, Ph.D.
Los Angeles

Written requests for permission to make copies of any part of this publication should be addressed to:

Permission Department
American Health Publishing Company
P.O. Box 610430, Department 10
Dallas, Texas 75261-0430
Facsimile: 1–817–545–2211

Library of Congress
ISBN 1–878513-37-0

Address orders to:

The LifeStyle Company™	In Dallas	1–817–545–4500
P.O. Box 610430, Department 70	Toll Free	1–888–LEARN–41
Dallas, Texas 75261–0430	Facsimile	1–817–545–2211
Internet address	www.TheLifeStyleCompany.com	
E-mail address:	LEARN@TheLifeStyleCompany.com	

Acknowledgments

We are grateful to the following colleagues for their significant academic contributions to this manual. Their invaluable support helped make this manual a reality. They are:

Kelly D. Brownell, Ph.D., Professor of Psychology, Professor of Epidemiology and Public Health, Director of the Yale Center for Eating and Weight Disorders, Yale University, New Haven Connecticut.

David Hager, M.B.A., Publisher of American Health Publishing Company, Executive Director of The LEARN Institute for LifeStyle Management, and President of the American Association of LifeStyle Counselors, Dallas, Texas.

Finally, a special thanks to our family and friends for their continued support and encouragement.

Table of Contents

Introduction and Orientation Lesson

Congratulations! By picking up this manual, you have taken an important first step in reducing the stress in your life. We hope you are as excited as we are about this novel program that you are beginning. The Mastering Stress Program combines our many years of research and clinical experience to bring you the best science has to offer in stress management.

Our Welcome

We hope you are looking forward to the journey you are about to begin. We have put together a program that is easy to follow, scientifically sound, safe, and effective. You already may be doing things in your life to help manage your stress. If you are, that's great! We will give you even more useful tools for managing stress. Imagine this program as a journey through a hardware store collecting valuable tools. The more tools a carpenter has, the more tasks and problems the carpenter can manage. You will have a toolbox filled with helpful stress management tools after completing this program.

Think of your journey as a working partnership. We will be right here, working with you along every step of the way. As partners, we will be here to cheer you on and pat you on the back as you succeed. And, we'll be right here to encourage and support you when times are more difficult. Trust and rely on the information in this manual. Read it and reread it regularly until it becomes second nature. Highlight sentences and sections that are important for you, and write notes in the margins. Use this manual as a workbook. If you experience a particularly difficult day, go back to a section that was helpful and work on it again. Use what you learn and learn what works best for you. Practice your skills daily.

Our Goal

This program is the result of many years of research and clinical experience. In recent years, researchers have learned more about stress than was known before. Our goal is to share this information with you in an upbeat, positive way that will help you master the stress in your life. Hundreds of people have used this program and are now using the tools they learned to cope with the stress in their daily lives.

"We live in a fast-paced world, and many people have come to accept high levels of stress as normal."

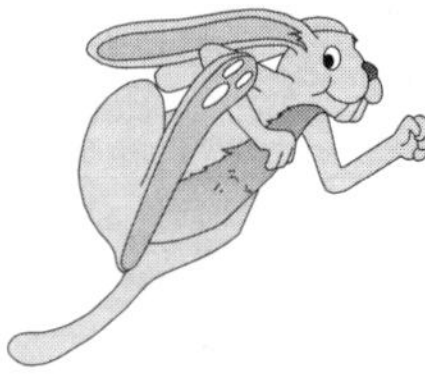

Stress is experienced by everyone. Our goal is not to eliminate the stress in your life, but to provide you with strategies that will enable you to reduce your stress to a manageable and healthy level. We have designed this program to be friendly and provide you with the essential skills for mastering stress. If you follow this program, it will work for you—now and in the future. We'll be right here working with you. Together, we will work toward reducing your stress.

High levels of stress may keep you from enjoying life. You may have tried other stress management programs in the past, yet certain events in life cause your stress levels to spiral out of control. If so, you're not alone. Because we live in a fast-paced world, many people have come to accept high levels of stress as normal. Although some stress is inevitable and even good, too much stress can be overwhelming and disabling. Our goal is to work with you as a team to help you learn the skills to master stress. In doing this, you will benefit from a happier, healthier, and less stressful life. So, without further delay, let us begin our stress management journey together by introducing you to Bob.

Meet Bob

Bob seemed to have it all. He was the classic success story. At the young age of 45, he owned a successful business, had a wonderful family, and lived in a beautiful new home. Bob was always striving for perfection, but it was making him miserable. Although he worked later and later each night at the office, he never seemed to get enough done. When he finally arrived home after work, his head would be pounding. Bob yelled at his kids so often that they began to shy away from him. He had difficulty focusing and felt drained at the end of each day. Nothing made Bob happy—not his business, not his family, not his new BMW sports car, and least of all, himself. Each day seemed to bring new irritations. One day, Bob suddenly looked around and realized that he was hurting everything and everyone that mattered to him. He was suffering from too much stress, and it was ruining his life.

Bob is not alone. Stress is the most common problem people face in today's busy world. You can't see it, hear it, touch it, or smell it. Yet, stress can threaten both your physical health and psychological well-being.

If you are at all like Bob, stress may be getting in the way of your enjoyment of life. Whether you are fighting perfectionism, taking on too much, or worrying about things you can't control, you are waging your own battle with stress.

Throughout this program, you will meet several people like Bob who are battling their own issues of stress. Our purpose in introducing them to you is twofold. First, it is important to realize that you are not alone. Second, learning from others' experiences can help you learn new ways to manage your own stress.

The Importance of Managing Stress

People react to stress in different ways. No matter how you currently react to stress, you can learn to master the stress in your life. Picking up this book was your first step toward that goal. As you journey through this program, you will learn important stress management techniques. For example, you will learn:

- How to identify the stressors in your life
- Techniques to help you relax
- Techniques that will help you be more assertive
- How to think more realistically
- How to better manage your time

When you finish this program, you will feel calmer and more in control of your life. Let's now turn our attention to understanding the basics of stress.

The Basics of Stress

Simply put, stress is a state of readiness. It is the mind and body's way of rising to an occasion and preparing you to do your best. Stress is a natural and necessary response—one experienced by all humans and even animals. However, too much stress can be harmful.

Stress is not—we repeat, *not*—a mental illness. Just as people's heights vary from short to tall, people's everyday stress levels vary from relaxed to "stressed out." Stress, no matter how extreme, will never make you "go crazy."

We all experience stress in different ways. What is stressful to one person may be challenging to another. Not all stress is bad. In fact, all of us need some stress in our lives to challenge and motivate us. Stress causes problems, however, when we are overstressed and unable to manage stressful situations. We cannot eliminate all stress, nor would we want to. Stress is part of being alive. The goal is to learn how to master it.

It may seem silly to state why we want to manage stress, but sometimes even the obvious must be addressed. This is especially true because stress often is considered "chic" in our fast-paced society. A common thought may go something like this, "I'm stressed and successful. If you're not stressed, how can you possibly be successful?"

The physical and mental responses that create stress are useful if they happen occasionally and in moderation. However, if

"What is stressful to one person may be challenging to another."

"Experiencing high levels of stress for long periods of time can affect your health."

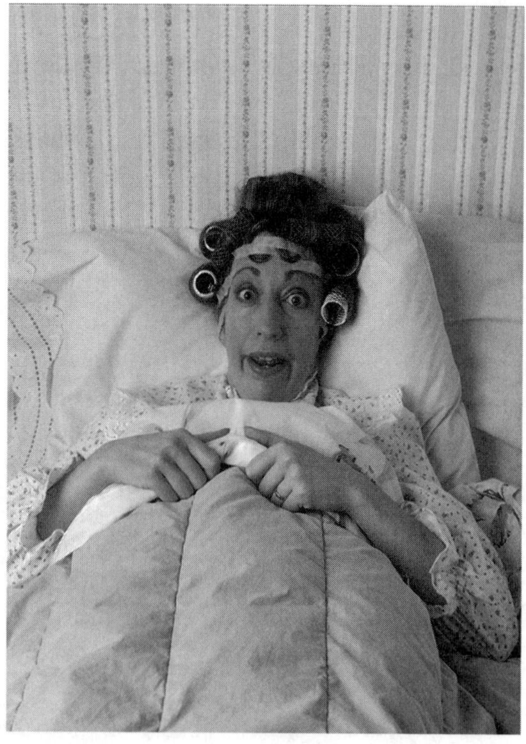

they happen all the time, they can have unpleasant effects.

Experiencing high levels of stress for long periods of time can cause you to lose sleep, feel fatigued, have trouble concentrating, and respond irritably to those around you. Prolonged stress can also lead to harmful "coping" behaviors such as putting things off and using substances to relieve stress. Also, too much stress causes inefficient use of our precious energy reserves and keeps us from doing our best.

In addition to the emotional and behavioral consequences of being overstressed, our bodies can also suffer. Long-term stress also can cause headaches, skin irritations, ulcers, diarrhea, and pain at the base of the jaw (Temporomandibular Joint Syndrome or TMJ). Too much stress can interfere with sexual function, inhibiting both desire and ability. Research also shows that long-term stress may significantly increase your chances of later developing heart disease, high blood pressure, diabetes, or immune system problems.

Although this list may look intimidating, you should not add to your stress by worrying about health problems. Being highly stressed does not mean that you will get these diseases. However, you may increase your susceptibility to these diseases over time. Clearly, managing your stress can have important health benefits, both mentally and physically.

Remember, it would be unrealistic and undesirable to eliminate all the stress in your life. Your goal is to become the master of your stress and not allow stress to control your life and behaviors. Our job is to help you achieve this goal. To this end, we will help you put together a toolbox of helpful stress management techniques. If you follow this program, work hard, and practice, these tools will last you a lifetime.

Your First Exercise

Finding the motivation to do a challenging task is sometimes difficult. Staying motivated can be even more difficult. Right now your motivation to work hard in a stress management program may be high. What will your motivation be like a week, a month, or a year from now? Although this is a 16-week stress management program, you will need to maintain and practice the skills you learn for a lifetime. Long-lasting stress management is not something you "go on" then "go off" after 16 weeks. Our focus here is making your new lifestyle habits permanent. As you change and the environment around you changes, you may need to try new techniques to keep your stress at a healthy level. But, you will need to practice continually and keep your skills ready to use when needed.

Before we go any further, we want you to stop and complete a simple exercise. This exercise is important, so take a few minutes and work through it carefully. You will refer to this exercise often throughout the program. Follow these three simple steps and complete this exercise before continuing on.

❶ Think about why you want to reduce the stress in your life. What is stress doing to the quality of your life? On the chart below, make a list of the negative effects in your life caused by stress. Maybe you lie awake at night worrying about everything you have to do, bicker with your spouse, or make careless errors at work. Examine your life honestly, and write down the negatives caused by stress.

❷ Think about how your life will improve once you have mastered stress. Maybe you will have fewer headaches, less trouble with that nervous stomach, or worry less about finances. Perhaps you will be able to sit down and enjoy relaxing with friends without worrying about how much you have to do. In the right-hand column of the chart below, list the positive effects you hope to experience when you have gained control over the stress in your life.

❸ Make a copy of your chart and place it in a prominent place, perhaps on the refrigerator or near your bed. When you find your motivation slipping, look at the chart, and think of the positive benefits you are working toward.

Negative Effects in My Life Caused by Stress	Positive Effects in My Life When I've Mastered My Stress
1	1
2	2
3	3
4	4
5	5
6	6

"Your first exercise."

By completing this exercise, you have begun to address your own motives and reasoning for beginning a stress management program. Now, we are going to take a much closer look at the notion of readiness and its effect on program success.

Is the Time Right for You?

People begin stress management programs for many reasons. Some begin a program because their spouse, employer, or physician asked them to. Others may feel overwhelmed and decide it's time to do something about their stress. Learning the skills to master stress takes time. It requires changing many lifelong habits. This calls for learning new skills and practicing them until you consistently apply them to your daily life. Many people struggle with the decision of whether or not to begin a program. Perhaps a more important question is *when* to begin a stress management program. We call this "readiness."

If you begin a program when the time is right, you will have the best possible chance of completing the program successfully. Starting a program when conditions are not ideal may result in your quitting the program, increasing your stress, and more importantly, thinking of yourself as a failure.

"The chances for success are better when the conditions are right."

Consider the hot-air balloonist. If he begins his voyage around the world when the weather is poor or his equipment is not ready, his chances of success are poor. On the other hand, if the balloonist starts his journey when the weather conditions are ideal and his equipment is in tip-top condition, his chances of success are much better. The same can be said for beginning a stress management program. Ultimately, you are the best person to decide when to begin a program. But, we can help you decide if the time is right for you.

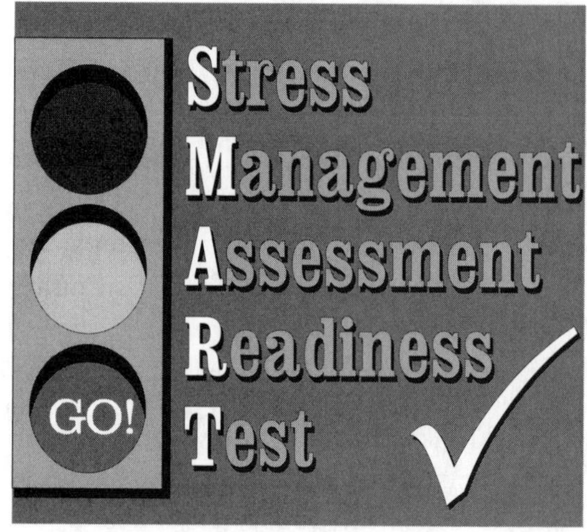

The first thing you need to do is ask yourself whether you are ready for the rigors of a stress management program. Consider how motivated you feel. What are your reasons for wanting to begin a program at this time? In Appendix A, beginning on page 405, we discuss stress management readiness and provide the Stress Management Assessment and Readiness Test (SMART). This tool gives you some guidelines for deciding if now is a good time for you to begin a program. The SMART will help you identify important factors when assessing your stress management skills and readiness. Take some time now and turn to page 405 to read through this important information on stress management readiness.

A Word About Motivation and Commitment

You are the only person who can change your stress level. The Mastering Stress Program can help, but the motivation and the time must come from you. You will be rewarded for your hard work and commitment to this program. People who have completed this program report that they are enjoying life more, and their friends and family enjoy being with them more.

In the lessons that follow, you will be learning new skills—new ways of thinking, acting, and organizing your life. The key term you will hear repeatedly is "practice." If you practice these skills, we are confident you will learn to master your stress. For most people, the benefits of starting a program far exceed the costs, such as time and changing behavior. We will now examine this concept more closely.

Weighing the Benefits and Costs

Consider the benefits and costs of starting a stress management program. Think about how your life will improve once you have learned to manage stress. Perhaps you will feel more relaxed, be able to sleep more restfully at night, improve your relationships with others, or be able to focus more clearly at work. Maybe you will be able to enjoy your free time with your family and friends without worrying about what you should be doing.

Considering the costs of starting a program is also important. For example, managing stress requires a commitment to self-monitoring that will take time out of your already busy schedule. You will need to set aside time each week to read this manual, fill out worksheets and forms, review your progress, plan your time, and

"Consider the benefits and costs of starting a stress management program."

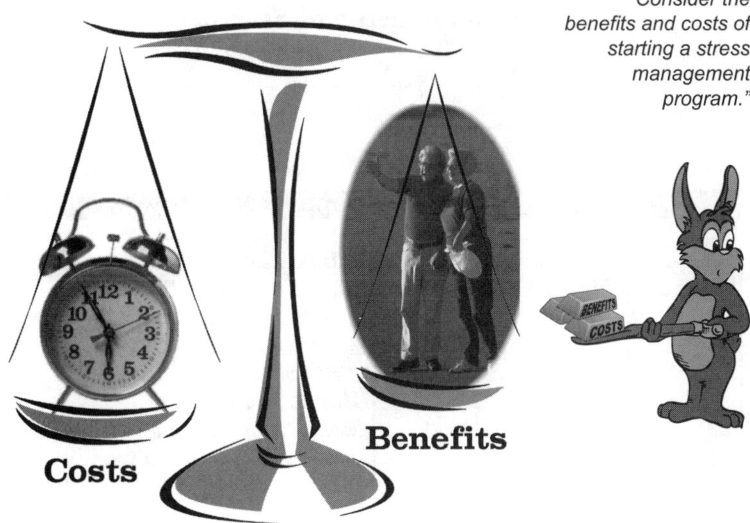

practice relaxation techniques. In addition, when you begin to address your stress triggers more assertively, friends, family members, and colleagues may ask why your behaviors have changed. Sometimes, these changes can initially create more stress.

Weighing the benefits and costs of starting a stress management program may help you measure your motivation. Below are examples from two individuals contemplating beginning a stress management program.

Meet John and Janet

On page 8, we provide examples from two individuals who are thinking about starting a stress management program. John wants to reduce the stress he feels to get everything on his list done each day. He also feels stress when his wife asks him to spend more time with the children. Janet spends a lot of time worrying whether she will be able to meet her boss's demands. She is tired of worrying and being upset all the time.

John and Janet weighed the costs and benefits of starting a program and came to

Costs and Benefits of Starting a Stress Management Program

John's Example

Costs	Benefits
Time to read this manual	Better relationship with wife
May challenge relationships by saying "no"	Spend more time with children
	Will be more effective with tasks
	Reducing stress will improve my health
	I'll be happier
	Improve my time management skills
	More self-confidence in my work

Janet's Example

Costs	Benefits
Time spent to read this manual	Reduce my worrying
Spend less time with my friends	Spend more time with children
Keeping self-monitoring records	Will be more effective with tasks
Hard work involved in learning new skills	Reducing stress will improve my health
Practicing relaxation	I'll be happier
Worrying about keeping up with a program	Improve my time management skills
	More self-confidence in my work

different decisions. For John, the list of benefits far outweighed the costs. He concluded that his motivation was high to begin a stress management program. For Janet, the decision was much different. She decided not to begin a program right now because the costs to her at this point outweighed the benefits. Weighing the costs and benefits of beginning a program helped Janet to admit that her motivation at this time in her life was not high. She was not discouraged, however. Janet was hopeful that by addressing her motivation she was much closer to starting and completing a program. About a year later, she was more motivated and successfully completed the Mastering Stress Program.

Let's look more closely at Janet's decision to wait. Was it a good or bad decision for her? Perhaps waiting increases the likelihood that she will be committed, motivated, and not resentful of the sacrifices she has to make to complete a program. Perhaps she had started programs in the past and later lost her motivation. Her decision to wait may have reduced the risk of another failed program.

Let's look at Janet's decision another way. Maybe she is telling herself that the time isn't right because the time isn't *perfect* for beginning a program. We know that certain times are better than others, but there's never a *perfect* time.

With the help of SMART, Janet may determine that her decision not to begin a program was based on her unrealistic expectations. In this instance, she may conclude, "This is not the perfect time for me to start, but a 'perfect' time may never exist. Perhaps I have just been putting off taking control of my stress." The SMART may also help Janet to see that the timing is sim-

Weighing the Costs and Benefits of Starting a Stress Management Program

Costs	Benefits

ply not right for her to begin a stress management program now. She may conclude, "I simply cannot commit the time right now to a program with all of the other things happening in my life." In this instance, her decision to wait was a good one.

Determining Your Benefits and Costs

Earlier, we asked you to explore the negative effects of stress and the positive effects of mastering your stress. We designed this exercise to help you see why it is important for you to address the stress in your life. Now that you have thought more about what you are losing by feeling stressed and what you will gain by learning how to better manage your stress, you are ready to move on.

You believe you need to manage your stress better, so the benefits are clear. Now, let's look at the real costs of starting a program. For example, if you already feel stressed and overworked, how will you respond to the new demand of self-monitoring your stress by filling out daily homework sheets? At first, learning new patterns of behavior may feel more stressful than keeping the older, more comfortable (though less healthy) ones. Take time now to identify the benefits and costs of starting a stress management program. List them on the worksheet provided on page 9. If the benefits on your list exceed the costs, this means that your motivation may be high and your chances of success are good. If the costs are greater than the benefits, you may want to explore ways to increase your motivation before starting a program.

A Bit about Expectations

Knowing what a stress management program can and cannot do for you is part of keeping expectations realistic from the start. The Mastering Stress Program teaches you skills to reduce your stress, not how to avoid stress altogether. Events such as divorce, death, and illness happen in life and add to your level of stress. Programs like this one will not make such problems disappear, but they can help you manage your reactions so that the stress does not control your life. If your expectations are reasonable and realistic from the start, you are less likely to become disappointed and give up. If, on the other hand, your expectations are unreasonably high and are unmet, you may become easily disappointed and quit the program.

Another part of realistic expectations is knowing that this program will require work. Every day, for the next few months, you will need to set aside time to read this manual, work through the lessons, monitor your stress and other behaviors, and practice the stress management techniques you learn. When the skills become part of your life, you won't have to work as hard. Remember, you are making changes that will become part of the way you live. As with many changes we make in life, at first they may seem more stressful than the old behaviors. In time, you will adjust to the new mind-set and behaviors and reap the rewards. Slow and steady progress is more likely to lead to lasting change. If you are patient and stay committed, change will follow.

Your Quality of Life

With many things in life, we tend to focus on a *single* result or *single* measure to assess change. This rarely, if ever, tells the whole story. We can measure progress in many ways. As you master the stress management technique we discuss in this program, your overall quality of life should improve. To help you track your progress, we have developed a Quality of Life Review. The first Quality of Life Review worksheet for you to complete is on page 11. Follow the directions on this simple worksheet and complete it now. You will refer to this worksheet in upcoming lessons. We will also ask you to complete this review several times during the program to see if the scores change. This will give you a clearer picture of how change comes in many different forms.

A Word on Medications

Although we will be talking about medications in a later lesson, we have a few words to share with you right now. Your doctor may have prescribed medication for you to help manage the uncomfortable feelings of stress. It is fine for you to continue taking this medication while working through the lessons in this program. You may also find that after completing this program you no longer need to take the medication. However, before you decide to stop taking or reduce your medication, you should talk to your physician.

About this Program

Although this program can help people deal with many feelings, it is not appropriate for every situation. If you are being treated for depression or anxiety, you should talk to your physician or mental-health professional before starting this program. If you determine that this program is right for you, here are some of the elements of the program you can look forward to in the weeks ahead.

This program consists of an Introduction Lesson, which you are reading now, followed by 16 weekly lessons and a Commencement Lesson. Most people complete one lesson each week, for a total of 16 weeks. Each lesson has a Knowledge Review and an assignment for the week. The review will help you assess whether you have mastered the key elements of the lesson. The weekly assignments will help you master the techniques discussed in the lessons.

Quality of Life Review

Please use the following scale to rate how satisfied you feel now about different aspects of your daily life. Choose any number from this list (1 to 9) and indicate your choice next to each numbered item below.

1 = Extremely Dissatisfied
2 = Very Dissatisfied
3 = Moderately Dissatisfied
4 = Somewhat Dissatisfied
5 = Neutral
6 = Somewhat Satisfied
7 = Moderately Satisfied
8 = Very Satisfied
9 = Extremely Satisfied

____ 1. Overall mood (feelings of sadness, anxiety, happiness, etc.)

____ 2. Sense of self-esteem

____ 3. Confidence, comfort in social situations

____ 4. Internal dialog (self-talk)

____ 5. Energy level

____ 6. Focus and concentration

____ 7. Ability to manage time

____ 8. Relationships

____ 9. General health

____ 10. Exercise and recreation

____ 11. Assertiveness skills

____ 12. Eating habits

____ 13. Overall quality of life

"The more you use your stress management tools, the better your skills and proficiency will become."

As we said before, life is full of unfortunate events—divorce, illness, death of a loved one—all of which can increase your stress. This program cannot cancel a divorce or bring someone you loved back to life. It can help you deal with your reactions to these situations so that stress does not control you—you become the master. The techniques you learn in this program can also help you find better solutions to other problems, such as the small, everyday hassles and burdens we all encounter.

Throughout the lessons, you will be practicing the techniques you have learned. Practice is crucial when you are trying to change old behaviors that have developed over many years. Change may seem hard at first. In time, these new habits will become part of your lifestyle. We have tested the principles in this program and have proof that they work. Hundreds of individuals are using these stress management tools to effectively manage their stress. These tools are not "magic cures," they are common sense techniques that work when they are practiced consistently. With regular practice, these techniques will help you make important lifestyle changes that will lead to greater health and an improved sense of well-being. The tools you gather as you go through this program will last you a lifetime if you practice and use them often. The more the carpenter uses his tools, the better his skills and proficiency become. The same holds for you. The more you use your stress management tools, the better your skills and proficiency will become.

Once again, welcome. When you're ready, turn to Lesson One and let's begin!

Lesson One

Welcome to Lesson One. Today you begin the Mastering Stress Program, which combines the best of what science and clinical practice have to offer. This is a lifestyle approach to stress management. By lifestyle, we mean it focuses on all aspects of living. Lifestyle is, after all, everything about the way we live. It embraces the most private thoughts we have in our minds and the behaviors we show to the outside world. Lifestyle is the interaction of our thoughts, feelings, behaviors, attitudes, goals, and personal values. It is the relationships among ourselves, our environment, and others.

The unique thoughts, feelings, and behaviors that most directly affect our level of stress are part of the greater fabric of lifestyle. We can no more focus on an individual's stressful behaviors than we can isolate a single thread in a tightly woven wool blanket, change that thread, and say we have a new blanket. Just as the blanket is made of all the interwoven threads—it consists of them all—so is the fabric of life and lifestyle. It is a complex interwoven fabric of all that we are. To change your level of stress, we must address the whole.

Throughout this program, we will introduce many stress management principles and techniques. Some, like diet and exercise, may seem odd to stress management, but they are key threads that make up who you are. We will work with you to help you find those techniques that work best for you. We'll suggest weekly assignments for you to practice that will help you become proficient at mastering your stress. Our intent is to make this program a working partnership. We are partners in this endeavor, so remember, you're not alone! Together, we can make this work and reduce the stress in your life.

The Mastering Stress Approach

We have developed this program to address many components of your life. This program is part of The LEARN LifeStyle Program Series™. The word LEARN is an acronym originally developed by Dr. Kelly D. Brownell of Yale University. It represents LifeStyle, Exercise, Attitudes, Relationships, and Nutrition. These components include the essential elements of

"The fabric of life is like the threads in a tightly woven wool blanket. To change your lifestyle you must address all of the threads of life."

stress management. Throughout each lesson in the Mastering Stress Program, we will focus on one or more of these important stress management components.

Although we are partners with you in this program, your role will be an active one. Each week you will read a new lesson and have homework assignments that include completing worksheets and forms. If you have difficulty with a particular lesson, it is fine to spend more than a week on that lesson—you're not running a timed marathon here. But, try not to let this be an excuse for you not to move on. If you spend two weeks on a lesson and are still having difficulty with the concepts, try moving on to the next lesson and coming back to the difficult material a little later.

Throughout this program, you will be trying many different techniques and new approaches to manage your stress. The exercises and assignments will help you practice the new techniques you have learned. It will be both exciting and challenging. So get ready to have fun, learn a lot, and work hard!

You may be using this program by yourself as a self-help program or with the assistance of a health professional in individual or group sessions. Although these sessions provide a great source of support, they should not be used in place of this manual. By using the manual, you can work at your own pace and at a time that works best in your schedule. You can refer to previous lessons in the manual and re-read them to better understand specific points. You may also have a specific need early on and may need to look ahead to a particular section. This is the beauty of using the Mastering Stress manual. Remember, use this manual as your personal road map to better manage your stress. Bend the corners of the pages, write in the margins, and highlight those sections that are important for you. Read the manual each week, and work diligently on the weekly assignments.

L LIFESTYLE
E EXERCISE
A ATTITUDES
R RELATIONSHIPS
N® NUTRITION

Working In Groups

The Mastering Stress Program is used throughout the world by health professionals counseling clients on stress management. You may be working with a health professional in either a group setting or in individual sessions. If you are a member of a group working with others who suffer from high levels of stress, you need to consider several important issues.

Being a member in a group can be a terrific experience. The group can offer individual members support, helpful ideas, encouragement, and many other positive benefits. To benefit from the group experience, each member must realize that cooperation and a team effort are important for the success of the group. As a member of a group, you have the opportunity to benefit from the group process. But, perhaps even more importantly, you have some key *responsibilities.* To help you better understand your responsibilities as a group member, we provide you with some helpful guidelines for you to follow.

In Appendix D on page 423, we give you some helpful guidelines for being a good group member. These guidelines were adapted from *The LEARN Program for Weight Management 2000*, by Kelly D. Brownell, Ph.D. of Yale University. If you are participating in a group program, take a few minutes now to read over these important guidelines. Seriously consider the advice in these guidelines. If you contribute and support the group, the group will support the other group members, including yourself. Group support and encouragement can be helpful in maintaining motivation and inspiration when times are tough. In addition, the group can often provide helpful suggestions for overcoming obstacles and roadblocks. Groups can also help you to remember that you are not the only person working on stress management issues.

"Being a member in a group can be a terrific experience."

A Word about Lifestyle Change

You now know that we view stress management as a process that includes changing thoughts, behaviors, and many other elements in your life. As we said before, this process includes more than just changing one specific area of your life—it embraces everything about you. For example, your job may be causing you a great deal of stress. Simply changing your job may or may not reduce your stress. You may need to address relationship issues, build your time management skills, learn some assertiveness techniques, increase your physical activity, or learn how to change your thoughts. By not addressing *all* lifestyle issues, you could find yourself in a vicious cycle of changing the wrong things and still feeling overstressed.

A lifestyle approach to stress management strives for a long-term solution to stress management—not a short-term fix.

"Visualization is a powerful tool that uses your creative imagination to help you see into the future—a future with less stress."

Lasting lifestyle change is not a quick fix, but it is, instead, an approach that involves establishing new habits and working hard to make them part of your daily life. By adopting a lifestyle approach, you will be developing new, sustaining behaviors. Can you visualize yourself emerging from this program a new person? Do you visualize yourself making *permanent* changes in your life to reduce stress? Let's spend a few moments talking about the importance of being able to visualize the "new" you.

Visualization

In the Introduction and Orientation Lesson, we talked about this program being a journey—a lifelong journey. Think back on journeys that you have taken before. Do you remember planning the journey in advance, visualizing where you would go and what you would do? Visualization is a powerful tool that uses your creative imagination to help you see into the future—a future with less stress. The way you imagine yourself or things to be often becomes reality. Philosophers have often said that all of your thoughts become your reality, and you are what you think you are. So, let's see how we can help you use this powerful tool in a positive way.

Through visualization, you practice "seeing" yourself acting or feeling less stressed. You must see and feel yourself achieving the results you desire in great detail, creating the scenario that will take you there, and practicing it over and over again. How will you get there? How will you feel once you are there? How are you going to maintain that positive feeling, behavior, or positive outlook? Remember, if you practice visualization regularly, it can be an effective way to change feelings and behaviors to more desirable ones.

The Mastering Stress Program is not something you will work on for 16 weeks and then stop. We designed it to help you make permanent changes in your life that will last a lifetime. Take a few moments and visualize how different your life will be in

My Vision of the New Me
1.
2.
3.
4.
5.

the future. Can you visualize yourself more relaxed and confident? If you're sedentary (i.e., inactive), can you visualize yourself being more physically active? Visualize yourself smiling more, laughing more, and being happier. See yourself setting aside time each day for yourself to learn, practice, and become a master at stress management skills. Do you visualize a different person than you see today? Will others see you differently? On the worksheet on the bottom of page 16, list five visualizations you have of the "new you" after you have learned to master your stress.

Keeping Records

One of the most important behaviors you will learn is keeping records. We cannot overemphasize the importance of record keeping. Throughout this program, you will be introduced to a variety of forms that will be helpful to you in changing key behaviors. Even if you dislike paperwork, don't ignore these forms. Those who keep good self-monitoring records do much better than those who do not. We will remind you often that keeping records is very important if you want the program to help you.

As mentioned earlier, we have developed many worksheets and forms for you to use in this program. Some of our clients enjoy the challenge of using all of the worksheets and forms we provide. Others do not. Don't feel compelled or stress yourself trying to complete all of the worksheets and forms. If you can do the worksheets without compounding your stress, that's terrific. We do encourage you, however, to at least give each worksheet and form a try to see how it works for you. You may not find a particular worksheet useful when we introduce it in the program. But, when a stressful event arises later, you may recall a worksheet or form that may help you through the stressful situation. Use the worksheets and forms as friendly helpers.

The first thing you will need is a folder or a three-ring binder in which to keep your forms. As you complete each recording form, file it in the folder. We will refer you back to many of these forms in later lessons. Also, from time to time, look over earlier forms to see how you have progressed. You are sure to be encouraged by your progress.

Why Record Keeping Is Important

Before we introduce your first monitoring forms, let's review some reasons why keeping accurate, detailed records is important.

❶ **Awareness.** Awareness is the key to changing lifelong habits. Most of our behaviors are automatic. We do them without thinking and are unaware of many of our long-established habits. Keeping records will help you become aware of your thoughts, feelings, and behaviors.

"Those who keep good self-monitoring records do much better than those who do not."

How much you learn about yourself by keeping good records will surprise you.

❷ **Staying motivated.** If you keep honest and accurate records, you are more likely to practice each technique as recommended. Even during a week's time of keeping records, you can see progress. You can give yourself credit for what you accomplish, and this can help motivate you to continue to work hard.

❸ **Learning skills.** Writing out the details in a structured way helps you to understand how each technique works and how it affects you. You will find this particularly true in the lessons on realistic thinking, where keeping good records is the key to learning this stress management skill. Try to imagine learning math skills without ever working a problem on paper—difficult, if not impossible. The same is true of stress management skills—you need to write them down and practice.

❹ **Identifying triggers.** The events in life that cause stress are known as "triggers," and they are different for everyone. Some of these triggers are life-changing events, and others are everyday occurrences, minor hassles that might not bother others but are stressful for you. Keeping records will help you to identify the triggers associated with higher levels of stress in your life. When you are unaware of your particular stressful triggers, your mind and body's responses can seem frightening and unexplainable. This can increase stress even more. Keeping records will help you identify your stress triggers, thus giving you a greater sense of control.

❺ **Learn how you respond.** It's difficult to know all about our own physical and emotional responses. For example, we may think that on any given day, we are either stressed or not—all or nothing. In fact, we experience many degrees of stress every day and respond to each one differently. Much of our response to stressful situations is just that, an automatic response, often without much thought. Learning how you respond to certain situations will help you become less reactive and more proactive in stressful situations—you become the master of your stress.

❻ **Increase control over your thoughts.** As we discuss in later lessons, most of our stress is the byproduct of our thoughts. Keeping track of your "automatic" thoughts will help you change those thoughts into less stressful ones.

In this lesson, we introduce two different monitoring forms. The first is the Daily Stress Record and the second is the Stress Change Worksheet. Before you begin to learn stress management techniques, you will need to learn more about how you react to stressful events. The forms in this lesson will help in this learning process. Let's look closely at each of these forms.

The Daily Stress Record

The Daily Stress Record is used to track your highest levels of daily stress. Feel free to make as many copies as you need of the Daily Stress Record on page 28. Every evening, sit down with the form and think back over your day. How stressful was it? Be sure to do this exercise every day and not just at the end of the week. Keep the form on your night stand or use another method to help you remember to complete the Daily Stress Record each evening. The following information will help you complete the Daily Stress Record accurately:

❶ In the first column, record the date.

❷ In the second column, record your average level of stress during the day. The "average level" means the overall, background level of stress you felt during the day as a whole. Was it a "good day" when you felt fairly relaxed most of the time? Was it a "bad day" when you were constantly tense, or did the day fall somewhere in between?

To help you measure your stress levels, you will be using the Stress Scale. This is a scale from 0 to 8, where 0 is no stress and 8 is extreme stress. We will be using this 0–8 scale at many points throughout the program. For now, it is important that you become familiar with it and practice assigning your responses to some point along the scale.

❸ In the third column, using the 0–8 scale, note the highest level of stress you experienced during the day. If nothing significant happened during the day and events did not stress you more than your average level, the numbers in the second and third columns may be the same. However, your stress level will likely have increased in response to at least a few things, small or large, that happened during the day. Using the 0–8 scale, write down the number that corresponds to your highest stress level of the day.

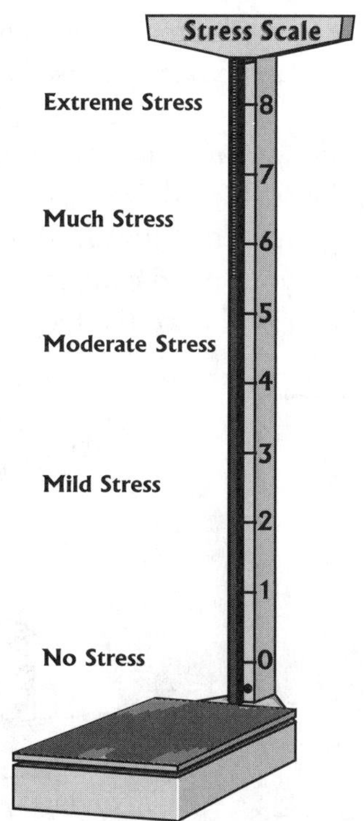

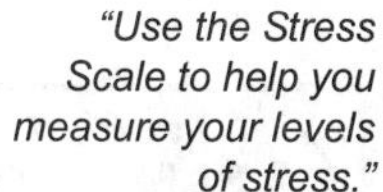

"Use the Stress Scale to help you measure your levels of stress."

❹ In the fourth column, write down the time at which you experienced the highest stress of the day. Patterns in this column may help you determine if there are certain times of the day that are more stressful than others. Discovering these patterns may help you better prepare for your high-stress situations.

❺ In the fifth and final column, write down the major stressful events that occurred during the day. This is the place to list the event or events responsible for the highest level of stress you listed in column three. The fifth column serves an important explanatory purpose. Say, for example, that you recorded your average stress level as 2 on Monday, but it rose to 5 on Tuesday. If you experienced a sudden rush of orders at work on Tuesday or returned home to find your cellar flooding, the increase in stress would be understandable. Unless you note the reasons on the form, however, you may not remember what caused your increased stress.

This points out an important purpose of the Daily Stress Record. It helps you gauge your feelings more realistically. When it comes to stress, your mind can play tricks on you. For example, how often have you said on Friday, "Boy, this was a terrible week?" Looking back at your Daily Stress Record, you may discover that only one day really went badly. In this way, record keeping can contribute to your peace of mind. We provide a sample Daily Stress Record on page 21.

At the end of the week, review your Daily Stress Record, and then identify the five stressors you experienced most often during that week. Write these five stressors in the space provided at the bottom of the Daily Stress Record titled "Stressors I Experienced Most Often." Once again, this self-monitoring will help you identify patterns to your stress.

You will be using the information you recorded on your Daily Stress Record to complete the next form, the Stress Change Worksheet.

The Stress Change Worksheet

As you progress through this program, you will want to keep track of your progress. Over the next several weeks, you should begin to notice a gradual drop in your level of stress. Again, remember that your mind can play tricks on you. You may not remember how you felt before the program, and you may not recognize your

Daily Stress Record—Lesson One

Name: *Jane's Example* **Week of:** *January 4, 2001*

Date	Average Stress Level	Highest Stress Level	Time of Highest Stress Level	Stressful Event Associated with Highest Stress Level
01-04	2	3	n/a	n/a
01-05	4	6	7:35 a.m.	Argument with wife, late for work
01-06	3	6	7:30 a.m.	Johnny sick at home
01-07	4	5	1:00 p.m.	Doctor's report Lost important file at work
01-08	4	4	5:30 p.m.	Traffic was terrible
01-09	5	8	10:30 a.m.	Parking ticket on the way to the gym
01-10	3	4	2:30 p.m.	Bought expensive gift for wife

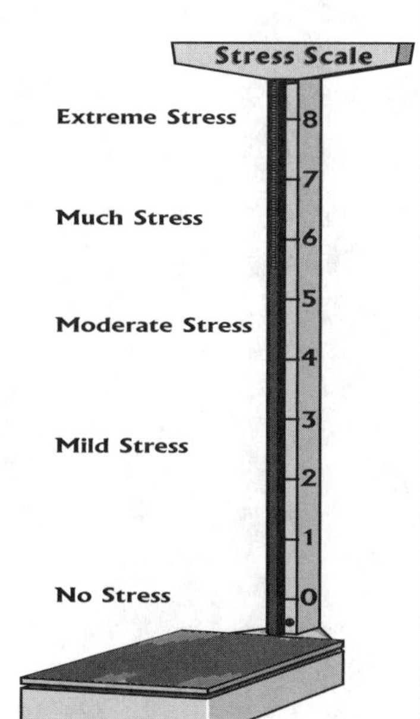

Stressors I Experience Most Often
1. Being late for work.
2. Heavy traffic.
3. Making a mistake at work.
4. Things that may make me miss work.
5. Not doing things perfectly.

Stress Change Worksheet

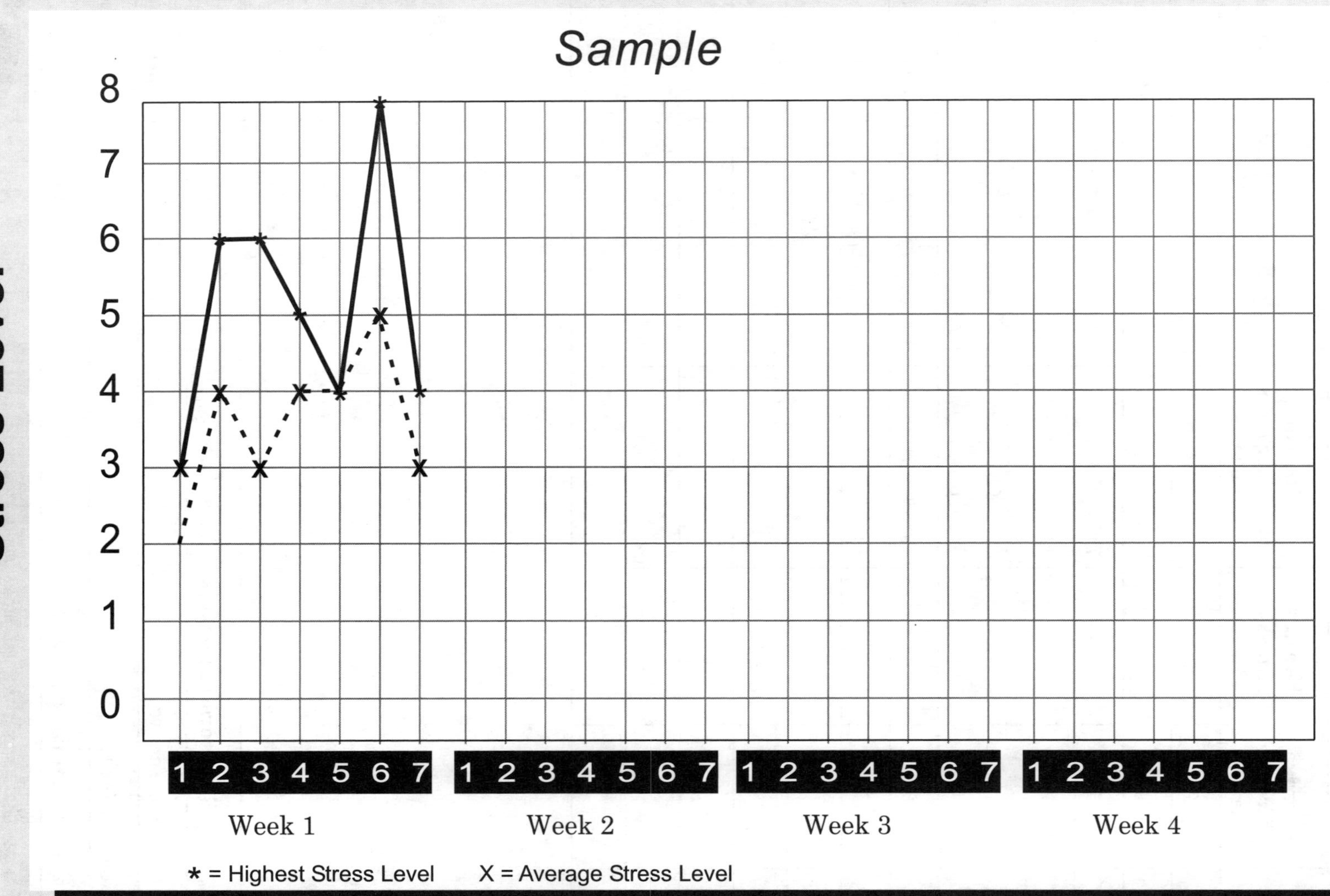

progress. This is again where record keeping can help.

On page 29, we provide you with a Stress Change Worksheet. The Stress Change Worksheet is a daily and weekly graph of changes in your stress level. At the end of each week, complete the Stress Change Worksheet by recording the Highest Stress Level and Average Stress Level from your Daily Stress Record. On page 22, we provide a sample Stress Change Worksheet from the sample Daily Stress Record on page 21.

By keeping a Stress Change Worksheet you can monitor your progress in the program. The facts are there before you, and no guess work is involved. The worksheet also enables you to see the natural ups and downs of the stress management process and gives a clear perspective of change. For instance, your stress level may be going down for weeks then, during week 5, it goes up and, during week 6, goes down again. The Stress Change Record helps you to see week 5 as just an exception and lets you take credit for the earlier changes. This can be a very helpful reality check for measuring progress when you are uncertain if you are making any changes. Post the worksheet in a place where you can see it each day—it can be a source of encouragement and motivation.

More on Motivation

As you begin the Mastering Stress Program, no doubt, your motivation is high. After all, you have just about completed your first lesson! As with any worthwhile endeavor, you will encounter peaks and valleys as you work through this program. At times, the weekly assignments will seem almost effortless, and you'll marvel at the progress you've made. Other times may be more challenging, and you may question whether you should continue. Let us say right up front, by all means, you should continue. Make yourself a promise (write it in the space above) that when times are challenging, you will continue with your program.

"Establishing techniques to help you stay motivated at the beginning of your program, when motivation is high, is important."

My Commitment to Continue

Even with the best intentions, you may still need help to keep the motivation going. We recommend self-control or reward techniques. Establishing techniques to help you stay motivated at the beginning of your program, when motivation is high, is important. These techniques will help you get through those inevitable times when you are challenged and motivation is lower. We divide these motivational techniques into social techniques and material techniques. You may want to experiment with each to see what works best for you. Let's look at each technique more closely.

Social Techniques

Social techniques involve enlisting the help of others. Others can help you with specific goals as you go through the pro-

"Social techniques involve enlisting the help of others."

gram or you may want to form a stress management partnership with another person. For example, to commit yourself socially, you could tell your friends and family that you are beginning a stress management program. You could ask them to discuss it with you and to encourage you from time to time.

You may enlist the support of one person to exercise with you regularly and another friend to discuss your thoughts or feelings. Better still, you could make a commitment with your spouse, significant other, or close friend that you will both follow the Mastering Stress Program. You can have them set aside time when both of you will talk about your progress. Moreover, each of you will have someone to turn to when times are difficult and you need encouragement. In Lesson Two, we'll give you some guidelines for deciding if a stress management partnership would work well for you.

Material Techniques

A second method of sticking with the program and reaching goals involves material rewards. These are more definite and concrete than the social techniques. For example, suppose you establish an exercise

My Social Techniques

____

____

____

____

____

____

____

____

My Material Techniques

____

____

____

____

____

____

____

____

goal of walking 30 minutes on Monday, Wednesday, Friday, and Saturday. When you make this commitment and your motivation is high, establish a self-reward system. You may want to put $50 in a jar and reward yourself each week that you reach your goal by taking $10 out and buying something special. On weeks that you do not reach your goal take $10 out and donate it to a charitable organization.

You may want to combine social and material techniques, perhaps by having a friend or relative issue the rewards. In the above example, you may agree to go walking with a friend. Give the $50 to your friend, and have him or her pay you if you reach your weekly goal, or if you don't reach your goal, donate the money to his or her favorite charity. This way, you can't cheat! You may be able to think of other creative ideas to help boost your motivation. It's better to do this now, when motivation is high, than wait until you get into trouble.

Self-control techniques may sound silly or childish, and in fact, they are no substitute for willpower. Still, during the course of long-term change, it is important to reinforce yourself along the way to maintain motivation. This helps ensure your ultimate success. In the spaces on page 24, list possible social and material techniques that you think may help you maintain motivation. We'll have you refer back to this list in future lessons.

Maximizing Your Success

Having almost completed Lesson One of the Mastering Stress Program, you are on your way to improving your quality of life. We conclude the first lesson by discussing some additional strategies for you to consider that may help maximize your success. Specifically, let's examine the benefits of enlisting the help and support of others.

"Sharing your plans to begin a stress management program with your family and friends can be helpful."

Friends and Family

Often, sharing your plans to begin a stress management program with your family and friends can be helpful. As we discussed earlier, those closest to you will be seeing you make changes in your life. So, take a minute or two to explain the program and answer any questions that they may have about it.

In discussing your program plans, you will be the best person to decide about how involved you want family and friends to be. You may just want them to know that you will be making changes in your life and they should be prepared for some changes in your routine. Also, you may want to let them know how they can best support your efforts. For example, you may find it helpful to ask for help with the chores or daily responsibilities. This may become easier to do after you learn how to better assert your wants and needs with those closest to you.

My Social Support Network

The People	How They Can Help

"Developing a social support network can help maximize your success."

Remember, you are involving others in your program to help you because you want to, not because you believe you have to.

Other Support

In addition to the work you will be doing on your own to reach your program goals, you may find it helpful to be part of a support group. Many find support groups helpful because they provide an opportunity to interact with others who may be dealing with similar issues. Remember, support groups aren't for everyone—ultimately, you must decide what works best for you.

Many individuals will find it helpful to turn to other professionals for additional support. As we discussed earlier, if you are feeling depressed or anxious, you may need to meet with a mental-health professional first. Then as a team, you can decide if beginning this program is appropriate as you address the other issues in your life. By dealing with these problems first, you are clearing the path to success. In the space above, list five possible sources of social support and how you believe each could help you with your stress management program.

Lesson Review

Congratulations! You have completed your first lesson and are now on your way to leading a less stressful life. We discussed several important "first steps" of your Mastering Stress Program in this lesson. We began by defining lifestyle and the importance of lifestyle in stress management. We discussed the importance of keeping good records and how those who keep records do better than those who do not. You'll hear us say this over and over again. We cannot emphasize enough, the importance of keeping good records! We introduced two records that you will be completing this week. If you do not complete these, we suggest you spend another week on this lesson and complete these before moving on to Lesson Two.

The Daily Stress Record should be completed at the end of each day. It is a record of your average stress and highest level of stress for each day. The Stress Change Worksheet is a graph of the changes in your daily stress level from week to week. This graph helps you keep the ups and downs of stress management in perspective by showing changes over time. Finally, we discussed techniques to help keep your motivation up as you go through the program. Self rewards and social support can be keys to success for some people.

This Week's Assignment

The assignment for this week is to begin monitoring your stress level by completing the Daily Stress Record. We provide you with a blank form that you may copy on page 28. Remember to do this at the end of each day. At the end of the week, plot this information on the Stress Change Worksheet for weeks 1–4 on page 29. Also at the end of the week, record the five stressors that you experienced most often during the week on your Daily Stress Record (page 28).

To measure your progress more accurately, you will need to know your current level of stress. Using the Stress Scale (0–8), use your best judgement. By the end of the week you'll be better able to evaluate your various stress levels. Remember, your willingness to complete these forms helps you determine your level of motivation and your ultimate success with this program. Good luck with your first week's assignment!

As we discussed in the Introduction and Orientation Lesson, each lesson ends with a Knowledge Review. We have designed each review to help you assess whether or not you have mastered the key topics for the week. Below is your first Knowledge Review. Circle "T" for true and "F" for false. After you complete the review, look in Appendix C (page 415) for the correct answer along with an explanation. Good luck with your first lesson!

Knowledge Review

T F 1. A lifestyle approach to stress management includes only changing the behaviors that cause you stress.

T F 2. To benefit from the group experience, each member must realize that cooperation and team effort are important.

T F 3. The Daily Stress Record is meant to be used to record your major stressful events of each day.

T F 4. Self-monitoring is a key to reducing your stress that can also help you keep motivation high.

T F 5. You should establish techniques to help improve your motivation as soon as you start to have trouble in this area.

T F 6. Involving your friends or family members in your stress management efforts is not a wise practice.

T F 7. Through visualization you practice "seeing" yourself acting or feeling less stressed.

T F 8. Social techniques involve enlisting the help of others, whereas material techniques involve rewards.

(Answers in Appendix C, page 415)

Daily Stress Record—Lesson One

Name:______________________________________ **Week of:**_______________

Date	Average Stress Level	Highest Stress Level	Time of Highest Stress Level	Stressful Event Associated with Highest Stress Level

Stressors I Experience Most Often
1.
2.
3.
4.
5.

Stress Change Worksheet

(Weeks 1 – 4)

Stress Level

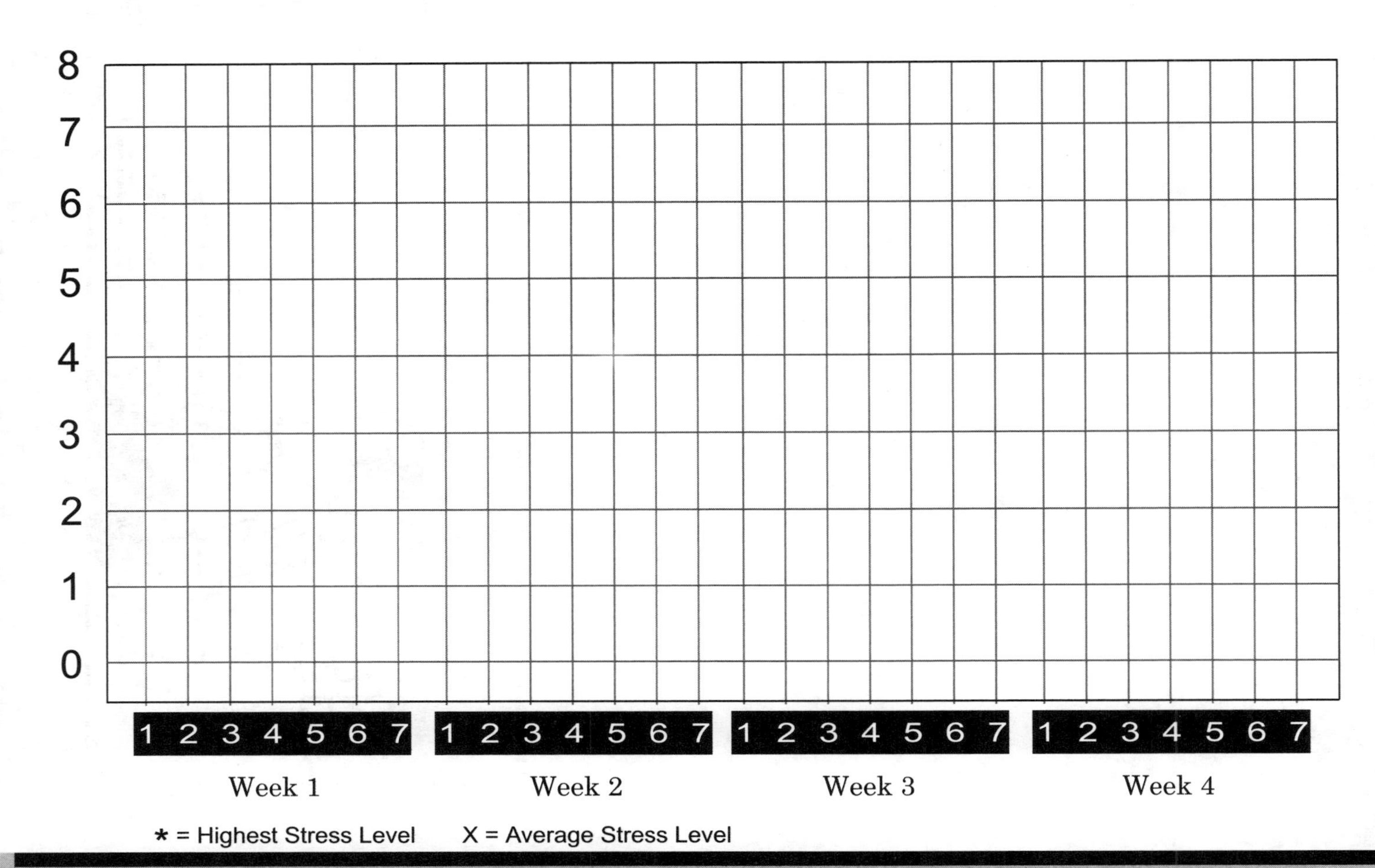

"I'm going to be late for work this morning. I was listening to my motivation tapes and suddenly found myself driving farther and faster than I ever imagined I could!"

Lesson Two

Welcome to your second lesson! We hope you are using the self-monitoring techniques introduced in Lesson One and that you are well on your way to mastering stress. Again, we cannot overstate the importance of self-monitoring. In this lesson, we will be discussing the Lifestyle and Attitude components of the LEARN acronym.

This lesson begins with a brief discussion on the difference between principles and techniques. In any behavior change program distinguishing principles from techniques is important. We then turn our attention to a review of the Daily Stress Record that you completed last week. You will be looking for patterns in your levels of stress. We then move on to discuss several key principles of stress that will help you better understand and identify the stress in your life. Most people are misinformed about the causes of stress. Being aware of your stress and its source will help you apply the appropriate techniques to reduce it. If you're ready, let's begin.

Principles versus Techniques

As you probably have guessed by now, this program is based on a dynamic process that involves your active participation. Over the next 15 lessons, we will introduce you to several methods designed to effect change in your life—change that reduces stress. Each method capitalizes on the specific ways in which we learn. We will introduce you to principles about stress to help you understand it more fully. Specifically, you will learn principles about the stress response systems and how they affect your body, mind, and behavior. You will also learn techniques or specific methods for handling stress. These techniques will be more meaningful to you if you understand the principles upon which they are based.

For example, you will learn the principle that your thoughts cause much of the stress in your life. You will learn a second principle that changing your thoughts can also change the stress you experience. To help you change your thoughts, we introduce you to several techniques.

Before you can change your thinking, you must first become aware of your thoughts, many of which are automatic.

The Daily Stress Record is the first step in this process of change. For the last week, you have been recording your average stress level and your highest level of stress each day. You should now have seven days of records. Let's now go back and review your Daily Stress Record and see what you can learn.

Reviewing Your Daily Stress Record

The main purpose for completing the Daily Stress Record is to help you gauge your feelings more realistically and record them as they happen. This helps you become aware of your feelings and how stressful they are for you. You can now review your records to see if any patterns exist.

Stress is something that builds up gradually over time and becomes so much a part of living that you may not notice specific stressful times. You may go through an entire day without even realizing your stress level stayed at a high level all day. Then, at the end of the day, you're surprised that you feel run down, your head may be pounding, and you yell at anyone in sight. If you experienced a day like this last week, your Daily Stress Record may have helped you identify the stress that caused these feelings. Remember, the first step in making change is awareness—you need to know where you are before you plan the route to your new destination. This process is similar to planning a trip to Disney World. You know that Disney World is in Florida. Your route of travel will be much different if you live in New York than if you lived in Utah. To assist in your search for patterns, we introduce you to Jane.

"Your Daily Stress Record can help you identify stressful events in your life that cause stressful feelings."

Meet Jane

Jane is a 27-year-old attorney. Having made the law review, she graduated at the head of her class two years earlier. People she knows adore and respect Jane. She is the type of person who offers to help anyone in need, even if it means working later and putting herself second. This happens at work and in her social life with friends. Although it's wonderful to be loving, supportive, and caring, it can also be a source of great stress. Always putting the needs of others first can often leave your needs unmet. This was happening to Jane, especially at work. She wanted to become a partner in her law firm and thought that doing more work for more people would help her get there faster.

Jane cannot say no, or more realistically, fears that if she does say no, she will not be liked as much. She believes this will keep her from becoming a partner. She has a hard time saying no to friends, fearing she will be disliked and have no friends. The result—Jane takes on too many projects at once. She then fights against her interests, her clients' interests, and her friends' interests to get everything done. Jane can reduce her stress by learning techniques that will help her say "no" at appropriate times. We call this assertiveness training. We'll cover assertiveness techniques in upcoming lessons. On page 34 is an example of Jane's Daily Stress Record. We'll refer to Jane's example as we help you search for patterns in your Daily Stress Records.

"Taking on too much, and not being able to say no, can cause great stress."

Searching for Patterns

Look at your Daily Stress Record or records from the past week. You are looking for patterns. Becoming more aware of the stressors in your life will help you to anticipate when a stressful event may arise. Knowing that a stressful event may be lurking around the corner is a key to planning and implementing stress reduction strategies—just in case. As your partners in this program, we will arm you with several stress management techniques to help avert stressful feelings. We cannot eliminate the stressful events in your life, nor would we want to. However, we can help you manage your stress level when stressful events present themselves. As you begin looking for patterns, consider the following:

Time. Look for times during the day when you experienced the highest levels of stress. Are there certain times during the day when your stress level goes up? For example, is your stress level highest as you pull into the parking lot at work? Maybe your stress is highest when you arrive home at night, when you first wake up in the morning, or when you pay your bills.

Look at Jane's Daily Stress Record on page 34. Do you notice any patterns in the times of the day when she experiences the highest levels of stress? Look carefully at January 8th, 10th, and 13th. Jane experienced the highest level of stress early in the morning when she thought she would be late for work or when she realized how much work she had to do. Do you recognize time patterns of stress in your life?

Daily Stress Record—Lesson Two

Name: Jane's Example **Week of:** January 8, 2001

Date	Average Stress Level	Highest Stress Level	Time of Highest Stress Level	Stressful Event Associated with Highest Stress Level
01/08	3	6	6:30 a.m.	Getting a late start for work
01/09	3	7	11:30 a.m.	I'm not ready for the 1 o'clock meeting. I'm going to get fired!
01/10	2	5	7:15 a.m.	I walked into my office and saw my messy desk.
01/10	4	7	6:45 a.m.	The bus was late. I have so much work to do!
01/11	3	7	1:00 p.m.	A partner asked me to do a special project—I said yes, but don't know when I'll get time.
01/12	2	5	6:00 p.m.	I have so much to do, I shouldn't go home yet.
01/13	2	4	7:00 a.m.	I'm so tired, I'd like to sleep in, but I have too much to do.
01/13	2	4	5:30 p.m.	Preparing food for friend's party—I should be at work.
01/14	2	5	10:00 p.m.	I can't sleep, I keep thinking of all the things I have to do at work.

Stressors I Experience Most Often
1. Not finishing projects perfectly and on time
2. Being late to work
3. Not being prepared for a meeting
4. Having too much to do
5. One of the partners may not like me and could keep me from becoming a partner

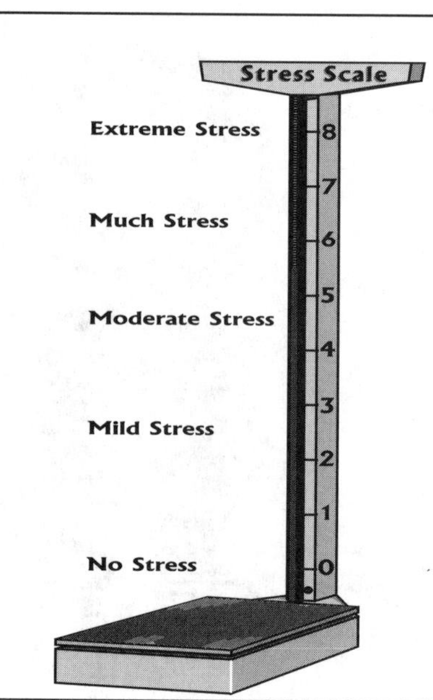

Day. Are there certain days of the week that are more stressful for you than others? For example, Mondays may be more stressful than Fridays. Sunday may be more stressful than Saturday, as you anticipate going back to work on Monday.

Look again at Jane's example. Do you notice her highest levels of stress are experienced on work days and on Sunday, January 14th, as she thinks about going back to work the next day? Can you find similar patterns in your Daily Stress Record?

Events. What events are associated with your highest levels of stress? Is there one specific event that is consistently associated with your highest stress levels, or are there several events that fit into this category?

In Jane's example, her highest levels of stress surrounded her work. Although Jane is a competent attorney and always does excellent work, her stress is related to her overcommitment to projects at work. This is magnified by her fear of not pleasing those to whom she has made promises.

Stressors. Pay close attention to the stressors you experience most often. Stressors are often related in some way. They may be related to work, family, finances, self-esteem, weight management, or a number of other issues. Review the five stressors you listed on your Daily Stress Record. Is there a pattern in the stressors you experience most often?

Now, look at the five stressors on Jane's Daily Stress Record. Do you recognize a pattern? The stressors Jane experienced most frequently are work related. She wants to please everyone so they will like her. She believes this will help her become a partner in the law firm.

The Principles of Stress

As you learned in the Introduction and Orientation Lesson, stress is a natural response to a threat or challenge. When you experience stress, your emotions may seem as out of control as a monster in a horror movie. The responses of both your mind

"Stress is a natural response to a threat or challenge."

and body are, however, logical and predictable. Learning more about them can help you regain your sense of control.

Stress is a natural occurrence and has a very useful function. Let's say, for example, that you were going to be a contestant on *The Wheel of Fortune* television show. If you feel no stress at all, you may not prepare for the contest, and as a result, you might do poorly. If, on the other hand, you feel extremely stressed, you may be too nervous to study. You may become confused and distracted when the cameras begin to roll. But, if you feel a mild amount of stress, you may study hard, prepare well, concentrate better, and be more confident when Pat Sajak asks you a question.

Stress in Humans

The belief that low levels of stress can enhance performance is relatively new. In fact, our basic understanding of stress has increased dramatically over the past 50 years. In the first half of the 20th century, stress researchers viewed all stress as negative or bad. Since that time, our views about stress have changed. We now know that there is "good" stress and "bad" stress. Understanding this notion is important in learning to master your stress. Now, let's look at some of these interesting advances that science has made concerning stress and stress management.

"Two people may experience the same event, but their individual stress levels may vary greatly."

Good Stress and Bad Stress

According to stress researchers today, stress is any challenge to the body's internal sense of balance. Stress can be anything that causes us to adapt, including happiness (birth of a baby) and sadness (death of a loved one). According to stress expert Paul J. Rosch, "Stress that results from something good or positive is *eustress*, and stress resulting from something bad or negative is

distress." This raises an interesting question. Does everyone view the same situation or event the same way? In other words, does everyone view the birth of a baby as positive? The answer to these questions is clearly no. What may be a positive and challenging event to one person may be negative and even threatening to another. To understand this concept better, let's now look at how individual differences in perception influence the assessment of a situation or event as stressful or not.

Sources of Stress

Researchers used to think that all individuals experienced stress in the same way. They believed the events in our lives cause stress. We now know this is not the case. Everyone experiences events differently. Two people may experience the same event, but their individual stress levels may vary greatly. Our perceptions of what we find stressful may differ based upon our unique individual beliefs and experiences. Certain situations, however, may be considered stressful by most people. Living with a chronic, debilitating illness may be an example.

You may not consider helping a friend with a dinner party to be stressful. In fact, some may consider it fun and relaxing—a change of pace from a long week. Do you remember Jane's Daily Stress Record? Her stress level increased when she helped prepare food for a friend's party. Why? She had overcommitted herself at work and at home. In other words, Jane's life circumstances all worked together to cause an otherwise enjoyable event to be stressful for her.

Internal and External Sources of Stress

Because stress varies with perception, both internal (thoughts) and external (environmental) events influence how much stress we experience. Internal sources of stress come from our thoughts, our attitudes, and our reactions toward a particular threat or challenge. External sources of stress may include factors such as pollution, constant noise, injury, surgery, or sitting in an airplane that is stranded on the tarmac for hours in a snow storm. Internal and external sources of stress also interact.

Interpersonal relationships are a good example of an internal stressor. We may believe that a conflict with a family member or friend is solely an external stressor, something we cannot control. Our thoughts and attitudes about the conflict are based on something internal or something we can control—our thoughts.

Why We Have Stress

Again, when we ask ourselves why we have stress, we often ascribe to environment factors—events in our lives. For example, we may believe our job, a relationship, or our workload are responsible for increased stress. Although these factors do contribute to the stress we experience, they're not the direct causes of the stress. Each of us has adopted a certain style of thinking; we have embraced unique attitudes, beliefs, and behaviors, all of which contribute directly to our level of stress. Although we have control over our thoughts and beliefs, it is important not to blame or condemn ourselves for having them. This will only add to the stress. Instead, we need

to learn how to change our thoughts, attitudes, beliefs, and behaviors. This is a key *principle* in stress management—changing your thoughts, attitudes, beliefs, and behaviors. You will learn many different techniques to do this as you go though this program. We will help you assemble a tool chest filled with helpful stress management tools. Now, let's look at some of the more common reasons for experiencing stress.

"Oh no, I'm so afraid that I'll lose my job!"

Perfectionism

The desire to do things perfectly can cause a great deal of stress. Logically, we all know that no one is perfect. Unconsciously though, we often believe that we should be. Jane is a good example. If her supervisor or anyone else in the office asks her to do something, she begins to worry about her performance. The worry probably results from an unconscious thought such as, "It will be a disaster if I make even one mistake. It will keep me from becoming a partner." Suppose one of your friends at work did a project and made a few small errors? Would that really be terrible? Would you think that your friend was a hopeless case and should be fired? Of course not. You would probably think, "It's too bad about the mistakes, but everyone makes them, and overall, she did a terrific job." When you realize that the same standard you apply to someone else is the standard you need to apply to yourself, you begin to address your perfectionism. Are you a perfectionist? Do you worry about doing a "perfect" job? Now turn to page 43 and, on the Reasons for My Stress worksheet, list at least one perfectionism attribute that increases your stress.

"I have to complete each of these reports PERFECTLY!"
OUT
IN

Worry

When we worry, all the possible outcomes to a situation swirl around and around in our minds. Often, the thoughts keep swirling—even when we know we can do nothing to change the situation. This tendency may come from the human need for control. Most of us have trouble accepting the notion that there are some things in life we simply cannot control. Rather than accepting this reality, we keep worrying,

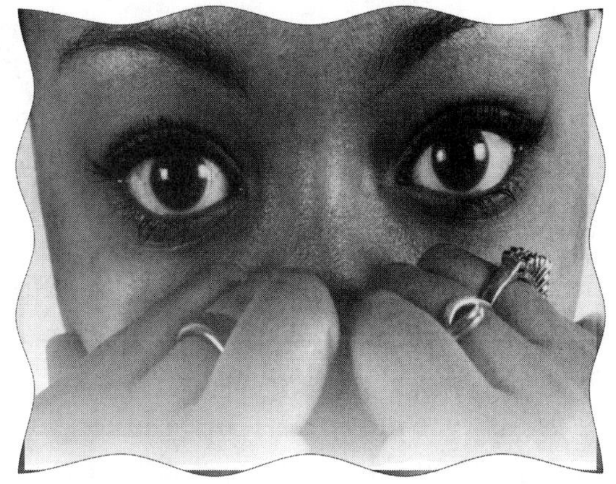

unconsciously hoping that somehow the worry will change things.

Breaking the cycle of worry is a matter of convincing yourself that you cannot control everything. Some events are going to happen whether you want them to or not, whether you worry about them or not. Your worrying will not affect these events or their outcomes. Yet, it does affect you; it can make your life unpleasant and greatly increase your stress. In extreme cases, worry can become chronic. If you find this happening to you, you may be suffering from a more extreme form of anxiety or obsessive thinking. Seeking the assistance of a mental-health professional may be wise.

Do you worry? If so, do you worry a little or a lot? Do you worry about things you cannot control? Look back at Jane's Daily Stress Record on page 34. On Sunday evening (January 14th), she began to think and worry about work the next day. This kept her from sleeping and increased her level of stress. Turn now to page 43, and on the Reasons for My Stress worksheet, list at least one thing in your life you worry about that increases your stress. It's fine to list more than one item on the worksheet.

Low Self-Esteem

People who suffer from low self-esteem often feel that they have no worth, competence, or value. Low self-esteem can be a chronic problem or can occur when we're reminded about something we do not like about ourselves. This often comes from a strong tendency to focus on what is wrong rather than what is right. Because of this negative self-assessment, people may feel sad or even depressed because they don't see themselves as measuring up. Their negative self-assessment may cause them to be irritable and angry. Low self-esteem creates more stress because it keeps a person from taking risks, setting goals, and being assertive. Having a negative body image or being overweight and feeling nothing can be done are examples of low self-esteem thinking.

The key to changing this negative style of thinking is to stop the negative self-assessment cycle. Instead, according to researcher and clinician Dr. Albert Ellis, individuals need to learn how to rate their

"I'm so stupid
I can't do anything
right. I'm such
a failure!!"
ERROR

"Breaking the cycle of worry is a matter of convincing yourself that you cannot control everything."

behaviors and not themselves. If they were to rate their behaviors alone, they would be less likely to see themselves as total failures—even if they failed to perform as well as they believe they should. We will show you how to do this in later lessons. Are there things in your life that make you feel like a failure? Do these thoughts lower your self-esteem? Turn to page 43 and, on the Reasons for My Stress worksheet, write down at least one thing you believe diminishes your self-esteem.

Anger

Many people under stress have a tendency to become angry and irritable, often for totally irrational reasons. Typically, they may hold beliefs that others are stupid or nasty and that they have to battle everyone else's incompetence. However, this style of thinking can increase stress and can even be physically harmful. Let's look at an example.

"To avoid feeling anger, try to put yourself in the other person's position."

Assume you are driving to a meeting, and you're a little late. Suddenly, a car in front of you changes lanes, gets right in front of you, and proceeds to drive slowly. Your immediate response may be to get very angry and start sounding your horn. This type of anger has become so common in our society, it even has a name—Road Rage. The thoughts that are likely to produce these responses include: "That jerk!" "He's totally inconsiderate!" "He's purposefully trying to make me late!" "I'll get even with him."

Now, try to put yourself in the other person's position. Have you ever driven anywhere slowly, perhaps because you were looking for something or you were thinking about something other than driving? Do you always watch out for other cars when you're in a hurry? Suppose the person who just cut in front of you is a physician rushing to a medical emergency. Would you have the same response? Gaining this perspective and considering other reasons for such behavior can help you reduce your anger, thereby reducing your stress. Are there things in your life that make you angry? Turning again to the Reasons for My Stress worksheet on page 43, list anything that comes to mind that makes you angry.

Shame and Guilt

Excessive feelings of shame and guilt can increase stress. This may happen when individuals focus on how bad they are for what they did, rather than accept responsibility and move on in a healthy way. Again, feelings of lack of control come into play. This is similar to what the person with low self-esteem feels—assessing him or herself as unworthy based on an act or a series of acts that were less than desirable. The stress level increases because feelings of shame and guilt focus on the consequences of a past choice and not on making better choices in the future. When we live in the past and try to control the consequences of past choices, we are trying to control things we can't control. Again, we can control our

choices, not the consequences. As Dr. Steven Covey would say, "When you pick up one end of the stick, you pick up the other end."

Are there things in your life that cause you to feel ashamed or guilty? If so, these feelings may contribute to your high level of stress. Turn to page 43 and list these things on the Reasons for My Stress worksheet.

Bad Habits

Bad habits range from spending too much money, biting your nails, and eating too much, to more severe problems, such as alcoholism, smoking, and substance abuse. These are behaviors you engage in over and over again, although you know they have a negative effect on your life and your health. Although we do not specifically address the treatment of addictions in this program, we will show you several techniques to help you stop the bad-habit cycle. We will also help you identify when a bad habit becomes an addiction for which you should seek professional help.

Many people develop bad habits as a way of coping with or reducing their stress. Unfortunately, developing bad habits rather than healthy coping skills causes even more stress. For example, imagine someone who overeats every time he or she feels stressed. In the short term, this person may feel more relaxed and comforted by the behavior. However, in the long term, this person will have the additional stress of dealing with the consequences of the chronic overeating—being overweight. In addressing bad habits, we will show you how to find healthy coping skills. List any bad habits you may have on the Reasons for My Stress worksheet on page 43.

Procrastination

Procrastination is another major stressor for many people. All of us procrastinate from time to time. But when it becomes part of daily living, it can increase stress. Those who procrastinate may have poor time management and/or problem-solving skills. They may also experience performance anxiety and perfectionism. As a result, procrastinators put off

"Some people develop bad and unhealthy habits to cope with stress."

"Procrastinators may hold beliefs about being entitled to a stress-free or work-free existence."

what they need to do, feel guilty about it, then procrastinate even more. This cycle leads to more stress.

Procrastinators may also hold beliefs about being entitled to a stress-free or work-free existence. This thinking leads them to indulge in more comfortable, desirable distractions. Often, discomfort, anxiety, or fear is at the heart of procrastination. We may fear that a task is too hard, uncomfortable to do, or that we lack the skills to do a good job. In later lessons, we will help you develop the skills to overcome procrastination. For now, list those things you often procrastinate about doing on the Reasons for My Stress worksheet on page 43.

Catastrophizing

People who catastrophize expect the worst possible outcome. For example, a noise in the house at night may cause the person who catastrophizes to immediately think a burglar who will cause harm or death is in the house. A call into the boss's office may lead to the "I'm going to get fired" thought. Look at Jane's Daily Stress Record again on page 34. Notice that on Tuesday (January 9th) her high level of stress for the day came when she was not prepared for a meeting and her immediate thought was that she would be fired. You can imagine how this style of thinking increases stress. At times, fearing the worst can be helpful. This is particularly true when danger is present. However, the person who chronically catastrophizes sees danger in every situation—real or imagined. These individuals need to learn how to differentiate between real and imagined danger. We'll show you how to do this later in the program.

Do you sometimes "fear the worst"? Is this fear often unwarranted? Turn again to the Reasons for My Stress worksheet on page 43. Write down experiences when you have feared the worst.

Taking on too Much

The person who takes on too much will often feel overstressed. Does this sound familiar? Jane is a perfect example of taking on too much. Often, a person who takes on too much has difficulty delegating responsibility and/or asserting his or her needs. Perhaps this person is a perfectionist and believes that nobody can do the job as well. Some may believe that asking for help implies weakness or that taking the time to show someone else takes too much time. "I can have it done by the time I show anyone else how to do it," is a common thought among those who take on too much. In addition, these people may fear that saying no to someone's request will result in a loss of approval from that person. Because of these styles of thinking, these individuals

"The person who takes on too much will often feel overstressed."

Reasons for My Stress	
1. Perfectionism	
2. Worry	
3. Low Self-Esteem	
4. Anger	
5. Shame and Guilt	
6. Bad Habits	
7. Procrastination	
8. Catastrophizing	
9. Taking on too Much	

often take on too much, thereby increasing their levels of stress. Remedies to this problem include learning how to delegate, assertiveness training, time management, and reducing perfectionistic demands.

Do you sometimes have trouble saying "no"? Do you often find yourself with too much to do? Most of us do at some point in time. Write down, on the Reasons for My Stress form on page 43, the circumstances where you find yourself taking on too much.

We have discussed many causes of stress. This list is not an exhaustive list, but it includes the most common stressors people experience today. You should now have a list of the main causes of your stress. As we said before, many people go through life being highly stressed, yet completely unaware of their high stress levels. How can we tell when we are overstressed? Let's look at some of the common symptoms of stress.

The Symptoms of Stress

When we experience symptoms that are uncomfortable and at times debilitating, we're likely feeling the effects of too much stress. We experience symptoms of stress in various ways including physically (the way our body feels), mentally (the way we think), emotionally (the way we feel), and behaviorally (the things we do). For example, we may feel a lump in our stomachs, our thinking may seem clouded and we're unable to focus, we may be easily agitated, or we may overeat or stop eating altogether.

Telltale Signs of Stress

Below is a list of some of the more common telltale signs of stress.

"High levels of stress can affect our bodies, the way we think and feel, and the things we do."

Physical symptoms. Sweaty palms, fatigue, racing heart, lump in the throat, stomach pain, shortness of breath, trembling hands, shaky voice, tingling toes and fingers, dizziness, and blurred vision are some of the physical signs of too much stress. Hence, the stronger your body is physically, the better your ability to cope with periods of high stress. If you're not physically active, you should be. In later lessons, we will give you guidance on how you can become more active.

Mental symptoms. Inability to concentrate, forgetfulness, reduced creativity, worrying, brooding, and inflexibility are often mental signs of high levels of stress.

Emotional symptoms. Anxiety, depression, low self-confidence, irritability, anger, cynicism, and loss of enthusiasm are some of the emotional symptoms of excess stress. Developing healthy attitudes and relationships are key strategies to overcoming these symptoms. We'll show you how to do this in upcoming lessons.

Behavioral symptoms. Procrastination and withdrawal are the most common behavioral symptoms of too much stress. Addictive or excessive behaviors including drugs, alcohol, smoking, overeating, and overspending are also common behavioral responses to high levels of stress. Compulsive behaviors including working, watching television, sleeping, and nail biting are other behavioral symptoms.

Do any of these symptoms sound familiar? Do you experience them? If so, how often? Write down four stress symptoms you experience and how often you experience them on the My Symptoms of Stress worksheet below.

When Stress Becomes Distressing

We want you to use the list of symptoms you just completed as a guide to help you recognize the stress in your life. However, remember that not all stress is bad. All of us need some stress in our lives to feel motivated and to focus on a task. Think of it this way. Suppose you have an important examination coming up. Stress, or your level of awareness, will enable you to assess how prepared you are to pass the test and how much you need to study. If you experience no stress at all, you may not be motivated to prepare yourself for the exam. Therefore,

My Symptoms of Stress

1. Physical	
2. Mental	
3. Emotional	
4. Behavioral	

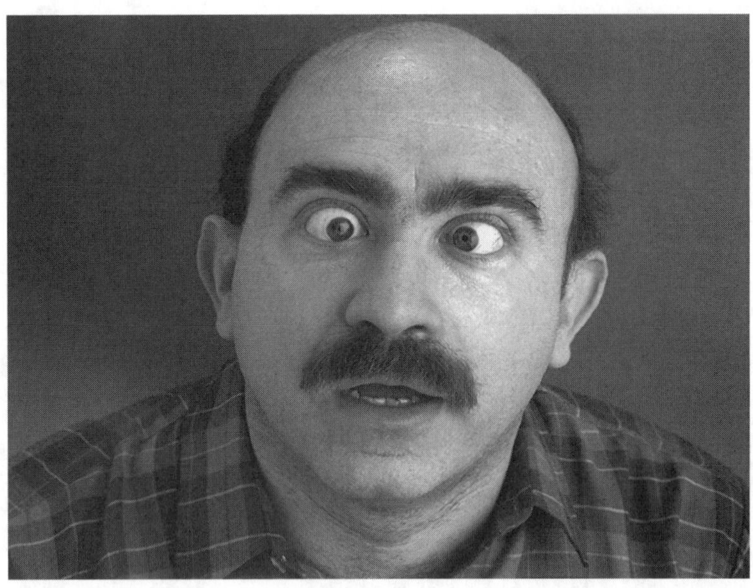

"Too often, people spend their time and energy trying to control the consequences of past choices—ultimately to no avail."

there is an optimal amount of stress that motivates an individual to perform his or her best.

When stress goes beyond this optimal point to excessive levels, it starts to become distressing and keeps us from doing our best. On a continuum of feelings, we can see that concern motivates, but worry debilitates. This is when stress begins to turn against us rather than work for us. For example, we can see how excitement and concern can be positive and even motivating. Problems occur when the stress changes to fear, depression, or withdrawal—the effects are no longer helpful.

The Important Role of Choice

We do not have control over everything that happens to us. In fact, we have very little control over the events in our lives. Hopefully, you are beginning to realize that we do have control over something very powerful—our choices. We have discussed the role of the environment in increasing the stress in your life. How you choose to react (an automatic thought or behavior) or respond (a proactive, conscious thought or behavior) to the stressful events in your life will ultimately determine the level of stress you feel. This program will help you learn how to *respond* rather than simply *react* to stressful events.

Yes, you do have the power to choose your responses to stressful events. You are constantly making choices, although many of them are automatic. You choose to think a certain way, eat a certain way, and behave a certain way. Mastering your stress involves learning to make better choices. The Mastering Stress Approach teaches you how to become aware of the choices you make. With this increased awareness, you can then make better choices that reduce your stress. Remember, worrying and dwelling on the consequences of past choices is unproductive and stressful. Too often, people spend their time and energy trying to control the consequences of past choices—ultimately to no avail. You are much better off using your energy to make good choices in the future that reduce your stress. Instead of blame, use past choices as examples of things to change. Learn from your experiences today to reduce your stress tomorrow!

Setting Reasonable Goals

Many people begin stress management programs with specific goals in mind. Some may pick up a book, read it over the weekend, and hope to significantly reduce their stress from then on. Others may attend a one-day stress management seminar, hoping it will teach them the "magic" of stress management. When these hopes fade and stress returns, feelings of failure and hopelessness may abound.

These examples highlight the importance of setting reasonable goals. As we said in the Introduction and Orientation Lesson, managing stress is a dynamic, life-

OUR GRANDPARENTS' GENERATION KEPT THEIR STRESS IN THEIR HEADS, GOT HEADACHES, AND CARRIED ON WITH LIFE.

OUR PARENTS' GENERATION SENT THEIR STRESS TO THEIR STOMACHS, GOT ULCERS, AND WALKED AROUND WITH STOMACHACHES.

OUR GENERATION JAMS OUR STRESS INTO OUR BACKS, CREATING A CYCLE OF EXPANDING, EXCRUCIATING PAIN THAT AFFECTS EVERY MUSCLE GROUP AND DEBILITATES THE ENTIRE BODY.

long journey. At this juncture on your journey, you may not know what reasonable stress management goals are. We could list some here, but they may not have much meaning. For now, we want you to focus your goals on keeping your Daily Stress Record and your Stress Change Worksheet.

A New Stress Change Worksheet

In Lesson One, you started completing the Stress Change Worksheet (see page 29). This worksheet covers the first four weeks of your stress management program. On this Stress Change Worksheet you recorded daily, your average level of stress and the highest level of stress for the day. On page 48, you will find a Sample Average Stress Change Worksheet. On this worksheet, you see two lines. The straight line represents what your average weekly stress would look like if you reduced the level of stress in your life exactly the same amount every week. Certainly, life doesn't happen in a straight line. The jagged line is more realistic and has ups and downs. You will experience weeks where your stress level continues to decline and others when stress may increase.

A helpful way to setting goals is to think ahead and select how much you would like to reduce your stress by landmark dates. Your anniversary may be at week 6, your daughter's birthday at week 11, and New Years at week 15 as shown on the sample worksheet. When you reach the dates you select, you can see if you are accomplishing what you expect.

Take a few minutes to pencil in some landmark dates on the Average Stress Change Worksheet in Appendix E on page 430. Remember, this is each week's "average" stress level, so you will be making one entry on this worksheet each week. Don't worry, we'll be sure to remind you to do this. When your landmark dates come around, compare them with your actual stress level. The process of change is slow,

"You're getting pretty good at this stress management thing."

Sample Average Stress Change Worksheet

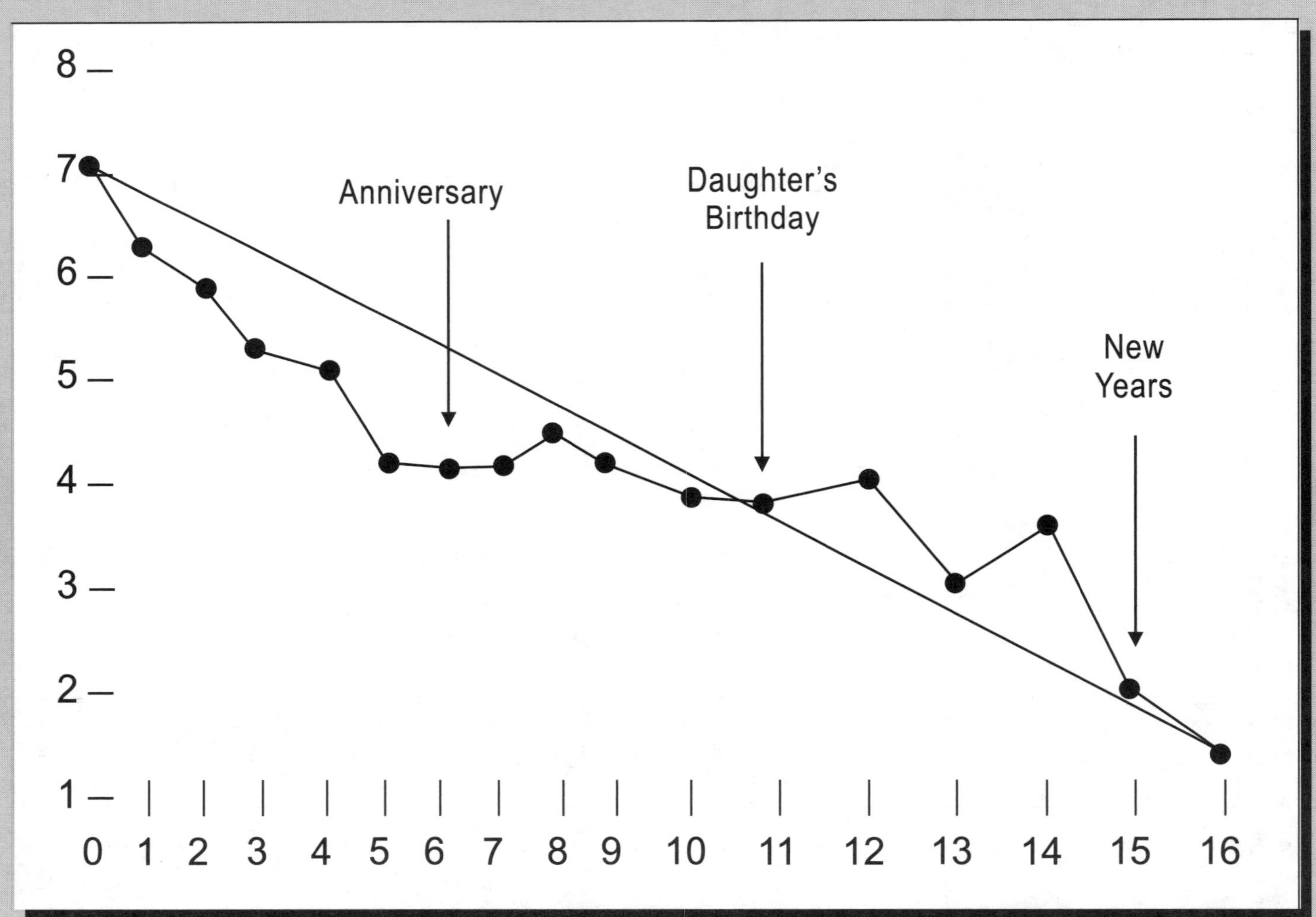

and there will be weeks when your stress level may rise a bit. Don't panic! Instead, look for patterns and trends, and try to figure out what you did differently that week. Use the less-than-perfect weeks as opportunities to reassess your weaker points and work on them. Use your strengths to help improve the areas that need more work. Finally, remind yourself time and time again that setting unrealistic goals is a setup for trouble. Remember, *slow and steady* progress is your goal.

Go back to your Daily Stress Record from last week. Calculate the average level of stress for the week. Record this average on the Average Stress Change Worksheet in Appendix E on page 430 for week 1.

A Word About Shaping Attitudes

Part of setting realistic goals involves gradually shaping your attitudes. We have all developed behaviors and beliefs over time and expecting them to change overnight is unrealistic. *Shaping* refers to making changes gradually, in a step-by-step fashion. For example, let's say that you want to begin reducing your stress by becoming more assertive at work. At first, you might try easier levels of asserting yourself, let's say with your co-workers and staff. After you have begun to master this and feel more comfortable with assertiveness skills and behaviors, you might try something more difficult such as assertion (not aggression) with your boss. You may find, however, that although you easily mastered the earlier levels of assertion, the higher levels of assertion require more effort. Don't be alarmed, remember shaping attitudes and behaviors is a gradual process. We'll provide you with what we call the "stepladder" approach to assertiveness training later in the program.

"Shaping refers to making changes in a step-by-step fashion."

It is now easy to see how shaping applies to goal setting. Setting realistic goals means to begin changing your behaviors gradually, with an attainable goal in sight, and then working up to the level you want. Being realistic, once again, will reduce the likelihood that you become disappointed if you do not make changes as quickly as you desire. Being unrealistic, on the other hand, you may view small, yet important changes as insignificant and not worth the effort. Being realistic also means recognizing there will be ups and downs as you change; try not to overreact to the downs.

Lesson Review

Congratulations! You've now completed your second lesson and should be more aware of stressors in your life. We started this lesson by distinguishing between principles of stress management and techniques. We then had you review your Daily Stress Record to search for patterns. By now, you are probably beginning to realize the importance of self-monitoring and looking for patterns in your stressful experiences. As you become more aware of these patterns, you will have an easier time recognizing and anticipating stressful events in your daily life.

In this lesson, we also discussed some common reasons for stress along with symptoms of high levels of stress. You learned that positive events can be stressful because they too require the body and mind to adjust to change. We also showed you that the sources of stress are both internal (our thoughts and attitudes) and external (environmental events). And finally, we discussed the power of choice and the importance of setting reasonable goals. We covered a lot of material, and we encourage you to reread any of the information you did not clearly understand.

This Week's Assignment

This week, we want you to continue self-monitoring by completing the Daily Stress Record. We provide you with a blank Daily Stress Record for this week on page 51. Remember to do this at the end of each day. At the end of the week, plot this information on the Stress Change Worksheet you began in Lesson One on page 29 and on the new Average Stress Change Worksheet in Appendix E on page 430. Also, watch for the five most common stressors you noted at the end of last week. By becoming more aware of your stress patterns, you will be better able to anticipate and manage them more effectively. Also, look for the five most common stressors you experienced this week. Write them down on your Daily Stress Record.

You will probably notice that it is easier to judge your stress levels this week as you become more aware of the role stress plays in your life. Use this progress to stay motivated and when you are learning other techniques in future lessons that may seem difficult at first. Good luck with this week's assignment!

Knowledge Review

T F 9. It is not necessary to review your Daily Stress Records because you diligently complete them each day.

T F 10. Patterns in your Daily Stress Records are coincidental and should be ignored.

T F 11. Low levels of stress are unhealthy and should be eliminated from our lives.

T F 12. The only stress that has an impact on us or requires us to adjust is the stress caused by negative events.

T F 13. Excessive and addictive behaviors are reactions to, as well as causes of, stress.

T F 14. Low self-esteem often results from a tendency to rate yourself instead of your behavior.

T F 15. Shaping refers to the weight loss associated with learning to master stress.

(Answers in Appendix C, page 415)

Daily Stress Record—Lesson Two

Name:________________________ **Week of:**______________

Date	Average Stress Level	Highest Stress Level	Time of Highest Stress Level	Stressful Event Associated with Highest Stress Level

Stress Scale

Extreme Stress — 8
7
Much Stress — 6
5
Moderate Stress — 4
3
Mild Stress — 2
1
No Stress — 0

Remember to complete the Stress Change Worksheet on page 29 at the end of the week by recording the Highest Stress Level and Average Stress Level from your Daily Stress Record.

Stressors I Experience Most Often
1.
2.
3.
4.
5.

"You've been working too hard. Instead of a heart beat, I'm getting a fax tone."

Lesson Three

You have now completed two weeks of the Mastering Stress Program. Are you becoming more aware of the events in your life that increase your stress? Is this awareness helping you to anticipate stressful situations? Most people going through this program begin to see a noticeable reduction in their stress levels from this increased awareness during the first few weeks. You may find this odd, especially since we haven't had you begin to make changes. This is the power of self-monitoring. You are becoming more aware of the stressors in your life by keeping good stress records. If you have been diligently keeping your Daily Stress Record, we applaud your efforts. More important, *you* are the one reaping the benefits of your hard work, and *you* deserve all the credit. If you have had difficulty keeping your Daily Stress Record, we recommend you reread Lessons One and Two and try harder to keep these records. Remember, those who keep self-monitoring records are more successful than those who do not. We want you to be successful with this program.

We begin this lesson by having you review your Daily Stress Record for last week. You will use a worksheet to help you discover patterns in your stress. We then introduce the Relationship component of LEARN by raising the notion of a stress management partner. Would you benefit from a partner in this program? We'll help you decide. In Lesson Two, we introduced you to some of the principles of stress. We'll continue this discussion with more insight into understanding stress and provide some suggestions as to why you may be stressed. You will be working through an exercise that will help you identify your unique stress triggers. We'll introduce you to the four states of feeling to help put stress into perspective. Then we discuss five important steps to mastering stress. Finally, we conclude this lesson by introducing you to a new monitoring form. Don't worry, it's not difficult. This sounds like a lot of material, but it is very interesting. So, if you're ready, let's forge ahead.

Reviewing Your Daily Stress Record

Take out your Daily Stress Records from last week. Do you recognize any patterns in your levels of stress? If so, what patterns are you beginning to see? Are any patterns related to the time of day? Does your stress occur in the morning when you're trying to get things accomplished so you can go to work? Perhaps you experience more stress at the end of the day when you're trying to wind down from a hard day. Other responsibilities such as family and chores at home may interfere with your plans to relax when you get home.

"Remember, the patterns you uncover now will become the foundation of this program in subsequent lessons."

What days of the week were most stressful for you? Do you see a pattern to your stress level on certain days of the week? On what day is your average stress level the highest? Are you more relaxed on your days off? Can you identify recurring events in your day that increase your level of stress? For example, are you finding yourself most stressed when you are working with your boss or when you are talking to your spouse? Are certain events during the week associated with higher levels of stress? Is there one specific stressor that is consistently associated with your highest stress levels or are there several events that increase your stress?

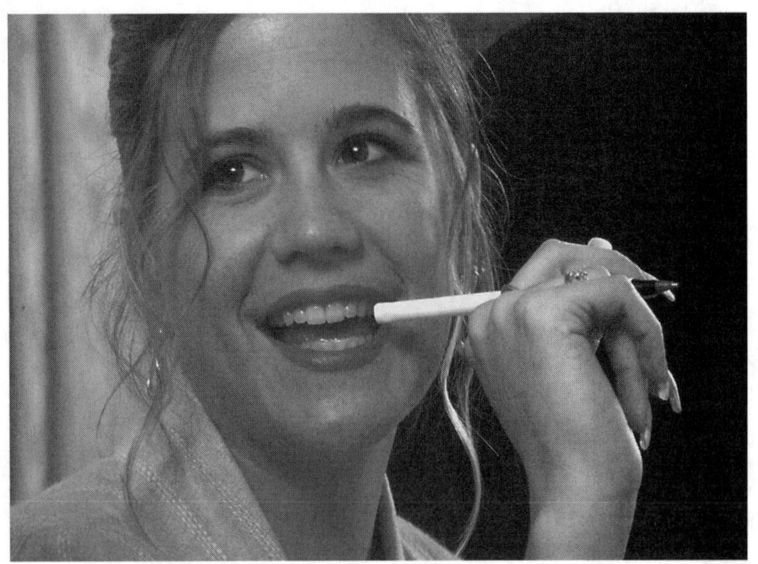

On page 55, is an example of Jane's Stressful Patterns Worksheet. This was prepared by Jane from her Daily Stress Record example on page 34. Take a few minutes to review Jane's Daily Stress Record and her Stressful Patterns Worksheet. Can you identify Jane's patterns of stress from her Daily Stress Record?

Now, it's your turn. On page 56, we provide the My Stressful Patterns Worksheet. This worksheet will help you sort your stressful patterns by time, day, events, stressors, and any other category you find helpful. Take time now to carefully review your Daily Stress Record from last week and complete the worksheet. Remember, the patterns you uncover now will become the foundation of this program in subsequent lessons. This is an important exercise, so when you've finished, we'll continue.

A Stress Management Partner

Different people have different preferences when it comes to making personal lifestyle changes. Some people like to engage others to work with them, such as family members or close friends. Others prefer to go it alone. Dr. Kelly Brownell of Yale University calls these two different types of individuals *social* changers and *solo* changers.

Social changers enjoy the companionship of another person on their journey of change. These individuals find it helpful to have someone to talk to about the program and the changes they are making in their lives. They enjoy the company, support, and encouragement when times are a little

My Stressful Patterns Worksheet

Name: Jane's Example Week of: January 4, 2001

TIME

Early in the morning as I think about my workday
Sunday night at bedtime

DAY

Weekdays (work days)
Sunday evening

EVENTS

Getting to work late
Not being prepared
Having too much to do
Not getting enough sleep

STRESSORS

Not having enough time to get things done
Not doing a good enough job
Thinking about being fired
Letting someone down who is counting on me
Not becoming a partner in the firm

OTHER

My Stressful Patterns Worksheet

Name: ______________________________ Week of: ____________

TIME	
DAY	
EVENTS	
STRESSORS	
OTHER	

difficult, and enjoy the compliments about the positive changes they are making.

Being either a social or solo changer is fine. The important thing to determine is what works best for *you*. Throughout this manual, we talk a lot about relationships and gaining support from friends and family members. This information is likely to help the social changer but not the solo changer. Social changers may be thrilled at the notion of having others involved in their stress management program. On the other hand, solo changers may become upset even thinking about involving anyone else, even when it's for the right reasons. Moreover, solo changers may feel uncomfortable when others ask them questions about the program.

Over the next week, think about yourself and how you relate to social or solo changing. Think of the people who would be willing to help you in this program. These and other helpful resources can be cultivated if you are a social changer. Again, we emphasize that if you prefer the solo path, this is perfectly fine. You may even fit somewhere in between. For instance, you may prefer to work solo on everything except physical activity. We will be discussing much about exercise and physical activity in upcoming lessons. Having an exercise partner may help you to become and stay more active.

Is a Partner Right for Me?

Developing a good program partnership can be a powerful source of motivation and inspiration. Often times, a program partner is also on the program, however, an excellent partnership can be formed with someone who is not going through the program. The key question

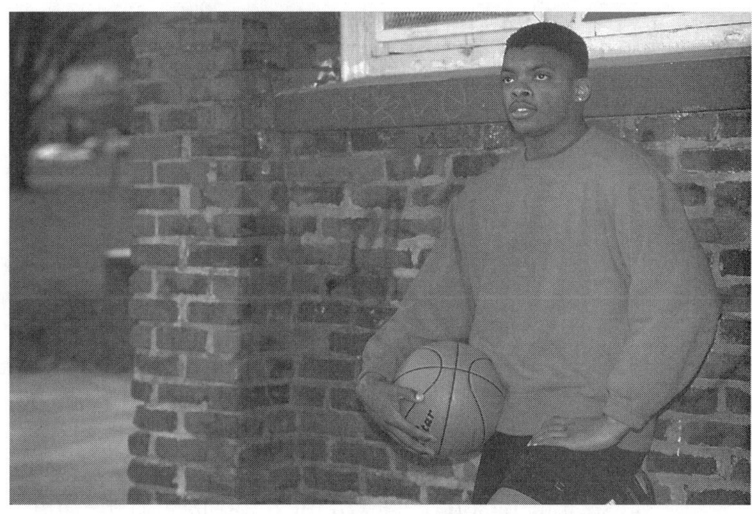

here is, how can you tell what is best for you?

"Some people like to make changes on their own and some like to involve others."

First, there are many different types of good program partnerships. Perhaps the most logical partner would be a spouse, partner, or close friend. But, our clients have formed other excellent partnerships. Examples include partnerships with co-workers, neighbors, family members, and other close friends.

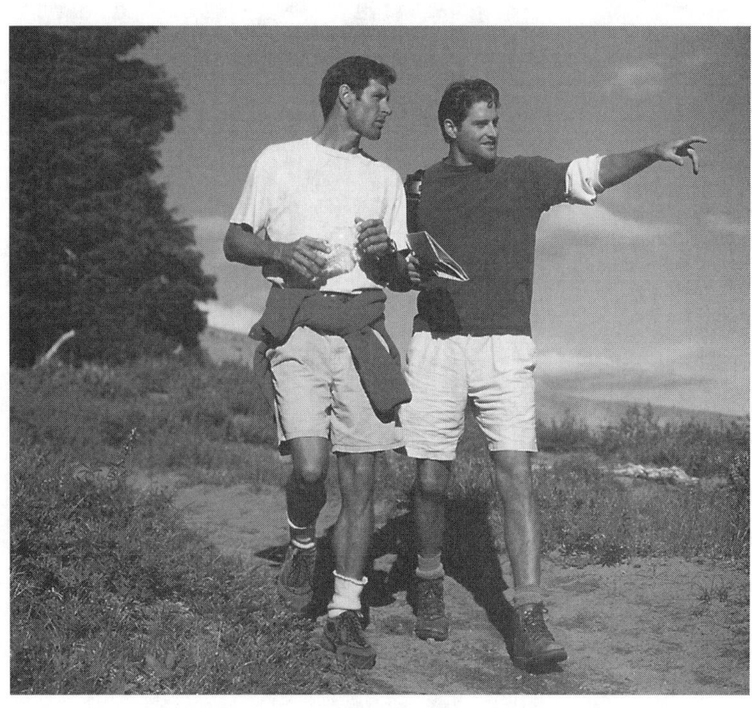

You may be one step ahead of us and already have a partner in mind. In Lesson Four, we'll give you a Partnership Quiz to help you determine if this person will be a good partner. A stress management partnership is like any other close relationship—both partners have to give and take. You cannot expect your partner to do all the supporting; you must also find helpful ways to support your partner. Time and effort are required on both sides to form and keep a working partnership. Think of this as you would a joint bank account. If one person makes all the deposits and the other person draws all the money out, chances are that the joint account won't last very long. If, on the other hand, both individuals continuously make deposits and withdrawals when needed, the account will continue to grow and last longer.

Would you benefit from a program partner? Ponder this question over the next week, and in the next lesson we'll give you some simple guidelines to help you decide. If you decide going solo is best for you, that's fine as well. Many people have successfully completed this program on their own. Let's now turn our attention to expanding your understanding of stress.

"You may not be able to easily change daily circumstances, but you can learn how to change the way you respond to them."

Understanding Stress

As you're reading this manual, you may be wondering why other people do not seem as stressed as you. Don't worry, you are not alone. Stress is not a disease or a sign of weakness. Stress isn't like a person's height, hair, or eye color—you cannot see it. Stressful feelings come from a combination of two sources:

❶ The world around you (your environment)

❷ The way you deal with the world (your thoughts)

In Lesson Two, on page 37, we discussed some common reasons for stress. Some of these reasons are environmentally driven and others are personality (thought) driven. Sometimes your life can be filled with so many stressful events that you are overwhelmed. But, stressful events are not enough to cause stress. We all know of people who don't get flustered, no matter how difficult the situation. They seem to have a personality that can deal with any situation—no matter how tough. Yet, other people seem to make "mountains out of molehills," no matter how trivial the event. Why is this?

You may think that a person's personality explains how he or she handles stress. Still, personality doesn't explain the whole story.

Why Am I Stressed?

Researchers are still trying to pinpoint the genetic components of stress. A specific stress gene is not likely to be found. A more likely possibility is that some people may inherited a tendency to be more emotional than others. This may explain why these individuals sometimes have difficulty with stress. On the bright side, however, this tendency probably makes them sensitive and caring individuals. The genetic factor only means that some individuals may be predisposed to feeling stress—they can learn to manage their stress.

Most of your stress probably comes from your environment and the way you have learned to deal with stressful situations over your lifetime. Therefore, to lower your levels of stress, you can either change the world around you or change the way you respond to the world—or both. These are two important stress *principles:* 1) changing your environment and/or 2) changing your responses to the environment around you. Surprisingly, changing your responses is often easier than changing what goes on around you. Yet, changing your environment is also possible.

In this program, you will learn how to consider both components of the stress equation. We show you different *techniques* of coping with the world around you and different *techniques* to help you change your thoughts and responses to that world. You will also learn skills that will help change the world around you, making it less stressful. Let's now consider the environment and what makes it stressful.

Stressful Environments

Many things in our world can make us feel stressed. We typically think of the big things—losing a job, death of a loved one, a serious car accident, or facing a serious illness. These are all events that, when they occur, can make us feel very stressed. In addition, we also need to remember those "daily hassles." These are the general, small events in life that can be annoying, irritating, and unpleasant. They can be an ongoing source of stress.

You may have uncovered some of these daily hassles as you searched for patterns of stress in your Daily Stress Record. Heavy traffic, overcommitment, unpleasant relationships, or noise around the house are examples. Because they are so common and tend to build over time, these seemingly small daily hassles often become more of a problem than major life events. Positive things can sometimes be stressful because of the negative aspects that go with them. Jane's Daily Stress Record from Lesson Two (page 34) is a good example. Preparing food for a friend's party and going to the party became stressful for Jane because of the extra time it took from her otherwise busy schedule. Yet, this would have been a perfect opportunity for her to forget about work, enjoy the company of her friends, and have a relaxing evening.

Some events in our lives are constant, ongoing sources of stress and have to do with circumstances in our lives. While we may not be able to easily change some of life's circumstances, we can learn to change how we respond to them. For example, you may not have as much money as you would like to have or may be financially overcommitted. While you may not be able to readily change your financial status, you do have the power to "choose" how you respond to the circumstances. You can choose to be happy or choose to be angry, sad, or depressed about the situation—the choice is yours! We will talk more about the power of choice later in this lesson.

Coping with Your Environment

The way you cope with stressful events and circumstances is part of your personality—the choices you make. You make choices from the things you have learned over your life. You have learned these things from parents, other family members, friends, teachers, and life experiences. Most people who are highly stressed tend to have two major beliefs:

1. They believe that their world is full of negatives.
2. They believe that they don't have as much control as they would like over the negatives in their lives.

If you can identify with these beliefs, just remember that it took you a long time to learn them. You are not going to unlearn them overnight. With hard work and practice, your outlook can change. We will not be looking deep into your past to try and determine what caused your original tendency toward stress. You will not be expected to spend hours on sofa regressing back to your childhood to blame your parents or your brothers or sisters. Instead, you will be learning practical skills to help you manage your stress, here and now. We will discuss these issues in more detail later. But for now, let's turn our attention to the factors that lead up to stress—challenges. Then, we'll look at how our bodies respond to these challenges.

Facing Challenges

When you perceive a potential threat or challenge, your mind and body prepare

"Most stress comes from your environment and and the way you respond to events that happen in your environment."

you to respond. The danger doesn't have to be real; anything you perceive as a threat or challenge can trigger your body and mind to get ready. Actual physical threats are not the only trigger. Potential failure or ridicule is also a major source of stress for most people.

The stressful triggers of our nomadic ancestors were more physical than mental. The nomads were constantly aware of the physical dangers of wild animals and other nomadic groups. Today, much of our stress comes from perceived threats that do not pose a direct physical threat. Feelings like having too much to do, having more bills at the end of the month than money, or thinking that your partner doesn't understand you may threaten your security. But, you may not feel physically threatened. Again, we want to emphasize that the danger does not have to be real—*perceived* danger can be as stressful as *real* danger. An example may help you understand how we respond to challenges.

Meet Mark

Mark is a 21-year-old student living in an eastern urban city. One night Mark is walking home from a late movie. His route took him down a dark, deserted alley. As Mark enters the dark alley, he is immediately on alert. His heart begins to beat faster and faster; his palms begin to sweat; and his eyes continually scan the area around him. Mark's mind and body are preparing him to take action in the event he is confronted with danger. Though it may not be immediately apparent, the purpose of Mark's stress is to protect him from danger. His mind and body are preparing him to respond. If a mugger were to suddenly jump from the shadows of the alley, Mark would be physically ready to respond quickly. This condition is referred to as the "fight or flight" response to stress.

The challenge of deadlines provides another common example of stress. Jane, who we introduced you to in Lesson Two, on page 32, is an excellent example. She began to experience stress one morning at 11:30 a.m. (see example on page 34) because she was not prepared for a 1:00 p.m. meeting. Jane's stress increased because of her perceived feelings of being a failure if she were not prepared. The threat is not the deadline itself. The threat to Jane is that one of her colleagues will criticize her for not being prepared. She also fears that this criticism will keep her from becoming a partner in the law firm. If Jane cared nothing about her colleagues or becoming a partner, she would not have these stressful feelings. But most of us do care about things that are important to us. Therefore,

My Stress Triggers

(Jane's Example)

TRIGGER	ENVIRONMENTAL	THOUGHT
Trigger 1: Getting a late start for work		✓
Trigger 2: Having too much to do and not enough time to get it all done	✓	
Trigger 3: Not being prepared for a meeting	✓	
Trigger 4: Taking on too much work	✓	
Trigger 5: Being fired and not becoming a partner		✓

most of us would feel stress in a similar situation.

This shows how our environment (approaching deadline) interacts with our thoughts (feeling like a failure) to produce a high level of stress. The closer the deadline, the higher the stress. The more Jane cares about her colleagues' opinions and becoming a partner, the higher her stress level. Jane's final level of stress will depend on a combination of her environment and her thoughts. We show you an example of Jane's stress triggers on the left.

Identifying Your Stress Triggers

We have repeatedly stated the importance of identifying your stress triggers, those situations or thought patterns that increase your stress. Think of triggers as the challenges in your life that increase your stress. You may have identified some of these triggers by analyzing your Daily Stress Records. Perhaps you are more likely to feel stressed when interacting with a specific person, say your mother-in-law! Maybe you feel stressed when you demand perfection from yourself at work. Once you identify the primary triggers in your life, you will be better able to plan coping strategies to lower your stress.

Look at Jane's example on the left. Now, list your five main stress triggers in the space provided on page 63. Identify each trigger as primarily an environmental or thought-induced stressor, although most stressors are a combination of both. We will refer to this list in later lessons.

The Four States of Feeling

Stress is one part of a continuum of feelings—a wide range of ways you may respond when faced with a threat or challenge. This continuum extends from excitement to depression, with stress and anxiety between, as shown on page 65. The four states are related, yet different. The one you experience at any given time depends upon your perceived ability to cope with the particular situation you are facing.

In any given instance, you may experience only one of the four feelings or combinations of two that are next to each other. An example might be excitement and stress

My Stress Triggers

TRIGGER	ENVIRONMENTAL	THOUGHT
Trigger 1:		
Trigger 2:		
Trigger 3:		
Trigger 4:		
Trigger 5:		

or stress and anxiety. You are not likely, however, to go back and forth between two feelings that are furthest apart, such as excitement and depression. Let's now take a closer look at the four states of feelings. To help us do this, we introduce you to Barbara.

Meet Barbara

Barbara is a 36-year-old, second-grade teacher. She has two terrific children and a wonderful, supportive husband. Barbara loves her work and adores her students. She works hard to gain the respect and consideration of her students and prides herself in the close relationship she enjoys with their parents. Barbara is constantly praising her students and enjoys the motivational challenge of communicating with them on their level.

Each year, Barbara's school honors an outstanding teacher with an annual "Teacher-of-the-Year Award." This award is presented to the winning teacher at the school's annual banquet. Although other teachers and parents constantly praise Barbara, she shuns being in the spotlight and reflects the comments back to her students. Secretly, Barbara has dreamed of winning the Teacher-of-the-Year Award. This year, Barbara's dream came true!

Excitement

You may be surprised at first that excitement—a positive response—is related to stress. Remember, we said that positive events can cause stress because of the negative aspects that go with them. Being excited is simply another way of responding to a challenge; it is a positive response. When you confront a situation for which you feel prepared, you get geared up for it; you expect your performance to be outstanding. The sensations you feel may be closely related to the sensations of stress: a rapid heartbeat, sudden burst of energy, or an upset stomach. You may even find yourself going from excitement to stress. You may feel excited at first, then tense about whether it will work out as you desire. We see this response often in athletes before a big game. Before the Super Bowl, the football players often have feelings of both excitement and stress. Remember, the purpose of these reactions is to prepare you for the challenge.

"Before the Super Bowl, the football players often have feelings of both excitement and stress."

When the principal told Barbara that she had won this year's Teacher-of-the-Year Award, she felt the excitement. Her heart started to pound, her palms began to sweat, a smile spread from ear to ear, and it was all she could do to keep from jumping up and down. She could hardly wait to dash home and tell her family.

Stress

Sometimes when you face a difficult challenge, you may feel that you can handle it if only you had the time or the help you needed—but you don't, and you feel overwhelmed. You may be afraid of failure or fear disappointing someone, possibly even yourself. You end up feeling constantly pressured to work harder, do better, and be perfect. You feel tense and irritable, your head hurts, and your stomach is tied in knots. This is the feeling of being stressed. As we said before, it's natural to go from feelings of excitement to feelings of stress, back to excitement, and so on.

Barbara's family was delighted to hear the good news about her award. They all knew it was well deserved. Her husband took the whole family out to eat in celebration. Later that night, after going to bed, Barbara began to think of the annual banquet where she would be presented with the award. As she remembered past recipients and their acceptance talks, Barbara was suddenly overcome with stress. The thought of giving an acceptance talk in front of students, parents, faculty, and administrative staff was overwhelming to her. She couldn't sleep all night.

Anxiety

If you perceive something dangerous is about to happen, and you believe that there is little you can do about it, you may become anxious. The danger could be anything from a physical attack to making a fool of yourself. Again, we want to emphasize that the danger does not have to be real—perceived danger can be as stressful as real danger.

You may fear an upcoming event like an important exam and be unable to get it out of your mind. Unable to clear the event from your mind, you worry about it constantly. The more you try *not* to think about it, the more you think about it. And the more you think about it, the more anxious you become. Inevitably, you become afraid of losing control.

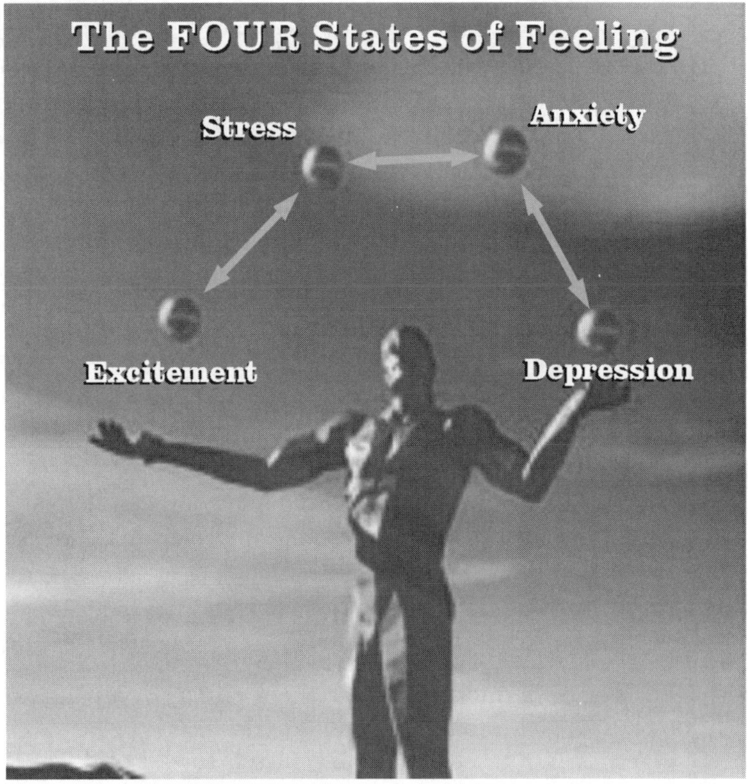

Although we designed this program to deal with stress, anxiety and stress are closely related. Most people who are highly stressed occasionally have feelings of anxiety—periods when they feel they are losing control. People who are primarily anxious, on the other hand, often show streaks of perfectionism and irritability—the hallmarks of stress. Thus, the techniques we discuss in this book are just as applicable to the anxious person. But remember, if you believe that you are experiencing anxiety, be sure to contact a mental health professional for additional help.

As the date of the school's annual banquet drew near, Barbara began to worry more and more. She would wake up in the middle of the night and begin to worry about what she would say. She feared looking foolish in front of everyone in attendance. Barbara worked through the stepladder technique for testing the reality of her fears along with probability testing.

Depression Questionnaire

Depression is a serious problem that can affect as many as 25 percent of women and 12 percent of men at some time during their lives. Also, in the past 50 years, the percentage of teenagers with depression has increased more than fivefold. Because of the increase in the number of cases of depression over the years, depression has been called the "common cold of mental illness." Unfortunately, the effects can be far more life threatening if left untreated. The following questions have been compiled to help provide a guide for determining whether a person may have a problem with depression.

Scoring

It is not possible to provide a scoring system here that can diagnose a depression reliably or categorize how serious a depression might be present. The diagnosis of a depression can only be determined by a health professional through careful assessment and/or the use of specific psychological testing instruments. Nonetheless, the following questions can help alert individuals to the possibility that a depression might be present. These questions, however, may not necessarily address the various forms of depressive problems.

Instructions

For each question below, check either a "yes" answer or a "no" answer in the space provided.

❑ Yes ❑ No 1. Do you find yourself so sad and depressed that it colors your entire life, and you can't seem to escape from it?

❑ Yes ❑ No 2. Do you find yourself no longer enjoying anything?

❑ Yes ❑ No 3. Do you have trouble concentrating on most tasks, such as work, reading, and other activities?

❑ Yes ❑ No 4. Do you have little or no energy and feel like you need to struggle to do anything at all?

❑ Yes ❑ No 5. Have your sleeping patterns changed? For example, do you have trouble falling asleep; do you wake frequently during the night; do you wake up early in the morning, and despite feeling tired, cannot fall back to sleep; or do you sleep more than usual?

❑ Yes ❑ No 6. Do you feel increasingly guilty, worthless, and hopeless?

❑ Yes ❑ No 7. Have you experienced a change in your eating patterns such as a poor appetite or overeating?

If you answer "yes" to four or more of the questions above, you should consider consulting a professional who deals with mental health. Please note that if the problems specified above last for at least two consecutive, weeks they can negatively affect many aspects of your life (e.g., family work, etc.).

Source: Adapted with permission from Marcus MD. Depression and weight control: Why is the link so strong? *The Weight Control Digest* 1995; 5:396.

These techniques helped her to reduce her stress and make an award-winning acceptance talk at the banquet. We'll introduce these techniques in later lessons.

Depression

A person who constantly perceives life as threatening or dangerous and begins to lose hope about ever controlling these threats, can slip into a state of depression. People who experience depression tend to be lethargic and believe that there is little hope that they will ever be able to change anything.

The causes of depression are still a mystery, but recent research has established both biological and psychological contributors. As with most disorders, including anxiety and stress, we seem to inherit a genetic tendency to be uptight, tense, or anxious. Early experiences in life may also teach us that life can be dangerous, threatening, or difficult to control. When we later experience similar circumstances in life, we may become extremely anxious and ultimately depressed with feelings of hopelessness. This is much different from normal sadness. This depressed state is associated with both chemical changes in the brain and distortions in the way a person feels and thinks. Fortunately, effective treatments exist for depression. Mental health professionals may recommend an antidepressant drug or brief psychological treatments. Such treatments may include cognitive-behavioral therapy lasting from 10 to 20 sessions.

Now, complete the Depression Questionnaire on page 66. This simple questionnaire is a guide for helping you determine whether you may have a problem with depression.

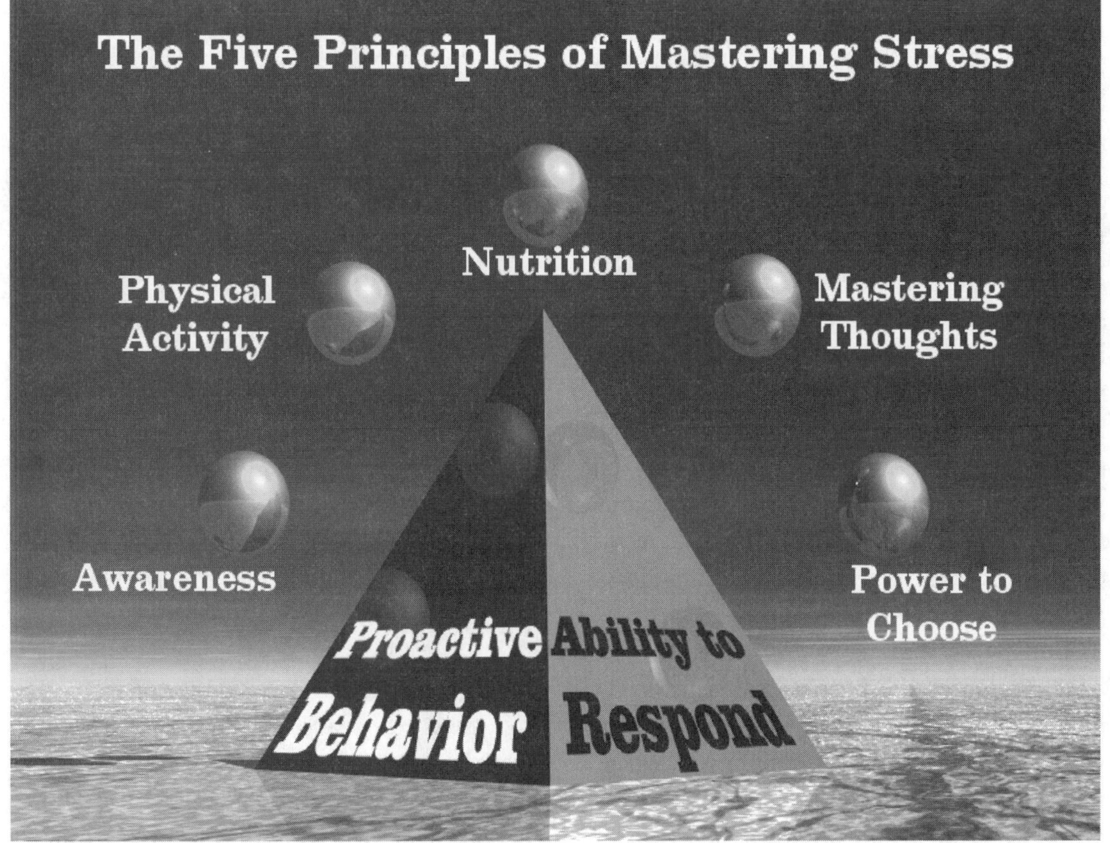

"The five principles of stress can provide you with the skills to be more proactive in your response to stressful events in your life."

Five Principles of Mastering Stress

We now want to turn our focus to looking at practical ways of managing stress. You'll be pleased to know that you are already well on your way to mastering some of these techniques! The five principles of stress that we discuss below can provide you with the skills to be more proactive in your response to stressful events in your life. Let's look closely at each of the five principles.

Awareness

For the past two weeks, you have been keeping a Daily Stress Record. You have also carefully analyzed your records, searching for patterns. This process has helped you to become more aware of when your stress level increases, what events increase your stress, and what your major stressors are. This information is key to the rest of this program and throughout your life. Don't panic, you won't have to keep daily records for the rest of your life. However, you will need to develop a self-monitoring system that keeps you on your toes. Some of our clients keep a Daily Stress Record during the first week of every month, while others may keep records every other month or quarterly. Again, we cannot overemphasize the importance of self-awareness. As we said at the beginning of this lesson, this awareness may have already helped you reduce the stress in your life.

Physical Activity

In Lesson Four, we discuss the three stress response systems that go to work to help us cope with stressful situations. The better these systems function, the better we cope with stressful situations. One response system is our physical response system.

Are you physically active every day? Recent research has shown many benefits associated with being physically active. In fact, inactivity is now considered a major risk factor for disease and early death. According to the recent Surgeon General's Report, *Physical Activity and Health*, roughly 60 percent of Americans do not exercise regularly. The good news is that you don't have to be a marathon runner or even go to a gym to improve your physical fitness. The more physically fit you are, the better you will cope with stress. We'll help guide you to becoming more active in later lessons.

Do you remember Mark and his journey down the dark alley on his way home from a movie? If a mugger were to jump from the darkness and begin to chase Mark, his physical fitness would play a key role in his ability to physically respond to this stressful situation. Again, we cannot overstate the importance of regular physical activity.

Nutrition

How is your diet? You may find this an odd question coming from a stress management program, but it is an important question for you to consider. We live in a fast-paced world in which good eating habits often give way to the drive-thru window at a fast-food restaurant. Like physical activity, good nutrition is a key component to a healthy body. Would you forget to put quality fuel in your car or care for its engine? Probably not, especially if you expect it to run well. We often treat our bodies with less care than we do our cars, and yet, we expect them to run efficiently.

Mastering Thoughts

Do you know where your feelings come from? You may think they come from your heart, from inside, or perhaps from events in your life. These are all common answers, but are not quite accurate. Our feelings come from our thoughts—yes, our thoughts. Many of our thoughts are automatic—we think without really thinking. These automatic thoughts that can lead to high levels of stress. By learning techniques to help you master your thoughts, you will learn to master your feelings. Here, we are talking about changing the dialogue that creates stress—the perfectionistic, catastrophic, and negative thoughts, to name a few. We also don't mean being positive all the time. This can be just as stressful as being negative. We mean being realistic and analyzing when your perceptions mirror reality.

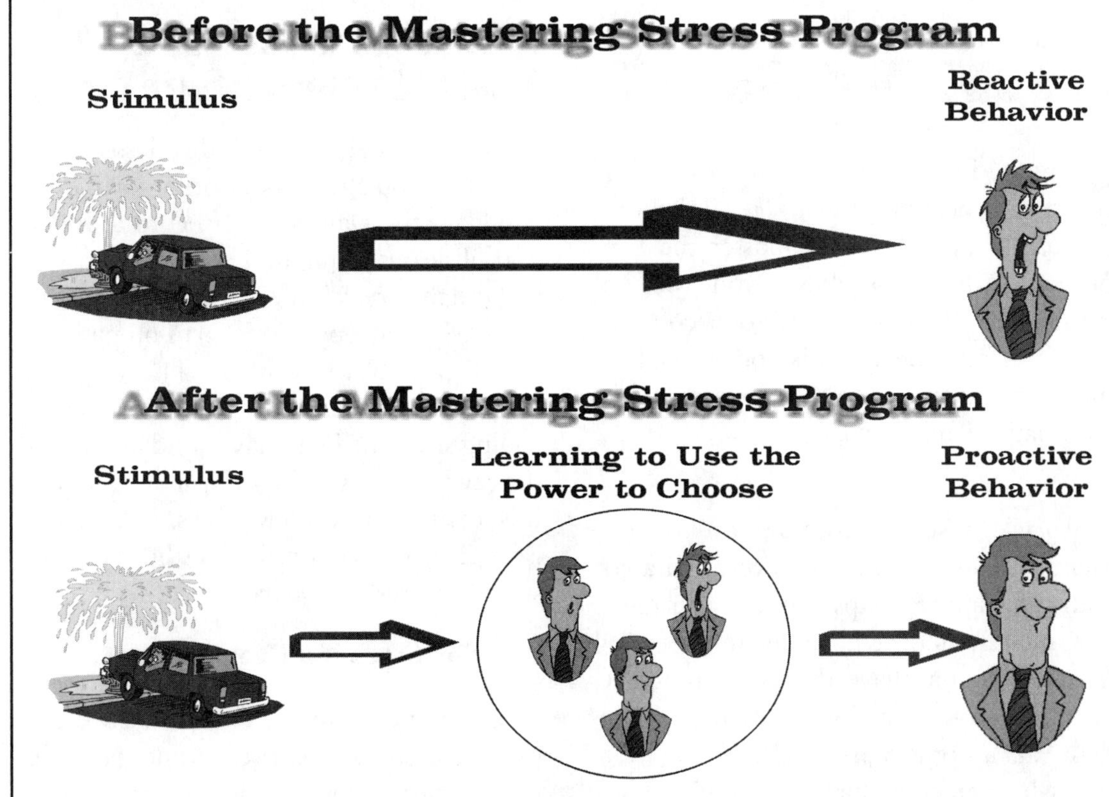

"The ultimate goal in mastering stress is to be less reactive and more proactive."

Power to Choose

In Lesson Two, on page 46, we discussed the important role of choice. Too often we spin our wheels trying to control things we simply cannot control, such as someone else's behavior, feelings, or mind. When our control efforts fail to produce the desired results, our level of stress increases. About the only things in life we can control are our choices. When we feel stressed, we often forget that we have the ability to choose the way we think, feel, and behave. Once you realize that you control your choices, the next step is to make the *right* choices for you. High levels of stress often come from making the *wrong* choices. Four key principles help us make the right choice. You're already familiar with the first principle, awareness. The more aware you are of your true self, the better choices you will make for yourself. In later lessons, we'll cover the remaining three principles for making the right choices.

Proactive Behavior

The ultimate objective in mastering stress is to become less *reactive* and more *proactive*. As you learn to master the five principles discussed above, you will be gaining the skills necessary to become a more proactive person. Like our thoughts, many of our reactions to life's events are automatic or reactionary.

To take just one example, do you remember the last time you were irritated with someone? Perhaps you lost your temper and shouted at a family member or friend. You may have deeply regretted it later, but your reaction seemed so sudden—an automatic reaction. You're not sure what you could have done differently.

Behavioral scientists have now demonstrated that there are many subtle cues, thoughts, and feelings that, even though they happen very quickly, come between the initial irritating event and your reaction. At each point, you actually have the power to choose what you are going to think and how you are going to react. The Mastering Stress Program will help you develop that *power* to choose. Then, you will be in control of your responses rather than having stressful reactions controlling you!

Putting it All Together

From the discussion here, you can see that Mastering Stress Program is all about learning and honing important stress management skills. These skills cannot be learned or mastered in a day, a week, or a month. By the time you finish this program, you will have learned these skills and be ready to practice them for the rest of your life.

Introducing a New Monitoring Form

At the beginning of this lesson, we promised you a new monitoring form. You can leave the Daily Stress Record at home and fill it out at night. The new form you will use this week is the Stressful Events Record. Make a copy of the form on page 75 so you can carry it with you. This way, you can fill it out whenever you notice yourself feeling stressed. That may sound like a burden, but do not worry. You will need to use this form for only a few weeks. Its purpose is to give you a better look at how you respond to stressful events.

The Stressful Events Record

Use the Stressful Events Record every time your stress level rises. Some days you may record many episodes of stress, while

Stressful Events Record

Jane's Example

Week of: *January 8, 2001*

Date	Starting Time	Ending Time	Highest Stress Level (0–8)	(a) Triggers	(b) Emotions (0–10)	(c) Thoughts	(d) Behaviors	(e) Physical Symptoms
01-08-01	6:30 a.m.	7:00 a.m.	6	Looking at clock and not being ready	Angry with myself	I have so much to do, I'll get further behind	Began rushing around, ran to the bus stop	Headache, upset stomach, sweating
01-09-01	11:30 a.m.	12:30 p.m.	7	Not being ready for the 1 o'clock meeting	Frustrated, angry for not working late last night	I won't be prepared, I'll make a fool of myself	Shut door to be alone, didn't answer the phone	Tight neck, upset stomach, tense
01-11-01	6:45 a.m.	7:30 a.m.	7	Late bus	Mad at the driver	I'll get further behind now	Biting nails, pacing	Tight neck and arms, upset stomach

Column ***Instructions***

(a) Write down the trigger (event) that caused your stress to rise. This column is likely to echo the "Stressful Event of the Highest Stress Level" column on your Daily Stress Record for the same day.

(b) Record the emotions you felt immediately after the stressful trigger. Examples may include, anger, fear, hopelessness, or frustration. Remember to record you initial feelings of emotion.

(c) Write down the thoughts that went through your head as your stress was increasing. For example, you may have thought, "I won't make it, I can't cope" or "I'm going to look foolish." No matter how silly the thoughts seem after the moment has passed, write them down.

(d) Write down your immediate behaviors to the stressful event. What did you do? Perhaps you started pacing, took a walk, threw something across the room, or started crying. Whatever the behavior, write it down.

(e) In the last column, record the major physical symptoms you experienced because of this stress. Physical symptoms such as, headache, nausea, pounding heart, or sweating are common symptoms of increased stress.

other days you may record none. On page 71, we provide you with Jane's example that she prepared from her Daily Stress Record on page 34. The following instructions will help you complete the Stressful Events Record.

- In the first column, record the date.
- In the second column, note the approximate time that your stress level began to increase.
- In the third column, note the approximate time that your level of stress returned to a normal level.
- In the fourth column, record the highest level of stress you felt during this episode. Use the 0–8 Stress Scale that you used on your Daily Stress Record.
- In column (a), write down the trigger (event) that caused your stress to rise. This column is likely to echo the "Stressful Event of the Highest Stress Level" column on your Daily Stress Record for the same day.
- In column (b), record your emotions immediately after the stressful trigger on a scale of 1–10, even if they seem extreme. For example, fear may not be the emotion you feel now when you think of being called into your boss' office, but at the time, you were very frightened.
- In column (c), write down the thoughts that went through your head as your stress was increasing. For example, you may have thought, "I won't make it, I can't cope," or "I'm going to look foolish." No matter how silly the thoughts seem after the moment has passed, write them down.
- In column (d), write down your immediate behaviors to the stressful event. What did you do? Perhaps you started pacing, took a walk, threw something across the room, or started crying. Whatever the behavior, write it down.
- In the last column (e), record the major physical symptoms you experienced because of this stress. Physical symptoms such as, headache, nausea, pounding heart, or sweating are common symptoms of increased stress.

Filling out the Stressful Events Record will help you identify your unique stress triggers and your reactions to them. You may have already begun to notice certain patterns to your stress triggers. The Stressful Events Record will now help you identify patterns in your reactions to these stressful triggers. Identifying your stress triggers and anticipating your automatic reactions will help you develop skills and strategies to become more proactive in your responses. This increases your ability to respond in a less stressful way. Think for a minute about these words, "ability to respond." Now, turn the phrase around and you get "response-ability." In other words, you become more responsible for your stress.

Lesson Review

Congratulations, you made it though this busy lesson. In this lesson, you reviewed your Daily Stress Record from last week and continued searching for patterns. We discussed how threats and challenges are met with a continuum of feelings, from excitement to depression, and how feelings can easily move along this continuum. You identified five triggers that cause you the highest stress. We introduced you to the five principles to mastering stress and showed you how they all work together to help you to become more proactive in your response to stressful situations. And finally, we introduced you to the Stressful Events Record. You will carry the Stressful Events Record with you during the day to record each event that causes your stress level to increase.

This Week's Assignment

This week, continue using the Daily Stress Record. We provide you with a blank form on page 74 for you to use or copy. Be sure to complete the Stress Change Worksheet each day on page 29 and the Average Stress Change Worksheet in Appendix E, page 430. Complete the "My Stressful Patterns Worksheet" on page 56 if you did not do so while reading the lesson. On page 63, be sure to list five of your most stress-causing triggers.

Make a copy of the blank Stressful Events Record on page 75. Carry this record with you, and every time your stress level rises, fill it out. Remember to record all events that increase your stress. On some days, you may have 10 entries and on other days, none at all. Be sure to complete each column. We have included the instructions for each column at the bottom of the form, or you can refer to them in the lesson on page 70. We highly recommend that you go back in the manual anytime you begin to have difficulty with any of the assignments.

Knowledge Review

T F 16. An effective program partnership requires both partners to participate in the mastering stress program.

T F 17. Because genetics predispose people to feeling stressed, some will not be able to learn to manage their stress.

T F 18. People who are stressed often feel that they don't have as much control as they would like over the negative things in their lives.

T F 19. A perceived threat or challenge can be as stressful as the real thing.

T F 20. It is possible to vacillate between a state of stress and anxiety when responding to challenging situations.

T F 21. Feelings come from your heart or from events in your life.

(***Answers in Appendix C, page 415***)

Daily Stress Record—Lesson Three

Name:__________________________________ **Week of:**______________

Date	Average Stress Level	Highest Stress Level	Time of Highest Stress Level	Stressful Event Associated with Highest Stress Level

Remember to complete the Stress Change Worksheet on page 29 at the end of the week by recording the Highest Stress Level and Average Stress Level from your Daily Stress Record.

Stressors I Experience Most Often
1.
2.
3.
4.
5.

Stress Scale

Extreme Stress	8
	7
Much Stress	6
	5
Moderate Stress	4
	3
Mild Stress	2
	1
No Stress	0

Stressful Events Record—Lesson Three

Week of: ____________________

Date	Starting Time	Ending Time	Highest Stress Level (0–8)	(a) Triggers	(b) Emotions (0–10)	(c) Thoughts	(d) Behaviors	(e) Physical Symptoms

Column	***Instructions***
(a)	Write down the trigger (event) that caused your stress to rise. This column is likely to echo the "Stressful Event of the Highest Stress Level" column on your Daily Stress Record for the same day.
(b)	Record the emotions you felt immediately after the stressful trigger. Examples may include, anger, fear, hopelessness, or frustration. Remember to record you initial feelings of emotion.
(c)	Write down the thoughts that went through your head as your stress was increasing. For example, you may have thought, "I won't make it, I can't cope" or "I'm going to look foolish." No matter how silly the thoughts seem after the moment has passed, write them down.
(d)	Write down your immediate behaviors to the stressful event. What did you do? Perhaps you started pacing, took a walk, threw something across the room, or started crying. Whatever the behavior, write it down.
(e)	In the last column, record the major physical symptoms you experienced because of this stress. Physical symptoms such as, headache, nausea, pounding heart, or sweating are common symptoms of increased stress.

**Stress Management Tip # 213:
When work becomes unbearable, grab the steam from your coffee and let it carry you away.**

Lesson Four

Welcome to Lesson Four. We begin this lesson with a review of your Stressful Events Record from last week. This is an important exercise and essential to the rest of the program. As promised, we will help guide you in the selection of a program partner if you are a social changer. Then, you will be learning about the three stress response systems. As you read through this section, you likely will recognize many of the responses you experienced over the last week and recorded on your Stressful Events Record. Now that you have been monitoring your stress closely with the monitoring forms, you should be more aware of your stressors and reactions. We then introduce you to the "Exercise" component of LEARN. You will learn the important benefits of physical activity and the key role that laughter plays in stress management. We then discuss the 10 characteristics of stress-producing thoughts and how you can begin to challenge these thoughts. We conclude this lesson with another Quality of Life Review. If you're ready, let's begin by reviewing your Stressful Events Record.

Reviewing Your Stressful Events Record

How did you do with last week's assignment of completing the Stressful Events Record? Carrying it with you each day allowed you to record stressful events immediately as they happened. Reviewing your comments will help you become more aware of your reactions to stressful events. Now, let's look at what you learned about *your* stressful events.

Reviewing the duration of your daily stressors is important. How long did each episode of stress last? Were there certain stressful experiences that lasted longer than others? For example, did you find yourself often stressed for short periods of time or did your stress level remain high for hours?

Now, look at the intensity of the stress you experienced. What stressors receive the highest stress scores, and how high are these scores? How do these scores compare

"Reviewing your Stressful Events Record will help you become more aware of your reactions to certain events."

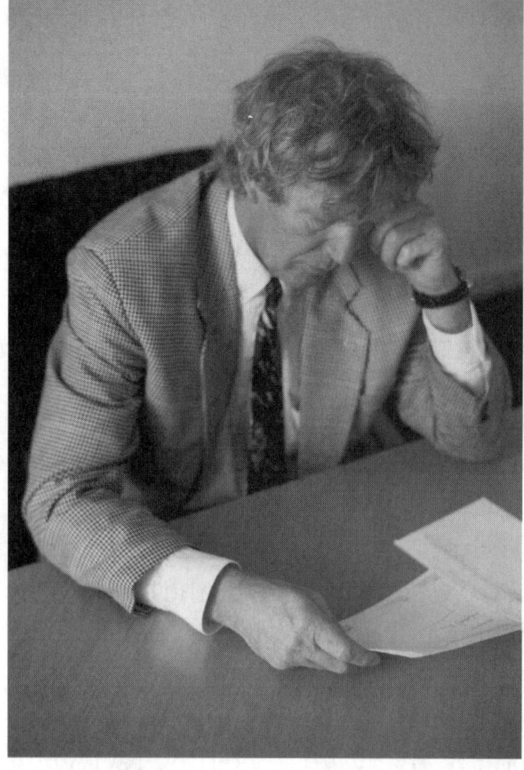

with the highest scores on your first Daily Stress Record from Lesson One? By the end of the week, could you begin to predict stressful events and the stress scores they might generate?

Remember, events do not cause stress directly, but they can trigger stress. What are your stress triggers? Do you have many or a few? How do the triggers on your Stressful Events Record, on page 75, compare with the triggers you listed on the My Stress Triggers worksheet on page 63 in Lesson Three? Do your stress triggers vary significantly by day? What thoughts are associated with them? Did your thoughts include not being able to do something well? Did you think someone may not like or approve of you? Carefully review your thoughts (self-talk) for each stressful event. This will be important to know as you continue through the program.

Lastly, what were the physical symptoms you experienced during the stressful episodes? Were your hands trembling, your heart beating fast, or did you feel tense and nauseous? Most people are unaware of the physical symptoms of stress. Knowing your physical symptoms will help you immediately recognize when stress is building. The sooner you know that your stress level is beginning to increase, the sooner you can take steps to reduce it.

Now that you have practiced recording your personal responses to stress, we can discuss the three stress response symptoms. As we go though this discussion, you may be able to recognize and identify more clearly the responses you experienced last week. But first, let's revisit the notion of a program partner. Keep in mind, however, that if you have decided to continue the program alone, that's fine too.

Choosing a Program Partner

In Lesson Three, we promised to give you some guidelines for choosing a good program partner. You were supposed to think of individuals that may be good partners.

Dr. Kelly Brownell of Yale University developed a Partnership Quiz to help individuals on a weight management program choose a good program partner. He developed this quiz after much research on the characteristics of a good program partner.

On page 79 is the Program Partnership Quiz. To take the Program Partnership Quiz, think of a person you believe would be a good partner. Then, answer the questions honestly. Answer each question either true or false. Beside each of your answers is a number. Write this number in the space to the left of each question number. After

Program Partnership Quiz

___1. It is easy to talk to my partner about stressful events in my life.

True—5 False—1

___2. My partner has always been stress *free* and does not understand my stress problems.

True—1 False—3

___3. My partner does things to increase my stress when he or she knows I'm trying to manage stress in my life.

True—1 False—5

___4. My partner never says critical things about my mood, even when I'm stressed.

True—3 False—1

___5. My partner is always there when I need a friend.

True—4 False—1

___6. When I become less stressed and more in control of my life, my partner will be jealous.

True—1 False—3

___7. My partner will be genuinely interested in helping me with my stress.

True—6 False—1

___8. I could talk to my partner even if I was doing poorly in my program.

True—5 False—1

____ **Total Score** (sum of questions 1–8)

If you scored between 30 and 34, you may have found the perfect partner. A score in this range indicates that you and this person are comfortable with one another and can work together.

If you scored between 24 and 29, your friend is potentially a good partner, but there are a few areas of concern. Try asking the partner to take the quiz and predict how you answered the questions. This may help you make a decision.

If you scored between 17 and 24, there are potential areas of conflict, and a program partnership with this person could encounter some difficult times. Think of another program partner.

If you scored between 8 and 16, definitely look to someone else as a partner. A program partnership in this case would be a high-risk undertaking.

Source: Adapted with permission from Brownell KD. Partnership quiz. *The LEARN® Program for Weight Management 2000,* Dallas: American Health Publishing Co., 2000.

answering all eight questions, total the number of your responses. Use the scoring guide at the bottom of the quiz to help you interpret your score.

This Program Partnership Quiz should help you choose a program partner. Once you have done so, be sure to discuss the possibility with the person you have in mind. In Lesson Five, we'll give you some helpful suggestions on communicating with your partner.

We want to emphasize again, that you do not need to have a program partner. We leave that decision entirely up to you. If you decide a partner would be helpful for you, the quiz should help in choosing a supportive partner. If you are not sure about going through the program with a partner, feel free to experiment. You can use the information in this manual to see if a partnership is beneficial to you. If it is not, proceed as a *solo* changer.

Understanding the Stress Response Systems

Stress is a response to threats and challenges, real or perceived, that occur in our environment. The word stress is a broad, poorly defined term often used to refer to a wide range of negative responses. As we discussed in Lesson Three, stress can evolve from a positive state of excitement. When we perceive a situation as having potential negatives—even while we experience something good—we cope by trying to eliminate the negative. Do you remember how excited Barbara was when she learned she had won the Teacher-of-the-Year Award in Lesson Three, on page 63? Her excitement later turned to stress as she began to worry about the negatives associated with giving an acceptance talk. She considered many possible ways to eliminate the negatives, such as not giving an acceptance talk, not showing up to receive the reward, and even declining the award. Instead, Barbara learned new coping skills (we'll discuss these in later lessons) that not only reduced her level of stress, but also helped to make the school's banquet a highlight in her life.

We can divide our reactions to stress into the following three interrelated response systems:

- Physical
- Mental
- Behavioral

Understanding the stress response systems and how they work together is important to understanding what stress is all about. This understanding will also help you to recognize stress in its earliest stages, allowing you to take steps to reduce the stress before it reaches higher levels.

Physical Response System

The physical response system includes all the changes that take place in your body when you feel stressed. Some of these changes can seem quite bizarre and frightening when they are unfamiliar to you. Rest assured, these responses are all natural, important, and harmless. However, if you are stressed for long periods of time, your body's immune system can begin to weaken, leaving you more susceptible to

disease. This is why stress management is a crucial issue for individuals with damaged or weakened immune systems.

When you perceive or anticipate a threat, your brain leaps into action. The brain sends messages to a section of your nervous system called the *autonomic nervous system* where it signals the release of chemicals that prepare you for action. This system has two branches: the sympathetic and parasympathetic nervous system. Let's look closely at each of these systems.

Sympathetic Nervous System

The sympathetic nervous system releases two chemicals, adrenalin and noradrenaline, from the adrenal glands of the kidneys. Fueled by these two chemicals, the activity of the sympathetic nervous system can continue for a long time. This activity increases your heart rate, breathing, and blood flow throughout your body. By tightening your blood vessels, your sympathetic nervous system directs blood away from places where it is not needed, such as skin, fingers, and toes. Blood flow is redirected toward larger muscle groups where it is needed more, such as arm and leg muscles. When you experience high levels of stress, your skin may look pale and your fingers and toes may tingle or feel numb. Meanwhile, this change in blood flow has primed your large muscles for action.

The rapid heart rate and fast breathing you experience when under stress helps provide more oxygen to your body. Though this is important for immediate action, the rapid change can make you feel as if you are choking or smothering and may cause chest pains. In addition, the reduced blood supply to your brain can make you feel dizzy or confused, cause blurred vision, or give you an elusive feeling.

Overall, stress affects most of the physical systems in your body. This process re-

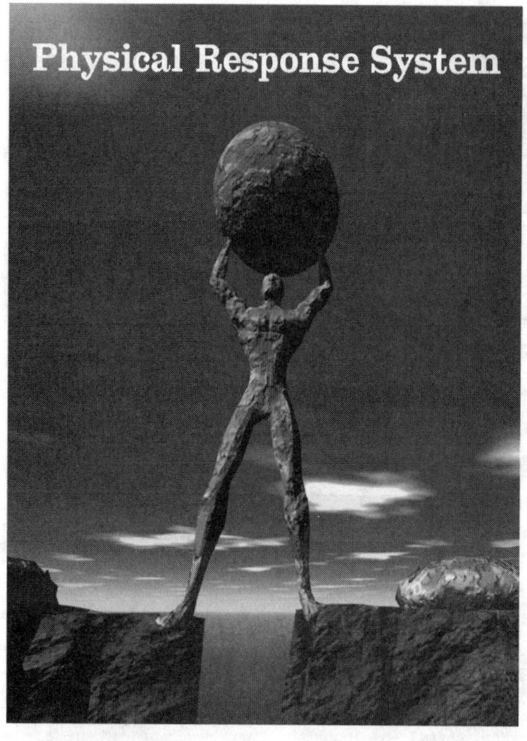

quires much energy and explains why you feel drained at the end of a stressful day. Rest assured, your sympathetic nervous system cannot get carried away and leave you in a state of high stress indefinitely. Your body has two safeguards to prevent this. First, other chemicals in the body will eventually destroy the adrenalin and noradrenaline released by the sympathetic nervous system. Second, the parasympathetic nervous system also functions as a built-in protector.

Parasympathetic Nervous System

When your body has had enough of the stress response or the threat has passed, the parasympathetic nervous system kicks in to restore a relaxed feeling. This may not happen as quickly as you would like, but it will happen. Your body will not allow your stress to keep increasing until you explode. You may feel keyed up and apprehensive, even after the initial stress trigger has passed. The reason is because the adrenaline and noradrenaline take time to dissipate. As long as they are still floating around in your body, you will still feel some degree of stress.

This slow recovery time serves an important purpose in the wild, where danger has a way of returning. Being prepared is a key to survival. In society, however, we must be careful not to use the lingering effects of stress as an excuse for inappropriate behavior, such as excessive drinking or overeating.

Other Physical Reactions

In addition to the effects on your automatic nervous system, feeling stressed produces a release of chemicals from your pituitary gland (a small area at the base of the skull). These chemicals travel to another section of your adrenal gland to release various corticoids and steroids that help to reduce swelling and inflamation. If stress is prolonged, the constant release of these chemicals in the circulatory system can damage your body and make you more susceptible to disease.

The physical responses that prepare you for action, and those involved in calming you down, are largely automatic. You cannot eliminate them altogether, nor would you want to. As we have said before, stress serves an important, protective function. Stress can lead to greater accomplishments and, under the right circumstances, can be enjoyable. In the short term, stress is not harmful, and small amounts of stress can actually have some benefits. However, if you experience high levels of stress for long periods of time, you are more likely to have physical problems. Obviously, learning to manage your stress is important to your physical well-being.

The Mental Response System

Your body is not alone in preparing for action when you face a challenge or threat. Your mind also gets into the act. The mental response system helps to change your focus of attention. When you are stressed, you tend to scan the environment constantly, looking for signs of danger. On one hand, this shift in attention is useful. If danger does exist, you will notice it quickly. On the other hand, you may be easily distracted and unable to concentrate on any one thing.

Worrying

As part of the scanning process, your mind considers many possible outcomes of a threatening situation. You may have anxious thoughts or, as most of us would put it, you worry. A little worrying is normal, and everyone does it. Many of us worry about the same kinds of things. Worrying is a main characteristics of people under stress; they have trouble turning off their worry.

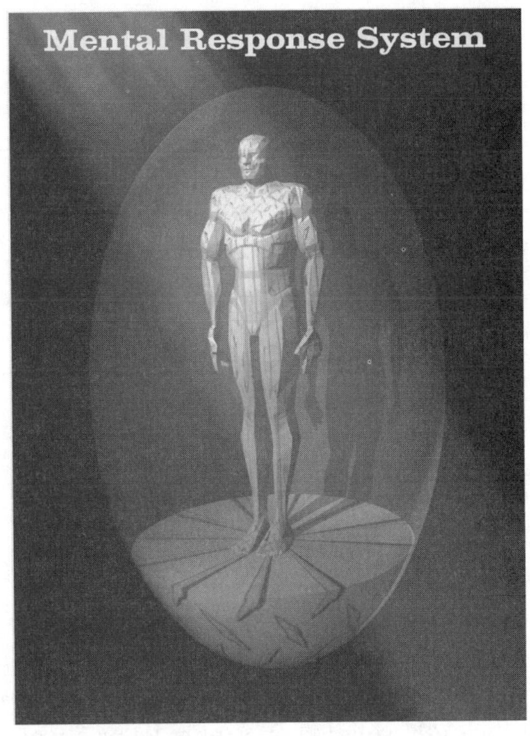

Sometimes, people feel they need to worry, fearing the lack of worrying might be irresponsible. For example, you may worry about finishing a report for work on time. Some worry or concern may help motivate you. You may say, "I will appreciate doing this now, so I can relax later." This concern is helpful. You could also tell yourself that you will never finish on time, your boss is going to hate it, or worse yet, your boss may fire you. Worrying may interfere with your ability to finish the report on time and do a good job. Avoid falling into the worry trap! Being responsible is an admirable quality. When you reach the point where your thoughts continually churn through your head and keep you awake at night, worrying is not helping you—it's hurting you.

Let's now apply these components of the mental response system to Barbara's example, from page 63 of Lesson Three, giving an acceptance speech for the Teacher-of-the-Year Award. As the initial excitement of winning the award wore off, Barbara began to worry about giving an acceptance speech. As the date for receiving the award grew nearer, she began to concentrate harder and harder on giving her acceptance talk. "What if I say something foolish?" "What will people say and think about me?" "Will they laugh at me?" These worries may be useful if they remind Barbara of the importance of her talk. However, if the worries become so strong that they interfere with her ability to sleep or function, she may have started a vicious cycle. Worrying could make Barbara miss classes or important deadlines, causing her to lose confidence in herself. Without confidence, she would certainly have difficulty giving her acceptance talk, and then she would feel even more stressed than before. Obviously, you do not want to let worry go this far. In later lessons, we will show you techniques and strategies to avoid falling into the worry trap.

The Behavioral Response System

Stress is likely to influence your behaviors. You may act irritably or try to avoid situations you fear could be stressful. Many people get jittery when they are under stress. You are probably familiar with your own nervous habits: pacing, tapping your feet, biting your nails, smoking, drinking, or snacking. Whatever your habit, you will probably notice yourself doing more of it when you are under stress. Most of these behaviors are simply ways of letting off some of the energy that has built up from physical and mental preparation and for avoiding uncomfortable situations. Still other behaviors, such as escaping from or avoiding unpleasant situations, are there to protect you. Taking a 20-minute walk is another example of a behavior you may engage in to help calm you down when stressful situations arise.

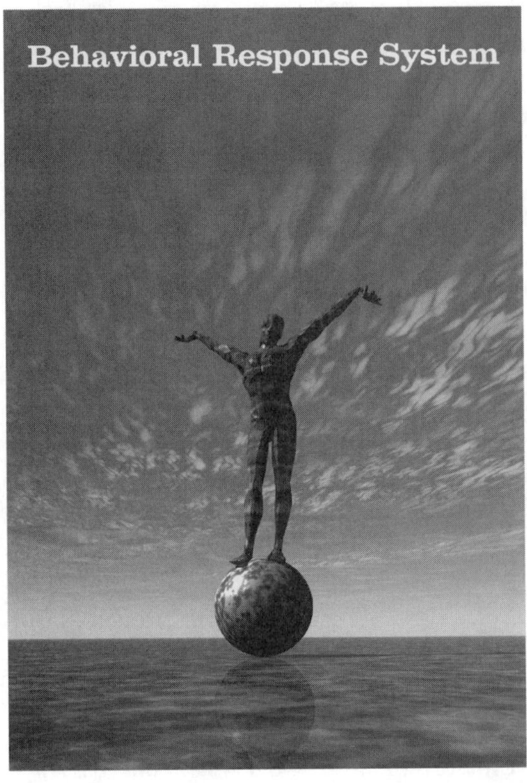

As with the other response systems, most behaviors are generally harmless and may even be beneficial when used in moderation. However, some behaviors such as smoking, drinking, or drug abuse can become very harmful. Even less harmful behaviors can become excessive and begin to interfere with your enjoyment of life.

The Stress Response Cycle

The physical, mental, and behavioral response systems each have unique purposes. Yet, they also closely interact. Any one system can affect the other, starting the entire stress-response cycle. For example, you may notice your heart beginning to pound. This, in turn, could trigger thoughts that something is wrong. You then begin to pace nervously back and forth. Alternatively, you may begin with a worri-

some thought about your children that may cause your heart to begin beating faster and your breathing to increase. You may then call or rush home to check on the kids. Your stressful thoughts may also trigger a nervous response in your stomach that may cause you to avoid a situation.

As you can see from the discussion above, each stress response system plays a key role in helping to prepare your mind and body for stressful events. Learning to recognize when each system begins to react to stressful situations is also key in managing your stress. If a stressful situation begins to smolder, you can douse it before the flames erupt. When a small fire does break out, you will want to put it out before it rages out of control. Your job is much like that of Smokey the Bear. Smokey's job is to first prevent fires from breaking out. He also constantly searches the forest keeping an eye out for smoke or small fires. Smoke is a prelude to a small fire, and a small fire is a prelude to a larger forest fire. You will be using the stress management tools you learn in this program to try and prevent stress in your life. But, when stress does begin to smolder, you will have other tools to help keep it under control.

At the physical level, you will learn to recognize tension in your body as it begins to increase but before it becomes excessive. You will learn relaxation skills to counter this physical response in Lesson Five. To address the mental component of stress, you will learn to recognize internal thoughts that begin to increase your level of stress. You will learn techniques to change your thoughts—more realistic ways of thinking about situations so they do not seem as threatening. Finally, at the behavioral level, you will learn and practice new skills to help you choose better ways of *responding* to situations—rather than automatically *reacting*. You will learn through experience that threats may not be threats at all; they may not be as bad as you fear.

"Physical activity is a critical factor in managing and reducing stress."

The Importance of Physical Activity

As we discussed in the Lesson Three, physical activity is a critical factor in managing and reducing stress. Moreover, studies show time and time again that regular physical activity is important for overall good health and longevity. Don't get nervous or worry! Increasing your physical activity does not mean that you have to start training for a marathon or spend hours each week at the local gym—it's far simpler than that. The goal here is to learn how to become more active, and make physical activity an important part of your lifestyle.

For years, we have been told that exercise has to be vigorous in order to be beneficial—"no pain, no gain." Thanks to new science and research, this is no longer the case. According to the American College of Sports Medicine and the Center for Disease Control and Prevention, even low levels of exercise can benefit health. Making modest changes in your activity level so that you become moderately active is sound advice. We will discuss how much physical activity you need to dramatically improve your health in upcoming lessons. For now, we want you to understand the important benefits of being physically active.

The Benefits of Being Active

The benefits of being physically active are important to overall health and stress management. Physical activity can help improve all three of the stress response systems that we discussed earlier in this lesson. Here are a few more of the many benefits of regular physical activity.

Increases energy. First, regular exercise increases cardiorespiratory fitness. This means that more oxygen is being circulated throughout the body and that the body is much more efficient in getting the oxygen to the muscles and other cells in the body that need it most. The more efficient your body, the better you feel. In simple terms, regular physical activity just makes

A Dozen Other Reasons to Exercise

The promise of thinner thighs or a slimmer midsection is what gets most people off the couch. And exercise can help you lose fat, preserve muscle, and keep off the excess weight you manage to lose. But if that's your only reason for moving, your're missing a lot. Here are a dozen others, including some concrete findings form selected studies. For more information, check out the 1996 Surgeon General's Report on Physical Activity and Health at www.cdc.gov/nccdphp/sgr/sgr.htm.

1 Sleep

A 16-week exercise program (30 to 40 minutes of brisk walking or low-impact aerobics four times a week) improved the quality, duration, and ease of falling asleep in healthy older adults.[1] Exercise may improve sleep by relaxing muscles, reducing stress, or warming the body.

[1] *J. Amer. Med Assoc.* 277:32, 1997.

2 Gallstones

Active women are 30 percent less likely to have gallstone surgery than sedentary women. In one study, women who spent more than 60 hours a week sitting at work or driving were twice as likely to have gallstone surgery as women who sat for less than 40 hours a week.[1]

[1] *N. Eng. J. Med.* 341: 777, 1999.

3 Colon Cancer

The most active people have a lower risk of colon cancer—in two studies half the risk—compared to the least active people.[1,2] Exercise may lower levels of prostaglandins that accelerate colon cell proliferation and raise levels of prostaglandins that increase intestinal motility. Increased motility may speed the movement of carcinogens through the colon.

[1] *J. Nat. Cancer Inst.* 89: 948, 1997.
[2] *Ann. Intern. Med.* 122: 327, 1995.

4 Diverticular Disease

In one of the few studies that have been done, the most active men had a 37 percent lower risk of symptomatic diverticular disease than the least active men.[1] Most of the protection against diverticular disease—pockets in the wall of the colon that can become inflamed—was due to vigorous activities like jogging and running, rather than moderate activities like walking.

[1] *Gut* 36: 276, 1995.

5 Arthritis

Regular moderate exercise, whether aerobic or strength-training, can reduce joint swelling and pain in people with arthritis.[1]

[1] *J. Amer. Med. Assoc.* 277: 25, 1997.

6 Anxiety & Depression

Getting people with anxiety or depression to do aerobic exercises like brisk walking or running curbs their symptoms, possibly by releasing natural opiates.[1,2]

[1] *J. Psychosom. Res.* 33: 537, 1989.
[2] *Arch. Intern. Med.* 159: 2349, 1999.

7 Heart Disease

In one study, men with low fitness who become fit had a lower risk of heart disease than men who stayed unfit.[1] In another, women who walked the equivalent of three or more hours per week at a brisk pace had a 35 percent lower risk of heart disease than women who walked infrequently.[2] Exercise boosts the supply of oxygen to the heart muscle by expanding existing arteries and creating tiny new blood vessels. It may also prevent blood clots or promote their breakdown.

[1] *J. Amer. Med. Assoc.* 273: 1093, 1995.
[2] *N. Eng. J. Med.* 341: 650,1999.

8 Blood Pressure

If your blood pressure is already high or high-normal, low- or moderate-intensity aerobic exercise—three times a week—can lower it.[1] If your blood pressure isn't high, regular exercise helps keep it that way.

[1] *J. Clin. Epidem.* 45: 439, 1992.

9 Diabetes

The more you move, the lower your risk of diabetes, especially if you're already at risk because of excess weight, high blood pressure, or parents with diabetes. In one study, women who walked at least three hours a week had about a 40 percent lower risk of diabetes than sedentary women.[1]

[1] *J. Am. Med. Assoc* 282: 1433, 1999.

10 Falls & Fractures

Older women assigned to a home-based (strength- and balance-training) exercise program had fewer falls than women who didn't exercise.[1] Exercise may prevent falls and broken bones by improving muscle strength, gait, balance, and reaction time.

[1] *Brit. Med. J.* 315: 1065, 1997.

11 Enlarged Prostate (men only)

In one study, men who walked two to three hours a week had 25 percent lower risk of benign prostatic hyperplasia (enlarged prostate) than men who seldom walked.[1]

[1] *Arch. Intern. Med.* 158: 2349, 1998.

12 Osteoporosis

Exercise, especially strength-training, can increase bone density in middle-aged and older people.[1] Bonus: postmenopausal women who take estrogen gain more bone density if they exercise.

[1] *J. Bone Min. Res.* 11: 218, 1996.

us feel better. This good feeling is due in part to the release of hormones responsible for improving mood. Many people can relate to the "high" they feel after they have engaged in physical activity. This improved mood can have a calming effect when stressful events arise. Exercise also improves the conditioning of our muscles. The better conditioned our muscles, the easier they are to relax. We'll be talking more about muscle relaxation in upcoming lessons.

Relieves tension. Physical activity is a great way to relieve muscular tension and muscle spasms. Aerobic exercise improves your cardiovascular efficiency and your metabolism. Your heart is strengthened, your resting pulse rate is lowered, and your cholesterol is likely to be lowered. This translates into a reduced chance of high blood pressure, heart attack, stroke, and a host of other diseases.

Fights fatigue. Exercise can help to fight chronic fatigue and insomnia. Immediately after you exercise, you feel alert and refreshed, not fatigued. An hour or so after you exercise, you will feel the relaxing effects of exercise and will be able to sleep more restfully.

Reduces anxiety and depression. Exercise is also effective in reducing anxiety and depression. Research in this area has shown that vigorous exercise, for 15–20 minutes, stimulates certain neurochemicals in your brain, which in turn elevate mood. Exercise is also a good outlet for stressful emotions such as irritability and anger.

Research as to the overall health improvements of regular physical activity, especially moderate-intensity activity, is relatively new. Researchers are learning more about the physical and mental benefits of exercise all the time, and there is still much to be learned. However, we do know enough to tell you that exercise is a powerful stress management tool. We will talk much about physical activity throughout this manual, but there is much more for you to learn than we can include in this manual. For more information about how to improve your fitness through lifestyle change, we suggest that you get a copy of *Living with Exercise 2001*, written by Dr. Steven Blair of the Cooper Institute in Dallas, Texas. This lifestyle activity manual is part of The LEARN LifeStyle Program Series™. For more information, you may call 1–888–LEARN–41 or on the Internet, log onto www.TheLifeStyleCompany.com. On page 87 is a chart that shows a dozen other reasons to exercise. This information came from an article by Bonnie Liebman and was published in the *Nutrition Action Healthletter*, a terrific publication from the Center for Science in the Public Interest.

HEALTH CLUB
INSTRUCTOR
OKAY, NOW TELL YOUR MUSCLES TO PICK IT UP.
SURE. BUT FIRST YOU TELL GRAVITY TO LET GO.
THAVES

For more information about this newsletter, you may call 202–332–9110 or log on to the Internet at www.cspinet.org.

Tracking Your Physical Activity

We cannot overstate the importance of regular physical activity. On your Daily Stress Record for the next week (see page 97) we have included a section at the bottom to record your physical activity. Make a conscious effort to accurately record *all* your physical activity for the week. Walking an extra block to work or parking in the far parking lot, where people with the new cars park, all count as exercise. Walking up stairs instead of taking the elevator or escalator also counts as physical activity.

On the bottom of your Daily Stress Record for the week, record each physical activity, how many minutes the activity lasted, your stress level before the activity, and your stress level after the activity. Remember, we're not asking you to necessarily increase your physical activity, just to monitor it and its affects on your level of stress.

Activity Monitoring Made Easy

How much regular physical activity do you get now? Most people who are asked this question, underreport their activity by as much as 50 percent. Let's face it, keeping track of every step is difficult—until now. We'd like you to consider purchasing a handy and helpful device called a pedometer. The newer versions make it simple to track your steps and calculate the distance you walked in a single day and the number of calories you burn from those steps. The use of a pedometer takes the guesswork out of trying to measure your activity.

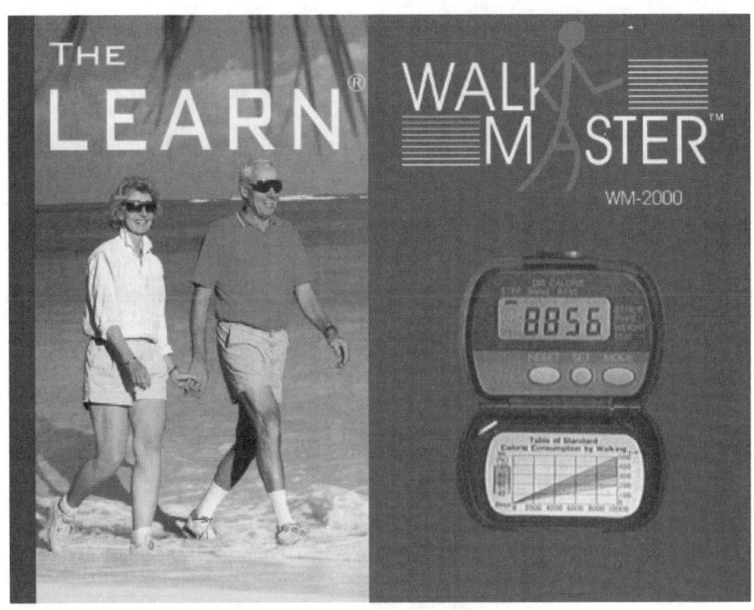

The LEARN WalkMaster™ is a handy, small pedometer you may want to consider purchasing. Many of our colleagues who study exercise use this type of pedometer themselves and with their clients/patients. The LEARN WalkMaster will log your progress if you're running the Boston Marathon, working in the yard, or strolling through the park. All of your activity will be tracked and stored, even the activity you don't think about. This feedback can be rewarding and motivational as you are reminded that any activity you do counts. For more information and ordering, call toll-free 1–888–LEARN–41 or log onto www.TheLifeStyleCompany.com.

The Role of Laughter

To demonstrate the value of activity in any form as a means to reduce stress, let's look at the benefits of laughter as a form of exercise. Laughter is one of the best stress-reducing exercises around, and as we all know, everyone can do it! Children laugh all the time, but many adults forget how to laugh. As laughter diminishes in adulthood, stress often intensifies. If you've forgotten how to laugh, we'll help you learn

"Children laugh all the time, but many adults forget how to laugh. As laughter diminishes in adulthood, stress often intensifies."

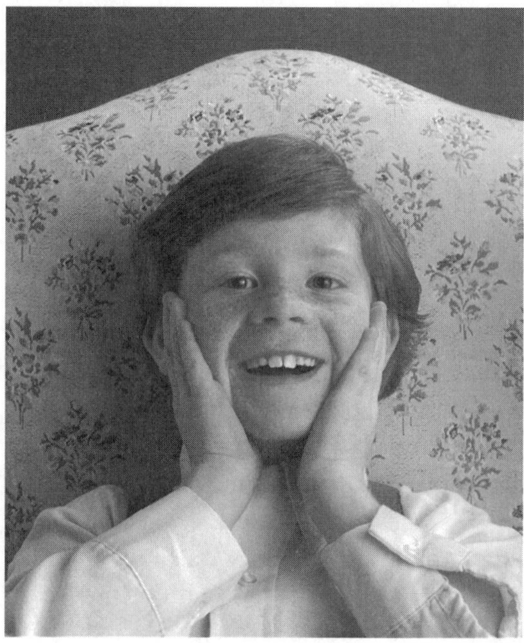

all over again. All you need is an appreciation for what is humorous and the desire to laugh. Have you stopped laughing? Do you remember things that made you laugh as a child?

According to William Fry of Stanford University School of Medicine, laughter, like exercise, causes huffing and puffing, speeds up the heart rate, raises blood pressure, accelerates breathing, increases oxygen consumption, gives the muscles of the stomach and face a workout, and relaxes the muscles that aren't used in laughing. Experts say that laughter provides a "total inner body workout," because of the complicated combination of physiological reactions. Laughter increases your metabolism, burning off calories. Also, laughter increases the levels of adrenaline in your system, leading to that "feel-good-all-over" sensation.

Things that make me laugh...

1. ______________________________
2. ______________________________
3. ______________________________
4. ______________________________
5. ______________________________

We also know that beyond the important physiological effects, laughter also has many psychological benefits. Laughter helps to relieve stress because it tends to improve our perspective. We have all experienced the value of laughter when we feel angry, stressed, or depressed about something. The ability to take a step back and find humor in uncomfortable situations is a valuable and healthy skill. Try it next time you allow yourself to become upset about something in your busy day!

MY LAUGHING EXERCISES

DAY OF THE WEEK	PLANNED LAUGHTER	YES	NO
Monday			
Tuesday			
Wednesday			
Thursday			
Friday			
Saturday			
Sunday			

In the space on page 90, list at least five things that make you laugh or used to make you laugh. You may include those things that made you laugh as a child or as a young adult, even if you haven't laughed in some time.

Schedule Laughter

Look again at your Stressful Events Record for last week. Can you find situations where you could have laughed to reduce your stress? Think about things that make you laugh—look at the list you just completed. Perhaps cartoons, a funny joke, or remembering a prank that you or someone else pulled when you were younger can make you laugh. In the space provided above, plan at least one laugh each day for the next week. Write down your plan here and at the end of the week, mark "yes" if you did the exercise or "no" if you did not do the laughter exercise. Good luck with your laughing exercise! When you're finished, we'll move on to the topic of your internal dialog.

Your Internal Dialog

We all have an inner dialog with ourselves in which we automatically make interpretations about everything we see, hear, feel, and touch. These interpretations are ongoing and are often subtle and unrecognized. They are, however, very powerful in determining our thoughts, feelings, reactions, and behaviors. We have already explained that events alone do not cause stress. Our thoughts about events determine whether we experience an event or occurrence as stressful or not. These thoughts are called irrational beliefs by cognitive behavior therapist Dr. Albert Ellis, founder of Rational Emotive Behavior Therapy. Dr. Aaron Beck, cognitive therapy founder, calls these thoughts "automatic thoughts." No matter how we label these thoughts, they are simply seen as stress-producing thoughts. These thoughts

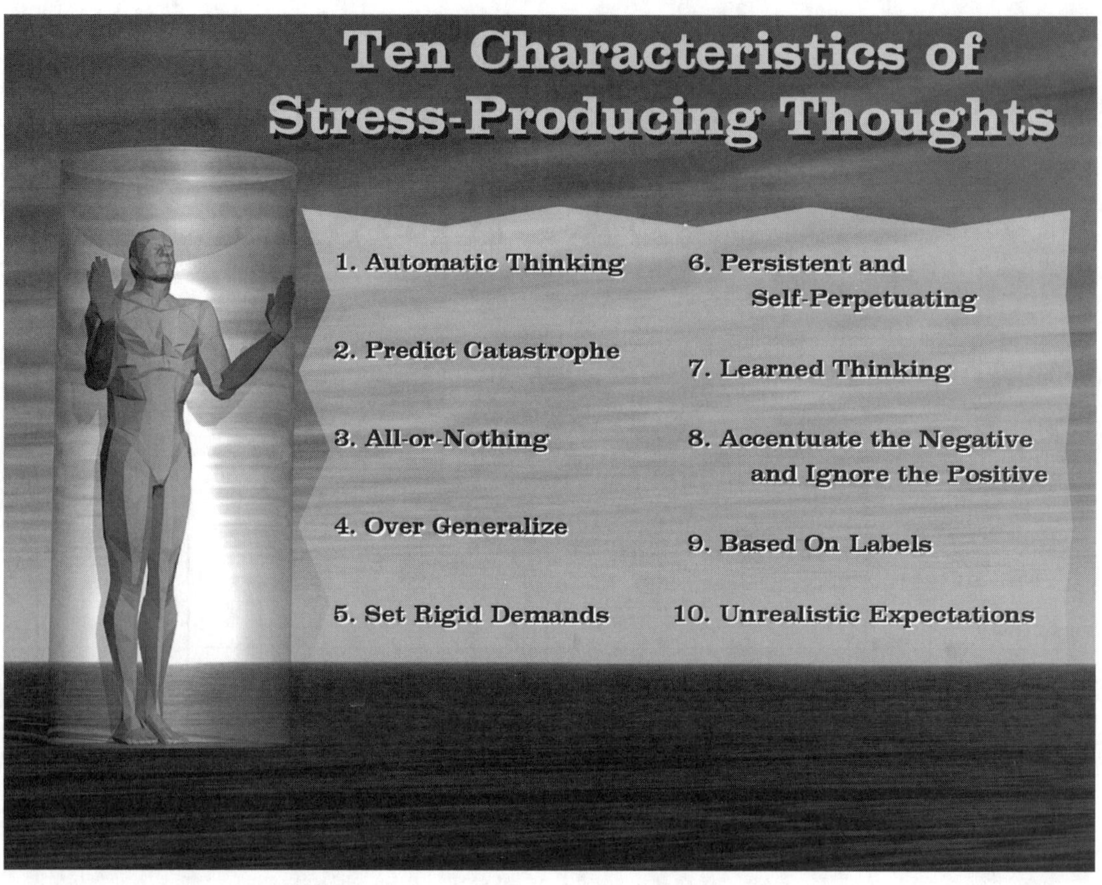
Ten Characteristics of
Stress-Producing Thoughts
1. Automatic Thinking
2. Predict Catastrophe
3. All-or-Nothing
4. Over Generalize
5. Set Rigid Demands
6. Persistent and
Self-Perpetuating
7. Learned Thinking
8. Accentuate the Negative
and Ignore the Positive
9. Based On Labels
10. Unrealistic Expectations

have 10 common characteristics. Let's look at these common characteristics.

Ten Characteristics of Stress-Producing Thoughts

❶ Stress-producing thoughts are experienced as automatic and appear linked to events. We then make the error of assuming that because they occur with the events, the events cause the thoughts.

❷ Stress-producing thoughts tend to "catastrophize." These are thoughts that predict catastrophe, the worst in every situation, and danger around every corner.

❸ Stress-producing thoughts are all-or-nothing thoughts. A simple mistake is viewed as complete inadequacy.

❹ Stress-producing thoughts are overgeneralizations: "I can *never* do anything right, *everyone* hates me, *nothing* will work."

❺ Stress-producing thoughts are rigid demands or rules for us and others to follow. Terms such as, should, ought, or must are examples: "I must be perfect;" "I ought to do better;" "I should have been more assertive." These statements often precipitate a sense of guilt or loss of self-esteem.

❻ Stress-producing thoughts are persistent and self-perpetuating. We have been practicing these thought for years, and thus, they are hard to turn off unless we actively practice challenging them.

❽ Stress-producing thoughts are learned. The early learning of these thoughts can explain the persistence of these thoughts, at least in part. Family, friends, and the media have conditioned us to interpret things a certain way.

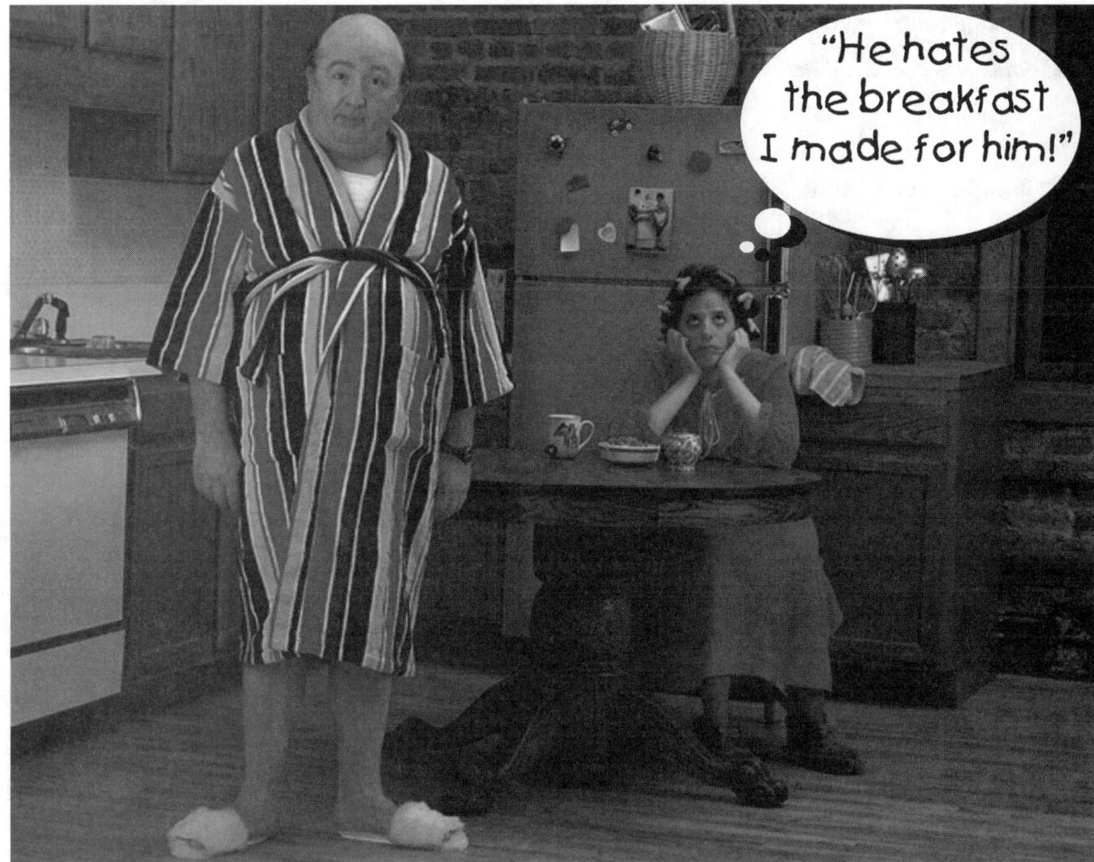
"He hates
the breakfast
I made for him!"

"We all have an inner dialog with ourselves, in which we make interpretations about everything we see, hear, feel, and touch."

8. Stress-producing thoughts often accentuate the negative and ignore the positive. One negative experience can lead to a negative self-evaluation, despite many positive experiences.

9. Stress-producing thoughts are based on labels. Instead of "I did a stupid thing," the stress thought is "I am so stupid."

10. Stress-producing thoughts are unrealistic overestimates or underestimates. For example, you may overestimate the size of a problem and overestimate the probability of a negative event happening. In turn, you may underestimate your ability to deal with the problem.

Challenging Your Stress-Producing Thoughts

By now, you are probably beginning to see how your *thoughts* contribute to your levels of stress. For example, thinking in catastrophic, rigid, or perfectionistic terms can increase your stress. Thinking styles that also contribute to stress include:

- Assuming the negative
- Catastrophizing
- Anticipating danger in non-threatening situations
- Overgeneralizing
- Perfectionism

These thinking patterns are learned early in life and are practiced over time. The good news is that you can learn to change your thinking patterns. Because you learned how to think in a stressful way, with practice, you can learn how to think in a less stressful way. In the next lesson, we will show you how to begin challenging the

Quality of Life Review

Please use the following scale to rate how satisfied you feel now about different aspects of your daily life. Choose any number from this list (1 to 9) and indicate your choice next to each numbered item below.

1 = Extremely Dissatisfied
2 = Very Dissatisfied
3 = Moderately Dissatisfied
4 = Somewhat Dissatisfied
5 = Neutral
6 = Somewhat Satisfied
7 = Moderately Satisfied
8 = Very Satisfied
9 = Extremely Satisfied

____ 1. Overall mood (feelings of sadness, anxiety, happiness, etc.)

____ 2. Sense of self-esteem

____ 3. Confidence, comfort in social situations

____ 4. Internal dialog (self-talk)

____ 5. Energy level

____ 6. Focus and concentration

____ 7. Ability to manage time

____ 8. Relationships

____ 9. General health

____ 10. Exercise and recreation

____ 11. Assertiveness skills

____ 12. Eating habits

____ 13. Overall quality of life

stress-producing thoughts by thinking realistically.

Quality of Life Review

In the Introduction and Orientation Lesson, we introduced to you the Quality of Life Review. As we described then, this tool helps you measure your progress in many different ways and at different times.

Take a few moments now to complete the Quality of Life Review above. How do your responses here compare to the responses on page 11 in the Introduction and Orientation Lesson? We will ask you to complete this assessment several times later in the program to see if the scores have changed, and to give you a clearer picture that change comes in many different forms.

Lesson Review

In this lesson, we helped you review your Stressful Events Record from last week. If you are a social changer, you worked through the Program Partnership Quiz to help you choose a good program partner. We introduced you to the three stress response systems and discussed how these systems can operate in a cycle. We talked about the importance of physical activity and the benefits of laughter. The 10 characteristics of our human stress-producing thoughts were discussed and we asked you to begin challenging *your* stress-producing thoughts. And finally, we concluded the lesson by having you complete another Quality of Life Review and compare your scores with the review you completed in the Introduction and Orientation Lesson. Congratulations, you are now one-fourth of the way through this program!

This Week's Assignment

This week, keep your Daily Stress Record as you have been, along with the Stressful Events Record. A blank Daily Stress Record is given to you on page 97 and a blank Stressful Events Record on page 96. Remember to keep track of your physical activity on the Daily Stress Record this week. As you record stressful events in your life this week, see if you can begin to identify which response system begins the process. Schedule your planned laughter exercises on the worksheet on page 91, and be sure to record whether or not you did the exercises this week. At the end of the week, be sure to record your stress change on the Stress Change Worksheet on page 29. This week will complete this worksheet. In Lesson Five, we'll give you another worksheet for weeks 5–8. Finally, be sure to record your average stress change on the worksheet in Appendix E on page 430.

Knowledge Review

T F 22. A program partner is necessary to help you get the most out of your stress management program.

T F 23. The physical response to stress may include symptoms such as increased heart rate, fast breathing, chest pains, and a choking sensation.

T F 24. The three stress response systems always act independently. It is impossible for one to affect the other.

T F 25. Physical activity is important for many health benefits but not all that helpful in stress management.

T F 26. Laughter is an important exercise to help reduce stress levels.

T F 27. Stress-producing thoughts often accentuate the negative and ignore the positive.

T F 28. Stress-producing thoughts are experienced as automatic.

T F 29. Because thinking patterns are learned early in life and practiced over time, it is impossible to permanently change thought patterns.

(Answers in Appendix C, page 415)

Stressful Events Record—Lesson Four

Week of: ____________

Date	Starting Time	Ending Time	Highest Stress Level (0–8)	(a) Triggers	(b) Emotions (0–10)	(c) Thoughts	(d) Behaviors	(e) Physical Symptoms

Column	***Instructions***
(a)	Write down the trigger (event) that caused your stress to rise. This column is likely to echo the "Stressful Event of the Highest Stress Level" column on your Daily Stress Record for the same day.
(b)	Record the emotions you felt immediately after the stressful trigger. Examples may include, anger, fear, hopelessness, or frustration. Remember to record you initial feelings of emotion.
(c)	Write down the thoughts that went through your head as your stress was increasing. For example, you may have thought, "I won't make it, I can't cope" or "I'm going to look foolish." No matter how silly the thoughts seem after the moment has passed, write them down.
(d)	Write down your immediate behaviors to the stressful event. What did you do? Perhaps you started pacing, took a walk, threw something across the room, or started crying. Whatever the behavior, write it down.
(e)	In the last column, record the major physical symptoms you experienced because of this stress. Physical symptoms such as, headache, nausea, pounding heart, or sweating are common symptoms of increased stress.

Daily Stress Record—Lesson Four

Name:____________________________________ **Week of:**____________

Date	Average Stress Level	Highest Stress Level	Time of Highest Stress Level	Stressful Event Associated with Highest Stress Level

Remember to complete the Stress Change Worksheet on page 29 at the end of the week by recording the Highest Stress Level and Average Stress Level from your Daily Stress Record.

My Physical Activity Record

Day of the Week	Activities	Minutes	Stress Level Before Activity	Stress Level After Activity
Monday				
Tuesday				
Wednesday				
Thursday				
Friday				

LAP
LAP
LAP
JIM DAVIS
6-3

LAP
LAP

AH
AH
AH
JIM DAVIS
6-4

WAH-
CHOO!

SNIFF

AH
AH
AH
6-5

WAH-
CHOO!

JIM DAVIS

Lesson Five

Congratulations! You have completed the first four weeks of the Mastering Stress Program. By now, you should be more aware of the triggers that increase the stress in your life. Through this awareness, your average level of daily stress should be decreasing. This is the power of self-monitoring. If you have been lax in monitoring your daily stress, we encourage you to keep a Daily Stress Record. Remember, self-awareness is an important key to making the right choices in your life. Again, we cannot emphasize enough the importance of keeping these self-monitoring records.

You should now also be more aware of how stress affects you physically, mentally, and behaviorally. Regular physical activity will help keep your body in shape to better handle stressful events. Incorporating laughter into your daily life and challenging your stress-producing thoughts should now be part of your daily stress-reducing activity. We hope you are pleased with your progress. You deserve the credit for your hard work and success.

This lesson is a bit longer than the past four lessons because it includes a review of your progress along with some interesting new material. We begin this lesson by reviewing the accomplishments you have made so far in the program. Then we have some exciting new material to share with you. We begin this new material by discussing some impressive new research on the importance of physical activity. Our attention will then turn to relaxation. We'll show you a technique to help you relax. Lastly, we introduce the notion of time management and the importance of learning how to manage your stress with respect to time. If you're ready, let's begin this lesson by looking at the important changes you have made. Reviewing your progress in the program at this time is an important step.

Reviewing Your Progress

First, we will look at your Quality of Life Review from the last lesson. We will then have you review the changes recorded on your Stress Change Worksheet over the past four weeks. The review of your progress over the first four weeks of the Mastering Stress Program is important before you continue. This review is pivotal for two reasons. First, it can be motivational as you

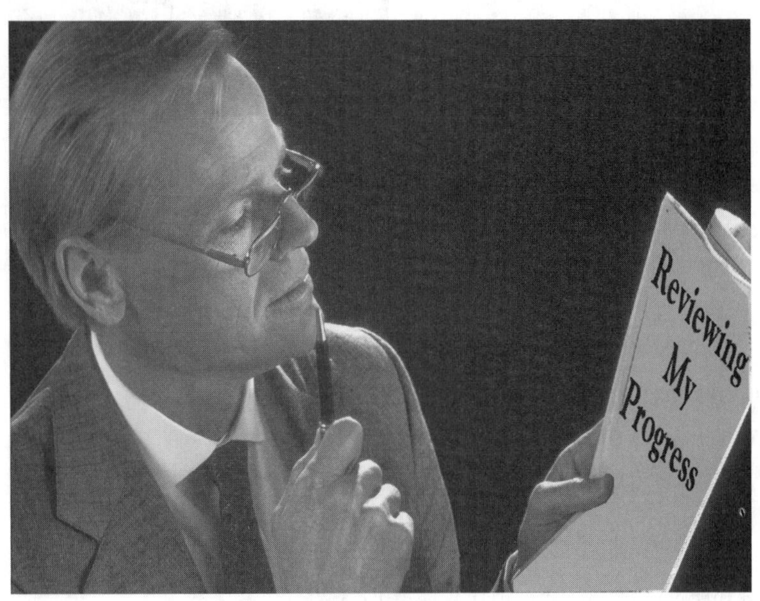

"Reviewing your progress in the program at this time is an important step."

review the progress you've made over just four weeks. A careful review of your progress can highlight the areas of the Mastering Stress Program that you have mastered and are using daily to lower your stress. This can be inspirational as well as motivational. Second, the review can help to identify other areas that may be giving you some trouble. Knowing the areas that need some additional work can help point you in the right direction to maximize your stress management efforts. Remember, this program is unique to other stress management programs. We designed the Mastering Stress Program to be a building-block approach to lifestyle change. Like building a house, the better the foundation, the better and longer lasting the structure.

Comparing Your Quality of Life Reviews

We want you to compare your responses at the beginning of the program to your responses in the last lesson. Turn to the Quality of Life Review on page 11 that you completed in the Introduction and Orientation Lesson. Next, turn to your Quality of Life Review from page 94 of Lesson Four. Let's now compare your responses.

Look at the Quality of Life Review Comparison worksheet on page 101. In column (b), record the scores from the Introduction and Orientation Lesson and in column (c), record your scores from the last lesson. Column (d) reflects the positive (+) or negative (-) change in your responses. The positive (+) numbers reflect increased satisfaction with life in the related category. The negative (-) numbers represent decreased satisfaction with life. If you have negative (-) numbers in any of the categories that we covered in the first four lessons, now is a good time to go back and review this material. Positive (+) numbers in the

categories that were covered in the first four lessons means that you have done well and are ready to move on. Do not get discouraged with negative (-) numbers in categories that we have not discussed. Simply note these areas for upcoming lessons.

This review is designed to help you measure your progress in different ways and at different times. Change comes in many different forms, so let's look at the changes you have made in the past month. If you are like most people who go through this program, your quality of life will have increased in at least one area, if not more. For example, you may have experienced improvement in your overall mood, concentration, energy level, or self-talk. These changes have occurred within a relatively short period. Just think what you have to look forward to over the next several weeks! Remember that not all changes occur at the same pace. Some aspects of your life may not change immediately. Be patient and trust that you will make more changes as we continue this journey together.

Quality of Life Review Comparison

(a) Category	(b) Score from Introduction and Orientation Lesson	(c) Score from Lesson Four	(d) Change in Scores (column c minus column b)
1. Overall mood (feelings of sadness, anxiety, happiness, etc.)			
2. Sense of self			
3. Confidence, comfort in social situations			
4. Internal dialog (self-talk)			
5. Energy level			
6. Focus and concentration			
7. Ability to manage time			
8. Relationships			
9. General health			
10. Exercise and recreation			
11. Assertiveness skills			
12. Eating habits			
13. Overall quality of life			

Reviewing Your Four-Week Stress Change Worksheet

You now have been tracking your progress for four weeks on the Stress Change Worksheets. On the Stress Change Worksheet on page 29, you have been recording both your highest and average stress levels on a daily basis. The Average Stress Change Worksheet on page 430 reflects your average weekly stress levels. Let's first look at the Average Stress Change Worksheet on page 430.

Over the past four weeks you may have noticed a gradual drop in your weekly average level of stress. If you have, good work! You may have also noticed the natural ups and downs of the stress management progress. Perhaps the change has not been as steady as you would have liked. This is perfectly natural, so don't get discouraged.

At this point, turn back to your Stress Change Worksheet on page 29. By referring to your Daily Stress Records, write on this worksheet the events during the week that caused your average weekly stress levels to go up. Remember that you are working with averages. A single stressful day may overshadow an otherwise stress-free week. For example, your stress level may have been going down for the first three weeks, then during week four it went up. The Stress Change Worksheet helps you to see week three as just an unusual occurrence and lets you take credit for the earlier changes. This can be a reality check for measuring progress, especially if you are uncertain about making positive changes. Let's look at an example to help show you the importance of this exercise.

Meet Sally

Sally is a 37-year-old homemaker from Omaha. Although Sally has a master's degree in business, she chose to stay at home and raise her family. Sally's husband, Tom, works for an insurance company and spends much of his time traveling. Sally and Tom have four children who are 5, 8, 10, and 14 years old.

As Sally's children became more involved in school activities, Sally began volunteering for various parents' organizations. Tom did very well in his company and was recently promoted to national vice president. Along with the promotion came more travel, work, and time away from his family. Sally found herself more and more stressed with these changes. Her four children were more demanding than ever, and she was constantly worrying about disappointing one of them by forgetting a school activity. With Tom being gone more often, she had much more to do around the house. Sally was overwhelmed and knew she needed to gain control of the stress in her life.

Sally began the Mastering Stress Program to help manage her stress. During her first four weeks in the program, she diligently made time to complete the self-monitoring assignments. Sally was amazed at how much better she felt by simply becoming more aware of the things in her life that caused her stress to increase. As you can see from Sally's Example Stress Change Worksheet on page 103, her overall level of stress did, indeed, decrease during her first four weeks in the program. However, she still experienced some stressful days as shown on her Stress Change Worksheet. These sudden increases in stress levels are natural and should be expected.

Look closely at Sally's Stress Change Worksheet. Although Sally experienced significant increases in her stress level during the third week, she was able to quickly gain control of her stress. This is the key. Notice that Sally uses physical activity to help lower her stress during week three.

Another Word about Self-Monitoring

We hope that by now, you see the value of keeping good self-monitoring records. Reviewing the records you keep is also important in recognizing patterns in your stress. You should be more aware of the specific stress triggers in your life now than you were four weeks ago. If you have not been diligent in keeping good self-monitoring records, a reality check may be in order. In the Introduction and Orientation Lesson on page 8, you made a list of the costs and benefits of beginning a program. Review this list and see if the benefits still outweigh the costs. Did you list "keeping self-monitoring records" as one of the costs of beginning a program?

If you find keeping records difficult, you're not alone. We provide many self-monitoring forms and worksheets throughout this program to help you. We provide the forms for your benefit if you find them useful. If you have designed a form that

Stress Change Worksheet

Sally's Example (weeks 1–4)

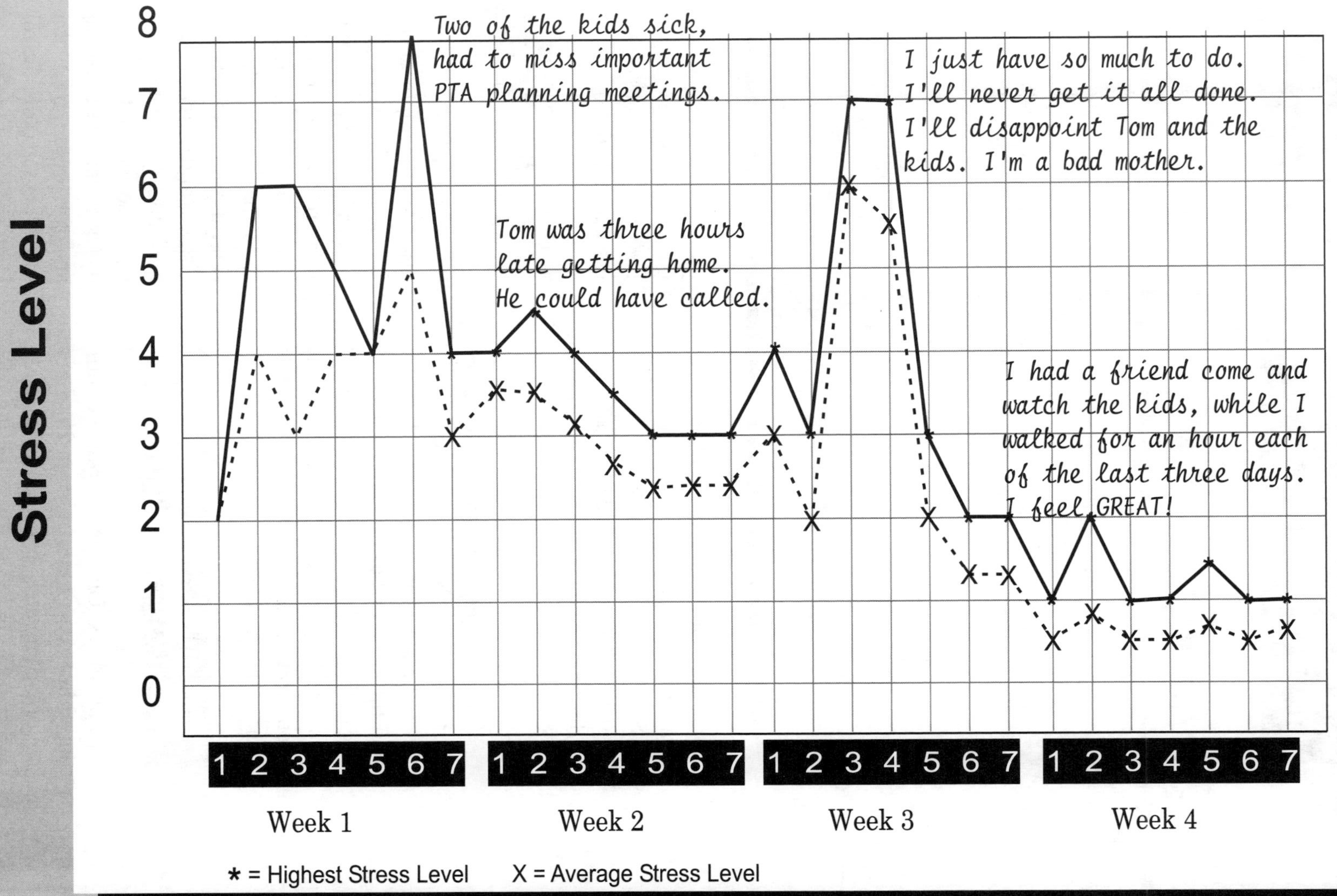

Stress Level

8
7
6
5
4
3
2
1
0

Two of the kids sick, had to miss important PTA planning meetings.

Tom was three hours late getting home. He could have called.

I just have so much to do. I'll never get it all done. I'll disappoint Tom and the kids. I'm a bad mother.

I had a friend come and watch the kids, while I walked for an hour each of the last three days. I feel GREAT!

1 2 3 4 5 6 7 — Week 1

1 2 3 4 5 6 7 — Week 2

1 2 3 4 5 6 7 — Week 3

1 2 3 4 5 6 7 — Week 4

* = Highest Stress Level   X = Average Stress Level

Costs and Benefits of Self-Monitoring

Costs of Self-Monitoring	Benefits of Self-Monitoring

works better for you, that's terrific. Take a moment to complete the Costs and Benefits of Self-Monitoring worksheet above. The more benefits you write down for self-monitoring, the greater your motivation to move on.

Also, take a moment now to turn back to the worksheet titled, My Vision of the New Me, in Lesson One, on page 16. Is that vision the same or has it changed since you began the program? Can you more clearly visualize the "new you," now that you have been working on stress management for four weeks. We hope so.

A New Stress Change Worksheet

The Stress Change Worksheet introduced in Lesson One, on page 29, should now be completely filled. This worksheet covered the first four weeks of the Mastering Stress Program. At the end of this lesson, we provide you with a new Stress Change Worksheet on page 127 that covers the next four weeks of the program (weeks five through eight).

Important Reasons to Be Active

In Lesson Three, on page 68, we briefly discussed the importance of regular physical activity in stress management. The physical response system is one of the three stress response systems that we introduced in Lesson Four, on page 80. Many studies show that regular physical activity plays a central role in reducing the risks for many diseases and increasing a person's longevity and independent function. Several studies have also shown that regular physical activity has important psychological benefits and can be a powerful tool in reducing stress. Let's explore the role of physical activity in overall health and well-being further.

Most people are surprised to learn of the many health benefits that are linked to physical activity. Most of us would readily agree that regular physical activity is good for us. Yet, only about 22 percent of the American population is active, 24 percent of Americans are totally inactive, and 54 percent are not active enough. The reasons behind this paradox are not exactly clear, but we do have some good insight into many common reasons why most people are inactive. Typical excuses include, "I don't have enough time," "I hate going to the gym," and "I'm too tired to exercise when I get home."

Why is America a nation of inactivity? Perhaps some answers lie in the fact that we live in the most technically advanced society on earth. More labor-saving devices have been developed and introduced into the American culture over the last 50 years than in all of human history. Hundreds of labor-saving devices keep us from being active every day: garage door openers, elevators, escalators, moving sidewalks, remote controls, computers, and much more. Drive-thru windows and home delivery of almost everything imaginable make it easy to live our lives with the push of a button. In today's dot-com world, you can have everything needed to live delivered to your home. The only activity required is the push of a few buttons on the keyboard and a short stroll to the door to greet the UPS delivery person when the goods arrive. Along with less activity come more health problems and more stress.

Another possible reason for inactivity may be that most people simply don't know of the many health benefits that accompany regular physical activity. Additionally, many people may not know how to go about achieving these benefits. How many times have you heard the saying, "No pain, no gain"? Many times, we're sure. Often accompanying this phrase is the aerobic formula of at least 30 minutes of activity at 80 percent of maximum heart rate, performed at least three times a week. If this is what comes to mind when you hear the terms exercise or physical activity, we have terrific news for you. You'll be happy to hear that this is not so. You can realize much gain without pain, and you don't have to sweat in a gym to gain the many health benefits of exercise. Let's look at one important study that shows the health benefits of regular physical activity and how easy they are to achieve.

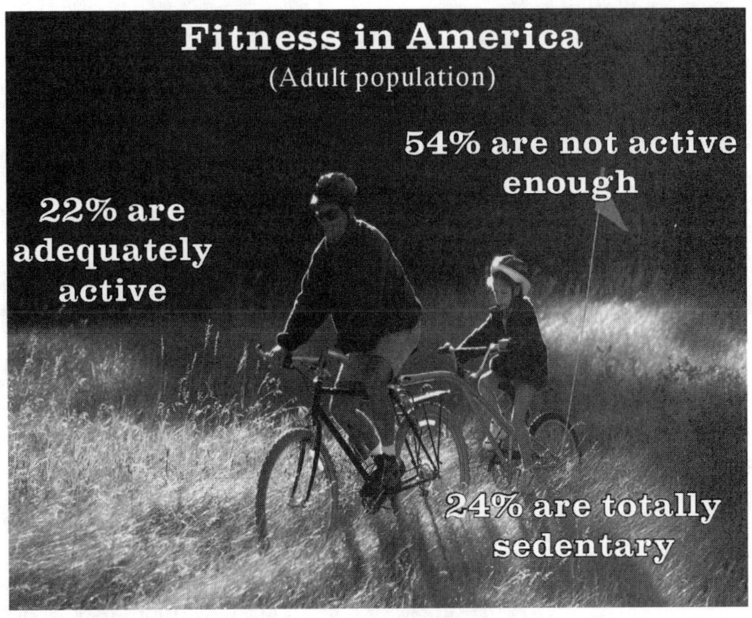

Fitness in America
(Adult population)
54% are not active enough
22% are adequately active
24% are totally sedentary

"Scientific evidence confirms the important benefits of regular physical activity. Yet, most people are virtually inactive."

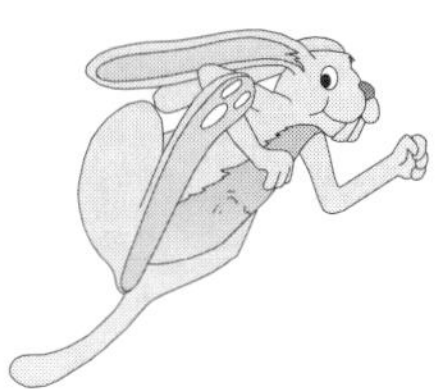

An Impressive Study about Exercise

Dr. Steven Blair and his colleagues at the Cooper Institute for Aerobics Research in Dallas, Texas, conducted an impressive study on physical activity. In this study, Dr. Blair and his team tracked the fitness and health levels of 10,224 men and 3120 women for an average of eight years. The study participants were divided into five different categories of fitness, based upon their performance on a treadmill test.

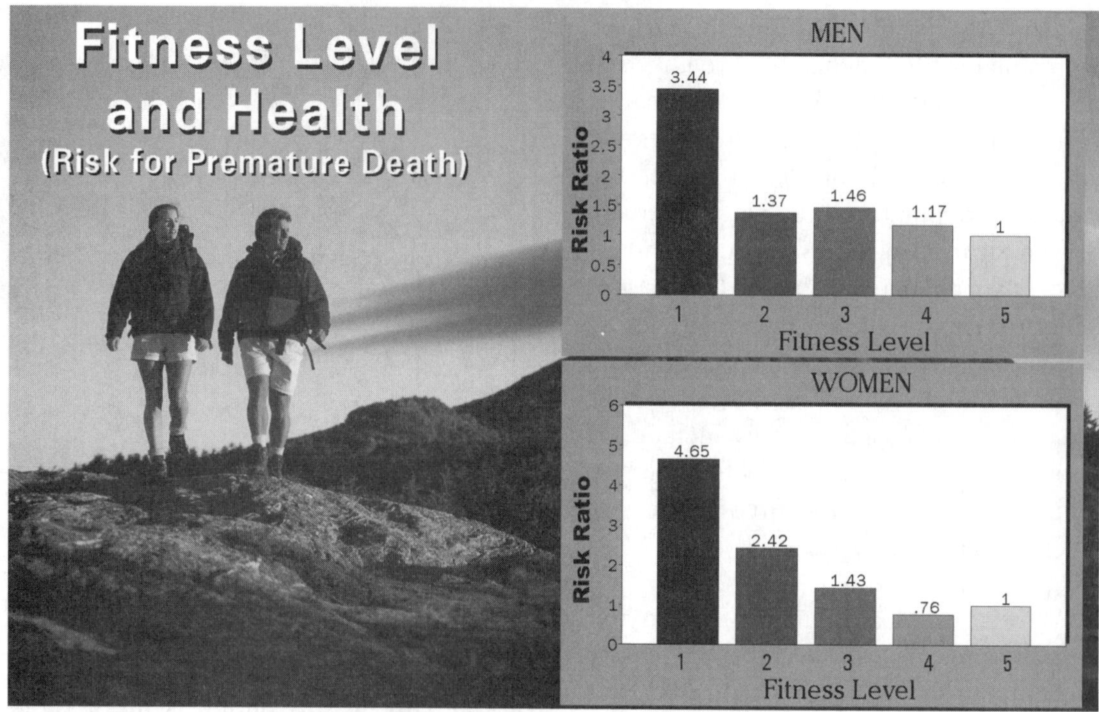

The five fitness categories of this study's participants ranged from Level 1 (very unfit) to Level 5 (highly fit). The graph above shows the relative risk ratio (representing premature death rate) of both men and women in the study. Look at the graph now and remember that the Level 5 group is the most fit group. On both graphs, the risk for the most fit people is given as a value of 1. The risk ratio for the other fitness categories are given in reference to this group. Let's look at an example.

The men in the level 3 category have a 46 percent greater risk of premature death from all causes than the men in Level 5. This may not seem like much of an increased risk, but look now at the Level 1 group. Men in this group have a 344 percent greater risk. As you can see, the risk ratio drops dramatically from the Level 1 group to the Level 3 group. Now look at the same risk ratios for women. Do you notice that the pattern is similar to the risk ratios for men? Studies by Blair and others show similar results, not only in risk of premature death from all causes but also in reducing the risks of other diseases, such as coronary heart disease, diabetes, hypertension, colon cancer, and improvements in mental health. Physical activity is also one of the predictors of successful weight loss and maintenance. Individuals who exercise regularly are more successful than those who do not.

Perhaps the real hallmark of the Blair study and similar studies is that they show you don't have to knock yourself out to reap the many health benefits of regular physical activity. You don't even have to buy a gym membership! Even small amounts of regular exercise, spread over the course of a day, can increase your fitness level and improve your health. Along with an increased fitness level comes an increased life span, improved physical heath, and improved mental health. This combination of health benefits is a strong and powerful stress management tool. Let's look now at how physical activity can help reduce stress.

Psychological Benefits of Physical Activity

In 1996, the U.S. Surgeon General released the first Surgeon General's report on physical activity. This report highlights the many physical benefits of exercise. More important, it also discusses the mental benefits of regular physical activity. The most notable conclusions of studies on physical activity and mental health include improved mood and general well-being; reductions in tension and confusion; and reductions in perceived stress, anxiety, and depression. Other mental benefits of exercise include higher self-esteem and self-efficacy, greater coping skills, and better cognitive functioning. Some evidence exists that suggests physical activity may protect against the development of depression, however, more research is needed to confirm this finding.

What does all this mean for you? Certainly, more research is needed to more clearly establish the links between physical activity and stress. But, we can conclude from the studies completed that a strong link exists between physical activity and stress.

The research on physical activity and mental health have included two interesting measurements: state measure and trait measure. State measures are used to reflect how a person feels at the present time (right now). This measurement is very useful in looking at changes that occur before and after a single bout of physical activity. Many people report improvements in transient moods, such as stress and anxiety and have temporary reductions in muscle tension. Studies have shown the reduction in muscle tension can last for two to six hours after a session of physical activity. Regular (daily) activity is necessary to experience the calming effect on an ongoing basis. This is a key reason we talk so much about physical activity throughout this manual.

How Much Activity Do You Need?

As we said before, you don't have to knock yourself out or go to the gym every day to gain the psychological benefits of physical activity. We encourage our inactive clients to first adopt lifestyle activity and our somewhat active clients to increase their activity. Lifestyle activity includes building small bouts of activity into your day, like starting with a two-minute walk. Lifestyle activity also includes recreational activities such as dancing, riding a bicycle, playing tennis, swimming, and a host of other fun activities. You should be as active as you can be while still having fun. To date, research has not identified an optimal time or duration of physical activity to improve a person's mental health status. Much more information is available on the amount of physical activity needed to achieve the physical benefits as reflected in the Blair study. We'll cover these new guidelines after we talk a bit more about lifestyle activity.

Lifestyle Activity

An important concept of lifestyle activity is for you to recognize any activity as exercise. Physical activity includes walking an extra block, taking the stairs instead of the elevator, raking leaves, or taking your kids to the park. If you do any of these activities you have been physically active. This should register as "exercise" in your mind. Make it a point to tell yourself, "Wow, I just exercised," every time you do some physical activity in your daily life.

What does all this mean? First, the work by Dr. Blair and others provides conclusive evidence that just about anyone can be-

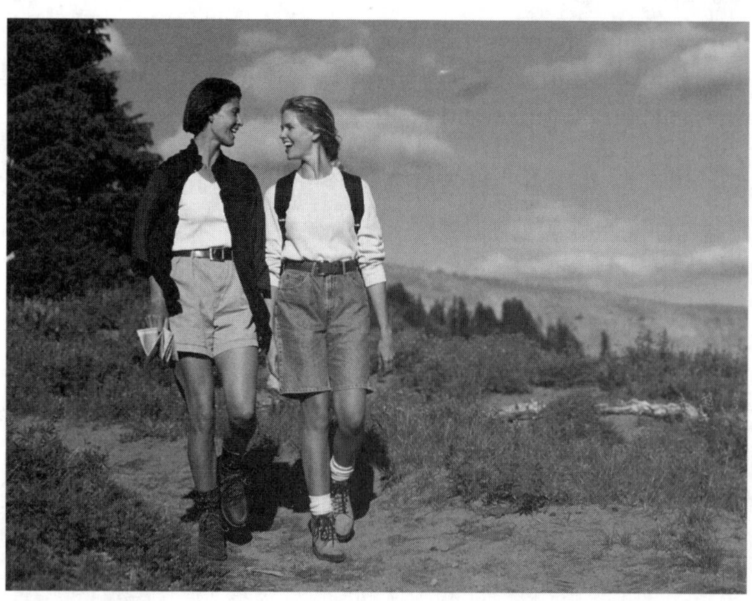

"The new activity guidelines for Americans recommend 30 minutes of cumulative, moderate-intensity physical activity on most days of the week—preferably every day."

come at least moderately fit. Individuals who accumulate about 30 minutes of brisk walking on most days of the week can reach the moderately fit category. Other studies on exercise and psychology suggest that physical activity may affect other factors related to stress management, including mood, self-esteem, well-being, and better coping skills. This suggests that individuals who are regularly physically active may have a much healthier mental attitude than those individuals who are inactive. When you do something that you recognize as physical activity, it sends a message that you have done something positive for yourself. This positive message may in turn motivate you to do something else that is positive, like keeping your Daily Stress Record and practicing your relaxation skills.

New Activity Guidelines for Americans

The work of experts in the field of exercise has provided much scientific support that regular, moderate-intensity physical activity can provide substantial health benefits. These health benefits include protection against several chronic diseases, such as coronary heart disease, certain cancers, osteoporosis, adult-onset diabetes, hypertension, depression, and of course, stress. How much exercise do you need to realize these important health benefits? Hold on, we'll get to this in a minute. But first, we have more good news.

In July of 1993, a new exercise formula was established for Americans. The American College of Sports Medicine (ACSM) and the U.S. Centers for Disease Control and Prevention (CDC) in cooperation with the President's Council on Physical Fitness and Sports published new exercise guidelines and recommendations for American adults. These new guidelines recommend 30 minutes of cumulative, moderate-intensity physical activity on most days of the week, preferably every day. The key word here is "cumulative."

This is terrific news! Can you find time for a five-minute walk? Most of us can. You've met the recommended guidelines if you incorporate six, five-minute walks into your daily routine. This is another good reason to track all of your daily activities. They all count, including vacuuming, sweeping, mowing, and walking the dog. Even walking into the dry cleaners instead of using the drive-thru window counts as activity. The accumulation of exercise can also come from activities, such as playing tennis, walking on the treadmill, playing baseball, jogging, riding a bicycle, or swimming. A brisk two-mile walk is another way to get in your 30 minutes of physical activity and reduce your stress. Do you remember Sally's Stress Change Worksheet example on page 103? Physical activity helped her reduce her stress when she felt out of control.

You can probably think of as many reasons to increase your physical activity as we can. Many people find it helpful to build physical activity into their daily life. We refer to this as lifestyle activity. We will provide you with some helpful ways to increase your lifestyle activity in upcoming lessons. If you want more help on increasing your fitness level, Dr. Steven Blair and his colleagues at the Cooper Institute for Aerobics Research in Dallas, Texas, have developed an excellent program to do this. This program is called *Living with Exercise 2001*. You can order a copy from LEARN—The LifeStyle Company by calling 1-888-LEARN-41 or by logging onto the web site www.TheLifeStyleCompany.com. Make regular physical activity an important part of your daily life. A problem many people have is forgetting to keep track of just how much activity they do in a day. If you have trouble tracking your daily activity, consider getting the LEARN WalkMaster that we discussed on page 89.

Communicating with Your Partner

In Lesson Four, we helped you work through the Program Partnership Quiz (page 79) to help you choose a good program partner. If you have decided to do the program alone, this is fine as well. Communicating is the first and most important step for starting a program partnership. You and your partner should have an open and honest discussion about whether you are both ready for a partnership. Is your partner willing to stick by you through the tough times? Are you willing to help your partner in return? Some degree of commitment is necessary from both of you. If you and your partner can agree to work together and communicate openly, you are on the way to a successful partnership. Here are some ideas for making this happen.

Tell your partner how to help. Do not expect your partner to read your mind. You may think he or she should know what you want or need, but most people are not good mind readers, so leave nothing to chance. Tell your partner what he or she can do. How do you want to be treated when you do poorly? Would you rather be scolded or encouraged? How often do you want your partner to check on your progress?

Make your requests specific. The more specific your requests, the easier it will be for your partner to respond. General requests such as "Help me with my program" put your partner at a disadvantage. A more specific request is better. Instead of saying "Don't nag me about being stressed out," say "If you think I am getting stressed, ask me if I would like to talk about

"Communicating in a positive way is the first and most important step for starting a program partnership."

"Ted! Are you unwound yet?"

what I am feeling." Keep your requests positive, rather than becoming critical and negative. Simple changes in wording can make all the difference. If your partner nags, you can say "It really helps me when you say nice things." Most people enjoy an opportunity to do something positive, so try this approach with your partner.

Reward your partner. Every partnership has two sides. For your partner to help you, you must help your partner. If you are going through this program together, you can find ways to help each other use techniques for mastering stress. If your partner is not on the program, be forward, and ask what you can do in return. Remember, it is important to acknowledge and reward your partner.

Use these techniques to start the ball rolling with your partner. Upcoming lessons will give you more ideas for working with your partner. It is important to lay this groundwork first.

Let's now move into a new topic, learning to relax.

Learning to Relax

In earlier lessons and this lesson, we discussed the important role of physical activity in stress management. The more fit your body, the better able you are to handle stressful situations. Anyone who has experienced stress, and that's everyone, knows that it can take a physical toll. When we are highly stressed, we spend much of our day feeling and acting tense. After a while, this state of tenseness becomes so common that we are not aware when our muscles become tensed. Instead, we feel only the products of that tension: fatigue, headaches, possibly back pain, and other symptoms. Managing your stress means breaking this cycle of muscle tension. Although regular physical activity helps to relieve stress and muscle tension, it isn't enough. You must first learn to identify the areas of tension in your body, and then you can learn relaxation techniques to help reduce muscle tension throughout your body.

Active Versus Passive Relaxation

Many forms of relaxation techniques and methods abound. We can divide these techniques into two categories: active relaxation techniques and passive relaxation techniques.

When you do something such as deep muscle relaxation or imagery to relax, you are practicing the more *active* forms of relaxation. You can also relax when doing *passive* activities. Many people find it quite relaxing to sit in a hot tub, listen to music, or read. We encourage you to do both active and passive forms of relaxation. Most people naturally practice the many forms of passive relaxation. However, few people regularly practice the more active forms. We cannot emphasize enough, the importance of practicing active relaxation.

In this lesson, we will begin by showing you how to practice relaxing your muscles in a quiet place. In later lessons, you will practice making this form of active relaxation portable, so you can take it wherever you go. This is why we like to teach active relaxation techniques to our clients. They can use this form of muscle relaxation anywhere, anytime, and in almost any stressful situation. The passive forms of relaxation are often less portable. For instance, if you are stuck in heavy traffic late in the afternoon, it's not practical to jump into a nice hot bath and relax. You need a relaxation technique that will help you in that situation.

Learning to Identify Tension

Tension, like stress, can be desirable at low levels. For instance, you could not write or use a keyboard if you could not tense the muscles in your hands. However, you don't need to tense other muscles in your body such as your neck, jaw, and back muscles; your hands are enough. Individuals who generally have high levels of stress often tense muscles throughout their bodies when they need to tense only one or two muscle groups. Consequently, learning to isolate the various muscle groups in your body is important.

Reducing Tension

Do you know how the various muscles in your body feel when they are tense? Most people would answer "yes" to this question. However, many of the same people experience tense muscles from stress without realizing their muscles are tense. For many people, stress levels build over time. Muscles that are continuously tense become the norm. Your first objective in this lesson is to learn how the different muscles in your body feel when they are tense. This will help you to recognize stress when your muscles begin to tense up needlessly. When this happens, you will want to take steps immediately to reduce the unnecessary tension.

Think of yourself as a firefighter. A firefighter's job is to spot and put out small fires before they get out of control and consume the entire building. Being sensitive to your own muscle tension is one way of spotting small spikes in stress. Your job is to spot even the slightest increase in muscle tension anywhere in your body and relax the tense muscles before they engulf your entire body with tension and stress.

Reducing unwanted tension through relaxation is a skill that requires a great deal of practice. Relaxation is not some kind of "psychological Valium" or handy crutch you can use when you are feeling uptight and then put away until you need it again. Instead, relaxation must be practiced often—at least twice a day at first, for 20 minutes each time. Don't get stressed over this revelation. The results will be well worth the effort.

You have probably heard of various relaxation techniques. These techniques usually have catchy names designed to snare the consumer and distinguish their "unique characteristics." Most of these relaxation techniques work in much the same way. In fact, you may have already tried some of them. Research has not shown that any particular technique is best for any one type of person or stress-related problem. Researchers have studied extensively the deep muscle relaxation technique we recommend here. Research and clinical testing have shown this technique works well for many people. Deep muscle relaxation of-

"Learning to recognize when your muscles tense needlessly is an important stress management technique."

fers many advantages over other forms of relaxation, and we encourage you to give it a chance to work for you. For example, this form of relaxation is portable—you can take it with you anywhere, and you don't need tapes, electricity, batteries, or any other equipment. Also, deep muscle relaxation has been recommended to treat:

"A stress manager is much like a firefighter. Your job is to spot small amounts of tension in your muscles and relax them before they engulf your entire body with stressful tension."

- Chronic muscle tension
- Neck and back pain
- Insomnia
- Muscle spasms
- High blood pressure

If you practice deep muscle relaxation regularly, you can significantly reduce the level of anger, anxiety, and other extreme emotions you experience. In later lessons, we discuss another form of relaxation known as visualization.

The purpose of relaxation techniques is to help you build a valuable new skill. If you have a favorite relaxation technique that works for you, it's fine to stick with it. The key is not the particular technique itself, but regular, consistent practice. It is also important to incorporate relaxation into your daily life. However, we highly recommend that you also try the deep muscle relaxation technique. As we said before, this technique has important advantages over other techniques.

Deep Muscle Relaxation

Feeling a warm sense of relaxation in your body and experiencing high psychological stress at the same time is impossible. This is why learning to relax is so important. As your body relaxes, your stress level decreases. Deep muscle relaxation is a process of tensing, then relaxing individual muscle groups. In this way, you will learn how each group of muscles feels when it is tense and when it is relaxed. Once you master these skills, you will then learn how to reduce unwanted tension in each muscle group. We begin with the 12 large-muscle groups. Then later in the program, we reduce this number, making your relaxation practices shorter and more portable. This is the beauty of deep muscle relaxation techniques. They work whether you're in the privacy of your home; on a busy, crowded freeway; or in a long line at the grocery store. The chart on page 113, Deep Muscle Relaxation, lists the 12 large-muscle groups and suggests ways of tensing them.

Getting Ready to Practice

Think of a sport that you enjoy. As an example, let's use tennis. Remember how

Deep Muscle Relaxation

Large Muscle Groups	Suggestions for Tensing Muscles
1. Upper Forehead	Raise your eyebrows and wrinkle your forehead.
2. Lower Forehead	Pull your eyebrows together. Try to get them to meet.
3. Eyes	Close your eyes tightly, but not too tight. If you wear contacts, be careful.
4. Lips	Press your lips together, but don't clench your teeth or jaw.
5. Back and Neck	Put your head back and press it against the back of a chair.
6. Shoulders & Neck	Shrug (drop) your shoulders, then bring your shoulders straight up until they almost touch your ears.
7. Chest & Breathing	Take a deep breath and hold it about 10 seconds, then release it.
8. Upper Arm	Tense your biceps and with arms by your side, pull your upper arm toward your side without touching. Try not to tense the lower arm while doing this—let the lower arm hang loosely.
9. Lower Arm	Make a fist, palm down, and pull your wrist toward your upper arm.
10. Abdomen	Pull your stomach in toward your back.
11. Thighs	Push your feet hard against the floor.
12. Lower Leg & Foot	Point your toes upward toward your knees.

clumsy you felt the first time you tried to hit that little ball over the net? If you had quit then, as you might have wanted to, just think of all the pleasure you would have missed. The same is true of learning how to relax. You may not "get it" at first. You may even feel as awkward trying to relax as you did trying to keep the tennis ball in play. But gradually, if you keep practicing, you will master the skills and become proficient in their use. Before we have you begin your first practice session, let's discuss some preparations you can make to help create the "right" practice environment.

First, choose a time and a place where you can regularly practice relaxation techniques. If you use a calendar, planner, or computer, schedule your practice sessions for the next week. If not, use the My Scheduled Relaxation Practice Sessions worksheet provided on page 125. Remember to be specific. We do not recommend that you try to sneak your practice sessions into spare moments when you are likely to be interrupted. Instead, choose a time when no one else is around or when you can ask others not to bother you for about 20 minutes. Now select a place. Eventually, you will be able to do your relaxation anywhere and at any time. But for now, when you're just starting, make it easy on yourself. Find a quiet room, pull the shades down, turn down the lights, and sit in a comfortable chair. A bed is fine as long as you don't fall asleep. Learning relaxation skills when you're asleep is difficult!

We recommend that you practice your relaxation skills once before your day begins and again toward the end of your day. You may need to get up a little earlier, but the few minutes of lost sleep will be well worth the extra effort.

Let's Begin

Do you have a quiet room and a comfortable chair? If so, you are ready to begin. First, spend a minute or two just settling deeper and deeper into the chair. Breathe slowly and evenly—in and out. Each time you breathe in, breath in through your nose with your mouth closed. Visualize the incoming fresh air as pure and stress free. Now, each time you exhale, breathe out through your mouth. Picture some of the tension leaving your body, like a bird gliding away as you exhale. Close your eyes and keep breathing, slowly and smoothly—in and out. If closing your eyes makes you uncomfortable, you can start by keeping them open and focused on one spot on the floor, ceiling, or wall.

When you feel calm and can concentrate, you are ready to start working with your muscles. Keep breathing evenly as you tense and relax each muscle group. As you inhale, tense your muscles, but don't hold your breath! Relax your muscles as you exhale. Let's now discuss four important factors to focus on as you do this exercise.

Tension

Begin with your upper forehead. As you breathe in, raise your eyebrows and wrinkle your forehead. Tense them to about three-quarters of their maximum tension—enough so that the muscles feel tight, but not so much that they are painful. Tense the muscles as you inhale. Holding the tension at three quarters of maximum, continue to breath—in and out—for about 10–15 seconds. This is about three breaths for most people. After about the third breath, relax the tension in your eyebrows and forehead as you exhale—visualize the tension rushing out of your muscles through your mouth.

Isolation

Isolating the tension to the specific muscle area as much as possible is important. In our present example, try hard to isolate the tension to your eyebrows and forehead. Make a quick mental check of the rest of your body to make sure that other muscles are not tensing too. At first, it is very likely that you will also tense other parts of your body such as your shoulders, stomach, legs, and toes. Even your breathing may stop. If you notice this happening, try to intentionally relax all other parts of your body except for the one or two muscles that you are trying to tense. Remember to keep your breathing smooth and even—in and out.

Concentration

As you continue the deep muscle relaxation, remember to keep breathing smoothly and normally— in and out. As you breathe, concentrate on the feeling in your eyebrows and forehead. Hold the tension for 10–15 seconds, or about two or three breaths. As you concentrate on the tension in your eyebrows and forehead, check other muscles to make sure they are not also tensing. Do not get discouraged if you find this difficult. You will do much better with practice.

Relaxation

The next time you exhale (about the third time), let the tension go. Relax the muscles quickly. You might want to think of your muscles as flopping, like a rubber band when it is released. Concentrate on this relaxed feeling. Notice how different relaxed muscles feel than tense muscles. Keep breathing normally. After three breaths or so, your muscles should be completely relaxed. You are now ready to start the process again, with the same muscles.

After you have practiced tensing and relaxing your eyebrows and forehead twice, take a break for a minute or so. During this time, keep breathing slowly and evenly—in and out. Each time you breath in, count to yourself (one, two, and so on). Each time you breathe out, say the word "relax" to yourself. Try to picture the words as you say them. If your mind wanders away from the word, gently turn it back.

After a minute or two, move on to the next muscle group. Using the chart for the large-muscle groups on page 113, repeat the process you used with your eyebrows and forehead, then move to the next group, and so on. Tensing the muscles for 10–15 seconds, then relax them for about three breaths. Remember to keep breathing evenly—in and out. Try to tense the muscles as you breathe in through your nose, and after 10–15 seconds, release them as you exhale through your mouth. Tense and then release each muscle group twice. Each time, focus on tension, isolation, concentration, and relaxation—letting the muscles flop when you let go. Remember to take a break after each muscle group. Relax for at least a minute before you move on to the next group.

We have provided the steps for deep muscle relaxation on page 118. You may refer to this list during your practice sessions. Your entire practice should take about 20 to 25 minutes. When you finish the last muscle group, give yourself some time to slowly reconnect with the world. Relax all of your muscles, then gently open your eyes. See how long you can keep the relaxed feeling as you go about the day's activities. Before you end your day, find time to do the exercise again.

The Relaxation Practice Record

As we said earlier, we recommend that you practice your relaxation exercises at least twice a day for the full 20 minutes each time. Remember that Beethoven did not master the piano in a single sitting. As

Relaxation Practice Record

(Sally's Example)

Week of: November 8, 1999

Date	Beginning Time	Ending Time	Tension Before (0-8)	Tension After (0-8)	Concentration (0-8)	Comments
11/08	6:00 am	6:25 am	6	5	1	Difficulty concentrating, this doesn't feel natural.
11/08	10:00 pm	10:25 pm	5	4	3	I'm tired, having trouble.
11/09	6:00 am	6:25 am	5	4	5	This feels much better I'm excited.
11/09	9:30 pm	9:55 pm	4	2	6	I'm getting the hang of this and I feel very relaxed.
11/10	6:05 am	6:30 am	6	4	5	Had trouble sleeping. Worrying about all I have to do today.
11/10	10:45 pm	11:10 pm	5	3	6	A busy day and I'm tired. Hard to concentrate.

with all forms of behavior change, self-monitoring is a key ingredient. Keep a record of your practice sessions so that you will not be as likely to forget to practice. Do you remember Sally, who we introduced earlier in this lesson on page 102? On page 116 is Sally's Example Relaxation Practice Record from her first week of practicing this relaxation technique.

We provide you with a blank Relaxation Practice Record on page 126 for you to record your practice sessions. Make as many copies of this form as you need. Record the date and time of your practice sessions, and rate your tension level before and after your practice session. Use the 0–8 tension scale on the form. This scale should be very familiar to you by now. Rate the tension and your concentration during the practice session. Be sure to include your thoughts in the comments column.

Your Daily Stress Record for this week is on page 124. We have included a place at the bottom of this form to record both the number of minutes you were physically active and the number of minutes you practice your deep muscle relaxation techniques. Be sure to record these times as accurately as possible.

Your tension levels should gradually drop and your concentration levels should rise. If you encounter any problems during a session or discover any techniques that work especially well, write them down. This will help you remember them for next time.

Try to do some "mini practice sessions" in addition to your main relaxation practices each day. You can practice when you have a few spare minutes. For example, on your lunch break, in the bathroom, at a traffic light, or during the commercials on

"This is my relaxation tape— it's the sound of ocean waves crashing onto the shore, snatching my boss's body off his beach chair and carrying him out to sea."

television. Try tensing and relaxing one or two muscle groups at a time. In particular, work on the muscles that have been giving you the most trouble. Also, as you go through your day, pay attention to which muscle groups are tensing up and try to relax them.

Physical Activity and Relaxation Worksheet

You reviewed your Stress Change Record earlier in this lesson. Hopefully, this exercise helped you to see the value of keeping such a record. In Appendix F, on page 432, we have included a Physical Activity and Relaxation Worksheet for you to record the number of minutes you are active each day and the number of minutes you practice relaxation techniques (for weeks five through eight). This is a record that you can complete at the end of the week by taking the information from your Daily Stress Record. When this worksheet is completed after week eight, you will be able to see clear patterns in your physical activity and relaxation practice. In Lesson Nine, we will review this worksheet.

Your Imaginary Bank Account

Imagine that you have a bank account. Each morning, at precisely the same time,

Deep Muscle Relaxation Technique

1. Close your eyes and breath slowly and evenly—in and out.
2. Breath in through your nose and out through your mouth.
3. As you breath out, relax your muscles.
4. When you are relaxed, begin with a specific muscle group.
5. Isolate the muscle group you're working on.
6. Check to make sure the rest of your body is relaxed.
7. As you breath in through your nose, tense the muscle group about three-quarters of maximum.
8. Hold this tension as you breath slowly and normally—in and out.
9. As you exhale after the third breath (or after 10–15 seconds), relax the muscle group quickly (flopping).
10. Visualize all of the tension and stress leaving your body as you exhale.
11. Repeat this exercise with the same muscle group, for a total of two times.
12. After each muscle group, sit quietly with your eyes closed, breathing deeply—in and out.
13. Each time you breath in, count, "one, two, three,..."
14. As you exhale, say to yourself, "relax," and picture the tension and stress leaving your body through your mouth as you breath out.
15. After a minute of relaxing (about 10–12 breaths) begin with the next muscle group. (Do each muscle group two times total.)
16. Remember to keep your concentration on your muscles and on your breathing—try not to think about anything else—nothing else at all!

$86,400 is deposited into the account for you to spend that day. This account carries no balance over from one day to the next. Every evening, at precisely the same time, whatever balance is in the account is lost forever.

If you had such an account, what would you do? Spend every cent, of course!

All of us have such a bank. No matter how rich or poor, short or tall, good or bad, we all have the same such account. It's called TIME. Every morning we are credited with 86,400 seconds for the day. Every evening, whatever we have failed to invest wisely is deleted. In this account, no balances are carried over and no overdrafts are allowed. If we fail to invest each day's time, it is lost forever—no going back, no carrying over until tomorrow.

The notion of "time management" is a misnomer. None of us can really manage TIME—we can only manage ourselves (our choices) with respect to time.

The term "time management" has become the common term used for managing ourselves with respect to time. To help in the understanding of this material, we too will use the term "time management" throughout the manual. But, keep in mind this brief discussion about what you can and cannot manage!

Managing Your Time

We can think of time as an ongoing series of decisions, both large and small, that give shape to each day. When you make decisions that you believe are not the best use of your time, you are likely to feel frustrated and stressed. In later lessons, we will be discussing techniques to help you become more aware of how you spend your time and how to better manage your time to accomplish the things in life that are truly important to you. To introduce you to the notion of time management, we first need to address some basic principles. To help you understand these basic ideas, we introduce you to Harvey.

Meet Harvey

Harvey is 32 years old and runs the family clothing company in Chicago. The company has been growing and now employs 30 people. This has made Harvey very happy, but also causes him more stress. As the amount of work increased, Harvey took on more responsibility. He didn't trust anyone else to do the tasks right.

Before long, Harvey had so many tasks that he did not know where to begin. Some

I'M GOING TO REEVALUATE MY PRIORITIES SOMEDAY, BUT THERE ARE A LOT OF OTHER THINGS I'VE GOT TO DO FIRST.
THAVES

days he spent far too much time doing unimportant things, and other times simply stared out the window, worrying about all the work he had to do. Although he worked longer hours, Harvey never seemed to get enough done. Soon, his relationships with friends and family suffered, he stopped exercising, he started eating junk food on the go, and he lost sleep worrying about all the things he had to do. Harvey was not happy. Eventually, he developed an ulcer.

When your house is on fire, it is unlikely that you stop to figure out how the fire got started or how you might prevent the next one. You have only one concern, deciding whether to fight or flee the flames. An old, Native-American proverb states, "The only reality is the present." Yet, if this were true and we paid attention only to the present, our lives would be out of control. We would spend every waking minute responding to things that are urgent enough to capture our attention. We would ignore or neglect all the other, perhaps even more important, things in our lives.

For many people, time pressures cause or aggravate stress. This creates the feeling that there is too much to do in a day. Most of us can identify with Harvey's situation. Harvey's example illustrates three typical problems associated with time pressures:

1. Taking on too much
2. Working inefficiently
3. Worrying about everything that has to be done

Taking on more responsibilities than you can handle does not mean that you are a bad worker. In fact, you probably work so well that it seems natural to try to do more. This is when the second problem sets in. When you have more tasks to do than you can do well, you become overwhelmed. You have less time to spend on each task and your ability to work efficiently suffers. When this happens, the third most common problem surfaces. Most people spend more time worrying about a task than it would take to complete the task. Learning a few simple time management techniques will help you avoid these problems.

Some people have no problem at all with time pressure. If this is true for you, you may find the sections on time management less important. For others, time pressure can be an overwhelming source of stress. Learning to manage time can be one of the most important stress management techniques for these individuals. Time management is no great mystery. This skill requires learning the difference between effectiveness and efficiency, important and

I THINK...
THEREFORE
I WORRY
THAVES

unimportant, and urgent and insignificant. Once these concepts and skills are mastered, you can get the most out of life without feeling stressed.

The two key skills of time management are designed to combat the problems described above. The first skill is not to become overcommitted. The second is to learn to organize your priorities. These two skills will enable you to accomplish the tasks that are *important in your life* without feeling stressed. This all comes back to the issue of feeling that you have no control over your environment. Good time management skills will help you better control the one thing in life you can control—your choices. The better your choices are for *you*, the less stress you will experience. Again, awareness is key. In later lessons, we will discuss alternative self-monitoring forms that will help you become more aware of how you invest your time, how you would have liked to invest your time, and how you can reconcile the two.

Which comes first, being overcommitted or being stressed? It's hard to say. People who tend to be stressed also tend to take on more than they can handle and end up feeling even more stressed. This state of affairs sneaks up on you with little warning. Saying "no" to all the requests and opportunities that come along can be difficult. Do you remember Jane, introduced on page 32 in Lesson Two? Overcommitment and time management issues were at the heart of her stress.

We will leave you with one final thought: time management takes time! If you find yourself saying or thinking, "I don't have time for time management," then you probably need time management the most. In the next lesson, you will begin recording your activities for a few days so that you will know what you are actually doing. Below are some final thoughts for you to consider as you think about time management.

- To realize the value of ONE YEAR, ask a student who failed a grade.
- To realize the value of ONE MONTH, ask a cancer patient who has less than 30 days to live.
- To realize the value of ONE HOUR, ask two lovers who are waiting to meet.
- To realize the value of ONE MINUTE, ask a person who missed the last flight home for a holiday.
- To realize the value of ONE SECOND, ask the person who just avoided an accident.
- To realize the value of ONE MILLISECOND, ask the person who won a silver medal in the Olympics.

"Two key skills of time management are not becoming overcommitted and learning to organize your priorities."

"I'm learning how to relax, doctor—
but I want to relax *better* and *faster!*
I want to be on the cutting edge of relaxation!"

Time is a valuable resource, even more valuable than the imaginary bank account we discussed earlier. Value it, treasure it, and invest it wisely. Yesterday is history, tomorrow is mystery, today is a gift—this is why it's called the *present.*

We don't want you to get the idea that you should feel stressed about keeping track of every second of every day—quite the opposite. Often, the best investment you can make of your time is to do something that is relaxing and reduces your stress. For you, this may mean reading a good book, taking a stroll through the park, going for a swim, or doing absolutely nothing. Investing time in yourself is important.

Lesson Review

This has been a long lesson, and you have finally made it to the end. We began this lesson by reviewing your progress over the past four weeks. You reviewed the self-monitoring forms that we introduced to you in the first four lessons. We reemphasized the importance of self-monitoring. We then spent some time discussing physical activity, its importance, and how easy it is to become moderately fit. The importance of communicating with your partner was then addressed. Deep muscle relaxation was a new stress management technique presented to you. You were introduced to the Relaxation Practice Record, which you will complete twice daily. Finally, we concluded the lesson by beginning our discussion on the importance of time management and its relation to stress. Although this was quite a long lesson, we hope you enjoyed its content.

This Week's Assignment

Continue to keep your Daily Stress Record including the physical activity and relaxation records on the bottom of this form. We have a new copy for you on page 124. Make a special effort this week to master the deep muscle relaxation techniques discussed in this lesson. Be sure to schedule your practice sessions on the form on page 125, and keep a record of your practice sessions using the form on page 126. At the end of the week (or daily, whichever works best for you) be sure to complete the Physical Activity and Relaxation Worksheet in Appendix F on page 432. Also, continue to complete the Stress Change Worksheet for week five on page 127. And finally, record your average weekly stress level on the worksheet in Appendix E on page 430. Good luck with this week's assignments.

Knowledge Review

T F 30. Reviewing your progress at regular intervals is an important step in mastering your stress.

T F 31. Your Stress Change Worksheet should reflect a gradual decrease in your levels of stress each week of this program.

T F 32. Regular physical activity can help improve both your physical and psychological well-being.

T F 33. You must exercise at least 45 minutes each day in order to experience any health benefits.

T F 34. Making specific requests to your partner about how he or she can help you in your stress management program is an effective way to communicate your needs.

T F 35. Passive forms of relaxation are more important in reducing stress than active forms of relaxation.

T F 36. One of the primary benefits of learning deep muscle relaxation is that it is very portable and does not require additional equipment to be beneficial.

T F 37. Deep muscle relaxation is a form of passive relaxation.

T F 38. While practicing deep muscle relaxation, it is important to hold your breath while you are tensing and relaxing the individual muscle groups.

T F 39. Three common problems associated with time management include taking on too much, working inefficiently, and worrying about everything that has to be done.

(Answers in Appendix C, page 415)

Daily Stress Record—Lesson Five

Name:____________________ **Week of:**__________

Date	Average Stress Level	Highest Stress Level	Time of Highest Stress Level	Stressful Event Associated with Highest Stress Level

My Physical Activity and Relaxation Record

Day of the Week	Physical Activity Record		Relaxation Record	
	Activity	Minutes	Time of Day	Minutes
Monday				
Tuesday				
Wednesday				
Thursday				
Friday				
Saturday				
Sunday				
This Week	Total Activity		Total Relaxation	

My Scheduled Relaxation Practice Sessions

week of: ____________________

Day	Time(s)	Place(s)
Monday		
Tuesday		
Wednesday		
Thursday		
Friday		
Saturday		
Sunday		

Relaxation Practice Record

Week of:_______________

Date	Beginning Time	Ending Time	Tension Before (0-8)	Tension After (0-8)	Concentration (0-8)	Comments

Stress Change Worksheet

(Weeks 5 – 8)

Stress Level

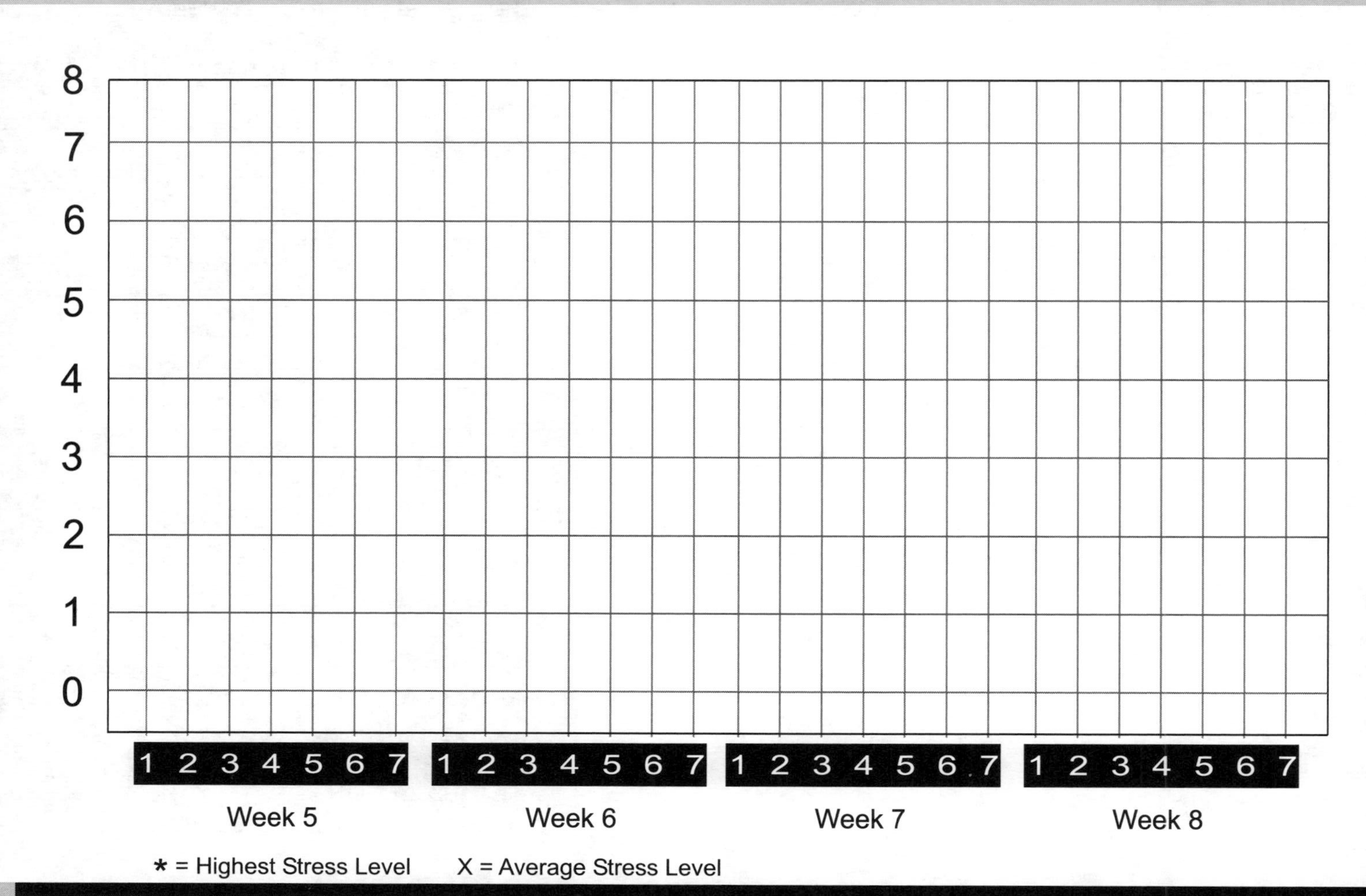

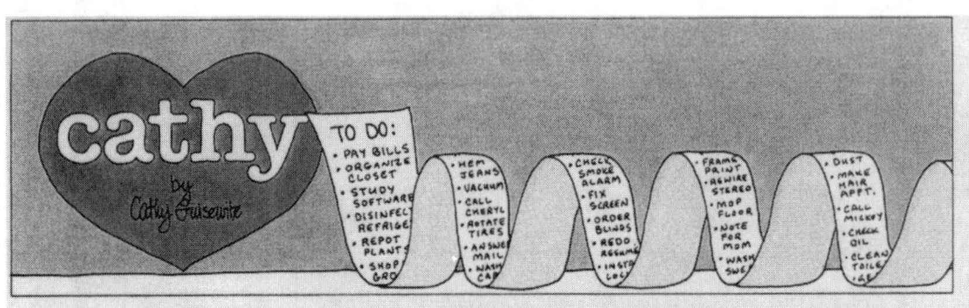
cathy
by Cathy Guisewite
TO DO:
• PAY BILLS
• ORGANIZE CLOSET
• STUDY SOFTWARE

I'M FINANCIALLY SECURE ENOUGH TO CHARGE OUT INTO THE WORLD AND BUY MY OWN HOME...

...BUT NOT QUITE WELL OFF ENOUGH TO HAVE A CLEANING PERSON.

I'VE PUSHED MYSELF TO A BRILLIANT POSITION OF RESPONSIBILITY AT WORK...

...BUT NOT QUITE TO THE POINT WHERE I GET AN ASSISTANT TO HELP WITH THE DIRTY WORK.

I HAVE THE CONFIDENCE AND DRIVE TO ORCHESTRATE A FABULOUS WARDROBE, SOCIAL SCHEDULE AND TRAVEL ITINERARY...BUT NOT THE MEANS TO HIRE ANYONE TO DO ALTERATIONS, WASHING, COOKING, SHOPPING, ORGANIZING, OR CLEANING UP....

I AM WOMAN.

I KEEP LEAVING MYSELF IN MY OWN DUST.
MENDIN
BILLS

Lesson Six

Welcome to Lesson Six. We hope your week of deep muscle relaxation practice went well. If you have not yet perfected your practice sessions, don't worry—it takes time. In Lesson Seven, we discuss some common problems people often have with deep muscle relaxation and how to overcome them. We begin our discussion this week by talking about the ABC's of behavior change. This discussion is a good lead-in to the topic of feelings and where they come from. We then introduce you to the notion of realistic thinking and a discussion on the power each of us have to choose our thoughts and beliefs. Here, you will learn techniques for controlling your mental response to stressful events. We'll introduce you to a new form for recording and challenging your initial thoughts to stressful situations. So, with all this in mind, let's begin this exciting lesson!

The ABC's of Behavior Change

Your daily behaviors (habits) have developed over your lifetime. They are the result of a complex interaction of biological, cultural, and environmental factors. Changing these lifelong behaviors takes time and practice. Understanding how your behaviors develop can be an important step in changing them. To do this, we will use the ABC approach. This stands for Activating events, Beliefs, and Consequences.

Dr. Albert Ellis, a clinical psychologist, developed an ABC approach to emotional and behavior change. The basic premise of this approach is that our *thoughts* lead to our emotions and behaviors—events do not. Let's take a closer look at the ABC's.

Activating Events

Events are the situations or occurrences in life that cause us to react emotionally. Examples include taking an exam, asking another person out on a date, or asking for a pay increase. Many people believe that the *events* cause stress. As you will soon see, they do not.

Beliefs

Beliefs refer to the actual *thoughts* we have about activating events in our lives. Our thoughts (beliefs) about the events trigger our feelings and subsequent behaviors.

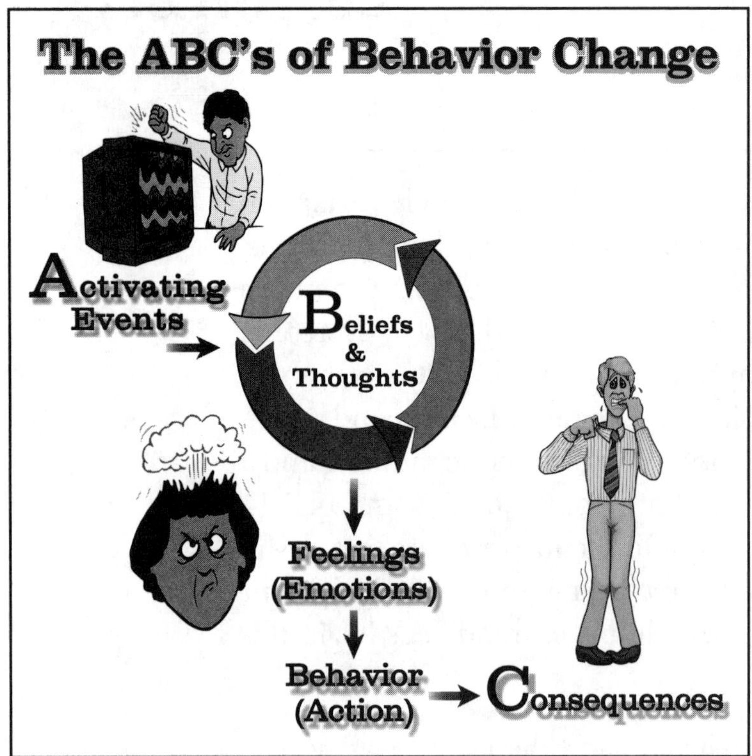

These thoughts or beliefs can be helpful and lead to healthy emotions and behaviors. However, our thoughts can also be irrational and stress producing, leading to unhealthy emotions and behaviors. The following are examples of irrational thoughts and beliefs that may increase rather than reduce stress:

"If I do poorly on this exam, I am a failure."

"If he rejects me, I am unlovable."

"If I don't get a raise, then the company doesn't value me as a person or employee."

Consequences

Consequences are the emotions and subsequent behaviors that result from the *beliefs* we have about certain *events*. Many people believe that the consequences occur directly from the events themselves, but this is incorrect. Examples of consequences that can result from stressful thoughts and beliefs include anxiety, depression, and procrastination.

As you can see, the way to change the consequences of a particular event to more positive feelings and behaviors is to change the *thoughts* that cause them. Later in this lesson we will introduce you to the notion of *realistic thinking*. Realistic thinking will help you change the way you think about the events in your life that are likely to cause stress. The more realistic your thinking, the less stress you will have.

Challenging the Mental Response System

We now come to an exciting juncture along your journey to mastering stress. In Lesson Five, you learned two important principles for reducing the physical effects of stressful situations. First, being *physically active* can help to improve your fitness level, which better prepares your body to handle stressful situations. In addition, regular physical activity can help keep your stress level down because it makes you feel better. Second, *deep muscle relaxation* can be used to reduce the physical stress (tension) in your muscles.

In this lesson, we begin to work on the mental aspect of stress management. A key principle to reducing the mental effects of stress is learning to *change your thoughts* or, in other words, learning to *choose* (control) your thoughts. If you can learn to control your thoughts and the tension in your muscles, you are well on your way to mastering stress. In the examples we discussed earlier in the program, you may have noticed how easy it is to make simple errors in thinking. Certainly, these errors are more easily noticed in others than in ourselves. In this lesson, you will learn to challenge your initial thoughts and learn techniques that will help you choose thoughts that are more realistic and less stressful. So, if you're ready, let's forge ahead.

Where Feelings Come From

Where do feelings come from? When we ask our clients this question, we get a wide range of answers. Most people believe that the events we experience in our lives determine our feelings and subsequent responses to those events. If this were true, then everyone would react in the same way to the same event. Yet, we all know this is not true. Actually, your *beliefs* and *thoughts* determine your feelings about an *activating* event, and these feelings trigger your actions (*behaviors*). Your behaviors, in turn, determine the *consequences* of what you choose to believe and think.

You are probably now pondering the next question, "Where do our thoughts and beliefs come from?" Many of our thoughts and beliefs are automatic, and as such, our responses also become automatic, given a particular event. Yes, believe it or not, you have the power to choose your thoughts and beliefs. This is why people can react so differently to the same event. Learning the skills and techniques to choose thoughts that are less stressful is critical to mastering your stress. Let's look at an example.

Meet Me at the Movie

Assume for a moment that you and a friend, Sarah, have agreed to meet at a movie theater to see a newly released movie. You and Sarah agree to meet at 6:30 p.m. for the 7:00 p.m. show. You arrive on time and are standing in front of the theater at 6:30 p.m. sharp. Try to picture the scene—traffic going by; the ticket lines getting longer; people standing in line, walking by, laughing and talking; the coolness of the air; and the sounds and smells around you. Imagine yourself pacing slowly back and forth, looking at the advertisements, and watching the other people going into the theater. It's 6:45, then 6:50, and still no sign of Sarah. As you look up at the ticket window, you notice the time is now 6:55 p.m. Still, Sarah is not there. Stop and ask yourself, "How would I feel?" What would your stressful emotions be, and how strong are they on the 0–8 scale? Most people say that they are either very worried or very angry (around a 6–7 on the scale).

Now imagine that Sarah comes running around the corner, and before you can say anything, she says, "I'm so sorry I'm late, but there was an accident right in front of me. I had to administer CPR and first aid until the paramedics arrived to take over. Thankfully, everyone lived, even the little girl I was helping." Now, how do you feel?

"It's not the events in our lives that cause stress, but rather our thoughts about the events that lead to stress."

At this point, most people say that their anger or worry disappears.

If we asked you what *caused* your emotions as you stood outside the theater, you would most likely say that you were worried or angry because Sarah was late. But, this is not true. Let's look at what happened. Obviously, Sarah was late before she showed up. She was still late even after she arrived. The event (being late) has not changed—Sarah was late in both instances. However, your emotions changed dramatically. So, it could not have been the event (being late) that caused your initial emotions. What changed was your interpretation of the event—your thoughts about it. You *chose* the thoughts, and the thoughts are what caused your emotions.

Before Sarah showed up, you might have been thinking something like, "She is always late," "She probably decided to go to the game instead," or "She is so irresponsible." These thoughts would have made you feel angry or frustrated. If you were thinking, "I hope she's okay," "Maybe her mother is sick again," "Maybe she had an accident," or "Could I have come at the wrong time?" you probably would have felt worried or a little anxious. In other words, *your thoughts* about Sarah's lateness—not the lateness itself—caused you to feel angry, frustrated, worried, or a little anxious. If you could have changed your thoughts while you were waiting, you could have saved yourself a lot of unnecessary stress. This is exactly what we are going to show you how to do in this lesson.

Changing Your Thoughts

Many of our thoughts are automatic. These automatic thoughts are the result of the complex interaction of our life experiences, and they often pop into our heads irrationally, without much detailed thought or review. Changing your automatic thoughts requires learning new skills that will help you examine your thoughts more objectively. Understanding five key principles about your thoughts will help you de-

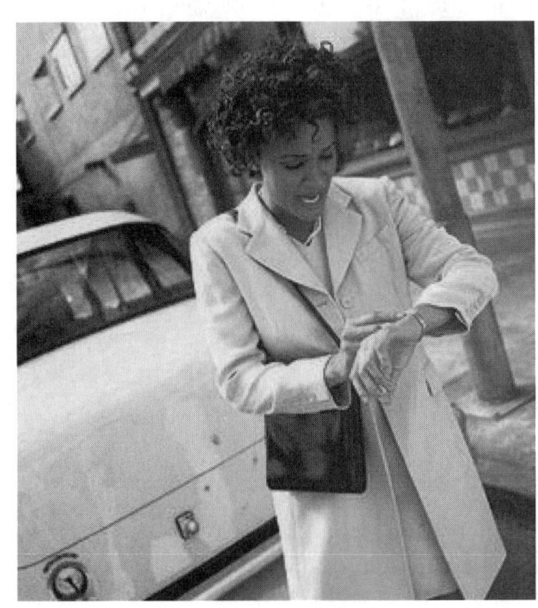

velop the skills necessary to begin thinking more realistically.

❶ Your emotional reactions are the direct result of your thoughts and beliefs about an event, not the result of the event itself. Two people can react differently to the same event because they have different thoughts and beliefs about the event.

Let's say that two people go up in an airplane for their first skydiving lesson. The first person excitedly leaps out of the plane because she thinks the experience will be a great feeling of freedom. The second person stays in the plane because he thinks jumping is too dangerous and that the jump might kill him. The relationship between events, our thoughts and beliefs, and the resulting emotional reactions is illustrated on page 130. Remember, this illustration shows our "automatic" reactions to events.

❷ Extreme beliefs cause extreme emotions. By changing your extreme beliefs, you can learn to control your emotional reactions.

❸ Many of your thoughts and beliefs may seem to be automatic—they come very fast, and you may not be consciously aware of them. You may simply "react" without any thought, but the thoughts are really there. Time and practice will help you identify your underlying thoughts and beliefs.

❹ Although it is not easy, you can "choose" or "control" your thoughts, thereby controlling your emotional reactions. Most people who are troubled by stress believe they have no control over their reactions. As we have said before, this is simply not true. You do have the power to choose your thoughts and beliefs. Your thoughts and beliefs are not easy to change; you have spent a lifetime developing them, and they have become a part of you. But remember, you *can* change them. Once again, awareness and practice are the keys to making this happen.

❺ Realistic thinking is different from positive thinking. Positive thinking asks you to look through rose-colored glasses and see the world as a wonderful place. But we all know the world is not always wonderful; this is why positive thinking never lasts long—we tend to disbelieve it. Realistic thinking, on the other hand, asks you to look at situations rationally and objectively. The key to changing your emotions is believing in your new thoughts.

The Power to Choose

As humans, we are gifted with four unique abilities: self-awareness, vision, principles, and independent determination. These four uniquely human gifts converge when we make choices in life. The better we understand each of these gifts, the better our choices. The better our choices, the happier, healthier, and less stressful we become. Let's look at each gift.

Self-Awareness. As humans, we are aware of ourselves. However, as we have said before, we are often unaware of our environment. This is why self-monitoring is so important. Self-monitoring helps you become more aware of your environment and your responses to it. Having kept a Daily Stress Record for five weeks, you are now probably much more aware of the stressors in your life than before your started this program.

Vision. In addition to self-awareness, we are gifted with vision—the ability to see (in our minds) beyond today. In Lesson One, on page 16, we had you look into the future and visualize a less stressful life. Vision is what creates tomorrow. As humans, we are gifted with a unique ability to visualize ourselves beyond the present. The better we are at vision, the better choices we make. The better you are at visualizing a more stress-free future, the more likely the vision will become a reality. A time-honored saying goes something like this, "You can always achieve what your mind can perceive." You will have an opportunity to see just how powerful vision is in Lesson Ten when we begin our discussion on imagery.

Principles. Each of us have a set of principles by which we are guided. These principles help us distinguish between what we believe to be right or wrong—they are our consciences. These principles guide our beliefs and thoughts and the degree to which our emotions and behaviors are in harmony with them. Being aware of your own principles is key to changing your beliefs and thoughts.

Independent Determination. Another uniquely human gift is the ability to act based upon our self-awareness, vision, and principles. Even in the harshest of circumstances, we have this independence. Imagine the captive prisoner of war. While his body may be confined and tortured, he still has the independence and freedom to choose his thoughts, beliefs, principles, and visions—he has an internal power to exercise his options.

Let's develop the idea of these four gifts a bit further. Consider people who have too much to drink and decide to get behind the wheel and drive home. These individuals lack the awareness of their physical state; they do not see themselves as a potentially lethal and deadly weapon. Now consider vision. Drunk drivers cannot visualize what might happen to them if they are stopped by the police or are involved in an accident. If they could visualize being imprisoned for

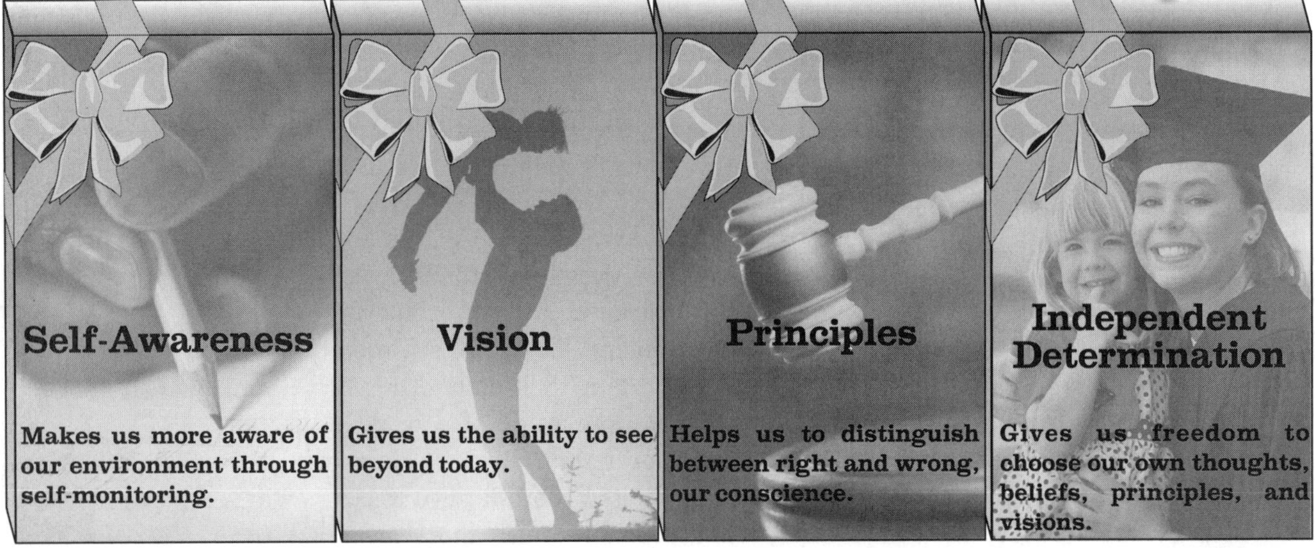
The Four Gifts of Human Ability
Self-Awareness
Makes us more aware of our environment through self-monitoring.
Vision
Gives us the ability to see beyond today.
Principles
Helps us to distinguish between right and wrong, our conscience.
Independent Determination
Gives us freedom to choose our own thoughts, beliefs, principles, and visions.

a long period of time or worse yet, being killed in an accident, they would be less likely to drive. Consider principles. Some people are guided by a strong set of principles. If they drink, they don't drive.

We have all heard the phrase, "Live for today, for tomorrow may never come." People who live by this philosophy lack self-awareness and vision. Moreover, this idea is unrealistic. Certainly, tomorrow may not come. However, consider this: tomorrow *always* comes, every day of your life, tomorrow will *always* come—except for one! This is reality and what realistic thinking is all about.

Realistic Thinking

By now, you should be convinced that your *feelings* (emotions)/behaviors are caused by your *thoughts* about an event and not by the event itself. The graphic illustration below shows this concept. Learning the skills and techniques to challenge your automatic thoughts and think more realistically will help you choose thoughts that are more realistic and less stressful. Let's look at some common problems people have when they allow their automatic thoughts to increase their stress.

Overestimating Probability

People who are highly stressed tend to make two types of errors in thinking. First, they overestimate how likely it is that an unpleasant event will happen. We call this overestimating the *probability.* Second, overstressed people often overestimate how bad the consequences will be if the event does occur. We call this overestimating the *consequences.* In this lesson, we will focus on the first of these errors—overestimating probabilities. In Lesson Eight, we discuss overestimating consequences.

No doubt, you can think of times in your own life when you have overestimated the probability of something bad happening. For example, if your boss says he wants to talk with you, you may immediately think, "He's going to yell at me." If your spouse is late coming home, you may immediately think, "She's had an accident." Or, if someone asks you to take on a new project, you may think, "I won't be able to do it."

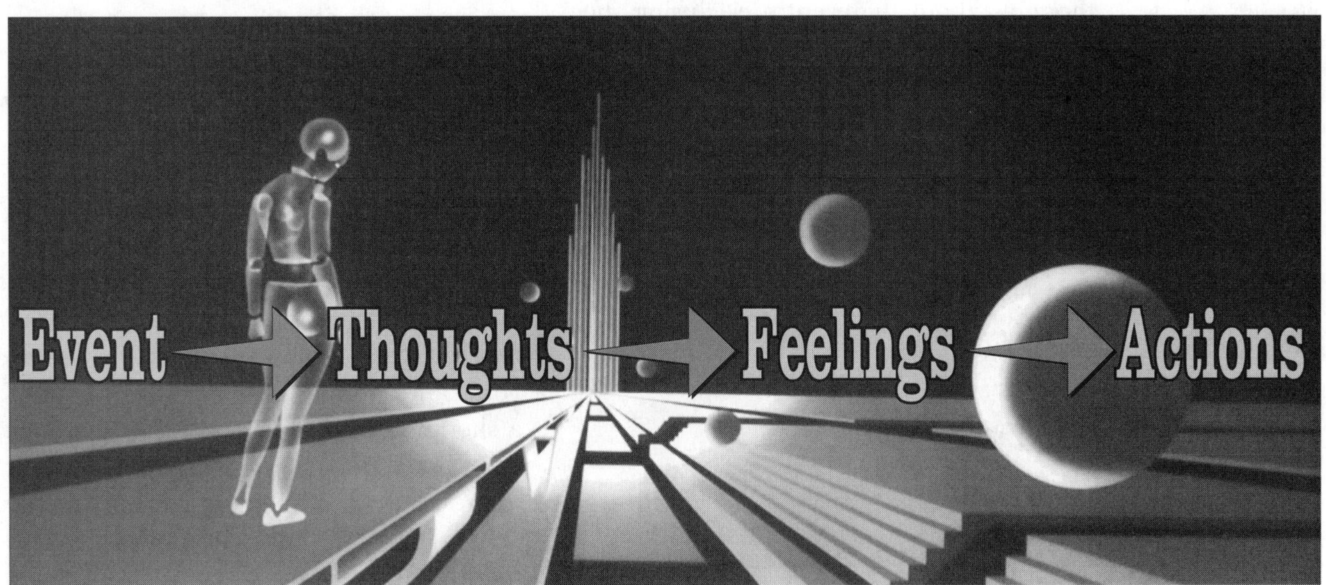

In each of these examples, you are assuming a very high (say 80 percent) probability that the negative event will occur. By thinking that your boss is almost certainly going to yell at you, you are thinking that there is no other possible reason you boss might want to talk with you. Realistically, there are many reasons your boss may want to talk with you—only one of which involves anger. So, you are overestimating.

Overestimating probability not only increases worry, it can also increase other negative emotions such as fear or anger. If a speeding driver cuts you off in traffic, you may think, "She did that intentionally to annoy me." Actually, the realistic probability that the driver's sole motive was to intentionally annoy you is much less than 100 percent and is probably quite unlikely. If you can learn to estimate and think about probabilities more realistically, you can reduce your stress.

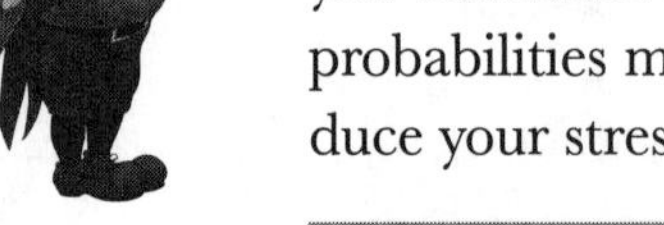

"The first step in changing your estimates is to identify your thoughts. Ask yourself what is making me feel this way?"

Changing Your Estimates

The first step in changing your estimates is to identify your thoughts. Remember, the event is not causing the stress, your thoughts about the event are causing the stress. Each time you notice your stress level increasing, ask yourself, "What is making me feel this way?" Let's say your boss has just scheduled a business meeting for this afternoon, and you are worried about it. Immediately ask yourself, "Why am I worried?" If you answer, "Because there is a meeting scheduled," remind yourself that events do not cause feelings. Ask a more specific question: "What is it *about* this meeting that is making me worry?" You may answer something like, "I might have to present a report." Now you have identified a stressful belief.

Even if your thought seems silly, be totally honest with yourself and identify the specific thought you have about the event. Sometimes, when you ask yourself a question, the answer may seem so silly that you will not want to admit that you actually had such a thought. But much of our stress is caused by silly beliefs that stay with us precisely because we never spell them out and realize just how silly they really are. Don't worry, having ridiculous thoughts does not mean that you are crazy. Denying that you have them can do more harm than acknowledging them.

Identifying Your Thoughts

Not all of your thoughts will be easy to identify. You may experience an emotion and not be able to determine its source. Try guessing a few likely thoughts. The simple process of considering and rejecting various possibilities may lessen your stress. This process may also lead you to the very thought that is really causing your emotion. For example, imagine that you came out of a shopping mall and found that someone had parked behind your car and blocked it in. You feel an immediate rush of intense anger. Practicing realistic thinking means that the first step would be to ask yourself,

"Why am I feeling angry?" If you cannot come up with an answer, make up a few possibilities, "This person is deliberately trying to make me late," "I am extremely inconvenienced," "This person is trying to take advantage of me in some way," or "This person has parked illegally." By brainstorming in this way, you may find that one of these thoughts rings a bell and is your underlying belief in the situation. Even if none of the possibilities ring true, looking at the reality of each one should help you to believe that there is no logical reason to feel angry.

Remember two other rules when you are identifying your beliefs about stressful emotions:

Rule #1

First, you should try to phrase your belief as a statement. Statements of supposed fact are usually responsible for negative feelings, yet we often don't realize this. Let's say, for example, that you come home some evening and find someone has burglarized your house. If you think to yourself, "Have I lost any valuables?" (a question), you probably would not be too stressed— instead, you may be concerned, inquisitive, or curious. These are emotions that are not too stressful. However, if you were to think, "I've lost everything" (a statement), then you would probably feel very stressed or panicked. In other words, extreme, negative feelings generally follow *statements* of negative occurrences. If you find yourself identifying a curious question as your thought or belief, then you probably have not identified the real thought.

Rule #2

The second rule to remember is that you should not let feelings or voluntary actions automatically become the subject of your thoughts. For instance, you might ask yourself the question, "Why am I feeling nervous about this meeting?" You might identify the thought, "Because I will be embarrassed." But remember, embarrassment is not a necessary outcome of the meeting. Your answer will depend on how realistically you think. It is not possible to look at how realistic this belief is because it depends on you. Instead, you should ask yourself, "What is it about the meeting that might make me feel embarrassed?" If you then come up with a statement like, "I haven't prepared my work properly," then this is a clear statement and belief that you can check in terms of how realistic it is. Similarly, if you come up with a thought regarding why you are feeling anxious about the meeting along the lines of, "Because I'm sure I'm not going to say anything" or "I know I'll say something stupid." These thoughts can be checked for reality.

Once you have *identified* your initial thought or thoughts, the next step is to ask yourself, "How likely is it that this will actually happen?" Generally, the lower the realistic estimate, the less intense your emotion will be. For example, let's assume your partner is late meeting you for dinner, and your initial thought is that he or she has had an accident. You will be far more worried if you think there is a 50 percent chance that your partner had an accident, than if you think there is only a 5 percent chance.

The goal here is to convince yourself that the probability of a negative outcome is as low as possible, but you must really believe it. If you tell yourself that there is no chance that your partner has had an accident, although you believe deep down that there is a high probability, you will not reduce your stress. The key is to change your

actual beliefs, not simply to change what you say to yourself.

You will need to look at the evidence and consider the alternatives to help answer the question, "How likely is it?" Look at evidence that is both positive and negative. By considering the alternatives, you will learn to think of all the possibilities, not just the initial one that increases your stress. In Lesson Seven, on page 153, we'll discuss techniques to help you begin to weigh the evidence for and against your initial stressful thoughts. For this week, we want you to begin practicing realistic thinking by asking yourself, "How likely is it?"

A Word about Probabilities

Some people find the idea of working with probabilities complex and difficult. So, we have included this short section to help you better understand probabilities. They are really quite simple to understand and use.

First, probabilities are always expressed as a percentage. Meteorologists use probabilities to predict the likelihood of it raining on any particular day. For example, "There is a 30 percent chance of rain today." Second, when the probabilities of *all* possible outcomes are totaled, their sum will equal 100 percent. Let's look again at our weather example.

Probability of rain	30%
Probability of no rain	70%
Total of all possible outcomes	100%

We can trace the origin of probabilities to games of chance. Take the coin toss at the beginning of a football game, for example. Let's assume that the Dallas Cowboys choose "heads" and the Philadelphia Eagles choose "tails." Given a single coin toss, what is the probability that the Cowboys will win the toss? You will agree that in this particular game of chance, two outcomes are possible:

- Outcome 1: The coin will land heads up
- Outcome 2: The coin will land tails up

There is an equal probability or chance that when the coin is tossed, it can land with either heads up or tails up. When *all possible* probabilities are considered, their total sum equals 100 percent. In our coin example, the probabilities are as follows:

Probability of heads up	50%
Probability of tails up	50%
Total	100%

Suppose we hand you a single die to roll. What is the probability that you will roll a six on the first roll? To determine this prob-

Estimating Probabilities Alternative Method
(0–10 scale)

10	= The event *will absolutely* happen
9	= The event is *extremely likely* to happen
8	= The event is *quite likely* to happen
7	= The event is *somewhat likely* to happen
6	= The event is *more likely to happen* than not happen
5	= There is an *equal chance* that the event may or may not happen
4	= The event is *less likely to happen* than to happen
3	= The event is *somewhat unlikely* to happen
2	= The event is *quite unlikely* to happen
1	= The event is *extremely unlikely* to happen
0	= The event will *absolutely not* happen

ability, you would divide the total number of rolls (in this case, one) by the total number of possible outcomes (in this case, six). The calculation would look like this:

$$1 \div 6 = 16.67$$

In other words, there is a 16.67 percent chance that you will roll a six on the first roll.

As you continue the Mastering Stress Program, we will ask you to *estimate* the probability of certain events actually happening. Your estimates will range somewhere from 0 percent to 100 percent. Some people would rather not work with probabilities. If you are one of these individuals, you may want to try the alternative method shown in the chart on the left. If you find using the 0–10 scale easier and more helpful than probabilities, feel free to do so.

Introducing a New Monitoring Form—My Initial Thought Record

No one said that changing your thoughts would be easy. You cannot simply read this lesson and say, "Okay, I'll think more realistically in the future." Your negative thoughts are deeply ingrained; they come automatically before you can stop them. If you want to replace them with realistic thoughts, you must commit to regular, formal practice. To do this, write down your initial thoughts. Then, challenge each thought by asking yourself, "How likely (probable) is it?" Writing out your thoughts may seem tedious at first, but it is the best way to identify your thoughts and look at them objectively.

My Initial Thought Record

On page 144 is My Initial Thought Record, a worksheet for recording your initial thoughts, estimating their probability, and recording your initial emotion. The worksheet is a bit trickier than the others you have used, so it is important that you use it correctly. Carefully read the instructions below, consider the example that follows on page 141, and practice. You will soon be a whiz at using the worksheet.

❶ In the first column, record the event—the stimulus that triggered your feelings of stress, tension, or anger. Include only the event, not your feelings about the event. For example, if a job interview stresses you, in this column you would write "job interview tomorrow," not "doing poorly at the job interview."

❷ In the second column, record your initial thought or belief. Ask yourself, "What is it about this event that bothers me?" Remember to be totally honest about identifying this belief, even if it sounds silly.

❸ In the third column, gauge the intensity of your emotions using the 0–8 scale. How worried, angry, or depressed are you as you start thinking about this event?

❹ The fourth column is the most important. In this column, you should record the realistic probability that your initial thought about the event will occur. Take what you have written in the second column and ask, "Realistically, how likely is this to happen?"

❺ Now that you have decided the realistic probability, how intense are your emotions about the event? Record the number in column five using the 0–8 scale. Ideally, having determined the realistic probability should make the intensity lower than it was in the second column.

When to Do the Exercise

You should fill out the Initial Thought Record each time you notice yourself *reacting* emotionally to an event that increases your stress level. Make several copies of this form and carry them with you. When you feel your stress rising, fill out the form immediately, if you can. If you can't, do it as soon as possible—no later than the end of the day. Write down your initial thought about the event that increases your stress right away. When doing this, remember to ask yourself this question, "What is it about this event that increases my stress?"

Your goal is to reach a stage where you automatically interpret events realistically, rather than automatically seeing them in a threatening way. In other words, you will eventually be able to do your realistic thinking in your head while the event is happening. At first, however, most people stumble through a stressful event any way they can, then sit down later to try to think more realistically about it. This will not reduce your stress during the day, but it does give you practice. The next time a stressful event occurs, you can start your realistic thinking a little sooner.

If you are like most people, you have some continuing worries—money, children, your health, and job pressures—practice realistic thinking with these as well. Long-term worries provide a good opportunity to try changing your thinking during the event—while you are worrying, instead of later.

Meet Tim

Tim is a 42-year-old sales associate for an international computer manufacturer. He is married and has four children. Tim and his family recently moved into a new house with a big mortgage. Last month, the sales in Tim's territory were way down from previous months. On Tuesday morning, last month's sales report was on Tim's desk when he arrived at work. Just seeing the envelope on his desk, caused Tim's stress level to shoot up. After about an hour of doing other things, Tim opened the en-

My Initial Thought Record *Week of:* September 4, 2000

Tim's Example

Event (1)	Initial Thought (2)	Initial Emotion (0–8 Scale) (3)	Realistic Probability (4)	Realistic Emotion (0–8 Scale) (5)
Tuesday morning—saw last month's sales report on my desk	My sales numbers from last month are going to be really terrible	7	70%	7
Later Tuesday morning—reading last month's sales report	Boy, my boss will really be angry over these numbers	7	20%	6
Driving home Tuesday evening thinking of telling Jan the bad news	Jan will start to panic over the money situation and the big house payments we now have	6	25%	5
Wednesday morning—hearing the message that my supervisor wants to meet tomorrow	He'll yell at me and maybe even fire me over these bad numbers	7	40%	5
Thursday morning—going to meet with my boss to discuss the sales report	I could be out of a job in an hour	6	50%	5

Instructions

1. In the first column, record the event—the stimulus that triggered your feelings of stress, tension, or anger. Include only the event, not your feelings about the event. For example, if a job interview stresses you, in this column you would write "job interview tomorrow," not "doing poorly at the job interview."
2. In the second column, record your initial thought or belief. Ask yourself, "What is it about this event that bothers me?" Remember to be totally honest about identifying this belief, even if it sounds silly.
3. In the third column, gauge the intensity of your emotions using the 0–8 scale. How worried, angry, or depressed are you as you start thinking about this event?
4. The fourth column is the most important. In this column, you should record the realistic probability that your initial thought about the event will occur. Take what you have written in the second column and ask, "Realistically, how likely is this to happen?"
5. Now that you have decided the realistic probability, how intense are your emotions about the event? Record the number in column five using the 0–8 scale. Ideally, having determined the realistic probability should make the intensity lower than it was in the second column.

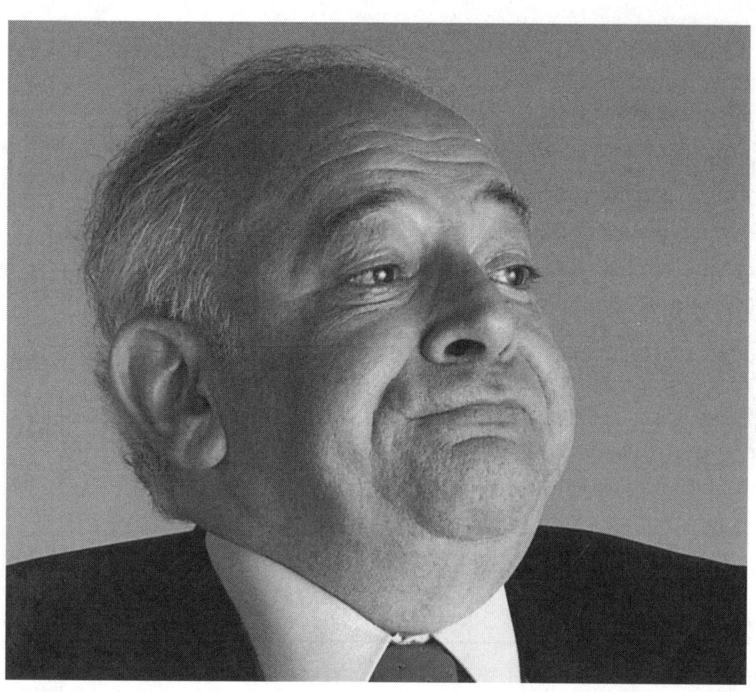

"Long-term worries provide a good opportunity to try to change your thinking during an event—while you are worrying, instead of later."

velope and read the sales report. Sure enough, Tim's sales for the previous month were down—down even more than he had thought. As Tim was driving home that same evening, his stress level increased again as he pondered the thought of telling his wife the bad news. The next morning, Tim had a message on his voice mail from his supervisor, requesting a meeting with Tim the next morning.

On page 141 is Tim's example Initial Thought Record. Review this example to see how Tim completed his Initial Thought Record. Remember to keep a copy of this record with you during the next week and record those initial thoughts that increase your stress immediately as they happen. In Lesson Seven, we'll take this process a step further. So, be sure to do this exercise.

Putting it All Together

After writing down his initial thoughts, Tim carefully identified his initial *automatic* thoughts that increased his stress. He then considered the *realistic* probability of his initial thought actually happening. In most cases, Tim's stress level decreased slightly after he considered his initial (automatic) stressful thoughts. This process helped Tim to realize that there is not always a 100 percent chance that his initial thoughts would, in fact, become reality.

When you record your initial thoughts this next week, ask yourself, just as Tim did in the example, "How likely is it?" This may seem a little awkward at first, but you will get better at the exercise with practice.

Lesson Review

We began this lesson by introducing you to the ABC's of behavior change. We used this as an introduction to the topic of feelings and where they come from. Our feelings (emotions) come from our thoughts and beliefs, and our behaviors result from these feelings. Most of our thoughts (and behaviors) are automatic. Yet, as humans we have the power to choose our thoughts, thus controlling our feelings and behaviors. To begin the process of changing your thoughts, we introduced you to the idea of realistic thinking. We then showed you an example of Tim and how he began the process of estimating the probability of his initial stressful thoughts. Learning to realistically estimate the likelihood of your initial stressful thoughts is an important first step in realistic thinking. The key message in this lesson is that events do not cause stress. Rather, our thoughts about the events cause the stress in our lives.

This Week's Assignment

In this lesson, we discussed the key role self-awareness plays in helping you change your thoughts about stressful events. Continue keeping your Daily Stress Record. We have provided you with a new record on page 145. Be sure to update your Stress

Change Worksheet for week six on page 127, and your Average Stress Change Worksheet in Appendix E on page 430. Continue your deep muscle relaxation practice sessions and record your sessions on the worksheet on page 146. If you are having trouble or find practicing deep muscle relaxation difficult, read ahead in Lesson Seven, beginning on page 147, where we discuss strategies for improving your relaxation skills.

Make copies of the My Initial Thought Record worksheet, on page 144, to carry with you. When you notice your stress increasing, take out the form and complete it as soon as possible. Remember to keep up your physical activity this week. Record your physical activity and relaxation practice sessions for week six on the worksheet in Appendix F on page 432. You may find it helpful to schedule a little time at the end of each day to review your day and complete any lesson material. Good luck with this week's assignment!

Knowledge Review

T F 40. Activating events are the main source of most people's stress.

T F 41. The basic premise of an ABC approach to behavior change is that our thoughts lead to our emotions and behaviors.

T F 42. Realistic thinking is not the same as positive thinking.

T F 43. Humans share four unique abilities for making choices in life: self-awareness, vision, principles, and independent determination.

T F 44. Most of our thoughts about stressful events are automatic and often trigger unrealistic and irrational estimates about something bad happening.

T F 45. The lower the realistic probability of an event, the greater the intensity of your emotion.

T F 46. The first step in changing your estimates about an event is to identify your thoughts.

T F 47. Consequences are the direct result of events beyond our control.

T F 48. Independent determination is the freedom to choose our own thoughts, beliefs, principles, and visions.

(Answers in Appendix C, page 415)

My Initial Thought Record				Week of:
Event (1)	Initial Thought (2)	Initial Emotion (0–8 Scale) (3)	Realistic Probability (4)	Realistic Emotion (0–8 Scale) (5)

Instructions

1. In the first column, record the event—the stimulus that triggered your feelings of stress, tension, or anger. Include only the event, not your feelings about the event. For example, if a job interview stresses you, in this column you would write "job interview tomorrow," not "doing poorly at the job interview."
2. In the second column, record your initial thought or belief. Ask yourself, "What is it about this event that bothers me?" Remember to be totally honest about identifying this belief, even if it sounds silly.
3. In the third column, gauge the intensity of your emotions using the 0–8 scale. How worried, angry, or depressed are you as you start thinking about this event?
4. The fourth column is the most important. In this column, you should record the realistic probability that your initial thought about the event will occur. Take what you have written in the second column and ask, "Realistically, how likely is this to will happen?"
5. Now that you have decided the realistic probability, how intense are your emotions about the event? Record the number in column five using the 0–8 scale. Ideally, having determined the realistic probability should make the intensity lower than it was in the second column.

Daily Stress Record—Lesson Six

Name:______________________________ **Week of:**______________

Date	Average Stress Level	Highest Stress Level	Time of Highest Stress Level	Stressful Event Associated with Highest Stress Level

My Physical Activity and Relaxation Record

Day of the Week	Physical Activity Record		Relaxation Record	
	Activity	Minutes	Time of Day	Minutes
Monday				
Tuesday				
Wednesday				
Thursday				
Friday				
Saturday				
Sunday				
This Week	Total Activity		Total Relaxation	

Relaxation Practice Record

Week of:________________

Date	Beginning Time	Ending Time	Tension Before (0-8)	Tension After (0-8)	Concentration (0-8)	Comments

Lesson Seven

This lesson continues our discussion of deep muscle relaxation. You have now been practicing deep muscle relaxation for two weeks. If you are like most people, you may be having some problems with practice—this is perfectly normal. We will discuss some common problems people experience with deep muscle relaxation and suggest ways to overcome them. Our next topic of discussion is relationships, which can be both a help and a hindrance in your stress management program. We then continue our discussion on realistic thinking by showing you how to look at the evidence for and against your initial thoughts. We conclude this lesson with a more in-depth discussion on time management and its relationship to stress management. We have much to cover in this lesson, so let's begin.

Improving Your Relaxation Skills

You have now practiced deep muscle relaxation for two weeks. Have you had any difficulties? Most of our clients have some trouble at first, but with continued practice, they overcome the hurdles and begin perfecting their skills. Everyone has heard the saying, "Practice makes perfect." When you first start learning to relax your muscles, *perfect* may not best describe your practice sessions. Below, we discuss five of the most common issues our clients encounter as they begin to practice relaxation skills and techniques. Along with a description of these issues, we'll suggest some helpful strategies to master them and improve your relaxation skills.

Worrying about Time

Some people find relaxation practice difficult because they worry about the amount of time it takes. They are often thinking about all of the other things they *should* be doing. If you find yourself worrying about time when you practice, then relaxation is *exactly* what you need! Try to purposely force yourself to spend time relaxing and enjoy the time you have to spend alone improving this important skill. This will help convince you that the world will not end if you drop out for a couple of 20-minute relaxation sessions each day. All

the things you have to do will still be there when you finish your sessions. More importantly, you will learn how to take time for yourself. The more you learn to relax, the easier it becomes to take time for yourself—worry free!

If you are having trouble stopping your worries, or if your mind wanders while you are trying to relax, we have a suggestion. Gently turn your thoughts back to your counting. Think of the word "relax" as you exhale. Concentrate on your muscles; visualize your muscles tensing up and then going limp as you relax each one. With practice, you will get better at concentrating. You will also become even better at doing your other work while feeling more relaxed.

Concentrating

"I wonder what the kids are doing."

As we just discussed, many people have trouble concentrating when they first begin learning relaxation techniques. Let's face it, spending time alone for 20 minutes, twice a day, to work on relaxation is a luxury. Most people have trouble keeping their minds on the task at hand—namely, learning to relax. If you find this happening to you, don't despair; you're in good company. This is perhaps the most common issue our clients confront. Overcoming this problem is crucial to your stress management program. Concentrating when your stress level is high and your muscles are tense is paramount to relaxing your tense muscles.

Picture your attention span (concentration) as a muscle. Like any muscle in your body, it becomes weak when it is not used and stronger when exercised regularly. As you exercise your concentration "muscle," it too will gradually strengthen. If your attention wanders during a practice session, try not to get angry or upset with yourself. Simply let the extra thoughts that enter your mind, go out with each breath—release them—blow them out. You can think about them later. You have more important things to do as you practice. Deliberately turn your attention back onto the road of relaxation, much like you would steer a car back onto a roadway. The more you do this, the stronger your concentration "muscle" will become. Soon you will begin to enjoy your relaxation practice sessions. As you become better at concentrating, your attention will wander less.

Isolating Muscles

Some people find it difficult to tense one muscle group and keep the rest of their body relaxed. They may feel fatigued after a stressful day because every muscle in their body is tense. The solution to this problem is to keep practicing. Like all skills, this one improves with practice.

Think of Beethoven writing his *Fifth Symphony.* How often do you think he wrote, rewrote, and repeatedly played each measure of this beautiful masterpiece? Try not to be too hard on yourself. Remember that you cannot perfectly isolate each muscle group in your body because they are all interconnected. If muscle isolation is difficult for you, lower your standards. In the beginning, relax most of the muscles in your body more than usual. Then try to tense the group you are working on more than usual. Like Beethoven, who became the master of the symphony, you can become the master of your muscles!

If you find your arms, stomach, or face tensing when you tense your legs, then you need to continue to practice isolating your muscles. We have confidence that with continuous practice, you'll do well. Learning to relax your muscles is a critical step for you to master in your stress management program. So, don't give up!

Feeling Frightened

This may sound like a paradox. Yet, some people feel even more stress when they try to relax. Does this sound familiar? If so, the sensations you feel as your body starts to relax may just be unfamiliar. This is common in individuals who have experienced stress over a long period. Perhaps you feel as though you're losing control, and because you feel uncomfortable, you stop. This is perfectly understandable. Realizing that relaxing is not dangerous but is, in fact, healthy is key. Your fear of losing control may be a major factor contributing to your overall level of stress, so overcoming this fear is important. You may want to try relaxation in gradual steps. For example, start by trying to relax with your eyes open or while a "safe" person is with you.

We introduced Jane to you in Lesson Two, on page 32. You may recall that Jane spent much of her day in a tense state because she overcommitted herself and had perfectionist expectations. She often experienced backaches, shoulder pains, and headaches as a result. Deep muscle relaxation was an important skill that helped Jane reduce her stress. After a few weeks of practice, she became a master of muscle relaxation. Yet, she too had trouble at first. Five minutes into her first relaxation session, Jane suddenly jumped up and started pacing the floor. She didn't like the feeling; it was strange to her. So, she ran away from the relaxed feeling.

We worked out a relaxation plan with Jane. She began practicing relaxation by sitting straight up in a chair. She kept her eyes open and stared at a spot on the floor. Gradually, she learned to relax this way. Jane then tried closing her eyes for 30 seconds until she became accustomed to the feeling of relaxing with her eyes closed. Then, over the next several weeks, she closed her eyes for longer periods. Eventually, she could complete an entire 20-minute practice session with her eyes closed.

Falling Asleep

The fifth most common issue people have when learning relaxation skills is that they become so relaxed, they fall asleep. If this happens to you, consider it a sign that

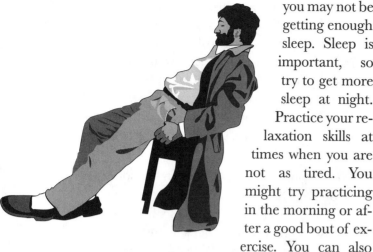

you may not be getting enough sleep. Sleep is important, so try to get more sleep at night. Practice your relaxation skills at times when you are not as tired. You might try practicing in the morning or after a good bout of exercise. You can also try practicing in a less comfortable chair or on the floor. If you sleep through your practice sessions, you are not going to learn much about relaxation. This brings us to another important topic—getting enough sleep.

The Importance of a Good Night's Sleep

A good night's sleep is important. Getting adequate sleep enables your body to recover from the stressors you experience each day. People often sacrifice sleep when they experience high levels of stress. Sleep deprivation is a common sign of a high stress level. Lack of sleep can cause accidents, low productivity at work, and general agitation.

People's needs vary when it comes to sleep. Most people need about six to eight hours of sleep each night. As we get older, we often require less sleep. If you wake up each morning without an alarm clock and remain alert throughout the day, you are most likely getting enough sleep. This means that your body is rested, and you are ready to rise. If you cannot awake without an alarm clock or you fall asleep during the day, then you may not be getting enough sleep. Consider contacting the National Sleep Foundation by phone (1–800–SHUTEYE) or on the Internet (www.shuteye.com) if you believe that you are not getting enough sleep.

Do You Have Trouble Sleeping?

If you have trouble sleeping at night, you may find that relaxation exercises help. Simply use the counting part of the deep muscle relaxation exercises. Breathe in and out evenly. Each time you breathe in, form a number in your mind (1, 2, and so on up to 10, then back down to 1). Try to visualize the number itself. Each time you breath out, form the word "relax" in your mind. Picture yourself sinking deeper and deeper into the mattress each time you exhale. You may have to repeat this several times—but try to persist. Worrying about not sleeping is the worst thing you can do. Remember, if worries intrude on your mind, don't get annoyed. Let them go and gently direct your mind back to counting and the word "relax."

Another helpful strategy for sleeplessness is realistic thinking. In Lesson Six, on page 135, we introduced you to this notion of realistic thinking. For the past week you have been writing down on the worksheet, "My Initial Thought Record," your initial thoughts about stressful events. This is the first step in learning this important skill. Later in this lesson, we will introduce you to the next step by showing you how to work through a realistic thinking worksheet. If you are having trouble sleeping, chances are that you are worrying about something, focusing your thoughts on a particular problem or issue. Writing your thoughts on paper and thinking about them *realistically* can help reduce your stress and help you get to sleep. You'll see how this works in an example later in this lesson.

The Important Role of Relationships

Do relationships add or reduce stress in our lives? You can probably guess that the answer depends on the relationship. All of us have experienced the true value of a good friend or family member. These individuals are supportive, anticipate our needs, and are sensitive to our current situation. Relationships are more stressful when they are inflexible, demanding, one-sided, or negative.

Some relationships can increase your stress. Most people have had relationships at some point in their lives that are truly unhealthy and may need to be abandoned. A cost-benefit analysis may help you decide which relationships contribute to your stress and which ones lower your stress. This is a good way to assess whether a relationship is meeting your needs. Don't be afraid to forego unhealthy relationships that you cannot repair. You may improve other relationships through better communication. Let's look at an example of how the cost-benefit analysis works.

Meet Ann

Ann is a senior at a large university. Her former roommate graduated at the end of the previous year. Ann invited Sue, a fellow classmate, to share her two-bedroom apartment. After living together for three months, Ann realized her stress level soared whenever she came home and when she thought about Sue.

At first, Ann thought Sue would be an ideal roommate. They shared many classes

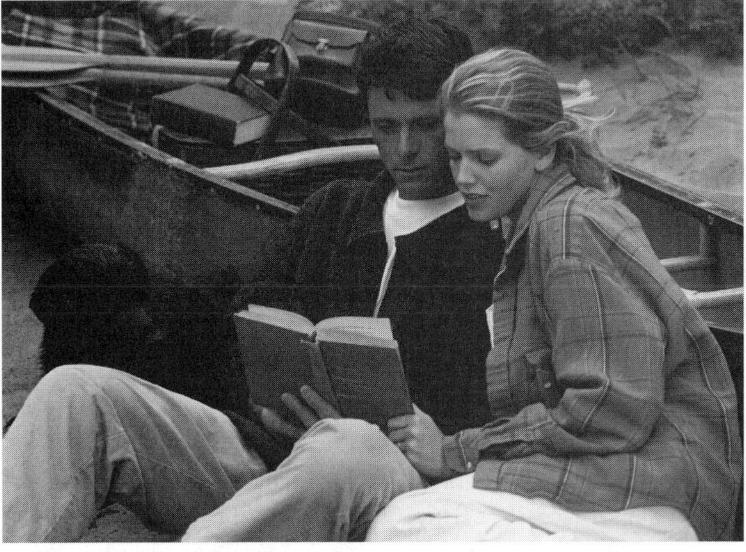

and had similar interests. They seemed to get along well. Ann focused on all the positives she thought Sue would bring to the relationship. Things seemed to work well with Sue—at first. Ann and Sue shared expenses and socialized together. They were there for each other for protection and companionship. As the semester continued, Sue became less interested in studying and began spending more time going out and partying with her friends.

"All of us have experienced the true value of a good friend or family member, however, relationships can become stressful when they are inflexible, demanding, one-sided, or negative."

Ann's needs in the relationship, such as privacy and quiet, remained the same, but Sue was no longer meeting her needs. Many nights, Ann would come home from class to find the apartment filled with smoke, loud music, and Sue's noisy friends. Sue would get angry with Ann when Ann would politely ask her to clean up after herself and her friends. Sue would accuse Ann of being "no fun anymore." Ann also found it disturbing when Sue would continually interrupt her while studying. Ann also became more annoyed with Sue's tardiness each month with her share of the rent. At this point, Ann's stress level began to increase, and it was beginning to affect her school work.

Ann completed an assessment of her relationship with Sue using the costs and benefits approach. Ann's example Relationship Assessment worksheet is shown below. After completing this worksheet, she realized that the costs of her relationship with Sue far outweighed the benefits. Ann discussed these issues with Sue. They decided to part as roommates, yet remain friends.

This decision was probably very good for both Ann and Sue. After living together, they saw that their needs were very different from what they had originally believed them to be. They were not able to satisfy each other's needs. Often, the need to have a relationship with another person causes individuals to stay longer than they should, increasing stress. By parting as roommates, Ann and Sue preserved their friendship.

Balance in a relationship is also important. We can easily begin to expect too much from a single relationship. Disappointment sets in when the other person does not meet our high expectations.

Building multiple, healthy relationships helps balance our expectations and social support system. This approach will keep you from becoming too dependent upon a single relationship for your social well-being.

The positives and negatives of any relationship may become imbalanced. If the negatives outweigh the positives, ask yourself if this is typical of the relationship. If it is, you may need to address the issues with the other person. Assess whether or not staying in the relationship is a healthy

Relationship Assessment

Ann's Example

Benefits (Positives)	Costs (Negatives)
Someone to talk to and do things with	Noisy, stays up too late talking on the phone
Someone to share the expenses	Leaves dirty dishes and clothes laying around
Protection, safety in a large city	Doesn't respect my desire for private time
	Eats all of my food without asking
	Pays rent and expenses late each month
	Much more interested in partying than studying

choice for you. This will require some assertiveness on your part. We will discuss assertiveness in later lessons. We have given you a Relationship Assessment worksheet on page 169. Make as many copies as you need to help you evaluate relationships that you believe increase your stress. Even if you don't believe any of your current relationships are adding to your stress, complete this exercise now for at least one relationship. This exercise can also help confirm a healthy relationship. Keep this tool in mind, even after you have completed this program. You may find it helpful in the future.

More on Realistic Thinking

In Lesson Six, on page 135, we introduced you to realistic thinking. You have now had a week to practice recording stressful events and identifying your initial stressful thoughts about those events. We can now go to the next step—learning how to weigh the evidence for and against your initial thoughts. You began this process in Lesson Six by estimating the realistic probability of your initial thought *actually* happening. You will now want to challenge that initial estimate by identifying probabilities.

Identifying Probabilities

As you know from Lesson Six, once you have identified your initial thought, the next step is to ask yourself, "How likely do I really think it is that this will happen?" Usually, the lower the realistic probability, the less intense your emotion will be. For example, if your partner is late and your initial thought is that an accident has occurred. Your initial (automatic) thought may be that this is a 100 percent probability. You will be far more worried if you believe there is a 100 or even 50 percent probability of an accident than if you believe there is only a 5 percent probability.

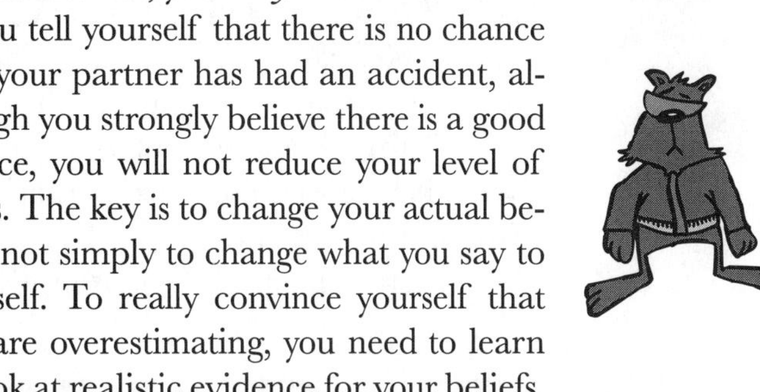

The goal is to convince yourself that the probability of a negative outcome is as low as possible. But, you *really* have to believe it. If you tell yourself that there is no chance that your partner has had an accident, although you strongly believe there is a good chance, you will not reduce your level of stress. The key is to change your actual beliefs, not simply to change what you say to yourself. To really convince yourself that you are overestimating, you need to learn to look at realistic evidence for your beliefs. By learning to always examine your thoughts against the evidence, you can start to think much more realistically. Remember, stress comes from our thoughts. This technique of weighing the evidence is one way to help make your thoughts more realistic. In this process, looking at four types of evidence will help you find a more realistic probability that your initial thought will occur. Let's now look at the four different types of evidence you should consider.

"The key to lowering your stress is to change your actual beliefs."

General Knowledge

The first type of evidence is to consider all of the facts, figures, and general circumstances about a situation. What have others told you about the incident? What has your actual experience been? What have you read, and what have you heard on the radio, television, or other media? A word of caution is in order here. Everyone believes they know the difference between *real evidence* and *wild imaginings*. People under stress often ignore the positive (real) evidence, focusing only on the negative (often wild imaginings). Be on the lookout for this tendency in yourself. Consciously try to focus on *all* of the evidence, not just the negative.

"Base your thinking on realistic evidence and not your initial, negative gut feelings. Look at all of the evidence."

Imagine that your partner is late for dinner. Your initial thought is that he or she has been seriously injured in an accident. You try to decide the realistic probability that he or she has been involved in an accident by reviewing the evidence. You may ask yourself, "How many cars are on the road in the city tonight?" Let's say you estimate 10,000 cars to be on the road. You then ask yourself, "How many of those cars are likely to have an accident tonight?" You may conclude that there are perhaps two. This means that there is a 2 in 10,000 chance that your partner will be involved in an accident. No doubt, this is lower than your initial thought.

You may think to yourself, "Yes, but I always think that my partner will be one of the two." This is precisely what we mean when we say that you need to stop basing your thinking or "gut feelings." Start basing your thinking on realistic evidence. Look at *all* of the evidence. Once you evaluate all of the facts, you will realize that your partner has about the same chance of being in a car accident at any given time as you have of winning the lottery!

Previous Experience

Another good way to challenge your estimates is to examine your past experiences. Has the situation occurred before? Consider the example of your partner being late for dinner. You might ask yourself, "How many times in the past has my partner been home late?" "How many of those times were because of an automobile accident?" "Would I have heard by now if he or she had been involved in an accident?" "Even if there was an accident, what is the probability that he or she would be *seriously* injured?" Your initial reaction may be something like, "Yeah, but there is always the first time." Again, what is the factual evidence? Answering this question will most likely help you further reduce your estimate of how likely it is that he or she has been involved in a serious accident.

When examining your experiences, remember not to focus on the negative. Suppose that your partner was involved in an accident once before and came home late. What about the other 50 times he or she has been late for other reasons? You are not thinking realistically if you focus only on one incident and ignore the other 50. You must examine *all* of the evidence. Then your initial thought will not seem nearly as likely as it did at first.

Consider Alternatives

Another strategy for learning to think more realistically is to think of all the possibilities, not just the first one that comes to mind. For example, what other reasons might cause your partner to be late for dinner? List all of the possibilities. Did you forget that he or she was going to do something after work? Perhaps he or she

- Got caught in traffic
- Had a flat tire
- Had to work late to finish a project
- Went shopping
- Met some friends

You know your partner's habits. Does he or she often lose track of time? Does he or she like to work late because the office is quiet after others go home? Clearly, an accident is only one of many possible reasons for your partner's lateness. Because so many other events are possible, focusing on one negative possibility does little more than increase your stress!

Examine all the evidence and list all the possibilities. This approach should help you assess the situation realistically. While it is possible that your partner may have had an accident, the probability is actually very low. If the evidence convinces you of this, your stress will be lower.

Changing Perspectives

A fourth way to evaluate the evidence is to view the realistic probabilities from someone else's perspective. For example, if the situation were reversed, and you were the one who was late for dinner, would you expect your partner to be stressed? If not, why? Also, suppose a close friend of yours called and was highly stressed because his or her partner was late and concerned about an accident. What would you say to your friend? Would you try to convince your friend that there may be another reason for the lateness? The answer to this question will often help you see how unrealistic your initial thoughts are. This will help you view the situation differently, with much less stress.

Changing perspectives is a good strategy for viewing evidence relating to social situations. These situations are often difficult to examine in other ways. Typically, no statistics or written facts about social situations are available. Imagine that two colleagues are talking loudly outside your office or that you are in line at a store and the customers in front of you are talking loudly. You may feel angry and think something such as, "They are totally inconsiderate." Now, try to change perspectives. Imagine that you are one of the people talking

"Examine all the evidence and list all the possibilities. This will help you realistically assess the situation."

Four Types of Evidence

General Knowledge

Focus on all of the evidence, not just the negatives.

"My business partner is running late for our lunch with a potential client, and I haven't heard from hi[m] yet."

Previous Experience

Consider previous experience, remember not to focus on the negatives.

"He's been late before because of traffic."

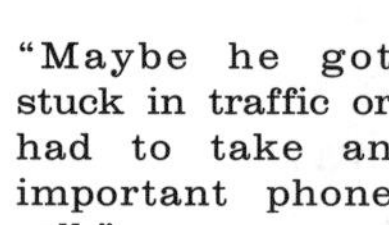

"Maybe he got stuck in traffic or had to take an important phone call."

Consider Alternatives

List all of the possibilities or alternatives, not just the first one that comes to mind.

"If a friend of mine was worried about his partner, I would say 'Relax, I'm sure he's just running late.'"

Changing Perspectives

Put yourself in the other persons place. Imagine a friend with similar problems, what would you say to them?

loudly. One of your colleagues is in his office or another person is standing in line behind you at the store. Are you talking loudly because you are totally inconsiderate? Could something else be going on? Perhaps you're excited about something and don't realize just how loudly you are talking. Putting yourself in the other person's place in this way can often reduce your extreme feelings very quickly.

The Realistic Thinking Worksheet

A Realistic Thinking Worksheet is provided on page 170. This is an expanded version of the Initial Thought Record that we introduced in Lesson Six, on page 139. Complete columns 1 and 2 the same way you did for the Initial Thought Record. Column 3 is the most important column on this worksheet.

You will record the evidence for and against your initial thought in column 3. Include all of the evidence you can think of that does or does not support your belief. Because this is realistic (not positive) thinking, you need to record the evidence that supports your initial belief. If you are being honest and are thinking hard, you are likely to find more evidence against your initial belief than for it. However, you may occasionally find that your initial beliefs are realistic and have much support. Here, the exercise may be telling you that feeling stressed about the situation is quite understandable. Perhaps you need to deal with the situation in a different way, such as trying to change it. An alternative is to accept the original thought and ask yourself, "What would happen if . . .?" In Lesson Eight, we will show you how to work through this thought process.

When you are listing the evidence on your worksheet, try to think of each of the four types of evidence we discussed earlier: general knowledge, previous experience, alternative explanations, and changing perspectives. Not all types of evidence will fit all situations. You may need to be clever and think up other alternatives for some situations. Remember to watch out for biases in your thinking and look at *all* of the evidence, not just the negative.

In column 4 of the worksheet, you will record two probabilities. In the top left-hand corner, record your *initial* probability *before* you consider all the evidence. You will record this probability on the row in which you recorded your initial thought. Be sure to list the evidence in column 3, and study it carefully. After careful consideration of the evidence, record your *realistic* probability in the lower right-hand corner of column 4. This answer will also be on the same row as your initial probability.

In column 5, you will record two emotions. Record your *initial* stress level in the upper left-hand corner of column 5 immediately after recording your initial thought and your initial probability. Use the 0–8 scale to record your initial stress. Record your *revised* stress level in the lower right-hand corner of the column after considering all the evidence and after you record your realistic probability in column 4. An example may help you better understand the Realistic Thinking Worksheet.

Meet Sharon

Sharon is a 38-year-old mother of two children. She works in the customer service center of a large credit card company. Sharon wanted to reduce her work schedule from five days to four days a week. This would allow her to spend more time with her two girls and be more involved in their school activities. When Sharon first thought about approaching her supervisor with this request, she felt very anxious (a 6 on the 0–8 scale). Sharon found herself worrying about this situation when she went to bed and night and because of this worry, had difficulty going to sleep. Working through the Realistic Thinking Worksheet helped Sharon reduce her stress and stop worrying about the situation. This exercise also helped Sharon return to her normal sleeping patterns.

Sharon's first step was to identify her negative expectations. She asked herself, "What is it about asking my supervisor that worries me?" Her answer (her initial thought) was that her supervisor would say no (100 percent probability). Then she realized that she was assuming a very strong chance (100 percent) that her supervisor would say no. As soon as she recognized this thought, she knew that she was overestimating. We have reproduced a copy of Sharon's Realistic Thinking Worksheet on page 159.

To come up with a more realistic estimate, Sharon looked at the evidence. She had no previous experience to consider. However, she did have some general knowledge about the situation. Another employee in a different department of the company had recently changed her work schedule from five to three days without difficulty. Sharon then told herself, "I am a good worker, and my supervisor doesn't want to lose me." She also said to herself, "This department isn't terribly busy now.

My co-workers would not miss me one day a week. Other people are available to cover for me when I'm not here."

Next, Sharon looked at the alternatives. She considered what her supervisor might say. "Maybe she'll say no," Sharon thought. "But maybe she'll say she will think about it or that we can try it temporarily and see if it works." Finally, Sharon tried to reverse positions. She tried to imagine what she would say if she were the supervisor and an employee asked her to reduce his or her work hours. Immediately, Sharon realized that she would be very fair and understanding. She would agree if at all possible. Sharon also realized that her supervisor was generally a fair and understanding person who had children of her own.

By challenging her initial thought, Sharon soon realized that her earlier estimate—100 percent probability that her supervisor would say no—was much too high. She revised her estimate. Her more realistic probability was closer to 20 percent. This new way of thinking about the situation helped reduce Sharon's stress level from 6 to 3.

Over the next week, use the blank Realistic Thinking Worksheet on page 170 to help you change your initial stress-producing thoughts to more realistic estimates. Let's now turn our attention to time management.

Time Management Continued

How do you spend your time? At the end of the day, do you feel satisfied that you invested your time in things that are truly important to you? Do you sometimes feel stressed at the end of the day as you think of all the things you didn't accomplish that you wanted to get done? For many people, learning time management skills can help reduce much stress. The first step to learning these new skills is to become more aware of how you spend your time. Take a few moments now to complete the Time Management Questionnaire above.

Time Management Questionnaire

(To answer each question, circle yes or no)

Yes	**No**	**Do you take on too much responsibility?**
Yes	**No**	**Do you have trouble delegating responsibility to others?**
Yes	**No**	**Is it difficult for you to say no to others?**
Yes	**No**	**Do you have trouble assessing your priorities?**
Yes	**No**	**Are you overly distracted by your environment?**

If you answer yes to just one of the questions on the Time Management Questionnaire, you may benefit from improving your time management skills. We will continue to work on these and other issues throughout the sections on time management in this and later lessons. For now, let's look at how you invest your time.

Investing Your Time

In Lesson Five, on page 119, we introduced the topic of time management. Two of the more common problems many people have with time management are overcommitment and organization. Many people take on more and more responsibil-

Realistic Thinking Worksheet
(Sharon's Example)

Today's Date:

(1) Event	(2) Initial Thought	(3) Evidence (How Do I Know?)	(4) Initial/Realistic Probability	(5) Initial/Revised Stress Level (0–8 Scale)
Want to ask my boss to reduce my work schedule from five to four days per week	She will say no	1. Another worker decreased her days. 2. My boss doesn't want to lose me. 3. Work is not too busy. She may say no, but may also think about it. 4. If I were the boss, I would be fair, and my boss is fair.	100% / 20%	6 / 3

ity and work longer and longer hours. They spend their life climbing the ladder of success only to discover when they reach the top that the ladder is leaning against the wrong wall. This is true of corporate executives, factory workers, homemakers, students, and people in other occupations. Time is the one resource of which *everyone* has the same amount. No matter the size of your bank account, the color of your skin, the language you speak, or anything else, *everyone* gets 24 hours in a day. The key is to invest your time wisely. Invest your time in the things in life that are truly important to you. This does not mean that you have to worry about every second of every day. Too often, people increase their stress by investing their time in the *urgent* and not the *important.*

The Minute and the Map

Our efforts to live less stressful lives can be illustrated by two powerful influences that help guide us through life—the *minute* and the *map.* Minutes symbolize our commitments, schedules, activities, goals, and appointments. We use minutes to measure how we invest our time. The map, on the other hand, reflects our vision, mission, principles, values, independent determination, and direction. The map is a blueprint of the things we truly believe deep inside and reflects the way we live our lives.

Stress begins to increase when the minute and the map become misaligned. This happens when what we *are* doing doesn't contribute to what we *want* to be doing in our lives. Stress can become more intense as the minute and the map become increasingly misaligned. When this happens, we often feel trapped and controlled by other people or circumstances. We begin responding to matters of urgency and are constantly putting out fires. We never make time to do what we know would truly make a difference in our lives. For some people this type of stress may be only discomforting. They may have trouble balancing what they *should do,* with what they *want to do,* with what they *are doing.* These individuals may feel guilty about what they are *not doing* and cannot enjoy what they *are doing.*

Some people know their lives are out of balance. They just don't have the confidence or skills to explore alternative ways of living. Perhaps they believe the cost of change is too high or they may be afraid to try. Living with the imbalance may be easier than trying to change.

Sometimes we become aware of the misalignment between the minute and the map in a dramatic way. When a loved one suddenly dies, for example, we may receive a wake-up call, as we begin to realize how uncertain the future is. Our physician

could diagnose us with a terminal illness. Our employer could eliminate our job because of corporate restructuring. Disagreement may threaten our marriage. We may discover one of our children is on drugs. In the absence of such wake-up calls, many people never really confront the critical issues of how they are investing their time. Imagine for a moment that your life is a wheel, a wheel must continuously be checked for balance so that it will run smoothly.

Life as a Wheel

Think of your life as a wheel. We all know that wheels can become unbalanced. When this happens, the ride becomes bumpy. If the wheel remains unbalanced, the ride worsens. Eventually, the unbalanced wheel can become dangerous and threaten the passengers' safety.

Life is much like a wheel. Our lives need balance. When we allow them to become unbalanced, life gets bumpy. If allowed to continue unbalanced, our lives become stressed. We become unhappy and unhealthy. This is why time investment is so important.

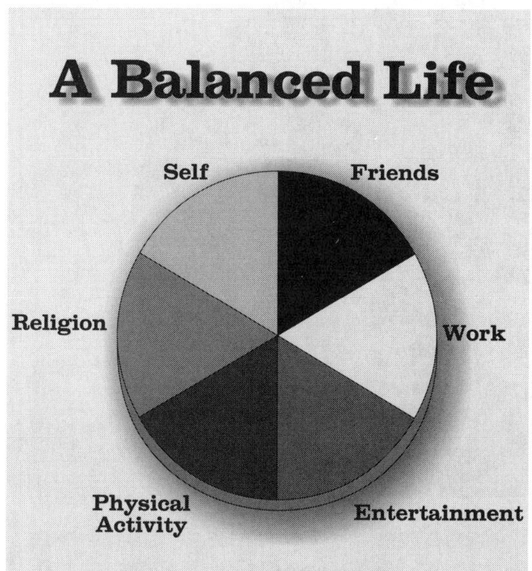

Revisiting Bob

We introduced you to Bob in the Introduction and Orientation Lesson on page 2. Although on the outside Bob seemed successful, he was very unhappy on the inside. He was investing most of his time in the *urgent* needs of his work. Yet, the things in life that were truly *important* to Bob were being left out. The time he was spending with his wife and children was stressful and tense. Bob no longer spent time being physically active and enjoyed the things in life that really made him happy.

On page 162 is an illustration comparing Bob's Urgent List with his Important List. Bob's important list reflects balance in his life. However, his urgent list shows just how far out of balance Bob's life had become. How is the balance in your life?

As with all other aspects of self-awareness, monitoring the way you spend time in your daily routine is important. To do this, we will have you record your activities for a

"Life is much like a wheel. Our lives need balance. When we allow them to become unbalanced, life gets bumpy. If allowed to continue unbalanced, our lives become stressed."

"All too often we spend our time chasing the urgent while letting the truly important things slip away."

few days so that you will have reliable information to act on. Before we continue, a word of warning: time management takes time! Before we get into tracking your time, a review of the evolution of time management may help you to see the importance of this activity.

The Evolution of Time Management

In an effort to align the minute and the map and balance their lives, many people turn to time management. Just three decades ago, fewer than a dozen reliable books on time management existed. Today, hundreds of books and articles abound on

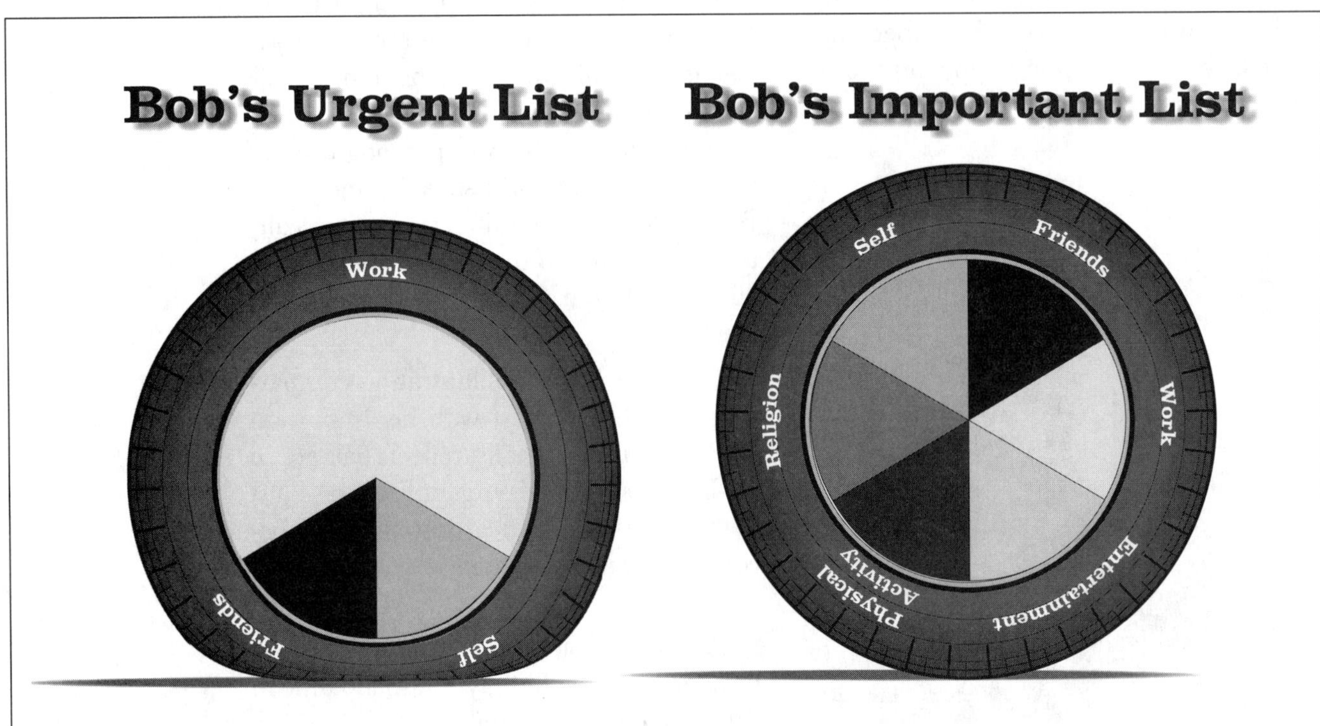

the subject. An almost endless supply of calendars, daily planners, computer software, and other time management tools can be found. Yet, the misalignment between the minute and the map continues for many people. Their lives continue to wobble and bounce like a crooked wheel, and they are more stressed than ever before.

First Generation

The first generation of time management tools consists of reminders and to-do lists. The notion here is to take each day as it comes. You keep track of the things you want to do and the things you actually get around to doing, such as attending a meeting, picking up the kids, writing a report, etc. Notes and checklists typify this classic time management technique. If you use this method of time management, you probably carry these lists with you and refer to them often so you don't forget to do something. At the end of the day, you are likely to check off the things you accomplished and carry the others over to the next day.

Second Generation

The second generation of time management focuses on planning and preparation. The key emphasis is on scheduling calendars and appointment books. Advance planning, achieving set goals, and personal responsibilities determine the success or failure of this view of time management. If you use this method, you plan meetings in advance, write them down, compare actual goals achieved with planned goals, and identify deadlines. You may even use a computer to keep track of your meetings.

Third Generation

The third generation of time management incorporates the planning process of the second generation and adds prioritizing and controlling. If you're using this as a time management tool, you may spend time clarifying your principles and values and setting priorities in your life. Perhaps

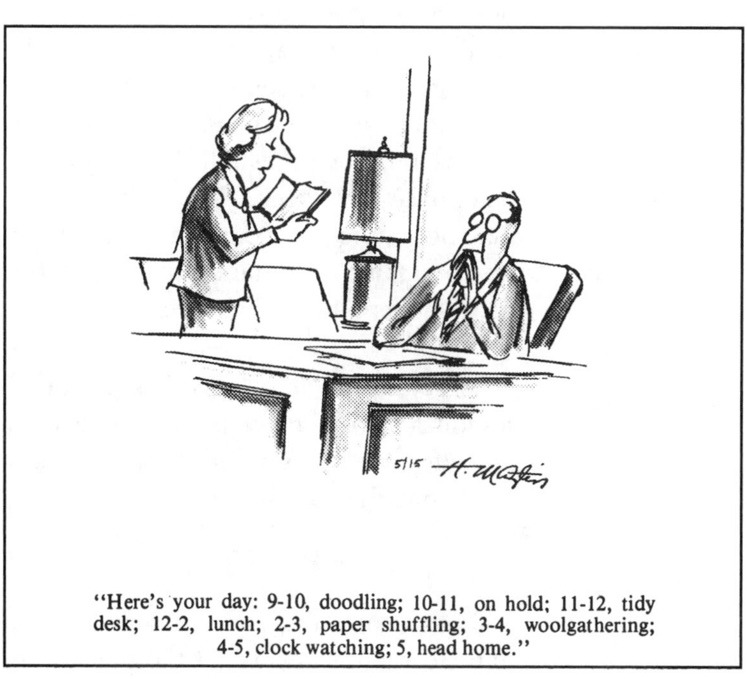

"Here's your day: 9-10, doodling; 10-11, on hold; 11-12, tidy desk; 12-2, lunch; 2-3, paper shuffling; 3-4, woolgathering; 4-5, clock watching; 5, head home."

you have asked yourself the question, "What do I really want?" You may have short-, medium-, and long-term goals to get what you want out of life. You probably prioritized activities on a daily basis. Electronic and paper planners with detailed forms for daily planning are at the heart of this time management process.

Efficiency versus Effectiveness

The evolution of time management has brought us much closer to achieving efficient lives. However, for many people, the misalignment between the minute and the map still exists. Stress in their lives remains high as they travel down the highway of life on unbalanced wheels. As a population, we may be getting more done in less time, but stress remains a constant reminder of this misalignment and imbalance.

A key to this imbalance lies in understanding the difference between efficiency and effectiveness. A simple illustration may help bring this together.

A Road Trip

Let's assume that we're all going to hop in the car and take a trip. Our journey begins in Denver and our destination is Los Angeles. We are determined to make this the most *efficient* trip ever taken and get our names published in the *Guinness Book of World Records.* We'll find the least expensive gas; drive at a speed that will optimize fuel consumption, while minimizing our time on the road; and eat at restaurants that offer the best food for the money. We get out our map, hop in the car, and away we go.

After three days on the road, we are all convinced that we will beat all records on efficiency. Around noon on the third day, we find ourselves alongside the road, staring at a sign. Our mouths are wide open, and we are all in a state of total shock. The sign beside the road reads, "Chicago, 20 miles."

You can think of *efficiency* as doing things right. *Effectiveness,* on the other hand, is doing the right thing. We can fill life, as in our road trip example, with the efficiencies of the minute. Yet, if we're ineffective (doing the wrong thing by following the wrong map) we may be going in the wrong direction. We could find ourselves in Chicago when our destination is Los Angeles. The result—more stress.

Where to Begin

Changing your habits with respect to time is like changing any other lifelong behavior. When you first started the Mastering Stress Program, do you remember how important it was to become aware of the stressors in your life? Time management is the same—awareness is the first step. To help you become more aware of how you invest your time, we have developed the Time Investment Worksheet. You have probably noticed that we refer to time as an investment. We do this because time is a valuable resource; if you invest it wisely,

it returns benefits that are important to *you*. Like other choices in life, each of us has the opportunity to choose how we invest this valuable resource.

The Time Investment Worksheet

On page 166 is an example of Bob's Time Investment Worksheet for one day. We have given you a blank Time Investment Worksheet on page 171. Make as many copies of this worksheet as you need for the next week. Typically, you will need only one worksheet for each day. Be sure to record your sleeping time as well.

You will need to allow 15 to 30 minutes to record everything you do in a day. Since you are already feeling overwhelmed, taking on another task may seem silly. You may be tempted to ignore the self-monitoring in favor of doing something else. However, remind yourself that this is only temporary and that it will serve an important purpose. Although it takes time now, eventually it will save you time by reducing your stress and helping you work more effectively and efficiently.

In other words, the time you save later will more than make up for the time you spend now. So your first step is to record everything you do over the next week. Try not to change your schedule to make it look better. Simply record what you are doing. Be sure to include both work and non-work days. Carrying the Time Investment Worksheet with you, keeping track of your time as the day progresses is best.

We have incorporated the information from the Daily Stress Record into the Time Investment Worksheet. This way, you won't have as many forms to carry with you for the next week. We have also given you a blank Daily Stress Record on page 172 if you prefer to keep this sheet separately. In any event, be sure to continue to record your daily physical activities.

On the Time Investment Worksheet, list the activity you are doing in the first column. You may need to list more than one activity in the one-hour time slot provided. Place a check in either the "urgent" or "important" column for each activity. In the next column, record your stress level as you do the activity. In the last column, record your feelings about doing the activity. Your goal for this week is to monitor the investment of your time, much like you monitor your bank account balance by keeping a check register. Being aware of how you currently spend your time is an essential first step in making changes. Good luck with the worksheet.

Time Investment Worksheet

(Bob's Example)

Today's Date: March 31, 2001

Time	Activity	Urgent	Important	Stress Level (0–8)	Thoughts
12:00–1:00 am	Sleep		✓	0	
1:00–2:00 am	"				
2:00–3:00 am	"				
3:00–4:00 am	"			3	Woke up, worrying about work
4:00–5:00 am	"				
5:00–6:00 am	"				
6:00–7:00 am	Wake up, watch the news-30 min walk		✓	6/4	Thinking about all I have to do today, the walk was terrific and relaxing
7:00–8:00 am	Feed kids breakfast, get ready for work	✓		5	Stress increasing because I have so much to do
8:00–9:00 am	Drive to work and prepare for the day	✓		7	Stuck in traffic, I'll never get everything done today
9:00–10:00 am	Meeting with secretary	✓		6	Go over Nation's contract
10:00–11:00 am	Meeting with department heads	✓		7	Problems in production are serious
11:00–11:59 am	Going over last month's financials	✓		7	We need to make more money to cover overhead
12:00–1:00 pm	Lunch meeting with bankers	✓		6	Negotiation of terms for a new line of credit
1:00–2:00 pm	"			8	This loan is going to cost a lot
2:00–3:00 pm	Took a 15-minute walk 20 minutes of relaxation exercises, then paperwork		✓	3	This feels great and relaxing, the flowers are beautiful. Feel more relaxed working at desk
3:00–4:00 pm	Worked on projects	✓		4	I'll never get this all done
4:00–5:00 pm	Worked on projects and returned phone calls	✓		4	I'll never get this all done—too much to do
5:00–6:00 pm	30-minute staff meeting then more work	✓		5	Still problems in production and now shipping
6:00–7:00 pm	Worked on projects	✓		4	By working late I'll get more done
7:00–8:00 pm	"	✓		5	"
8:00–9:00 pm	Drove home and ate dinner with wife		✓	4	Relaxing drive, enjoyable
9:00–10:00 pm	Read the paper and more work at home	✓		5	Making some progress
10:00–11:00 pm	More work	✓		5	Making some progress
11:00–11:59 pm	Watched the news and bed		✓	4	It feels good to get into bed and relax

Lesson Review

At last, we have reached the end of this lesson. We hope you enjoyed the new material. In this lesson, we discussed ways to improve your deep muscle relaxation skills. You learned some new ways to overcome common issues with this form of relaxation. We discussed the importance of getting enough sleep and provided some helpful hints if you find yourself having trouble sleeping. We also discussed the importance of healthy relationships. Although relationships are often resources for stress reduction, at times certain relationships can be stressors. We expanded the process of realistic thinking. You learned to challenge your initial stressful thoughts by carefully evaluating the evidence for and against these thoughts. The lesson concluded with a discussion on the topic of time investment (time management). We introduced you to a new monitoring form to help you become more aware of how you are currently investing your time.

This Week's Assignment

Continue to practice and perfect your deep muscle relaxation skills. Review the relationships in your life that may be contributing to your stress levels. Assess the costs and benefits of these relationships. Complete the Relationship Assessment Worksheet carefully. We say carefully because we do not want you to think impulsively when you are considering leaving a relationship. Take time to honestly review the positives and negatives of your relationships. Think carefully about the needs that brought you into the relationship and what keeps you there.

Carry the Realistic Thinking Worksheet with you and immediately record stressful events that increase your level of stress as they happen. Practice your realistic thinking every opportunity you have by using the worksheet. This is an important skill to master in this program. Any time you feel your stress level increasing over the next week, take out your worksheet!

"My calendar is way overbooked and I'm three months behind in my work — *I don't have time to attend a time management seminar!*"

Also, carry your Time Investment Worksheets with you during the week and complete them during the day. Remember to keep track of your physical activity this week. Keep up your deep muscle relaxation practice sessions and record your physical activity and relaxation practice sessions for week seven on the worksheet in Appendix F on page 432. And finally, remember to update your Stress Change Worksheet for week seven on page 127 and your Average Stress Change Worksheet in Appendix E on page 430. Good luck with this week's assignment.

Knowledge Review

T F 49. Taking the time to practice relaxation is not advisable if you are very busy each day.

T F 50. Concentration is paramount to relaxing when your stress level is high and your muscles are tense.

T F 51. Getting adequate sleep is important for your body to recover from daily stressors.

T F 52. All relationships are positive sources of stress relief.

T F 53. A good way to challenge your estimates when thinking realistically is to examine your past experiences.

T F 54. Changing perspectives is a good strategy for viewing evidence related to social situations.

T F 55. The level of stress in the last column of the Realistic Thinking Worksheet ideally will be less than the level of stress you experienced with your initial thought.

T F 56. Investing your time in the urgent items is a good way to lower your stress.

T F 57. Individuals who don't think they have time to practice time management skills are the ones who need these skills the most.

(See Answers in Appendix C, page 415)

"Before we begin our Time Management Seminar, did everyone get one of these 36-hour wrist watches?"

Relationship Assessment

Realistic Thinking Worksheet

Today's Date:

(1) Event	(2) Initial Thought	(3) Evidence (How Do I Know?)	(4) Initial/Realistic Probability	(5) Initial/Revised Stress Level (0–8 Scale)

Time Investment Worksheet

Today's Date:

Time	Activity	Urgent	Important	Stress Level (0–8)	Thoughts
12:00–1:00 am					
1:00–2:00 am					
2:00–3:00 am					
3:00–4:00 am					
4:00–5:00 am					
5:00–6:00 am					
6:00–7:00 am					
7:00–8:00 am					
8:00–9:00 am					
9:00–10:00 am					
10:00–11:00 am					
11:00–11:59 am					
12:00–1:00 pm					
1:00–2:00 pm					
2:00–3:00 pm					
3:00–4:00 pm					
4:00–5:00 pm					
5:00–6:00 pm					
6:00–7:00 pm					
7:00–8:00 pm					
8:00–9:00 pm					
9:00–10:00 pm					
10:00–11:00 pm					
11:00–11:59 pm					

Average Level of Stress Today	
Highest Stress Level Today	
Physical Activity Today	
Relaxation Practice Today	

Daily Stress Record—Lesson Seven

Name:____________________________ **Week of:**____________

Date	Average Stress Level	Highest Stress Level	Time of Highest Stress Level	Stressful Event Associated with Highest Stress Level

My Physical Activity and Relaxation Record

Day of the Week	Physical Activity Record		Relaxation Record	
	Activity	Minutes	Time of Day	Minutes
Monday				
Tuesday				
Wednesday				
Thursday				
Friday				
Saturday				
Sunday				
This Week	Total Activity		Total Relaxation	

Lesson Eight

Here we are at Lesson Eight. This lesson marks the halfway point in your stress management program! We hope you are enjoying the program and that you are well on your way to reducing stress in your life. We begin this lesson with a review of your Realistic Thinking Worksheet from last week. Did you have any difficulties completing the worksheet? If so, a short review may help with any problems you encountered. We'll then look at your Time Investment Worksheet from last week. To do this, we will review Bob's example from Lesson Seven, on page 166.

We discussed the benefits of being physically active in Lessons Four on page 86 and Five on page 105. We shared the good news about how you can achieve a moderate fitness level by accumulating about 30 minutes of activity on most days of the week. In this lesson, we expand our discussion of physical activity by talking about "lifestyle activity." We'll look at ways you can build small bouts of physical activity into your daily routine and talk about the common barriers most people face when it comes to regular physical activity. We expand our discussion on realistic thinking then we will move on to the topic of assertion and its value in stress management. Finally, we conclude this lesson with another Quality of Life Review. If you're ready, take out your Realistic Thinking Worksheets from last week, and let's begin.

Reviewing Your Realistic Thinking Worksheets

For the past week, you used the Realistic Thinking Worksheets to help you think more realistically about stressful events in your life. Many of our clients have difficulty learning how to use the Realistic Thinking Worksheet at first. Identifying the thoughts in our lives that increase stress is not easy. It takes dedication and a lot of practice. Let's look at some examples that may help you become more proficient at using the Realistic Thinking Worksheet.

"Realistic thinking is a a step-by-step approach to evaluate your thoughts and beliefs about certain events. It takes into account the possibility that both positive and negative things can and do happen."

Were you able to assign a more realistic probability to your initial thoughts after you carefully considered the facts and evidence? Were you able to identify alternative thoughts about the stressful events and assign more realistic probabilities to these alternative thoughts? As you considered more realistic probabilities, did your stress level decrease? If not, don't worry. You may still need more practice at this skill. Eventually, completing this worksheet should help you reduce your stress. If you are still having trouble with the worksheet, continued practice will help. Don't worry you won't need to carry a Realistic Thinking Worksheet around with you for the rest of your life. Eventually, you will be able to do this exercise in your head. However, when you find your level of stress increasing over a particular event, you may need to work through this exercise on paper.

I KNOW 12 HOURS IN THE CAR MAY SEEM LIKE A LONG TIME, BUT I BROUGHT ALONG SOME SELF-IMPROVEMENT TAPES TO MAKE IT GO FASTER. YES SIR, FOR THE NEXT 1,000 MILES WE'RE GOING TO WORK ON YOUR SELF-IMPROVEMENT.
REAL LIFE ADVENTURES©GarLanco. Reprinted with permission of Universal Press Syndicate. All rights reserved
WISE ALDRICH
3-17

Caution: Beating your head against steering wheel may cause airbag to go off.

As we mentioned earlier, many of our clients find working through the realistic thinking worksheets challenging. They often find that it works well in certain situations and not so well in others. If this sounds familiar, you are in good company. We continue to work with our clients until this exercise becomes easier and feels more natural. Sometimes it takes several weeks for our clients to master this skill. The good news is that once they master this skill, it becomes a very valuable stress management tool. If you are still having difficulties with this skill, be patient. Continued practice will help make this a helpful resource for you to use.

Let's now review your worksheets from last week. Look at the stressful events you encountered last week and your initial thoughts about these events. Compare the *initial* probability of your initial thought coming true with the *realistic* probability you assigned to the thought, after carefully weighing the evidence for and against the initial thought. Were your realistic probabilities lower than your initial probabilities? If so, congratulations! If you are able to lower the probability of an initial stressful thought, your stress level should also be lower after completing this exercise. If your realistic probability was not lower than your initial probability, consider these questions.

❶ Recalling the stressful event, what was it that increased your stress? Did you correctly identify the thought about the event that increased your level of stress?

❷ If you correctly identified the initial thought, did you carefully consider all of the facts and objectively review the evidence for and against your initial thought? Did you consider the four types of evidence we discussed in Lesson Seven, beginning on page 153, as you considered the facts? Did you take into consideration your general knowledge about the event and your initial thought? Were you able to relate prior experiences or past experiences of others you know to the event and your initial thought? Did you consider all possible alternatives to your initial thought? Did you try changing perspectives by thinking about how you would help someone else with the same event and initial thought use this technique to lower his or her stress?

Now compare your initial stress level with your revised stress level for each event. Were your revised stress levels lower than your initial stress levels? If they were, then the exercise was successful in lowering your level of stress. If not, how do the initial and revised stress levels compare with your initial and revised probabilities? You should notice some consistency in the probabilities and stress levels. You may have encountered a stressful event that was as stressful after you weighed the evidence for and against your initial thought as your initial thought. This may indicate that your stressful thought was realistic and justified. If this happened, we'll show you later in this lesson how to deal with such situations. On page 183, we begin our discussion about "What Would Happen If." Continue to practice through the realistic thinking techniques. Try to work through as many stressful events and thoughts as you can over the next week. As we have said before, practice, practice, practice!

Remember to distinguish between realistic thinking and positive thinking as you review your Realistic Thinking Worksheet.

Realistic thinking is a step-by-step approach to evaluate your thoughts and beliefs about certain events. This approach takes into account the possibility that both positive and negative things can and do happen. Positive thinking, on the other hand, ignores the possibility that something negative can happen. This approach focuses on an unrealistic view of the world. Realistic rather than positive thinking is in your best interest because bad things can and do happen. We will return to this subject later in this lesson. Again, we want to highlight that this is a complex exercise, and you need to be patient learning this stress management technique. Later is this lesson, we will share additional examples of this technique that will help you to better understand the worksheet and its purpose.

Reviewing Your Time Investment Worksheet

You have now had time to practice using your Time Investment Worksheet for a week. Let's discuss what the information means. You will be looking for several things as you review your worksheets from last week. The first are *patterns* of stressful events. These patterns will tell you whether your high levels of stress follow a regular course from day-to-day. The second are *triggers* or events that initiate your stressful reactions. Some patterns may not be recognized after only a week of keeping the worksheets. This is why continued monitoring is important. Let's begin by searching for patterns.

Searching for Patterns

The Time Investment Worksheet includes columns for time, activity, urgent vs. important, stress level, and thoughts. Can you find any patterns? Let's look at each of the columns more carefully. To do this, we will use Bob's example from Lesson Seven, on page 166.

Time. Are your high levels of stress grouped around certain times during the day? Your high-stress periods may vary depending upon the day of the week. Most people have more time commitments during their work days than on their days off. We copied only one sample day from Bob's first week of keeping his worksheets. However, a clear pattern of stress emerged after reviewing his worksheets for the full week. On many nights before a workday, Bob would often wake up thinking about work. During most work day mornings, his first thoughts were about all he had to do that day. If you find your stress level increasing during certain times of the day, try an alternative activity. Try practicing deep muscle relaxation, taking a short walk, or anything that will help you think about something pleasant.

Activity. Do certain activities increase your stress? More important, are there certain activities that help lower your stress? Crowded subways, traffic jams, and packed elevators may all contribute to your stress. Do you find yourself working on so many projects at the same time that you have a hard time focusing? Doing more than one thing at a time insures that nothing gets the attention it deserves. Do you eat at your desk while you are working, or do you take a break and relax while eating lunch? For most people, enjoying stress-reducing activities takes a back seat to many other activities. Seeing a pattern in activities that increase your stress is a sign that you need better ways of coping with stress. In later lessons, we discuss ways to take stress-breaks during the day. Bob found that taking a 15-minute walk was a good way to help lower his stress level during the day. During these walks, Bob carefully observed his surroundings as he walked. This activity helped break the stress-producing cycle. More important, this stress-reducing activity helped Bob increase his physical activity and his overall fitness level

Urgent vs. Important. Count the number of check marks in the urgent and important columns. Which column has the most marks? If the urgent column has more checks than the important column, this is a strong indication that you could benefit from improved time management skills. When you spend most of your day on the urgent matters, the truly important things in your life get left behind. You may forgo regular physical activity, nurturing relationships, eating healthy, entertainment, and other important activities. This cycle can leave you feeling exhausted and overstressed at the end of a long day. Look at Bob's example on page 166. Clearly, most of Bob's day was spent dealing with urgent matters. The urgent matters even followed him home!

Thoughts. Did your stress level increase when you had additional tasks to complete? Did you wake up at night worrying about all the things you had to do? Other thoughts may also be involved when the urgent matters outnumber the important. Examples include thoughts of resentment, hostility, frustration, and anger.

Patterns In My Stress

On page 196, we provide a Patterns in My Stress worksheet to help you review and evaluate daily patterns in your stress. Take time now to review your Time Investment Worksheets from last week and look for patterns. Write these patterns down on the Patterns in My Stress worksheet. We will refer back to this worksheet in upcoming lessons.

High-Risk Situations— Triggers for Stress

What are your triggers for increased stress? Thinking about work, driving in heavy traffic, or having a difficult conversation with a close friend may increase stress in your life. Coming home after a long day at work to energetic young children or concerns about financial matters may trigger your stress. Most of us have well-defined stress triggers. Do you know your triggers?

The notion of high-risk situations becomes very important at this point in the program. Throughout this program, you are learning techniques for avoiding or coping with high-risk situations that increase your stress. An important first step in this process is to identify your stress triggers. The information you have learned from your Realistic Thinking Worksheets, your Time Investment Worksheets, and from increasing your self-awareness, holds key information for developing these techniques later in the program. You can learn to predict the situations that increase your stress and develop alternative strategies.

Triggers are generally a combination of elements included in your Time Investment Worksheets and Realistic Thinking Worksheets. Look at the patterns you discovered and wrote down on your Patterns in My Stress worksheet, on page 196. This worksheet may also include important factors to help you identify your stress triggers.

"Identifying your stress triggers will help you cope with or avoid high-risk situations that increase your stress."

Make a list of the five most significant triggers that increase your stress on the My Stress Triggers worksheet on page 197. We will refer to this list of your stress triggers in later lessons. After you complete this list, compare the triggers you listed here with the stress triggers you listed on page 63, in Lesson Three. Is your list different now? Are you more aware of the real triggers that increase your stress now than you were a few weeks ago?

Time Management and the Important

All of us deal with both urgent and important matters. In our daily routines, one of these elements will dominate how we invest our time. When we allow our daily life to become dominated by urgent matters, our stress levels increase because the important matters get left behind. As the important matters dominate, we spend more time planning and preparing with less stress. When important matters direct our daily lives, we spend less time putting out fires and more time doing things by choice rather than default. Our maps and minutes become more aligned.

Identifying the Important

We all know that life is not always neat, logical, and predictable. To think that urgent matters will never surface is unrealistic. The classifications of urgent and important are more a matter of degree than of type. Among the many urgent and important issues that we all face, how do we know what to do when? This is the challenge of time investment. How we deal with what is most important at any point in time is a key factor in investing our time wisely.

The first step is to identify the things in life that are truly important to you. As you contemplate this issue, it may be helpful for you to think of the following questions:

- Do you feel energized throughout the entire day? Or, do you lack the energy to do the things you would like to do?
- Do you have a clear sense of purpose and direction that inspires you to jump out of bed enthusiastically every morning? Or, do you lay in bed each morning, delaying getting up because you don't know what you want to accomplish?
- Do you have close and satisfying relationships with others? Are you able to work effectively with others at work to accomplish a common purpose?
- Do you spend quality time with members of your family at home or do you feel challenged by frequent misunderstandings?
- Are you financially secure? Are you able to meet your and your family's

daily needs or are you barely scraping by?

- Are you constantly learning new things and gaining new perspectives and skills? Do you have a passion to do something but can't find the time to do it?

Each of us has unique life-needs. If these needs are not met, it is easy to fall into the "urgency trap" and become increasingly stressed. Take a few moments now to write down at least 15 things in life that are truly important to you on the Important Matters Worksheet on page 198. List five items under each of these categories: physical matters; mental matters; and relationship matter. On page 180, we have reproduced Bob's example worksheet.

More on Physical Activity

We have discussed the importance of physical activity for overall health and stress management. Many people have a misconception about exercise. For years, Americans were told that in order to get any benefit from physical activity, we had to exercise for at least 30–60 minutes, on at least three days a week. In addition, we were told the exercise intensity had to be at least 80 percent of maximum heart rate. As discussed in Lesson Five on page 105, new research has shown this is simply not true. Overall fitness can be improved significantly by incorporating at least 30 minutes of incremental activity into your daily lifestyle. This is referred to by exercise specialists as "lifestyle activity." Throughout the Mastering Stress Program, we offer many suggestions on becoming more active. However, developing new lifelong habits to become and remain physically active is beyond the scope of the program. If staying physically active is difficult for you, we suggest that you get the *Living with Exercise 2001* program, developed by Dr. Steven Blair, at the Cooper Institute in Dallas, Texas. This book is designed to help individuals increase their physical activity by making permanent lifestyle changes. For totally in-

"When we allow our daily life to become dominated by urgent matters, our stress levels increase because the important matters get left behind."

Important Matters Worksheet

Bob's Example

Physical Matters:

1. Regular outdoor exercise
2. Joining a local golf club and playing regularly
3. Eating a healthy diet
4. Getting a good night's sleep
5. Taking regular vacations

Mental Matters:

1. Read novels for enjoyment
2. Take cooking class to learn new dishes
3. Learn a foreign language
4. Take a college course each year to advance my career
5. Learn to use the computer for personal finances

Relationship Matters:

1. Spend quality time each week with my wife
2. Take an active role in my children's activities
3. Develop a better working realtionship with Martin at work
4. Develop closer relationship with male friends
5. Communicate more with my parents

active individuals, Dr. Blair suggests beginning with a two-minute walk and increasing by one minute per week until you can complete a 30-minute walk. Dr. Blair's program can be ordered by calling 1–888–LEARN–41.

We know that physical activity in an important way to reduce stress. Yet, we often find reasons not to be physically active. Let's take a look at some of these barriers and explore some possible solutions to overcome them.

Barriers to Being Physically Active

Barrier: *I really don't like to exercise; it's not fun.*

Solution: Find activities you enjoy doing or explore new activities. You don't know if you will like them unless you try. Walking through the neighborhood, dancing, bowling, or working in the yard are all activities that get you up and moving. Doing something is better than doing nothing. You may not like being active at first. If this is so, it's a strong signal that you need to be more active. As you become more active, you will find activities that you like and enjoy more.

Barrier: *I just don't have the time to exercise.*

Solution: As we discussed in the time management section, time is about choosing the things in life that are truly important to you. If exercise is important to you, you need to find time each day to be active. Begin with a two-minute walk and increase your time from there. Physical activity does not require much time. Any amount of time spent exercising is a good start. Any increase in physical activity such as taking the stairs, parking farther away, or stretching at your desk counts. Finally, develop the habit of scheduling time for exercise just as you would for any other important activity. At age 100, Eubie Blake said, "If I'd known I was gonna live this long, I'd have taken better care of myself."

Barrier: *I am too self-conscious about my body to exercise in public.*

Solution: There are two parts to this solution. First, try not to focus on how you look, but on what you are doing for your health. Try, for just 30 minutes, not to rate or judge how your body looks. If you still feel uncomfortable, try walking in your house, in your backyard, or wherever you have more privacy.

Barrier: *Change happens slowly, and I am too impatient to wait for my fitness to improve.*

Solution: Focus on several ways to measure change, not just on your ultimate goal of fitness. For example, focus on your improved sense of mental and physical well-being. You can feel these benefits right away. Record your stress level before and after exercising. Many people notice the benefits of exercise after the first week. Remember to set realistic activity goals so you won't become discouraged!

"If you don't like to exercise, try to find new activities like working in the yard."

More on Realistic Thinking

After a week of practicing realistic thinking, you should feel that you are making progress. You may still be overestimating the probability that bad things will happen. If so, don't worry. This is perfectly natural. Your estimates will become more realistic with each day of practice. Continue to work on this important skill. Let's now expand our discussion on realistic thinking. To do this, we introduce you to another common error in thinking that many people encounter. This is the error of *overestimating* the consequences of a negative event. You might think of it as making mountains out of molehills.

To highly stressed people, life seems to pack a double whammy. First, they believe that unpleasant events are likely to happen. They also believe that the consequences of those events will be absolutely horrible. We call this blowing things out of proportion, or "catastrophizing." People who catastrophize automatically expect the worst possible outcome. If these individuals are awakened by a noise in their house at night, they immediately assume that it is a burglar who is going to harm or kill them. If they are called into the boss's office, they immediately think they are going to be fired.

Most people who assume the worst are unaware of their assumptions. They never identify the consequences they are imagining. The consequences stay at a subconscious level where they cannot be disproved. In other words, the unrealistic consequences are like the unrealistic probabilities we discussed in Lesson Seven on page 153. They lurk in the darkness of your mind, ready to jump out and cause harm, until you bring them out and see them for what they are.

I WANTED TO KEEP YOU FULL TIME, CATHY, BUT I WAS VETOED BY UPPER MANAGEMENT.
YOU ARE UPPER MANAGEMENT, MR. PINKLEY.

BUT THIS WAS FROM UPPER UPPER MANAGEMENT!
THIS IS A SMALL COMPANY. THERE IS NO UPPER UPPER MANAGEMENT.

AH, BUT IF WE CUT COSTS ENOUGH TO MAKE A PROFIT, WE'LL SELL OUT TO A BIG CONGLOMERATE WHO WILL HAVE AN UPPER UPPER MANAGEMENT... AND IT'S THOSE GUYS! THOSE GUYS WANT YOU OUT!

I DEMAND TO SPEAK TO THE HYPOTHETICAL BIGWIG WHO OUSTED ME!
GOOD LUCK! THOSE PEOPLE NEVER STAND UP AND TAKE THE BLAME.
Guisewite

What Would Happen if . . .

You can identify the consequences of your assumptions by asking yourself a simple question. Ask yourself, "What would happen if the thing I'm worried about really comes true?" As we said before, realistic thinking is not positive thinking. We have to admit the possibility that bad things can happen. In the last lesson, we showed you how to identify the realistic probability of negative things happening. You most likely discovered that the chances of bad things happening are far less than you might have initially thought, yet they are still possible. The next step is to accept that possibility. Then ask yourself, "If my worst fears come true, what would *really* happen? How bad would it really be?" The answer to these questions will produce the expected *consequence* to your first belief or the "catastrophe." This becomes your *next* thought or belief to challenge. Therefore, you are now able to examine the realistic evidence for this second belief. Most often, you will find that the consequences would not be as bad as you initially thought. The same rules that apply to your probability of an event happening, also apply to the likelihood of a terrible consequence. The key here is to phrase the consequence as a realistic statement without emotional or reactionary words.

"If my worst fears come true, what would really happen? The answer to this question will reveal the expected consequence to your initial belief or the catastrophe."

Let's return to the example in which your partner is late getting home from work. Your initial thought is that he or she has had an accident. When you think realistically, you may realize that the chance of this actually happening is very small (less than 1 percent). But, that's still a chance. So, your next step is to ask yourself, "What would really happen if my spouse had an accident?"

Talking to yourself may or may not come naturally. You do not have to do it aloud, although there is nothing wrong with this if it makes you feel more comfortable. All you have to do is ask yourself questions and answer them with realistic statements. Although talking to yourself has a bad reputation, it is actually very useful. Get into the habit of mentally asking and answering questions as you practice realistic thinking.

Ask yourself what would really happen if your spouse had an accident. You might immediately answer, "He or she would be killed." What does this answer remind you of? You're right, it is an overestimation of probability. Remind yourself that most accidents are not serious enough to kill or maim people. As you now know, overestimating the consequences is simply overestimating the probabilities that lie behind your original thoughts.

Asking yourself, "What would really happen if...?" is just another way of identifying your next thought. Many people find that asking one question opens a Pandora's box. One thought leads to another and then another. Identify all your thoughts, no matter how frightening or silly they seem, until you reach the bottom of the box.

If you think realistically, you will eventually learn to cope—even if your spouse were hurt or killed in an accident. This may sound callous, but it is a realistic fact. Humans can cope with an amazing amount of difficulty. When you reach the answer that is at the bottom of all the questions you are asking, you will usually find that it is not as horrible as you feared. Let's revisit Tim's example that we introduced in Lesson Six, on page 141.

Read through the following transcript of a counseling session Tim had with his counselor. This example illustrates how identifying your initial thoughts then reviewing all of the evidence can help you to think more realistically. The superscript letters refer to the places on Tim's Expanded Realistic Thinking Worksheet on page 185, where he completed the worksheet. Follow along on Tim's worksheet as you read through the counseling session.

Tim's Counseling Session

Tim: Sales were down last month.[a] I'm worried that I won't be able to get my sales back, and they will be bad again this month.[b]

Counselor: How likely is it that your sales will be down again?

Tim: Well, I know I'm usually good at my job.[c] In the past I've had times when my sales went down for one month but then went back up the next month.[d] So, another bad month isn't very likely—maybe 10 percent.[e]

Counselor: Let's assume they *are* down again this month. What would happen?

Tim: My boss would fire me.[f]

Counselor: It sounds like you are assuming there is a 100 percent probability that your boss would fire you. How likely do you think that really is?

Tim: Humm . . . I'm generally a good salesman. I know of other guys who have had bad months and didn't get fired. Once my sales were down for three months, and they kept me on.[g] So, I guess it's not all that likely that I would be fired—maybe 1 percent.[h]

Counselor: Okay. But let's not stop here. What would happen if you *did* get fired?

Tim: That would be awful. We would lose everything.[i]

Counselor: Why? Why would you lose everything, Tim?

Tim: Well, I wouldn't have a job, and we wouldn't be to afford the new house.

Expanded Realistic Thinking Worksheet

(Tim's Example)

Today's Date:

(1) Event	(2) Initial Thought	(3) Evidence (How Do I Know?)	(4) Initial/Realistic Probability	(5) Initial/Revised Emotion (0–8 Scale)	(6) Consequence
[a]Sales were down last month	[b]Sales will be down again this month.	[c]I'm usually very good at selling. [d]My sales have been down before, but returned again.	50% / [e]10%	7 / 6	[f]I will be fired
	[f]I will be fired.	[g]I'm generally good at selling. Others weren't fired after bad months. I wasn't fired when sales were down for 3 months.	100% / [h]1%	6 / 4	[i]We would lose everything
	[i]We would lose everything.	[j]We do have some money saved up, and we would be okay for a while.	100% / 5%	4 / 3	[k]I'll never find another job
	[k]I'll never find another job.	[l]I am a good salesman. I have had the highest sales in the company. I could even draw unemployment.	80% / almost 0	3 / 2	[m]We could survive and I'd find another job

Counselor: Do you have any money saved?

Tim: Yes we do. We have some money in savings and some investments in mutual funds. I guess we would be okay for a while.[j] But, I'll never be able to find another job.[k]

Counselor: And what would happen if you didn't find a job right away.

Tim: Well, as I said, we do have some money saved up, so we could pay our bills for a while. I am a pretty good salesman. I have had the highest sales in the company for three of the last five years. I could even draw unemployment for a while if I had to.[l] But, eventually, I'm sure I would be able to find a job somewhere.[m]

Counselor: So, in other words, there seems to be only a small chance that your sales will be down again this month. And, even if they are, there is only a small chance that you would get fired. And, even if you did, you would probably find another job soon because you are good at your job. Even if you didn't find another job soon, you know that you and your family would survive. So, it doesn't sound as bad as it first seemed. How much stress do you feel now?

Tim: Not much at all.

In reviewing Tim's Expanded Realistic Thinking Worksheet on page 185, notice that the *consequence* of each initial thought becomes the next initial thought. You should also notice that this process of identifying new thoughts and consequences continued until Tim finally agreed (and more importantly believed) that his initial thought of sales being down last month may not be so bad after all.

As we said earlier, you may have difficulty completing this worksheet properly at first. So, let's look at another example of the type of questioning involved in realistic thinking. The case of Irene provides another good example of how one question can lead to another and another, until the bottom line is reached. Although an expert asks the questions in the example, you can do the same kind of questioning yourself.

Meet Irene

Irene is in her late 20's. She takes care of three children in her home as a way to supplement her family's income. One day, Irene's three-year-old daughter, Sue, bit one of the children while playing a game. Irene was worried that the child's parents would withdraw him from her care. Follow along with Irene's example worksheet on page 188 as we listen in on her counseling session.

Irene: My daughter bit Robert, one of the children I sit for. I'm worried that his parents will take Robert to another sitter.

Counselor: Why would they do that?

Irene: Because Sue bit him.

Counselor: Has Sue ever bitten anyone before?

Irene: No.

Counselor: Do you think Robert's parents would understand that the children were playing a game?

Irene: Probably. They're real nice people.

Counselor: Do you think Robert wants to leave?

Irene: No. He likes coming to my house and enjoys playing with the other children.

[Note: Here, the counselor has been asking Irene to look at different types of evidence—particularly, her past experience and the general knowledge she has about Robert's family.]

Counselor: So then, looking at all the evidence, how likely do you think it really is that Robert's parents will change sitters?

Irene: Oh, I guess around 20 percent.

Counselor: Okay. Now, let's assume that Robert's parents did decide to take him somewhere else. What would happen?

Irene: That would be terrible! We just couldn't afford it!

Counselor What do you mean you couldn't afford it? Would you starve?

Irene Well, no. We wouldn't starve, but it would be hard.

Counselor How much do Robert's parents pay you each week?

Irene: About $50.

Counselor: Do you and your family buy little luxuries or do extra things that cost money, like going out to dinner, renting videos, or buying new clothes?

Expanded Realistic Thinking Worksheet

(Irene's Example)

Today's Date:

(1) Event	(2) Initial Thought	(3) Evidence (How Do I Know?)	(4) Initial/Realistic Probability	(5) Initial/Revised Stress Level (0–8 Scale)	(6) Consequence
Sue bit one of the children	Robert's parents will withdraw him.	Other parents have withdrawn their children for less, Robert's parents are very proactive and nice.	80% / 60%	7 / 4	We couldn't afford the loss; it would be terrible.
Robert's parents withdraw him	We couldn't afford the loss; it would be terrible.	Every time we lose a family, it's difficult finding a replacement, but not impossible.	60% / 20%	4 / 3	We wouldn't be able to make up the loss and may go out of business.
We couldn't afford the loss; it would be terrible.	We may go out of business.	There are things we can do to save money. Other parents might bring their children to our center.	50% / 10%	3 / 2	We would survive, although it may be hard at first; we wouldn't starve.

Irene: Sure, we do things like that.

Counselor: So, if you lost $50 a week from Robert's parents, could you cut back on a few of those things to save money?

Irene: I guess so. It probably wouldn't be that hard.

Counselor: Do you know other parents who may want you to keep their children if you had an opening?

Irene: Oh yes. I have inquiries all the time about keeping children.

Counselor: So again, if Robert's parents changed sitters, how hard would that be?

Irene: I guess it wouldn't be as bad as I first thought. We could just cut back on a few things until I found another child to take his place. I don't think I would have any problem finding another child to care for.

As you can see in Irene's example, her stress level went from a 7 to a 2 after she worked through the realistic thinking worksheet with her counselor. With the help of her counselor, Irene continued to challenge her initial *negative* thoughts until she realized that realistically, things would not be as bad as she had first imagined. This is the power of the realistic thinking worksheet. To highlight the importance of mastering this technique, let's work through one more example.

Sally's Counseling Session

Do you remember meeting Sally in Lesson Five on page 103? You may recall that Sally is a homemaker from Omaha with three children. Let's listen to the counseling session between Sally and her counselor as they discuss the telephone calls Sally gets from her mother.

Sally: My mother is always calling just when I'm in the middle of doing something important. It makes me so angry, and I find that I get short with her.

Counselor: Let's try and look at what you just said in a more realistic way. When you say that she always calls in the middle of something important, it implies 100 percent of the time. In other words, you are implying that she calls every time you are doing something important. Is that true? How likely is it really, that she will call you when you are doing something important?

Sally: Well, I suppose that when I think back over the last 10 times she has called, most of the times I was just watching TV or reading. She called once when I was making dinner, and it burned because she interrupted me. Another time, I was busy with some work I needed to get finished for the PTA when she called. I guess that makes it about 20 percent of the time.

Counselor: Okay, great. That's the first part. Now, let's go a bit further. Ask yourself, "What if she calls at an inconvenient time?"

Sally: Well, I know that one of my first thoughts is that she doesn't think anything I do is important. But, before you say anything, I know that is a major overestimation since she obviously doesn't know what I'm doing when she calls. However, I suppose I also think that it's a major interruption and inconvenience to have to stop at that point.

Counselor: A major inconvenience sounds pretty extreme. What is the evidence that it is so major?

Sally: When I was doing my work for the PTA meeting, I forgot where I was and it took me 10 minutes to work it out again. I guess that's not so bad. After all, it's only 10 minutes. The time that dinner burned was really not too bad either; it was just a little burned. Part of that was my fault anyway, because I could have turned the stove down before I went to the phone.

"Answering a phone call and not being able to tell someone you are busy, may be a sign that you need to work on your assertiveness."

Counselor: So, it sounds like even when she does interrupt, it is an inconvenience, but not a major one.

Sally: True, and I know what you are going to say next. Even if it is a major inconvenience, it's not the end of the world. I have handled plenty of bigger problems than this before.

From this point, Sally and her counselor went on to discuss assertiveness training. This training helped Sally feel more comfortable telling her mother that she could not talk when her mother called at an inconvenient time. We begin our discussion of assertiveness later in this lesson.

An Expanded Realistic Thinking Worksheet

In questioning Tim, Irene, and Sally, the counselors challenged the probability that negative events would happen. The counselors also challenged the likelihood of the dire consequences each of our sample clients imagined. You can learn to do this yourself. You have already been challenging your probability estimates using the Realistic Thinking Worksheet. We will now introduce you to an Expanded Realistic Thinking Worksheet, shown on page 199. This is the same worksheet that we used as an example for Tim and Irene.

The first five columns of this new form are the same as those on the worksheet you completed in Lessons Six, on page 144, and Seven, on page 170. You will record the event, your initial thought about the event, and the evidence to support the initial thought. Then you will add the probability (initial and realistic) and your emotional intensity (initial and revised). The expanded worksheet includes a sixth column. In this column, record your initial answer to the question, "What would happen if my initial thought actually did occur?" This is your initial consequence of your initial thought. Write this consequence in the last column. But wait, you're not finished yet!

In the next row, in column 2, below the place where you wrote your initial thought, write the consequence from the preceding line again. Now start the whole process over, as if this were your initial thought. In other words, challenge the consequence the way you challenged your initial thought. Ask yourself, "What would happen if this new possibility (my previous consequence) really occurred? In answer to this, you will come up with another consequence. Record it, then start a separate line and challenge that consequence as an initial thought. Keep going until you can't go any further. This usually happens when you can't think of any other consequences or you reach a very low stress level. After completing your worksheet, you should read back over the whole exercise, and realize just how unlikely it is that anything really bad will happen. Remember, the likelihood of each consequence depends on the likelihood of the preceding belief.

This process will become clearer to you if you study the examples we provided earlier of Tim and Irene. As you can see, a single event has the potential to produce a page or more of thoughts. Make several copies of the Expanded Realistic Thinking Worksheet. Don't be afraid to use as many as you need. Eventually, you will not need the sheets at all. You will be able to do all the challenging in your head. Yet, as with the other skills you are learning, this one takes practice.

Asserting Yourself

Relationships can become a major source of stress in your life. A lack of assertiveness can put more strain on a relationship than being more assertive. Learning and practicing assertiveness skills helps you stand up for your rights and won't allow others to take advantage of you. Many people confuse assertiveness with aggressiveness. You can think of aggression as asserting your rights with little regard for another person's rights or feelings. Assertiveness, on the other hand, is asserting your rights while respecting others' rights and feelings.

See if this scene sounds familiar. A friend or co-worker asks you to do something that you really do not want to do. Still, you give in and agree to do it anyway. Then later, another friend finds out and scolds you by saying, "Why in the world did you agree to that? You have got to be more

assertive!" You now feel confused. Maybe you should have stood up for yourself. On the other hand, you did not want to seem pushy and selfish. You may not have asserted yourself because you thought it would cause stress, but it turns out that not asserting yourself is causing stress.

We don't have the space in this program to fully discuss all aspects of assertiveness training. Several popular books are available that cover the topic in detail if you feel that you need more help with assertiveness. In addition, assertiveness training courses are often conducted at community health centers, educational institutions, and other public facilities. We will, however, provide you with general idea about being more assertive. In addition, we will provide you with some basic assertiveness techniques that may work well for you.

Most people do not act assertively because they do not know the best words to use to get their point across. They may have tried to be assertive in the past, but were misunderstood. Most people do know how to be assertive. They just don't feel comfortable asserting themselves or aren't sure when it is appropriate. People in the second scenario usually allow others to walk all over them. They are worried that if they are assertive, others may become angry with them or will not like them.

If you belong to the first group, you may find it useful to learn some strategies to help you become assertive in a competent, but non-threatening, manner. We will discuss some simple strategies in upcoming lessons. If you fall into the second group, then you need to address your lack of assertiveness as a type of avoidance. In other words, you may be avoiding situations because you are afraid to assert yourself. We will provide you with strategies and techniques you can use in avoidance situations in upcoming lessons.

What Is Assertiveness?

Before discussing how to be assertive, we want to clear up any misconceptions about assertiveness. Being assertive does not mean always getting your way. Rather, being assertive means developing an understanding of your rights in a situation and asking others to respect those rights. At the same time, you need to respect the rights of others and take those into account when deciding to act.

The key is to use assertiveness only when it is appropriate. At certain times, you really should insist on having your way, even if it causes inconvenience to someone else. At other times, you may have to put your own needs aside because the other person's

needs are more important. The trick is to learn the difference. Realistic thinking techniques, which you should be more comfortable with by now, can help in this process. Let's explore how these techniques can be helpful in Steven's example.

Meet Steven

Steven is a 28-year-old clerk who has had some difficulty being assertive at work. He wanted to ask for a week off from work a month after he had taken a week-long vacation. He needed this time to help his father who had just returned home from the hospital. Steven's initial thought was that his boss would say no. Realistically, however, he had to admit that he had no idea what his boss would say. Therefore, the probability of a negative answer was only about 50 percent. So Steven asked himself, "What would happen if my boss does say no?" His fear, he realized, was that she would consider him lazy and would fire him.

In fact, the evidence showed that Steven's boss had praised him in the past for his hard work. So, even if she said no to the time off, she would be highly unlikely to fire him. Moreover, she was not likely to consider him lazy. Based on his realistic thinking, Steven realized that he should ask for the time off because there was a chance he would get it. Whether he did or not, his boss would be unlikely to think badly of him or fire him. In addition, Steven felt he had a right to ask for the time off. After all, he had an important reason for his request.

In this example, realistic thinking helped Steven overcome his reluctance to assert himself. If you find yourself in a similar situation, ask yourself realistic thinking questions such as, "How likely is it that this person will be angry at me?" and "What is the worst thing that could happen if I ask?" Realistic thinking is one of many techniques you can apply to assertiveness. We will introduce more techniques to you in the lessons that follow. Until then, practice using realistic thinking to begin to assert yourself at appropriate times.

Quality of Life Review

Once again, it is time to complete another Quality of Life Review. As we discussed in the Introduction and Orientation Lesson on page 11 and in Lesson Four on page 94, this review will help you to measure your progress in different ways at different times.

Take a few moments now to complete the Quality of Life Review on page 194.

Quality of Life Review

Please use the following scale to rate how satisfied you feel now about different aspects of your daily life. Choose any number from this list (1 to 9) and indicate your choice next to each numbered item below.

1 = Extremely Dissatisfied
2 = Very Dissatisfied
3 = Moderately Dissatisfied
4 = Somewhat Dissatisfied
5 = Neutral
6 = Somewhat Satisfied
7 = Moderately Satisfied
8 = Very Satisfied
9 = Extremely Satisfied

____ 1. Overall mood (feelings of sadness, anxiety, happiness, etc.)

____ 2. Sense of self-esteem

____ 3. Confidence, comfort in social situations

____ 4. Internal dialog (self-talk)

____ 5. Energy level

____ 6. Focus and concentration

____ 7. Ability to manage time

____ 8. Relationships

____ 9. General health

____ 10. Exercise and recreation

____ 11. Assertiveness skills

____ 12. Eating habits

____ 13. Overall quality of life

After you have completed this assessment, compare the results with your responses on page 94, in Lesson Four. Has your quality of life improved over the last four weeks? We hope that it has.

Lesson Review

We began this lesson by reviewing your Realistic Thinking and Time Investment Worksheets from last week. You reviewed your Realistic Thinking Worksheet to see if the probability and stress level of your initial thought declined as you realistically considered your initial thought. You reviewed your Time Investment Worksheets and searched for patterns around time, activity, urgent vs. important matters, and thoughts. This review should help you become more aware of stressful situations and patterns in your life. Our attention then turned to high-risk situations, and you worked through an exercise to identify your stress triggers. We reviewed the notion of urgent vs. important matters that we all deal with on a day-to-day basis. You completed the Important Matters Worksheet to help you identify things in your life that are truly important. We discussed physical activity and common barriers many people have to being more active. In addition, we discussed possible solutions to overcome these barriers. Our lesson continued by taking a more in-depth look at realistic thinking. Here, we had you consider consequence of what would happen if your initial thought actually happened. We also introduced you to an Expanded Realistic Thinking Worksheet. Finally, we introduced the topic of asserting yourself and how using assertiveness skills at the appropriate times can help lower your stress. We have much more to discuss on this subject in upcoming lessons.

This Week's Assignment

Begin using the Expanded Realistic Thinking Worksheet on page 199. Make as many copies as you need for the upcoming week. Continue monitoring how you spend your time on the Time Investment Worksheet. We provide a blank worksheet for you on page 200. We also provide you with a new Daily Stress Record for this lesson on page 201. Be sure to continue to record your physical activity and relaxation practice sessions on this form. Also be sure to complete your Stress Change Worksheet in Lesson Five on page 127, the Average Stress Change Worksheet in Appendix E on page 430, and the Physical Activity and Relaxation Worksheet in Appendix F on page 432 for week eight.

Record keeping this week will be important for the next lesson. In Lesson Nine, we will spend time reviewing your progress in the program. One final note—remember to keep up your physical activity!

Knowledge Review

T F 58. Learning how to think realistically and completing the Realistic Thinking Worksheet isn't necessary if you can think quickly.

T F 59. The four types of evidence are general knowledge, prior experience, consideration of alternatives, and changing perspectives.

T F 60. You should try to spend most of your day doing urgent matters because they are critical to your happiness.

T F 61. It's best to avoid all high-risk, stressful situations when you are learning to master your stress.

T F 62. A person who jumps to conclusions about an event, assuming the worst possible outcome, is catastrophizing.

T F 63. The mind can cope with anything, including tragedies and catastrophes.

T F 64. Being assertive is the act of voicing your rights and feelings to others appropriately and respectfully.

T F 65. Assertive behavior does not generally reduce stress disorders, but it will make you feel better.

T F 66. Overall fitness can be improved significantly be incorporating at least 30 minutes of incremental activity into your daily lifestyle.

(Answers in Appendix C, page 415)

Patterns in My Stress

Time-Related Patterns:

Activity-Related Patterns:

Urgent vs. Important Patterns:

Thought Patterns:

Other Patterns:

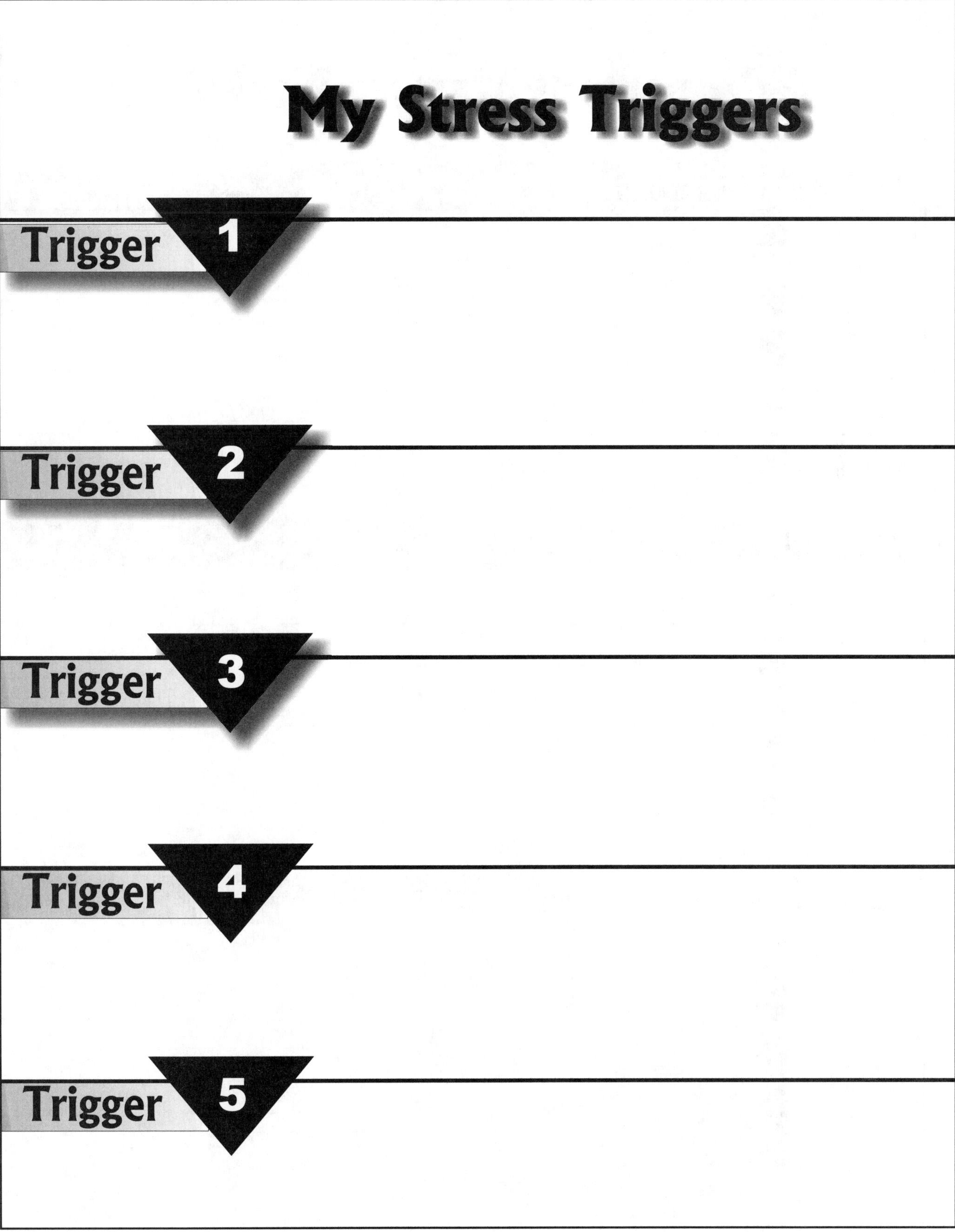
My Stress Triggers
Trigger 1
Trigger 2
Trigger 3
Trigger 4
Trigger 5

Important Matters Worksheet

Physical Matters:

1.
2.
3.
4.
5.

Mental Matters:

1.
2.
3.
4.
5.

Relationship Matters:

1.
2.
3.
4.
5.

Expanded Realistic Thinking Worksheet

Today's Date:

(1) Event	(2) Initial Thought	(3) Evidence (How Do I Know?)	(4) Initial/Realistic Probability	(5) Initial/Revised Stress Level (0–8 Scale)	(6) Consequence

Time Investment Worksheet

Today's Date:

Time	Activity	Urgent	Important	Stress Level (0–8)	Thoughts
12:00–1:00 am					
1:00–2:00 am					
2:00–3:00 am					
3:00–4:00 am					
4:00–5:00 am					
5:00–6:00 am					
6:00–7:00 am					
7:00–8:00 am					
8:00–9:00 am					
9:00–10:00 am					
10:00–11:00 am					
11:00–11:59 am					
12:00–1:00 pm					
1:00–2:00 pm					
2:00–3:00 pm					
3:00–4:00 pm					
4:00–5:00 pm					
5:00–6:00 pm					
6:00–7:00 pm					
7:00–8:00 pm					
8:00–9:00 pm					
9:00–10:00 pm					
10:00–11:00 pm					
11:00–11:59 pm					

Daily Stress Record—Lesson Eight

Name:________________________________ **Week of:**______________

Date	Average Stress Level	Highest Stress Level	Time of Highest Stress Level	Stressful Event Associated with Highest Stress Level

My Physical Activity and Relaxation Record

Day of the Week	Physical Activity Record		Relaxation Record	
	Activity	Minutes	Time of Day	Minutes
Monday				
Tuesday				
Wednesday				
Thursday				
Friday				
Saturday				
Sunday				

"Psssst—you should be back at the office! Vacations are for lazy people! What have you accomplished today?"

Lesson Nine

Congratulations! You are now halfway through the Mastering Stress Program. Are you more aware of the stressors in your life now than you were at the beginning of the program? Do you now see how your thoughts influence your stress more than the stressful events that happen in your life? Are you having success in changing your thoughts to lower your stress levels? We hope the answers to all of these questions are yes.

We begin the second half of the program by reviewing the progress you have made. This review is important for two reasons. First, it helps you to become more aware of your progress. Our clients often make great strides in their stress management programs during the first two months. Yet, they may not realize the important lifestyle changes they have made. Secondly, an objective review of your progress may also highlight areas that may need additional work. The more skilled you are in the techniques now, the better you will do in the upcoming weeks. This review typically inspires our clients to continue working hard to master their stress management skills.

A Word of Caution

Some people who use the Mastering Stress Program make great strides in reducing their stress during the first eight weeks of the program. This can lead them to believe that stress is no longer a problem in their lives. When this belief surfaces, some may question the need to continue with the program. Still others may feel as though they have made little progress during the first eight weeks. If you are having similar thoughts, put them aside—NOW! Giving up or quitting the program now would be like buying a brand new BMW, parking it in your driveway, and never driving it again. All the hard work that went into paying for the car would be wasted. Moreover, you would never have the chance to experience the wonderful innovations, gadgets, and thrills of driving one of the world's great driving cars. With that said, let's begin your progress review.

We'll begin your progress review by looking at your Stress Change Worksheet for weeks five through eight. Next, we'll turn our attention to your physical activity

LONG AGO I DECIDED MY LIFE WOULD BE A SUCCESS IF I COULD MAKE JUST ONE PERSON HAPPY. I PICKED ME.
THAVES

and relaxation worksheets. Are you more physically active now than you were at the beginning of the program? Have your thoughts and behaviors about physical activity changed? Are the relaxation exercises now part of your daily stress management routine? We hope relaxation techniques are now second nature for you.

We then turn our attention to some new and interesting topics. In the Lifestyle category of LEARN, we'll introduce you to the topic of procrastination and discuss three ways most people typically put off things. We then introduce the topic of nutrition. We discuss the importance of good nutrition for overall good health, well-being, and stress management. In the relationship category, we bring up the touchy topic of families. Families can be both a help and a hindrance in a stress management program. We revisit the topic of relaxation, and we'll show you how to identify low levels of tension in your muscles. The lesson concludes with a review of your Expanded Realistic Thinking Worksheet and your Quality of Life Review from Lesson Eight. We have much material to cover in this lesson. So, if you're ready, let's begin with a pep talk.

"Focus on your progress—you should be able to use your stress management tools whenever you encounter stressful situations."

A Midpoint Pep Talk

Before starting your review, let's revisit some important points. Change is a process—it happens over time; it is always evolving. If you find yourself having stressful thoughts or engaging in stressful behaviors, be patient. Your thoughts and behaviors have developed over your lifetime; changing them takes time and practice. Try focusing on the progress you have made over the past eight weeks.

Let's say, for example, that your stress increases when you're in heavy traffic or when a careless driver cuts you off. Do you recognize this as stress more readily now, than before you began the program? Are you able to change your thoughts about why the driver may be driving recklessly? Are these new thoughts less stressful? If so, we congratulate you. If not, don't be discouraged. You may need to practice the techniques discussed in previous lessons a little more. If you can think of other examples of positive change in your life, pat yourself on the back. Recognizing that you are making important progress is essential. Simply being aware of the stressors in your life is progress. These changes and your new level of awareness are significant. Do not overlook or dismiss this progress. You deserve the credit for your hard work.

Another key point to remember is that change often happens slowly. Unfortunately, we don't have drive-thru windows for stress reduction in today's fast-paced world. Try to remember that your behaviors and thought patterns develop over a lifetime. Lifelong habits take time to change, but you can master the changes. With these things in mind, let's review your progress. You may be surprised with the progress you have made!

Reviewing Your Stress Change Worksheet

You have been tracking your progress for eight weeks on the Stress Change Worksheets. In Lesson Five, you reviewed your Stress Change Worksheet for weeks one through four, on page 101. Let's now do the same thing for weeks five through eight. To do so, you will be referring to your Stress Change Worksheet on page 127.

Over the past four weeks you may have noticed a decrease in your average weekly stress level. If you have, good work! You may have also noticed the ups and downs of your weekly levels of stress. These changes may not have been as steady as you would have liked, but remember, this is perfectly natural. So don't be discouraged.

At this point, look at your Stress Change Worksheet on page 127. If you experienced increases in your stress levels during any week, you should have noted the causes directly on your worksheet. If you didn't do this, look back over your Daily Stress Records and try to look for patterns during times of increased stress.

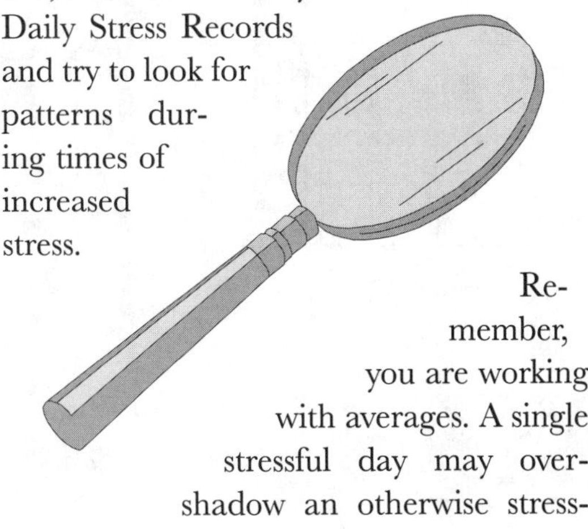

Remember, you are working with averages. A single stressful day may overshadow an otherwise stress-free week. For example, your stress level may have been going down for weeks five, six, and seven. Then, during week eight, it went up. The Stress Change Worksheet helps you to see week eight as an exception and allows you to take credit for the progress in the other weeks. This can be a reality check for measuring progress, especially if you are uncertain about the changes you have made. Do you remember Sally's Stress Change Worksheet example from Lesson Five, on page 103? Let's now look at Sally's Stress Change Worksheet for Lessons Five through Eight on page 206.

Sally's Stress Change Worksheet

You may recall that Sally is a 37-year-old homemaker from Omaha. She chose to stay at home to raise her children and take care of her family. Sally's husband, Tom, works for an insurance company and spends much of his time traveling. Sally and Tom have four children, ages 5, 8, 10, and 14 years.

Sally began the Mastering Stress Program to help her manage her stress. As we saw in Lesson Five, on page 103, Sally's overall level of stress decreased during her first four weeks in the program. However, Sally did experience natural increases in stress during that period.

Let's look at Sally's Stress Change Worksheet Example on page 206 for weeks five through eight. Sally's overall level of stress decreased during weeks five through eight. If we look closely at her worksheet, we see the times during weeks five and seven when Sally did experience high levels of stress. Toward the end of week five, Sally received a message from her son's teacher. She immediately thought the worse. She feared that her son, Michael, had gotten in

Stress Change Worksheet

Sally's Example (Weeks 5 – 8)

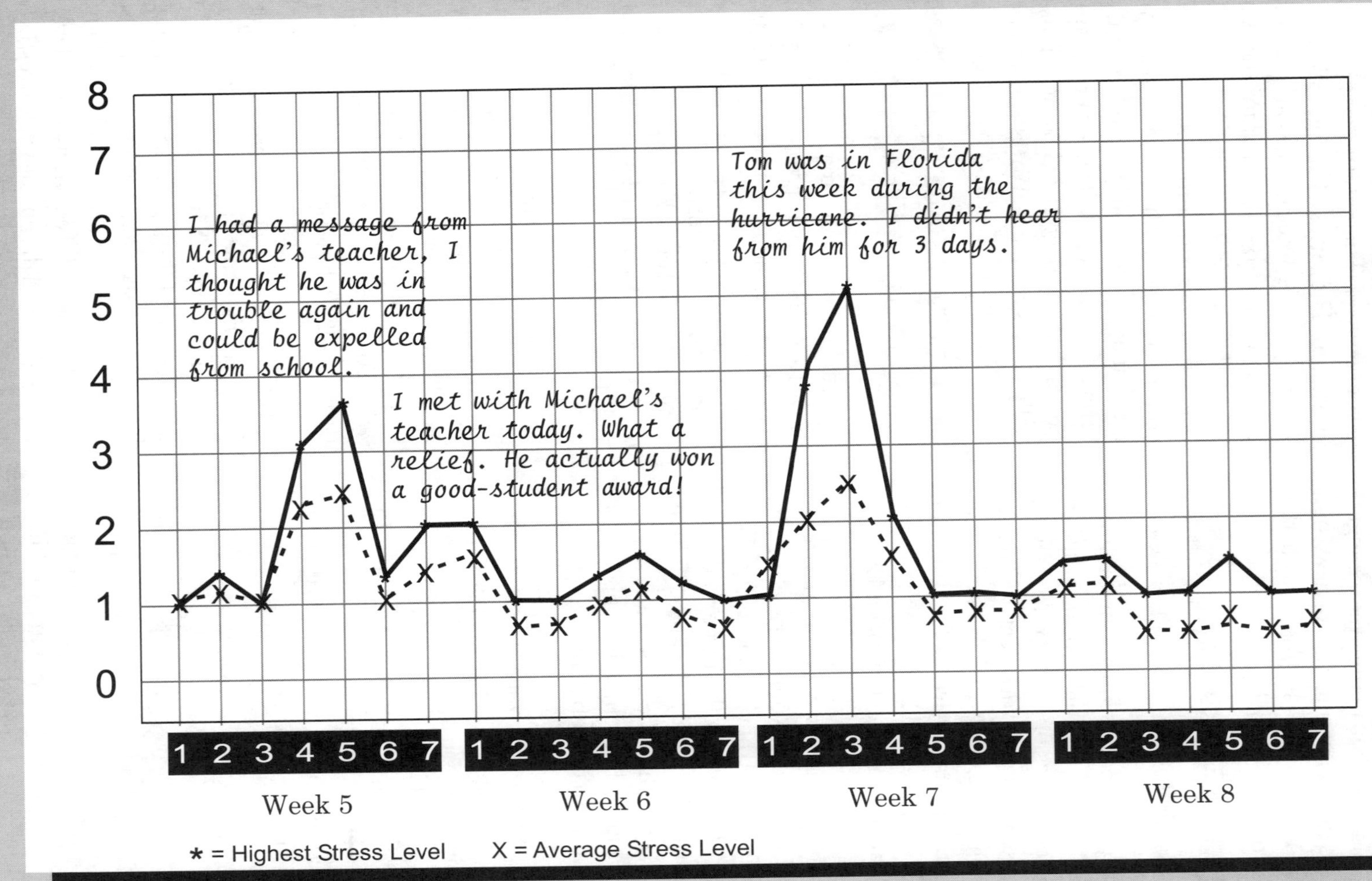

Stress Level
8
7
6
5
4
3
2
1
0
I had a message from Michael's teacher, I thought he was in trouble again and could be expelled from school.
I met with Michael's teacher today. What a relief. He actually won a good-student award!
Tom was in Florida this week during the hurricane. I didn't hear from him for 3 days.
1 2 3 4 5 6 7
Week 5
1 2 3 4 5 6 7
Week 6
1 2 3 4 5 6 7
Week 7
1 2 3 4 5 6 7
Week 8
* = Highest Stress Level
X = Average Stress Level

trouble again and was expelled from school. Sally's meeting with Michael's teacher was the following Tuesday, yet her stress level stayed high through the weekend. When she met with the teacher, she was delighted and relieved that Michael was to be awarded a good-student award. Sally was frustrated with herself for fearing the worst. She had worked through her Realistic Thinking Worksheet, yet she still allowed her thoughts to be catastrophic.

When Sally reviewed her Stress Change Worksheet, she realized two important things. First, Sally realized that she had indeed made real progress (compare her worksheet on page 206 with the one in Lesson Five on page 103). Second, she realized that she had learned techniques and skills to help her decatastrophize the teacher's message. Although she did experience stress when Michael's teacher called, she realized that it was less than it would have been before she learned these techniques. Her new stress management tools were definitely paying off.

During week seven, Sally's husband Tom was traveling in Florida. A terrible hurricane cut all communication off. Sally's stress level soared. After hearing that Tom was fine, Sally became angry with herself for allowing her stress level to get so high. Sally realized that if she had worked through the Realistic Thinking Worksheet more carefully, her stress level would not have risen so high. She was pleased that she was able to make these important discoveries on her own. Sudden increases in stress levels are natural and should be expected.

A New Stress Change Worksheet

By now, you should have completed the Stress Change Worksheets on page 29 and

page 127. These worksheets covered the first eight weeks of the Mastering Stress Program. At the end of this lesson, on page 227, we provide you with a new Stress Change Worksheet that covers the next four weeks of the program (weeks 9 through 12). We hope the review of your first eight weeks helped you identify the important progress you have made.

"Sudden increases in stress levels are natural and should be expected, but your stress management tools will help your stay in control."

Reviewing Your Physical Activity

We introduced you to the Physical Activity and Relaxation Worksheet in Lesson Five. Since then, you have been recording your physical activity and the length of time you practice deep muscle relaxation. You should have four weeks recorded on your Physical Activity and Relaxation Worksheet in Appendix F, on page 432. If you have been recording your activity and relaxation time, congratulations! If not, now is a good time to go back and complete this worksheet. This information is an important part of your stress management program. Let's now look at this worksheet and see if you can identify any patterns in

"Be sure to include programmed activities such as tennis, cycling, jogging, or dancing as part of your cumulative activity each day."

your physical activity and relaxation practice sessions.

First, let's begin with your physical activity over the last four weeks. Did you remember to track *all* of your physical activity? Remember, physical activity is not limited to a two-hour workout at the local gym. Several five-minute walks throughout the day also count. If you now park your car in the faraway spots where the people with new cars park, count the extra steps as exercise. The current exercise guidelines recommend 30 minutes of *cumulative* physical activity. This activity should be done on most days of the week, preferably every day. The key word here is "cumulative."

Be sure you include programmed activities, such as playing tennis, cycling, jogging, or dancing. Household chores like vacuuming, raking leaves, and walking the dog also count. You don't need to feel overwhelmed by the idea of exercising 30 minutes each day. All activity counts. This is why many people benefit from the use of a pedometer such as the LEARN WalkMaster, discussed on page 108, in Lesson Five.

Do you notice a pattern between your stress level and the activity you recorded each day? Were you more or less likely to exercise when you were feeling stressed? Were there certain days of the week when you were more active than others? On days that you were more active, what was your average stress level?

Reviewing Sally's Physical Activity and Relaxation

Let's look at Sally's example. Turn to page 209. Although Sally was always busy taking care of her family, she realized that she didn't get as much exercise as she thought. After realizing this, Sally tried to become more active. Looking at her physical activity record, we can see that during this four-week period, Sally was generally very active. You may notice that at the end of week five and the beginning of week seven, Sally's exercise routine slipped. Now look back at Sally's Stress Change Worksheet on page 206. Do you notice any patterns between her physical activity and her stress levels? When stress levels increase, it may be a sign to exercise. Remember that exercise can help reduce stress!

Look again at Sally's example on page 209. How consistent was Sally in her relaxation practice sessions? Can you find any patterns between her relaxation practice and her stress levels as reflected on her Stress Change Worksheet on page 206?

Reviewing Your Relaxation

Now let's look at your relaxation practice sessions. Deep muscle relaxation is a skill that requires a great deal of practice. We recommended that you practice this technique at least twice a day for 20 minutes each time. During this four-week pe-

Physical Activity and Relaxation Worksheet

Sally's Example (weeks 5–8)

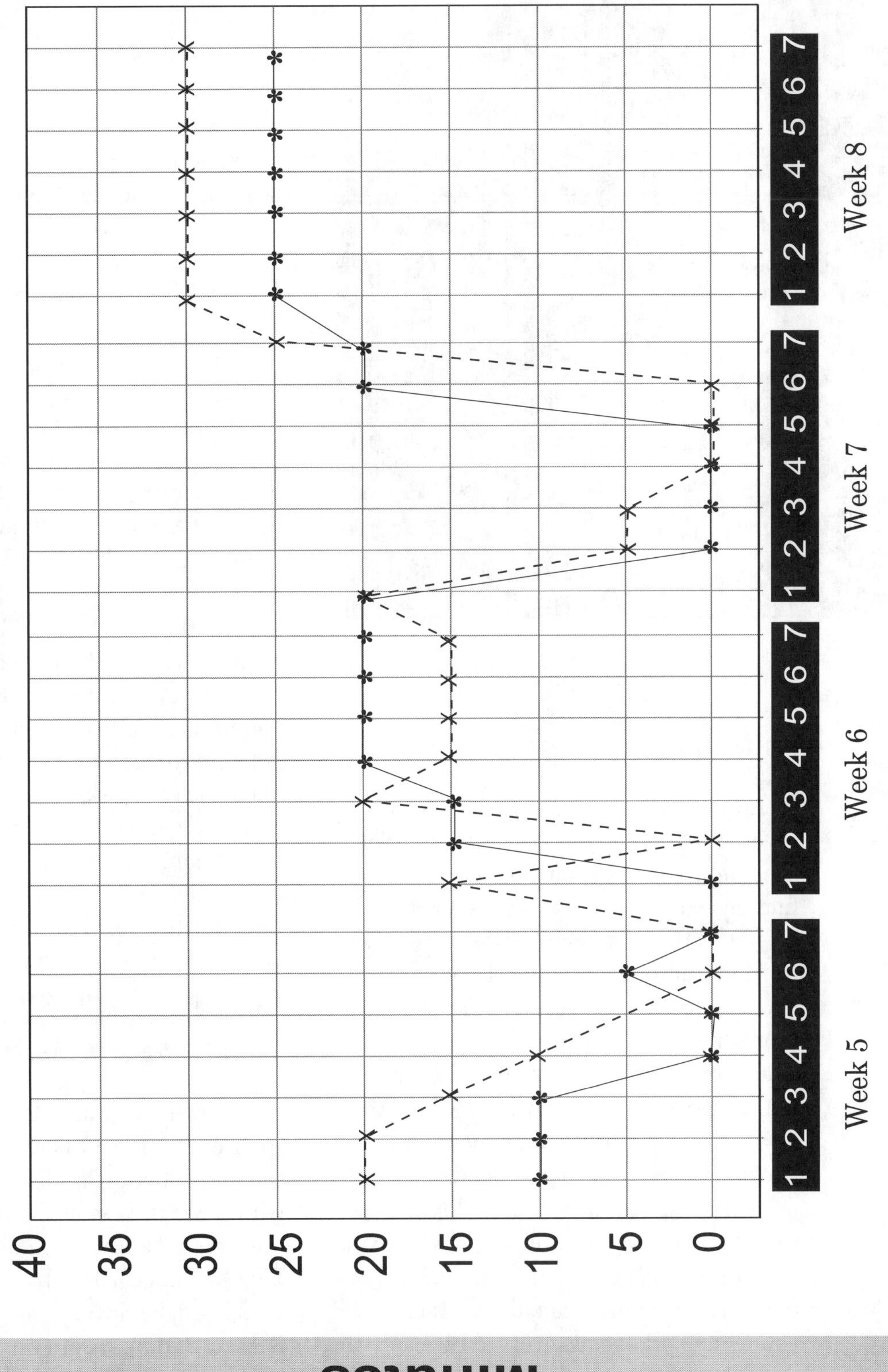

Minutes

40
35
30
25
20
15
10
5
0

1 2 3 4 5 6 7 | 1 2 3 4 5 6 7 | 1 2 3 4 5 6 7 | 1 2 3 4 5 6 7

Week 5 Week 6 Week 7 Week 8

*** = Physical Activity** **X = Relaxation Practice**

"Beethoven didn't master the piano in a few weeks or even months. He spent a lifetime practicing to become a master."

riod, we hope that you have included this practice in your daily routine. It is an important step in stress management.

Look at the relaxation portion of the Physical Activity and Relaxation Worksheet in Appendix F, on page 433. Can you find any patterns between your stress levels on your Stress Change Worksheet in Lesson Five, on page 127, and how much relaxation you practiced each day? Were you more or less likely to practice this technique when you were highly stressed? Many people forego relaxation practice when they need it most—during stressful times. Are you able to see your stress level decrease after your relaxation practice? Finally, are there certain days of the week when you were more likely to practice? Look for ways to increase your relaxation practice if you're not practicing every day. Later in this lesson, we'll show you how to make this relaxation technique portable. You will learn to use this technique anytime and anywhere to reduce stress. The more proficient you are, the better it will work for you. And the more you practice, the more proficient you become.

Now, let's look at the consistency of your relaxation practice sessions. Was your relaxation practice consistent over the four-week period or did you find yourself practicing less as the weeks progressed? You may have become bored or found that practicing twice a day was awkward. If so, don't despair. This is common among individuals learning this skill. But with practice, you'll become much better! Think of an activity or sport you have tried to master. Remember our analogy of Beethoven learning to play the piano. Practice is the key to mastering any skill.

Use the My Stress Management Program Review on page 223 to write down your review comments and the patterns you find on your Physical Activity and Relaxation (page 432) and Stress Change (page 430) Worksheets. Once you have completed the second column of the review form, use the third column to plan your goals for the next four weeks. We'll return to this program review in Lesson Fourteen to see if you have met your goals.

Comparison of Your Quality of Life Reviews

We want you now to compare your responses on your Quality of Life Review in the Introduction and Orientation Lesson with those in Lesson Eight. You may recall that you did a similar comparison in Lesson Five (see page 101). To help with your review, we have given you a Quality of Life Review Comparison on the right. Turn back to the Quality of Life Review on page 11, in the Introduction and Orientation Lesson, to complete column b. Next, turn to your Quality of Life Review on page 194, in Lesson Eight, to complete column c. Let's now compare your responses.

Record the scores from the Introduction and Orientation Lesson in column (b). In column (c), record the scores from Lesson Eight. Column (d) reflects the change in your responses as either positive (+) or negative (-). The positive numbers in column (d) mean that your quality of life has improved. The rows with negative values need more work. If you have negative numbers in any of the categories we covered, go back and review this material. Positive numbers in the categories we covered mean that you have done well and are ready to move on. Do not get discouraged with any negative numbers in categories we have not discussed. Simply note these areas for upcoming lessons.

This short review will help you measure your progress in different ways. Change comes in many forms. Let's look at the changes you have made in the past month. Most of the people who go through this program have positive numbers in at least one area.

As you review your progress, remember that these changes have occurred within a short period. You have more to look forward to in the next few weeks!

Not all changes occur at the same pace. Some aspects of your life may not have changed. Be patient, and trust that you will make more changes as we continue this journey together.

We have now finished our review of your progress in the program. We hope you have clearly identified the progress you have made. If you completed the reviews and set goals for the next four weeks, stand

Quality of Life Review Comparison

(a) Category	(b) Score from Introduction and Orientation Lesson	(c) Score from Lesson Eight	(d) Change in Scores (column c minus column b)
1. Overall mood (feelings of sadness, anxiety, happiness, etc.)			
2. Sense of self			
3. Confidence, comfort in social situations			
4. Internal dialog (self-talk)			
5. Energy level			
6. Focus and concentration			
7. Ability to manage time			
8. Relationships			
9. General health			
10. Exercise and recreation			
11. Assertiveness skills			
12. Eating habits			
13. Overall quality of life			

up and cheer for yourself. We're all cheering you on! If you skipped over this review or didn't keep the records to complete the reviews, you're missing an important part of the Mastering Stress Program. We encourage you to backup and do this review—it is important to you!

Before we conclude this lesson, we will want to help you review your progress from last week. However, since we have already devoted so much time to reviewing your progress in this lesson, we thought that you would enjoy covering some new and interesting material. If you would prefer to review your progress from last week, it's fine to jump to "Reviewing Your Expanded Realistic Thinking Worksheet," on page 220. If not, let's move onto the topic of procrastination.

Introducing Procrastination

In Lesson Two, on page 41, you learned that procrastination is a common behavior that increases stress. Procrastination may result from one or many situations. The figure below illustrates the procrastination-stress cycle. The cycle begins with an initial task that produces excitement or some stress. As stress builds, procrastination, begins to kick in. In an effort to postpone the task, other priorities are set, further increasing stress. Guilt about avoiding the task causes even more stress, leading to more procrastination and soaring stress levels.

"When procrastination becomes part of your everyday pattern of living, it can be a serious problem."

Perhaps you have had an important task that you really didn't want to do. If you're like most of us, you probably found every excuse under the sun not to do it. Suddenly, everything else became much more important. Right? The *important* task then became even more *urgent*. This most likely increased your stress. You may have become irritable to those around you at the slightest mention of the task. You may have felt a surge of stress when you thought about that horrible project you knew you had to do—sometime. If this scenario sounds familiar, you may benefit from learning important skills to help you avoid the procrastination pitfall.

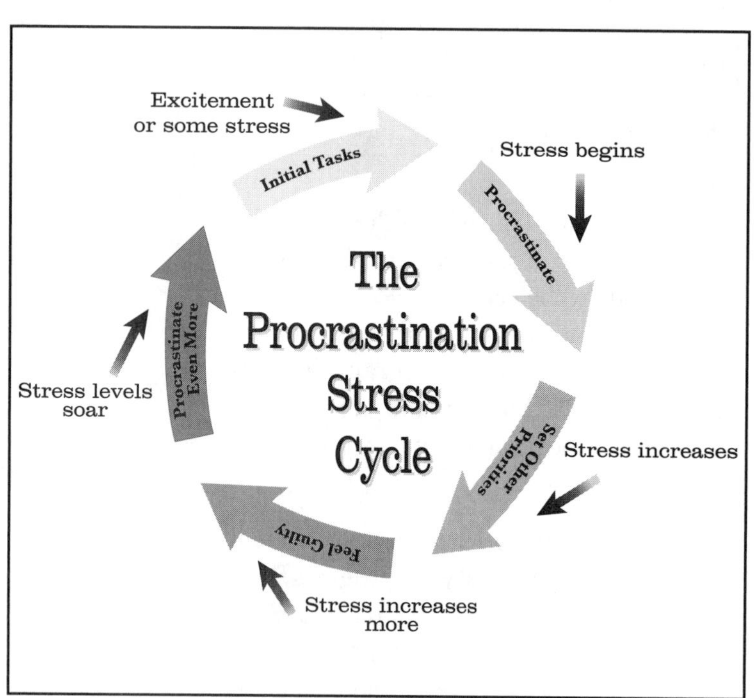

Everyone procrastinates from time to time. But when procrastination becomes part of your everyday pattern of living, it can be a serious problem. Procrastinators put off what they need to do and find something else to do to relieve their guilt. When they feel guilty, they procrastinate even more. This sets up a vicious cycle that greatly increases stress levels.

Procrastination Types

The first step in conquering the procrastination cycle is to discover why you put things off. Three primary types of procrastination exist. They include the following:

❶ **Type I procrastination.** You may dislike doing a particular task or project. This may lead to negative feelings about the task that build up over time. Common thoughts that accompany such tasks include, "I remember doing this last time and disliked everything about it. I still have plenty of time to get it done, so it can wait."

❷ **Type II procrastination.** You may expect to feel stress or anxiety about the finished product. "When I finish this, I'll be depressed. I don't want to know the final outcome." These or similar thoughts commonly occur when a person fears the worst in completing a project.

❸ **Type III procrastination.** You may not know where to begin. The more you think about the task, the longer you let it go, and the more overwhelming it seems. Common thoughts that accompany an undesirable task include, "Man, I don't even know where to begin. I'll think about it some more, and maybe I'll start tomorrow."

Let's now look at an example of the first type of procrastination.

Meet David

David is a 32-year-old accountant. He is a tax partner in a large, national public accounting firm. He is married and has two children. David's wife is a travel agent. David handles all of the household financial matters, including the preparation and filing of the annual tax returns. David works a lot of overtime during tax season. His wife, Mary, also works a lot of overtime booking her clients' summer vacations during this time of year. Being the accountant in the family, the responsibility of filing the tax returns falls on David. When April 15th finally rolls around, the thought of preparing his own tax returns is an unpleasant thought. So, each year, he files an automatic extension. When the deadline for the automatic extension comes along, David still dislikes the thought of preparing their tax returns. David and Mary's tax returns are not complicated. It takes just a few hours to prepare each year. Yet, David procrastinates year after year. On August 15th, David files yet another extension. As the *last* day to file a tax return draws nearer, David's stress level starts to climb. He continually thinks about the unpleasant task that lies ahead. When he thinks about doing the tax returns or when Mary asks him about

it, he becomes irritable and snaps at those around him. He feels guilty for not getting it done sooner.

Type I Procrastination—Disliking a Task or Project

People procrastinate for many reasons. Discomfort, anxiety, or fear may be at the heart of procrastination. One may fear that a task is too hard, uncomfortable to do, or that one lacks the skills to do a good job. This style of thinking leads to avoidance or finding other more comfortable and desirable things to do. Psychologist and researcher Dr. Albert Ellis studied the links between specific thoughts and procrastination. Let's take a closer look at some thoughts that often lead to procrastination.

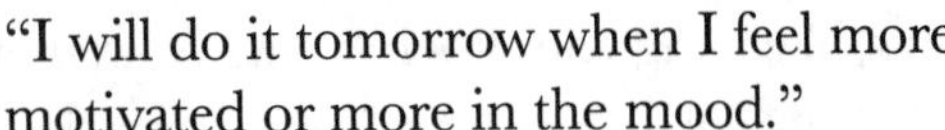

"I will do it tomorrow when I feel more motivated or more in the mood."

"It won't really matter if I put off this project, so it doesn't matter if I put off starting it."

"This task can wait until tomorrow, but my plans for today can't."

"I always procrastinate and it turns out all right, so why not do it again."

"I should be able to enjoy this day, I shouldn't have to do what I don't want to do."

"People procrastinate for many reasons. One such reason is that people may dislike a particular task so much that negative feelings build up over time."

"I don't know how to do this task properly or perfectly, so I will wait until I know how."

"It won't affect anyone if I'm late, so I'll just keep putting it off."

Many procrastinators believe that they are entitled to a life free of work and stress. Unfortunately, we all know life is not this way. So, learning skills to overcome procrastination can help you get through those unpleasant tasks and keep your stress level low. We will help you develop these important skills in upcoming lessons.

The example of David and his tax return illustrates type I procrastination, disliking a particular task or project. Some tasks, like filing your tax return, are an inevitable part of living. They have to be done. Are there tasks in your life that you simply dislike doing? Do you procrastinate doing these tasks? If so, write these tasks down on the worksheet titled "Tasks I Dislike and Procrastinate About Doing" on page 224. For now, complete the first two columns. In the first column, list those tasks you dislike doing. In the second column, write down what you dislike about the tasks.

David's Example

On page 215, we have provided an example of David's procrastination worksheet for preparing his tax return. Notice how David challenged his dislikes, then provided stepwise goals for completing the tax return. Use this example as a guide to help you complete your worksheet on page 224. In the next two lessons, we will help you develop skills to overcome the other two types of procrastination. Until then, monitor your thoughts related to putting off things and try to categorize them into one of three classifications of procrastination discussed earlier. Try to record your *specific* thoughts.

Remember that when all is said and done, we all have tasks that we dislike doing. We just have to roll up our sleeves and get them done. Also, remember that you can *choose* to like or dislike something. If we attack these unpleasant tasks with a specific plan, we can avoid much unnecessary stress. You may even learn to like doing something you used to dislike doing.

Overcoming Type I Procrastination

Below are some steps you can follow to help you overcome this type of procrastination and save yourself unnecessary stress.

Step 1: Admit that you don't like doing the task or project and that you often procrastinate when faced with the task. Recognizing and admitting

Tasks I Dislike and Procrastinate About Doing

(David's Example)

Task	What I Dislike (Why I Procrastinate)	Challenging My Dislikes	Stepwise Goals
Preparing tax returns	1. I'm tired of doing tax returns all the time. 2. It takes too much time. 3. I'd rather be doing other things. 4. I still have time to complete them.	1. I enjoy my work as a tax accountant. 2. Our tax returns aren't really that difficult once I get started. It doesn't really take that much time. 3. I can still do other things I enjoy and get the returns done—they HAVE to be done sometime. 4. The extension does give me more time, but I really get stressed thinking about getting them done.	1. Beginning with February 1st, I'll set aside one hour each Tuesday and Thursday evening at home to work on my taxes. 2. For each hour I spend during the week on my tax return, I'll give myself a free hour on the weekend to do whatever I want; Janet will help me with this. 3. If I don't spend two hours a week on the tax return, I will get up early Saturday and Sunday morning to make up for it. 4. If I get my tax return completed and filed by April 15th, I'll take a day of vacation by May 1st and do something fun.

that you are procrastinating is an important step. It's okay to dislike doing some things in life. So, go ahead and admit it to yourself.

Step 2: Write down the reason(s) why you dislike the task and why you procrastinate. You may think of a single reason or many reasons.

Step 3: Challenge your dislikes and the reasons for putting things off. Sure, some things in life are unpleasant, and we can all think of a thousand other things we'd rather be doing. However, for each unpleasant task, we can usually think of a positive reason to go ahead and get it done. On the worksheet on page 224, challenge each of your dislikes that you listed in the first column. In the third column, write a *positive* reason for getting the job done quickly.

Step 4: Set specific stepwise goals for completing the task. An example may be to work on the task 30 minutes in the evening every Monday, Wednesday, and Thursday. You may also want to make plans or pacts with friends or relatives to help you accomplish the task. Finally, reward yourself for meeting your goals. In the last column of the worksheet on page 224, list stepwise goals for each task you listed in column one.

The Importance of Good Nutrition

You may be wondering why three psychologists are talking about nutrition in a stress management program. The answer is simple. Nutrition is a key component of good health, and good health is a key ingredient of stress management. Poor nutrition can lead to both physical and psychological ill health. In the next lesson, we'll give you a short quiz to help you assess your diet. For now, let's look at the components of a healthy diet.

The U.S. Department of Agriculture (USDA) and the Department of Health and Human Services (HHS) have developed researched-based dietary guidelines for Americans. Following these guidelines will help you achieve and maintain optimal health. Let's review these seven guidelines.

❶ **Eat a variety of foods.** This strategy will help you get the energy, protein, vitamins, minerals, and fiber you need for good health. Remember, the healthier your body, the better able you are to cope with stressful situations.

❷ **Maintain a healthy weight.** Over one-half of the U.S. adult population is overweight or obese. Weight-related problems and stress go hand-in-hand. The relationship between stress and overweight is interesting and complex. It is not clear if stress is a cause or consequence of overweight. However, maintaining a healthy weight will help reduce your chances of having high blood pressure, heart disease, a stroke, certain cancers, and type II diabetes (the most common kind of diabetes).

❸ **Choose a diet low in fat, saturated fat, and cholesterol.** Reducing fat in your diet helps to reduce the risk of heart attack and certain types of cancer.

❹ **Choose a diet with plenty of vegetables, fruits, and grain products.** Fruits, vegetables, and grain products provide vitamins, minerals, fiber, and complex carbohydrates that your body needs. These foods are also low in fat, and choosing these foods can help keep your fat intake low.

❺ **Use sugars only in moderation.** Diets that are high in sugars can add many unwanted calories to your diet and provide few nutrients. Moreover, sugars can contribute to tooth decay.

❻ **Use salt and sodium only in moderation.** Studies have linked high-sodium diets to high blood pressure.

❼ **If you drink alcoholic beverages, do so in moderation.** Alcohol can easily add many calories to your daily diet, but almost no nutrition. Some people turn to alcohol when faced with stressful events in their lives. Not only can this strategy increase a person's risk for overweight, but it also can lead to other health problems, including addiction, and can cause accidents.

We will talk more about nutrition in upcoming lessons. For now, we want you to be aware of the components of a healthy diet.

Nutrition and Stress Management

What you eat can affect how you feel, and eating well will help your body handle stress more effectively. A healthy body responds better to the inevitable stressors in life. Good nutrition is important to maintaining good health.

"What you eat affects how you feel, and eating well will help your body handle stress."

Each time you face a challenge or a threat (a stressor), your body produces adrenaline. Adrenaline is a stimulant that energizes your body to handle challenges and threats in your life. This needed energy comes from the nutrients in your body, and these nutrients come from the foods that you eat. Too much stress and a poor diet can simply drain your body of valuable energy, leaving you fatigued, apathetic, irritable, and susceptible to a variety of diseases of a weakened body. Your body may be unable to handle additional stress.

Besides following the USDA and HHS dietary guidelines, avoiding foods that aggravate your stress response system may be helpful. For example, caffeine can produce a stimulant effect similar to adrenaline. Caffeine is found in many foods and drinks including coffee, tea, chocolate, and sodas (especially cola drinks). Too much caffeine can have the same effect on your body as too much stress. Limiting your caffeine intake, especially when you are under stress, is a good idea.

Alcohol can also aggravate stress because of its depressant effect. People often rely on caffeine to pick them up and alco-

"The red blobs are your red blood cells. The white blobs are your white blood cells. The brown blobs are coffee. We need to talk."

hol to bring them back down again. Refined flours and sugars can also aggravate your stress-response system. Eating plenty of complex carbohydrates like fruits, vegetables, and grain products is recommended by dietary professionals and the Food Guide Pyramid. Complex carbohydrates are quickly converted into glucose (your body's energy source) to provide your body with a good supply of energy.

It is also important to remember to make certain that your body has enough vitamin C, found in fruits (especially citrus fruits) and vegetables. Your adrenal glands (which produce adrenaline) use vitamin C during periods of physical stress.

The key to maximizing your nutrition for stress management, has two components. First, avoid foods that aggravate your stress response. Second, increase your body's stores of nutrients that are need to handle stressful situations. We'll discuss these issues in upcoming lessons.

How Your Family Can Help

Families can be a terrific source of help and support for your stress management program. They can also be a hindrance! Harmony between you and your family, however, requires a special effort from all involved. Communication is the first step. You must take the first step and talk to your family members. Let each person know exactly how you feel about reducing your stress and how they can help. This can sometimes be difficult, yet it is a necessary process. You must clearly express your needs.

A similar responsibility falls upon your family members. You may only have a cursory notion of how your family feels about your stress. Encourage your family members to express their feelings to you openly and honestly. This process will likely give you much relief because everyone's feelings are expressed. Once this occurs, open and positive communication can help provide ideas for everyone involved as to how they can help.

Your family can support you as you work on achieving your stress management goals. As you begin to assert yourself more, let your family know that you may be asking for additional support. This may mean delegating more responsibility. It may take a while for your family members to adjust to the change. Don't worry! This is a normal reaction to the new situation they are facing.

If you have not already done so, now may be a good time to meet with your family members and discuss your stress management program. Let them know your needs and expectations. Think about specific ways that your family can provide support. For example, you may want to let them know just how important it is for you to have time alone twice a day to practice your relaxations skills. You may need help with household chores. Let each family member know how he or she can help. You may not need any direct help from family members. Yet, communicating the fact that you may need additional time to yourself to do weekly reading and homework assignments is still important. Remember to be direct. Tell your family how they can help you and include them in your change process. In return, ask what you can do for your family.

"Families can be a great source of help and support, but you must take the first step and talk to them."

More on Relaxation

We introduced deep muscle relaxation in Lesson Five, on page 112, and in Lesson Seven, on page 147, we gave you some tips on improving your relaxation techniques. By now, you have more than four weeks of practicing these techniques. Are you finding it easier to relax while sitting in a comfortable chair in a quiet room? If not, don't worry. This is not a contest; you do not have to take the next step right away. Continue practicing the deep muscle relaxation techniques. You may also find it helpful to go back to Lesson Five, on page 112, and reread the section on deep muscle relaxation. This will be very important in the next lesson as you learn to take this relaxation technique with you.

Identifying Low-Level Tension

One main reason for learning relaxation is to enable you to identify tension in your daily life as early as possible. This is better than waiting until it turns into a full-blown headache or other physical problems. Until now, we have had you focus your relaxation exercises on big, obvious changes in tension. You have been tensing your muscles to three-quarters of their maximum, then flopping them to zero tension. In real life, muscle tension is rarely as obvious as this. Consequently, learning to identify tension at a much lower and subtle level is important. Learning this stress management technique is a skill that will allow you to lower tension before it gets out of hand.

As you practice your deep muscle relaxation techniques this week, tense each muscle group three times instead of twice. The first time, tense the muscles to three-quarters, then drop the muscle down to zero tension, just as you have been doing. The second time, tense the muscles only to about one-half of your maximum (moderate tension). Then drop the muscles down to zero tension. The third time, tense the muscles to only one-quarter of their maximum tension (mild tension) before flopping them to zero. While you are holding your muscles at the one-quarter level and breathing normally, try to think about all the times during the day when you feel this degree of tension.

The more you practice with these varying levels of tension, the sooner you will start to notice when your muscles tense up during the day. You will begin to notice *mild*

tension. This is important because mild tension is much easier to lower than higher levels of tension. The earlier you notice tension, the sooner you can do something about it.

Reviewing Your Expanded Realistic Thinking Worksheet

Let's now take a few minutes to review your progress from last week. Last week, you began challenging the probability of your initial thoughts of stressful events by using the Expanded Realistic Thinking Worksheet on page 199. In addition to assessing probability estimates, this expanded worksheet helped you challenge the likelihood of dire consequences ("What would happen if my initial thought actually occurred?"). The answer was your initial consequence of your initial thought. You then wrote this consequence in the last column. In the next row, below your initial thought, you wrote the consequence from the preceding line.

You then started the whole process over, as if that were your initial thought. In other words, you challenged the consequence the way you challenged your initial thought. You then asked yourself, "What would happen if this new possibility (my previous consequence) really occurred? In answer to this, you came up with another consequence. You recorded it, then started a separate line and challenged that consequence as an initial thought. You kept this process going until you reached zero emotion or could not think of another consequence.

In doing this exercise, did you find that a single event can produce a page or more of thoughts? Many of our clients find this to be the case. Were you able to challenge these thoughts and arrive at a place of zero emotion or no more consequences? If this exercise seems a bit overwhelming, don't worry. This too is a skill that requires much practice; in time, you can challenge your thoughts and beliefs more effectively. As you do so, you should also experience a reduction in the number of possible consequences.

You may have also noticed that although you said, "The consequences would not be that great," you may not have really believed it in your heart. Don't get discouraged, this happens at first. In time, you will actually start believing the words you are writing (or saying). Eventually, you can do most of the challenging in your head and may not have to write down all your beliefs. Once again, practice is the key.

Lesson Review

The main focus of this lesson was a midway review of your progress. We hope this review was helpful. Were you surprised by your progress? Are you motivated and inspired to continue to work hard? Did you uncover any areas that need additional work? The lesson then focused on the topic of procrastination. We discussed type I procrastination—disliking a task or project and provided you with some strategies to overcome putting things off. We talked about the importance of good nutrition and its importance in stress management. Seven dietary guidelines were discussed that were designed to help you optimize your diet. We then turned our attention to your family and how they can help you with your stress management program. Several strategies were suggested to help you benefit from family involvement. We discussed a new three-step deep muscle relaxation technique that will help you recognize small levels of tension in your muscles. We concluded this lesson with a review of your progress from last week. Congratulations, you have made it through another lesson!

This Week's Assignment

During this next week, continue to keep your Daily Stress Record and your Time Investment Worksheet. Blank forms for this lesson are provided on pages 225 and 226. Remember to use the information from your Daily Stress Records to complete the new Stress Change Worksheet on page 227 and the new Physical Activity and Relaxation Worksheet in Appendix F, on page 433. Keep a copy of the Expanded Realistic Thinking Worksheet with you and use it when you feel your stress level increasing. A blank copy is provided on page 228. Also, monitor your thoughts related to procrastination this week. Thoughts of procrastination may show up on your Daily Stress Record or your Time Investment Worksheet. Keep an eye open for them. Make several copies of the worksheet titled, "Tasks I Dislike and Procrastinate About Doing," on page 224, to help you overcome Type I procrastination.

"Life is stressful. It's not easy juggling marriage, career and a full TV schedule!"

One final note. Take time this week to reflect upon your progress. Reward yourself for all the hard work you are doing.

Knowledge Review

T F 67. If you have not made significant changes in reducing your stress so far, it is unlikely that you can reduce your stress.

T F 68. The primary purpose of reviewing your progress is to help you to see all the progress you have made since beginning the Mastering Stress Program.

T F 69. Change is a process and takes time.

T F 70. The three types of procrastination refer to a dislike for doing a particular task, fearing the end, and not knowing where to begin.

T F 71. Procrastinators often believe that life should be easy.

T F 72. One strategy to overcome procrastination is to challenge the thoughts that lead to putting things off.

T F 73. Nutrition is not really all that important for stress management.

T F 74. Families are rarely a source of help and support for individuals in a stress management program.

T F 75. It is not really important to learn to identify low levels of tension in your muscles.

(Answers in Appendix C, page 415)

"We're all being sent to auctioneering classes. If we learn to talk faster, we should be able to accomplish more at meetings."

My Stress Management Program Review

Worksheet/Activity	Weeks 5–8	My Goals for Weeks 9–12
Stress Change Worksheet	**Review comments:** **Patterns uncovered:**	**Goals for week 9:** **Goals for week 10:** **Goals for week 11:** **Goals for week 12:**
Physical Activity	**Review comments:** **Patterns uncovered:**	**Goals for week 9:** **Goals for week 10:** **Goals for week 11:** **Goals for week 12:**
Relaxation	**Review comments:** **Patterns uncovered:**	**Goals for week 9:** **Goals for week 10:** **Goals for week 11:** **Goals for week 12:**

Tasks I Dislike and Procrastinate About Doing

Task	What I Dislike (Why I Procrastinate)	Challenging My Dislikes	Stepwise Goals

Daily Stress Record—Lesson Nine

Name:________________________________ **Week of:**____________

Date	Average Stress Level	Highest Stress Level	Time of Highest Stress Level	Stressful Event Associated with Highest Stress Level

My Physical Activity and Relaxation Record

Day of the Week	Physical Activity Record		Relaxation Record[1]	
	Activity	Minutes	Time of Day	Minutes
Monday				
Tuesday				
Wednesday				
Thursday				
Friday				
Saturday				
Sunday				

[1] **Remember to tense each muscle group three times—the first at ¾ of maximum tension; the second at ½ of maximum tension; and the third at ¼ of maximum tension.**

Time Investment Worksheet					
					Today's Date:
Time	**Activity**	**Urgent**	**Important**	**Stress Level (0–8)**	**Thoughts**
12:00–1:00 am					
1:00–2:00 am					
2:00–3:00 am					
3:00–4:00 am					
4:00–5:00 am					
5:00–6:00 am					
6:00–7:00 am					
7:00–8:00 am					
8:00–9:00 am					
9:00–10:00 am					
10:00–11:00 am					
11:00–11:59 am					
12:00–1:00 pm					
1:00–2:00 pm					
2:00–3:00 pm					
3:00–4:00 pm					
4:00–5:00 pm					
5:00–6:00 pm					
6:00–7:00 pm					
7:00–8:00 pm					
8:00–9:00 pm					
9:00–10:00 pm					
10:00–11:00 pm					
11:00–11:59 pm					

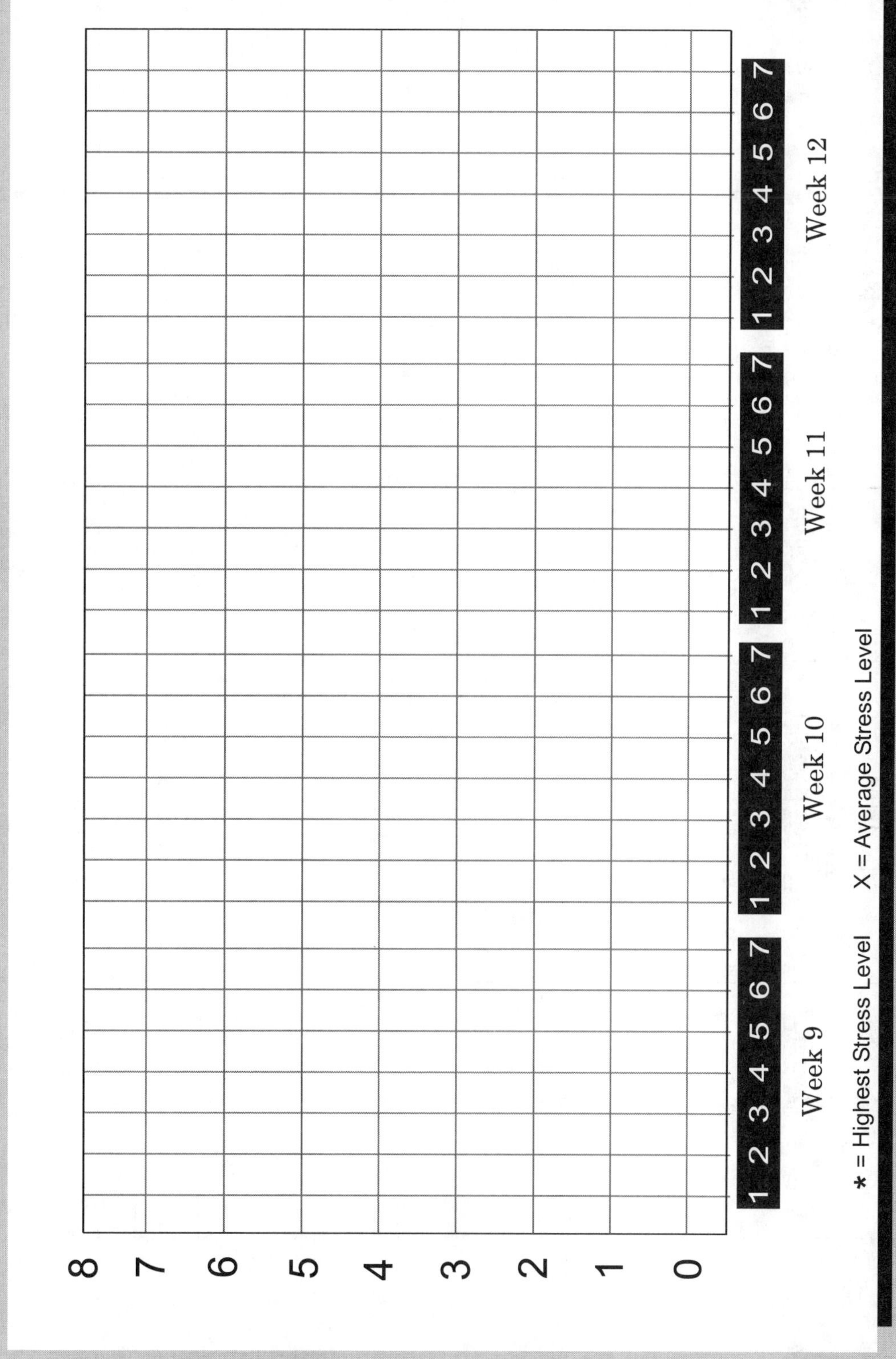

Stress Change Worksheet
(Weeks 9 – 12)
Stress Level
8
7
6
5
4
3
2
1
0
1 2 3 4 5 6 7
Week 9
1 2 3 4 5 6 7
Week 10
1 2 3 4 5 6 7
Week 11
1 2 3 4 5 6 7
Week 12
* = Highest Stress Level
X = Average Stress Level

Expanded Realistic Thinking Worksheet

Today's Date:

(1) Event	(2) Initial Thought	(3) Evidence (How Do I Know?)	(4) Initial/Realistic Probability	(5) Initial/Revised Stress Level (0–8 Scale)	(6) Consequence

Lesson Ten

Here we are at the beginning of Lesson Ten. We have covered much material in just nine short weeks. Many more exciting topics lie ahead. During the past nine weeks, you have added many new tools to your stress management toolbox. Like any craftsperson, you have probably found certain tools that work best for you in certain situations. We'll add more tools in this lesson. Let's begin by continuing our discussion on procrastination.

More on Procrastination

In Lesson Nine, on page 212, we introduced the topic of procrastination and its role in increasing stress. Three types of procrastination were introduced in last week's discussion, and we took an in-depth look at type I procrastination—a dislike for doing a task or project. Let's now focus on type II procrastination, and see what happens when individuals procrastinate by putting things off because they fear the end.

Type II Procrastination—Fearing the End

Some people put things off because they fear the outcome. They don't necessarily mind doing the task itself. They simply do not want to face the perceived consequences after they finish. Does this sound familiar to you? Thoughts of type II procrastination may include, "I won't be happy when I'm finished," "I will feel more stress when I finish," or "No matter how hard I try, my supervisor will not like my results." People in this situation put things off, believing that their delay tactics will reduce or eliminate their stress. Unfortunately, this is not so. In fact, this often leads to even higher levels of stress and can send a person's stress level soaring. The interesting thing about this type of procrastination is that the person fears a *perceived* outcome. In these situations, the *actual* outcome is usually far less stressful than the individual's *perceived* outcome. How often has your perception of an event been more stressful than the actual event itself? You can probably see how realistic thinking can help overcome this type of procrastination. Vicki provides a good example of how type II procrastination can increase stress.

Meet Vicki

Vicki is a 28-year-old, second-grade teacher in a suburban neighborhood of Chicago. She is married and has a 4-year-old daughter. Her husband, Jack, is an attorney in a large law firm in downtown Chicago. Vicki enjoys the professionalism of her job, and she is always concerned about her appearance. Almost every weekend, she goes shopping for new clothes. Vicki and Jack keep separate checking accounts, but they have agreed on who will pay certain household expenses. Each month, when Vicki's bank statement arrives, a blanket of fear spreads over her, and her stress level soars. She buries her bank statement at the bottom of her mail pile, hoping that it will somehow magically disappear. Still, she knows it is there!

"When people put things off, their delay tactics usually create more stress rather than reducing it."

Vicki puts off opening her bank statement because she doesn't want to balance her account. She fears that she has overdrawn her account by spending too much on clothes. If she overspends, she will have to ask her husband to cover her overdrawn account. To Vicki, asking Jack for money would be unbearable.

Overcoming Type II Procrastination

Do you find yourself thinking or behaving like Vicki? If so, can you think of some stress management techniques you have learned that may help you overcome this type of procrastination? In particular, the realistic thinking techniques can be very helpful. Consider, for example, an important task or job you have to do, and you fear that no matter how hard you try, your effort won't be good enough. How likely it is that you will do a poor job? Even if you do a poor job, so what? How bad will that really be? Also, consider how realistic your thoughts are about the perceived outcome. Consider all of the evidence and weigh it carefully. Let's listen in as Vicki and her counselor talk about her fear of balancing her bank account. Follow along the discussion by looking at Vicki's example Expanded Realistic Thinking Worksheet on page 231.

Vicki's Counseling Session

Vicki — "Every month when my bank statement arrives, my stress level almost goes through the roof. I hide it at the bottom of my mail pile, somehow hoping it will go away, but it never does. I hide my statement to avoid looking at it and having to balance my account."

Counselor — "Can you please share with me why it is difficult for you to balance your account?"

Vicki — "Well, I spent too much money this month on clothes, and I just

Expanded Realistic Thinking Worksheet

(Vicki's Example)

Today's Date:

(1) Event	(2) Initial Thought	(3) Evidence (How Do I Know?)	(4) Initial/Realistic Probability	(5) Initial/Revised Stress Level (0–8 Scale)	(6) Consequence
Balancing my bank statement at the end of the month.	I have overdrawn my account by spending too much money on clothes.	I bought a lot of clothes this month. But, I haven't overdrawn my account over the past year.	100% / 30%	7 / 5	I can't manage my money.
I can't manage my money.	This would be horrible.	Jack would look terrible if the bank called him to tell him that I had overdrawn my account.	80% / 70%	5 / 4	I would be a horrible, irresponsible person.
I would be a horrible, irresponsible person.	I would have to ask Jack for help.	Jack would have to help me cover the overdraft. I could get Jack to help set up an overdraft protection plan at the bank. I've helped Jack with problems before, I'm sure he would be happy to help me, if I would only ask him.	60% / 20%	4 / 3	Jack would need to help me manage my money.
Jack would need to help me manage my money.	This wouldn't be so bad!				

know that my account will be overdrawn."

Counselor "Is there a chance that you won't be overdrawn? In the past year, how often has your account been overdrawn?"

Vicki "No way, I know that I spent too much money last month. But, now that I think about it, I haven't been overdrawn at all during the last year. This month is different; I'm sure it's overdrawn, and well, you know what that means."

Counselor "What does it mean to you?"

Vicki Well, it means I am unable to manage money."

Counselor "Really? You just said that you have not overdrawn your account during the past year. Doesn't this sound like you manage your money quite well?"

Vicki "Well yes, but this time seems more important!"

Counselor "It sounds as if you are being a bit unfair to yourself by thinking you have overdrawn your account this month, especially since you really don't know whether or not you are overdrawn. Now tell me, why is the possibility of overdrawing your account this month so important?"

Vicki "I guess that I manage my money quite well most of the time. Jack just got a promotion at work, and one of his new clients is the bank that handles my account. If I overdraw the account, he'll know right away, and that would make him look bad."

Counselor "Let's step back a minute and look at all of the evidence. How likely do you think it really is that you are unable to manage your money?"

Vicki "Oh, I guess around 30 percent."

Counselor "Okay now, let's assume that it was determined that you were not able to manage your money. What would that mean?"

Vicki "That would be terrible! It would mean that I was a horrible, irresponsible person."

Counselor "What do you mean? How could that make you a horrible or irresponsible person?"

Vicki "Well, I would have to ask Jack for money to cover my account and that would be horrible!"

Counselor "Has Jack ever needed any kind of assistance from you in all your years of marriage?"

Vicki "Well, yes, several times, but not for money."

Counselor "When Jack needed your help, did you accuse him of being a worthless, irresponsible person, as you just did yourself?"

Vicki — "Certainly not. Jack is human like everyone else. When he asked for help I was happy to be there for him, and actually, was even delighted that he asked for *my* help."

Counselor — "It sounds like you would feel a lot better if you treated yourself as well as you did Jack."

Vicki — "You're right, I never thought of it that way. Maybe I wouldn't be horrible if I needed help managing my money."

Counselor — "Also, working on your spending is something you could work on if you wanted to. Jack may be happy to help you if you asked him to. You could also check with your bank about setting up some kind of overdraft protection. Let's now get back to your original belief: would you be a horrible person if you were not able to manage your money?"

Vicki — "I guess I wouldn't be horrible. I would just be someone who needed a little help with spending money on clothes. Perhaps I could ask Jack and not be too uncomfortable. I could also ask for tips on how to better manage my spending."

Stress and Eating

The relationship between stress and eating is both interesting and complex. Many overweight people report that they eat when they feel stressed. Food is often used as a source of comfort for these individuals. For some, eating helps distract them from the stressful feelings. For others, eating is a long-standing habit that is triggered by negative moods. No matter what the mechanism, these individuals eat more when they feel stressed.

For yet another group of people, stress can have the opposite effect; they stop eating. This behavior can lead to a host of other health problems. Inadequate nutrition can affect your immune system, weakening your body physically and tire you mentally. In Lesson Four, on page 80, we discussed how your body physically responds to stress. Having a well-nourished body is an important stress management technique. But, eating too much and becoming overweight can increase stress.

To better understand the relationship of stress and eating, we have to know whether

stress causes eating or vice versa. Unfortunately, little research exists in this area. We do know that some people may eat when they feel highly stressed. But, if eating makes them feel guilty, ashamed, or unhappy, additional stress may result. This additional stress can, in turn, lead to even more eating, and the vicious cycle continues. For the person wanting to lose weight, the Mastering Stress Program may be helpful. It may be even more helpful for long-term weight maintenance. However, if you have difficult with weight management and need to lose weight, we highly recommend that you obtain a copy of *The LEARN Program for Weight Management 2000,* written by Dr. Kelly Brownell of Yale University. You can order a copy of this manual by calling toll free 1–888–LEARN–41 or by logging onto the Internet site at www.TheLifeStyleCompany.com.

Although the exact relationship between stress and eating may not be clear, one thing is certain: eating a healthy and balanced diet, without overeating, is a powerful stress management tool.

More on Good Nutrition

In Lesson Nine, on page 216, we introduced you to the dietary guidelines for Americans. Following these simple guidelines can help you achieve and maintain good health and less stress. In Lesson Eleven, on page 263, we will introduce you to the Food Guide Pyramid. The pyramid is a useful tool to help guide you in making healthy dietary choices. Providing a comprehensive healthy eating plan is beyond the scope of this program, yet we believe good nutrition is important component of a stress management program. If you have not already done so, we suggest that you obtain a copy of *The LEARN Healthy Eating and Calorie Guide* to help you optimize your diet. Ordering information can be found in the Supplemental Resources and Ordering Information in the back of this manual. How does your current diet rate? To get an idea about how good your diet is, take a few minutes to rate your diet. This is a fun exercise and provides valuable insight into your eating habits.

Rating Your Diet

The Rating Your Diet Quiz is on page 234, in Appendix G. This quiz was developed by the Center for Science in the Public Interest and published in the *Nutrition Action Healthletter.* Take a few minutes now to complete the quiz and score your answers. We will have you take this quiz again, later in the program, to see how your diet has improved.

Better diets will receive higher scores on this quiz. By taking the quiz, you will be able to see what choices for each question contribute to or subtract from the overall total score. Just taking this quiz can be educational because it may help provide new ideas for healthy food choices. You will have a chance later in the program to take the quiz again and compare your scores. Good luck with the quiz!

Prediction Testing

We hope that by now the question, "How likely is it?" automatically comes to mind when a stressful thought crosses your mind. You'll recall that the purpose of asking yourself this question is to assign the answer a realistic probability of coming true. Taking into account as much realistic evidence as possible is an important first step in answering the question, "How likely is it?" Many of our clients have trouble when they first begin weighing *all* of the evidence for or against their initial stressful thought. They often focus on the negative and ignore the positive evidence. To help overcome this tendency, we suggest a technique called prediction testing. Don't let the term scare you; it's quite simple and very helpful. This is how it works.

In prediction testing, you first predict what you *think* will happen in a given situation. Then you compare your prediction with what *really* happened. As you do this repeatedly, you will find an abundance of realistic evidence. Let's look at an example.

Assume that you have a report to prepare for work. You will be presenting the report to a committee of your peers next week. At first, you feel excited about the assignment. But then, you begin to think about the presentation and get nervous. Your stress begins to increase. How do you confront these stressful thoughts?

The first step is to identify your thoughts. Once you identify three or four stressful thoughts about the assignment, challenge each one. Consider the following predictions:

1. "I will forget my material."
2. "I will sound as if I don't know what I'm talking about."
3. "I will say something wrong."
4. "No one will like me."

Now comes the prediction testing. After you give the report, think about what actually happened. Did your predictions about what you feared would happen, actually come about? Did you, in fact, forget anything? Did you sound convincing? Did you say something that was wrong? Did anyone say that they didn't like you? You can an-

"In prediction testing, you first predict what you think will happen. Then you compare your prediction with what really happened."

swer the first question by looking at your notes. Another way to assess the outcome is to ask for input from those who read the report and attended the meeting. Ask someone you know and trust to be objective and honest with you. Don't seek praise, applause, or a ticker-tape parade down Madison Avenue. You want genuine, honest feedback.

Getting honest answers to these questions gives you valuable, realistic evidence. Be prepared because sometimes the evidence can be negative. If a co-worker tells you that you could have sounded more sure of yourself, you may feel uncomfortable or even angry for a moment. Yet, this input can be very useful. So, use the information to your advantage. Ask more questions to find out the basis of the person's observations. Be specific. You may ask, "What did I say or not say that gave you this impression?" Also, ask the person what you could have done to sound more confident. Did you say "ummmm" too many times? Did you stare at your notes instead of making eye contact with the audience? These problems are easy to correct once you know about them. Some of the most brilliant people we know are also the most humble. They genuinely seek input on how to improve what they do. Do you remember our discussion in Lesson Two, on page 46, about self-awareness, and how the more self-aware you are, the better choices you will make in life? This is a perfect example. Discussing your report with your co-workers helps you become more aware of your performance. When you solicit this type of input, be sure to gather information from more than just one person. This will help you get a clearer and more objective viewpoint.

Continue to challenge your thoughts about the evidence. What if your report didn't sound like the State-of-the-Union Address. "What will really happen if you didn't sound completely convincing?" Not much, right? Chances are that those who attended the meeting will forget your demeanor and remember the topic you discussed and the important points you made. But, if you find yourself making negative predictions about your presentation, such as, "Because I didn't sound convincing, my supervisor won't approve my proposals," you can test them as well. Right? If your proposals are approved, you have overestimated the significance of not sounding sure of yourself. If not, ask your supervisor for feedback on why your proposals were not accepted. The reasons may have nothing to do with your report or presentation.

Prediction testing is not restricted to work-related issues. This technique is very helpful to test your beliefs about everyday events, including personal and professional relationships. In these situations, collecting objective evidence may be a little more difficult. With a little creativity, you can come up with some terrific ideas.

Our experience suggests that most of the evidence you are likely to collect from prediction testing will be positive. You spoke clearly, not too fast, and not too slow. You got the statistics right. Everyone liked your charts. And, your prediction that you would forget your material did not come true. Look at this evidence and remember it. The next time you are asked to give a report, you have much evidence to suggest that you will do just fine. This realization can keep your stress level under control.

In the next lesson, we will continue our discussion of prediction testing and provide a more formalized approach. We introduce the topic here so that you can be thinking about upcoming events where you may be predicting negative consequences. You will be introduced to the Prediction Testing Worksheet in the next lesson.

Conquering Negative Events

Life is not always a bed of roses. At times in your life, bad things will happen. As with other events in your life, the "event" does not cause the stress. Your thoughts about the event and how you respond to the event determine how much stress you feel. When this happens, remember that the goal is not to eliminate stress. Your goal is to be the master of stress and not vice versa.

Your supervisor may ask you to redo a report; your child may fall off a swing and break his or her arm; a friend or loved one may die; your spouse may ask for a divorce; you may lose your job and have no money. When we think realistically, we accept the inevitable fact that bad, and sometimes tragic, events do happen. This is a part of living. It's perfectly natural to feel and experience the negative feelings that accompany tragic events in our lives. However, dwelling on these negative feelings and allowing them to take control of your life can become a problem. The key is to know how likely these types of events are to occur. And, if something bad does happen, ask yourself, "How bad is it really?" When a negative event occurs, most people have two responses. The first response typically includes upset feelings. The second response is often worrying that the same event may happen again. Let's look more closely at the first response.

Responding to a Negative Event

Assume something bad does happen. You work hard preparing a report, and your supervisor tells you that it needs to be rewritten. It's natural to feel upset, sad, or perhaps even angry at this news. But, how you choose to respond to this event will directly affect your level of stress. Again, it's not the *event* itself that is causing the stress, it's your *response* to the event.

"Negative things can happen to you. How you choose to respond to these negative events will directly affect your level of stress."

Let's assume that you choose to respond positively. You will try your hardest, yet you still fear that your supervisor may also reject your rewritten report. You may be predicting a 100 percent probability that you will write another bad report. Now, you have to ask yourself, "What if I do write another bad report?" You might answer, "My supervisor will think I'm a bad employee." At this point, look closely at the evidence. What comments have you had from your supervisor in the past? Have you had to redo reports before? Do your co-workers have to rewrite reports? How long have you been working for the company? From here, you continue to weigh the evidence and challenge your thoughts. By doing this, you are likely to discover that perceived negative events are not nearly as bad as they may seem at first. Let's take this process to the extreme.

Assume that your work has not been satisfactory to your supervisor. Even though you try hard and believe that you are doing a good job, your supervisor doesn't think so. Let's assume that this prediction is 100 percent accurate. Your co-workers do not seem to be having the same difficulties as you are with your supervisor. Now, what is the worst that can happen? Well, you could get fired or even decide to quit. How bad would that really be? Could you find another job? What is the probability that you could find another job that you liked, where your supervisor appreciates and respects your work? How bad would that really be? Not bad at all, right? Look at the Expanded Realistic Thinking Worksheet on page 239 to see how to work through this example. What may initially seem to be a tragic event in your life, may in fact, turn out to be an unexpected gift.

"I learned about stress management from my kids. Every night after work, I drink some chocolate milk, eat sugary cereal straight from the box, then run around the house in my underwear squealing like a monkey."

What If it Happens Again?

The second typical response to a negative event is worrying even more that it can happen again. Psychologists call this a "recency effect." In other words, people remember best those things that happened recently. When you think realistically, however, you must to take into account ***all*** of the evidence. You may have written a poor report last time, but you also may have written excellent reports the previous 19 times. In this case, the chance that you will write another bad report is 1 in 20, or 5 percent. It's a good idea to record the many successes you have in life on a Prediction Testing Worksheet. Too often, we remember only the negative and forget all the terrific accomplishments we make. The old adage, "We are our own worst critics," is all too often true.

In Lesson Eleven, we'll continue our discussion of prediction testing. On page 249, we provide you with a Prediction Testing Worksheet. Use the worksheet this week to test, predict, and evaluate negative events in your life. Also, remember to record your successes!

Expanded Realistic Thinking Worksheet

(Bad Report Example)

Today's Date:

(1) Event	(2) Initial Thought	(3) Evidence (How Do I Know?)	(4) Initial/Realistic Probability	(5) Initial/Revised Stress Level (0–8 Scale)	(6) Consequence
Report needs to be rewritten.	My boss will believe I am a bad employee.	The boss has criticized others for bad reports in the past. I have been asked to revise reports before, and he didn't think I was a bad employee.	90% / 20%	7 / 3	Hopelessness

In the first column, record the upcoming stressful event such as, "Preparing and presenting a report for work." In the second column, record your predictions about this event. Remember to be as specific as possible. For example, "I will forget at least a quarter of my material, and I will sound as if I don't know what I'm talking about." In the third column, record how you will test your predictions after the event occurs. Examples may include, "Check notes to see whether I forgot anything. Ask Bill how I sounded." Finally, in the last column, record the outcome of your test.

A Paradigm on Perfection

In Lesson Two, on page 38, we listed perfectionism as a common cause of stress. We introduced procrastination in the last lesson and discussed how perfectionism can often lead to procrastination. If you say to yourself, "I must be perfect" or "I must do this task perfectly," on some level you know that this is not possible. Despite what you have heard in the past, perfection simply does not exist. It is an illusion! Think about this for a minute. Suppose you do something you believe to be perfect. If you look at it again in a day, a week, or a month, you'll find some way to make it better. This is why nothing is ever perfect. As humans, we are dynamic—constantly changing. Our environment is also dynamic and, like us, is constantly changing. So if perfection is part of your vocabulary, banish it from your mind right now.

"Recording past success puts negative events into perspective."

Doing an excellent job is possible, but doing a perfect job is not. Seeking the ideal relationship is a noble goal, but finding the perfect relationship is unrealistic. If you expect perfection, you're setting yourself up for disappointment. The more we expect, the more disappointed we are when we do not meet those expectations. This can lead to avoiding tasks, relationships, and many other worthwhile pursuits in life. Striving for excellence or a great job is a more realistic approach and may help prevent procrastination and disappointment.

Logically, we all know that no one is perfect. Unconsciously, however, some people often believe that they should be. Putting yourself in someone's shoes is a good way to gather realistic evidence against these thoughts. For example, if your supervisor asks you to do a special project, you may immediately begin to worry that your performance will not be good enough. Worrying probably results from unconscious thoughts such as, "It will be a disaster if I make even one mistake." But, what if a co-worker did the same project and made a few small errors? Would that really be so terrible? Would you think that your co-worker was a hopeless case and should be fired? Of course not. You would probably think, "It's too bad about those mistakes, but everyone makes them, and overall, the person did a terrific job."

Clearly, perfectionism can increase stress. It can bind like a pair of handcuffs or shackles, keeping you from taking on a challenge. It's a setup for failure and stress. Think of the stress you might experience if you told yourself, "This must be perfect; I cannot accept anything else." What if you know that you can't make it perfect? You may avoid the task altogether, or you might procrastinate until you believe you can achieve perfection. Think also of the stress you may feel while doing the task and the effect of that stress on your performance. If you tell yourself you must achieve perfection when you give a presentation to your supervisor, you energies become focused on how far you may be from perfect rather than on doing a good or even terrific job. Obviously, this is not where you want your focus to be.

Introducing Imagery

Now is a good time to introduce the topic of imagery. Imagery is a powerful stress management tool and is helpful in reducing the intense emotions often associated with stressful events. This process involves learning to imagine or visualize yourself mastering a stressful situation.

The imagery we discuss here was introduced by Dr. Maxie Maultsby, Jr. in 1971, as Rational Emotive Imagery (REI). This method of imagery is based upon the techniques of Rational Emotive Behavior Therapy, developed by Dr. Albert Ellis. Here's how it works.

First, imagine a stressful event. Think of a stressful situation you have experienced, or one that you perceive would be stressful for you. Imagine all the unpleasant emotions and feelings associated with this event. Try to imagine the environment surrounding the event. Are you inside a building, outside, or perhaps in an airplane? Who are the people around you? Are they friends, business associates, family, strangers, or a combination? What do you hear, see, smell, taste, or feel? Close your eyes and picture the situation as best you can.

When you have a clear image of a particular event, make yourself feel as *uncomfortable* as you can. Yes, we said uncomfortable. Let yourself feel the emotions of anger, anxiety, worthlessness, shame, or depression. Although these emotions are

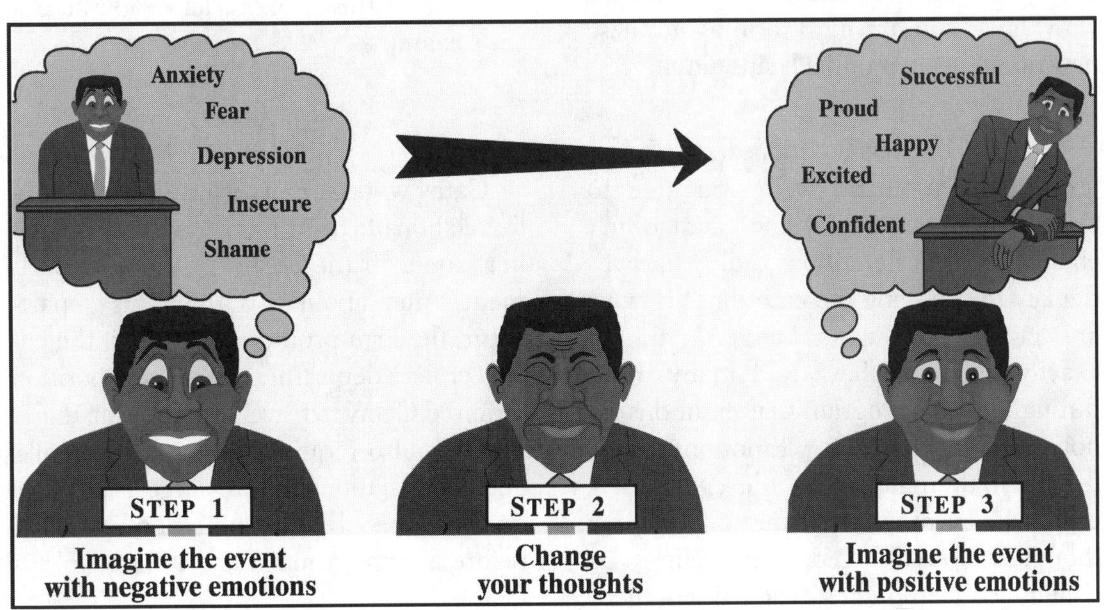

"The key to changing your emotions about an event is to change your thoughts about the event."

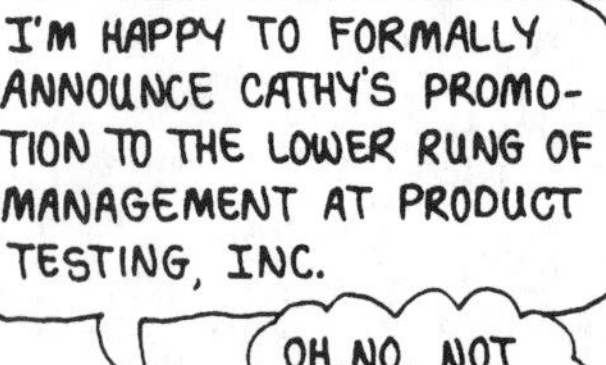

painful, force yourself to feel them—don't avoid them.

Now that you are feeling these intense emotions, force yourself to change these emotions. Instead of feeling angry, make yourself happy and cheerful. Feel excitement instead of anxiousness. Imagine yourself confident and in control of the situation, like Superman fighting Lex Luther. Picture yourself feeling proud and everyone around thinking highly of you. If you have difficulty changing your emotions right away, continue to practice. Changing emotions so radically is difficult; it takes time and practice. Before you continue with this lesson, try hard to imagine these new emotions in a difficult situation.

How did the new emotions feel? If even for a brief moment, were you able to change your emotions? The event didn't change, but your emotions did. What was the key to changing the emotions? If your answer is "my thoughts changed," you are exactly right. We have said many times throughout this program that emotions do not come from events. Emotions come from our thoughts about the events. Between the event and the emotion are your thoughts. You changed your feelings by changing the thoughts that caused them without realizing why. In this imagined stressful situation, you convinced yourself that something was different. Either you were different or the situation was different.

We want you to use this technique before, during, and after you experience stressful events. This is not an easy task at first, but with patience and practice, most people master this technique. Once you learn this new skill, you can replace stressful feelings with new, healthier, and happier beliefs at will. This is the power of choice; you become the master of your thoughts and the master of stress! To help you better understand this process, let's look at Cathy's example.

Meet Cathy

Cathy works for an advertising and public relations firm in New York. She began her career in the creative writing department. After about a year in this department, the firm promoted Cathy to the client services department. The new position required Cathy to travel a lot, but she didn't mind. It also required Cathy to give talks and presentations before large and small groups of people. The thought of speaking before a large group was very stressful for Cathy.

Visual Imagery Worksheet

(Cathy's Example)

Today's Date:

Event	Visualized Uncomfortable Emotions	Visualized Pleasant Emotions	What Changed?
Making an advertising presentation to ACME Building Company	Fear and discomfort	Concern and motivation	My thoughts: 1. I don't have to do a perfect job. 2. A fumble does not mean I am incompetent. 3. I have valuable information to communicate.

Cathy practiced the imagery techniques each day to help her manage the stress associated with public speaking. At the beginning of each day, before she went to work, Cathy would imagine a public speaking situation in vivid detail. She would imagine the trip to the airport, the flight, and the ride to the client's office. Cathy visualized arriving at the client's office and meeting the people there. She would then imagine the sounds of quiet conversation in the room, the heat of thc bright lights, and the smell of fresh coffee brewing in the back of the room. She then imagined walking to and standing at the podium, staring at the blank faces in the room, and beginning to speak. As she got in touch with these feelings, she found herself getting quite anxious.

After imagining as many uncomfortable, unpleasant, and stressful emotions as possible, Cathy would then force herself to change these feelings. She imagined her feelings changing from stress to concern—concern for her client's needs and how she could be a valuable resource in fulfilling these needs. This was very difficult for Cathy to do at first. The process took about 10 minutes for her to change her stressful emotions. With practice and hard work, Cathy became quite good at using this imagery tool.

How did Cathy change her thoughts or self-talk so that she could feel a healthier emotion? Cathy said to herself, "It won't be the end of the world if I don't do a perfect job. My audience will probably understand if I fumble, and if they don't, it does not prove that I am incompetent." She also would think to herself, "What would it feel like to focus on what I was saying versus how I was saying it, would it make me less anxious?" The answer was yes, because she was very good at her job and believed in her abilities as an advertising manager. On page 243 is a sample of Cathy's Visual Imagery Worksheet.

You can probably see the importance of realistic thinking in this visual imagery exercise. Cathy was able to assess the probability that her audience would understand a fumble, but she also decatastrophized what would happen if she fumbled and the audience didn't understand. As a result of this daily practice, Cathy was able to speak in front of large groups with concern for her clients and passion for her topic without feeling stressed.

Cathy's example illustrates how the process of imagery can help to change stressful emotions to feelings that are actually helpful and less stressful. You too can choose to respond to events in your life in a similar way. As you know, changing your thoughts

Alternative Responses to Stressful Situations

Event	Stressful Emotion	Healthier Emotion
Failing an exam	Depression	Sadness
Fight with friend	Rage	Irritation
Work presentation	Anxiety	Concern
Rejection	Shame	Disappointment

is the key to changing how you respond to stressful events. On page 244 is a list of Alternative Responses to Stressful Situations that illustrates some helpful and less stressful responses to stressful events. Review this list and see if you can think of other less stressful and healthier emotions.

Stress on the Job

Virtually everyone has experienced job-related stress. Whether you are the President of the United States, a housewife in Nebraska, or a farmer in Iowa, chances are that you too have experienced stress on the job. High levels of job-related stress can result from overcommitment; having a fast-paced, demanding position; working long hours; relationship issues with your supervisor or co-workers; and a host of other factors. Having too little to do or boredom with your job can also increase your stress. Stress at work also may be the result of a person's perceived inability to control her or his environment or destiny. Thoughts like, "I cannot do all this work in time" or "I'll never get a promotion" are common.

Either of these thoughts can increase stress. The sad reality of job stress is that it doesn't stay there; it follows you home. This, in turn, can lead to increased stress at home, which, like work-related stress, doesn't stay at home; it follows you back to work. You can easily see how this stress cycle can spin out of control. This is just one of the many reasons why understanding the causes and effects of job-related stress is important. Let's look at a few statistics.

You don't need a psychology degree to realize that stressed employees are less effective and productive than employees who are not stressed. Some experts estimate that stress-related claims cost more than $150 billion annually in lost productivity and workers' compensation claims (*Journal of Occupational & Environmental Medicine*, 1997). This is a staggering figure. The Center for Corporate Health (1997) estimates that between 60–90 percent of all medical office visits are for stress-related disorders. The Center also estimates that as much as 80 percent of all disease and illness is initiated and/or aggravated by stress. In addition, The National Safety Council estimates one million employees are absent every work day in the U.S. due to stress-related problems. In recent years, we have witnessed the horrifying effect of stress in the workplace, in school, and at home.

Many studies have shown that employee stress can lead to serious problems, including the following:

- Violence
- Absenteeism

- Employee turnover
- Employee distraction
- Carelessness and accidents
- Substance abuse
- Depression
- Anxiety
- Increased health care costs
- Decreased employee loyalty, motivation, and productivity

Over the next week, think about the impact your job has on your level of stress. In the next lesson, we will probe a little deeper into the issue of job-related stress and give you a handy tool to help you identify stressors in your job.

Lesson Review

You have now completed your tenth lesson! In this lesson, we reviewed your Expanded Realistic Thinking Worksheet to look for patterns in your stressful thoughts. We then introduced prediction testing for making predictions about the outcome of a particular event, then compared the actual outcome with the predictions. We discussed type II procrastination—fearing the outcome of a task, and provided you with strategies for overcoming this type of procrastination. You were introduced to visual imagery, and we showed you how this technique can be helpful in reducing stress. Finally, we addressed the all-important issue of work-related stress and its potentially harmful effects on both employee, employer, and co-workers.

This Week's Assignment

This week, use the Prediction Testing Worksheet on page 249 to test the predictions you make about potentially stressful events. You may need to make several copies of this worksheet during the week. These worksheets can provide valuable insight into the reality of stressful situations. Also, try using visual imagery this week to review a past stressful event or in preparation of a *perceived* stressful event. Remember, the visual imagery technique is used to reduce the intensity of negative emotions to healthier, more adaptive emotions. We suggest you practice this every day. The Visual Imagery Worksheet on page 248 may be helpful as you practice this technique. You may find this difficult as first, but soon it will become much easier to do!

We also have included at the end of this lesson, a Time Investment Worksheet, a Daily Stress Record, and an Expanded Realistic Thinking Worksheet. Don't feel compelled to complete all of these worksheets. Use the ones you find the most helpful. We have provided them for you as a convenience. Some of our clients like to complete all of the forms each week. Others find it more helpful and less stressful to complete only some of the forms and worksheets. And still others develop their own worksheets. What works best for you is fine.

Be sure to complete the Stress Change Worksheet in Lesson Nine, on page 227, the Physical Activity and Relaxation Worksheet in Appendix F, on page 433 for week 10, and the Average Stress Change Worksheet in Appendix E, on page 430. Good luck with this week's assignment.

Knowledge Review

T F 76. Type II procrastinators put things off because they fear the outcome

T F 77. Because the relationship between stress and eating is not clear, trying to eat a balanced diet will not help you manage stress.

T F 78. To do prediction testing properly, you must make highly specific guesses about the outcome of an event.

T F 79. Your thoughts about a negative event and how you respond to the event determine how much stress you feel.

T F 80. When using realistic thinking, you must consider only the negative evidence.

T F 81. Perfectionism always leads to increased performance due to the pressure you feel.

T F 82. The technique of Rational Emotive Imagery is based on the idea that events alone cause stress in our lives.

T F 83. Imagery involves learning to imagine or visualize yourself mastering a stressful situation.

T F 84. When used correctly, imagery should help you change all stressful emotions into positive emotions.

T F 85. Stress on the job is unrelated to stress experienced at home and should, therefore, be treated separately.

(Answers in Appendix C, page 415)

Visual Imagery Worksheet

Today's Date:

Event	Visualized Uncomfortable Emotions	Visualized Pleasant Emotions	What Changed?

Prediction Testing Worksheet

Today's Date:

Event	Prediction	Test	Outcome

Time Investment Worksheet					Today's Date:
Time	**Activity**	**Urgent**	**Important**	**Stress Level (0–8)**	**Thoughts**
12:00–1:00 am					
1:00–2:00 am					
2:00–3:00 am					
3:00–4:00 am					
4:00–5:00 am					
5:00–6:00 am					
6:00–7:00 am					
7:00–8:00 am					
8:00–9:00 am					
9:00–10:00 am					
10:00–11:00 am					
11:00–11:59 am					
12:00–1:00 pm					
1:00–2:00 pm					
2:00–3:00 pm					
3:00–4:00 pm					
4:00–5:00 pm					
5:00–6:00 pm					
6:00–7:00 pm					
7:00–8:00 pm					
8:00–9:00 pm					
9:00–10:00 pm					
10:00–11:00 pm					
11:00–11:59 pm					

Daily Stress Record—Lesson Ten

Name:____________________________________ **Week of:**____________

Date	Average Stress Level	Highest Stress Level	Time of Highest Stress Level	Stressful Event Associated with Highest Stress Level

My Physical Activity and Relaxation Record

Day of the Week	Physical Activity Record		Relaxation Record[1]	
	Activity	Minutes	Time of Day	Minutes
Monday				
Tuesday				
Wednesday				
Thursday				
Friday				
Saturday				
Sunday				

1 **Remember to tense each muscle group three times—the first at ¾ of maximum tension; the second at ½ of maximum tension; and the third at ¼ of maximum tension.**

Expanded Realistic Thinking Worksheet

Today's Date:

(1) Event	(2) Initial Thought	(3) Evidence (How Do I Know?)	(4) Initial/Realistic Probability	(5) Initial/Revised Stress Level (0–8 Scale)	(6) Consequence

Lesson Eleven

We begin this lesson with a brief discussion on motivation. At this pont in the Mastering Stress Program, our clients typically notice a marked reduction in their day-to-day stress. As we discuss, however, this can become a double-edged sword! We conclude our discussion on the topic of procrastination with the third type of procrastination—not knowing where to begin. We'll review the topic of imagery, then continue our discussion on prediction testing and introduce you to the Prediction Testing Worksheet. The **N** (Nutrition) component of the LEARN acronym comes up again in this lesson as we introduce you to the Food Guide Pyramid. Again, we bring up the all-important topic of relaxation and introduce you to some advanced relaxation techniques. The lesson concludes with a simple exercise to help you take stock of your physical activity. This is an exciting lesson with many important topics to discuss. Let's begin by talking about motivation.

Revisiting Motivation

Many people begin stress management programs with high levels of energy, determination, and passion for learning how to master stress in their lives. They realize the importance of mastering their stress. As they begin their program, motivation is high. Many are determined that nothing will derail their efforts. They are committed to keeping records, learning new skills, and practicing sound stress management techniques each day. Yet, as time passes, record keeping, practicing, and learning new techniques may become more difficult. This can be especially true when individuals have been successful in reducing the stress in their lives. They may think that they have learned all there is to know about stress management and do not see the need to continue with the program. For others, continuing to find and commit the time necessary for stress management may be an increasing problem. Some may find the advanced techniques of stress management more difficult than the easier, less complex skills they learned earlier in the program. This double whammy of increased difficulty and less time can lead to feelings of frustration. The notion of quitting the pro-

"Viewing motivation as the difference between the benefits and costs can help you make an informed decision about continuing your stress management program."

gram may be a frequent thought. "I'm working harder and seeing less progress than when I started" and "I just don't have the time any more" may be common thoughts. If these thoughts sound familiar to you, you're not alone. Learning to master your stress is hard work. But, as we have said many times before, the time you invest now will pay big dividends over the rest of your life. Let's revisit your motivation.

When Motivation Wanes

Decreases in motivation are often contributing factors to the increased difficulty of maintaining lifestyle changes. We often hear statements from our clients like, "I've lost my motivation, and I'm looking for ways to get it back." Looking at motivation in this light may suggest that something is wrong with the *person* who lacks motivation. Let's look at motivation another way. Do you remember completing the exercise of weighing the benefits and costs of beginning a stress management program in the Introduction and Orientation Lesson on page 9? Chances are that the benefits far outweighed the costs when you began the program.

Viewing motivation as the difference between the benefits and costs of stress management is a helpful way of looking at motivation. Assume, for example, that your primary motivation for beginning the Mastering Stress Program was to help you overcome stress at work. Let's say that the stress you now experience at work is much less than when you began the program. When you have conquered the major stressors in your life, *motivation* may fade. Statements such as "I'm much less stressed now, although I still have *some* stressors in my life," may overshadow your original objective of mastering *all* the stress in your life, now and in the future. If most of the benefits of a stress management program have been realized, the cost to continue the program may be too high. Viewed this way, the issue is not *motivation*. Instead, an informed decision has been made that the costs to continue the program may *now* exceed the expected benefits.

When Times Become Difficult

We said at the beginning of this program that changing lifelong habits is not always easy. Planning for and expecting difficulties is important. The more important question is *when,* not *if,* you will have trouble practicing your stress management techniques. Expecting difficulties will help you plan strategies for getting back on track. Focusing on these strategies when difficulties arise is much more helpful than feeling bad or beating up on yourself.

Review the Costs and Benefits

Reviewing the costs and benefits of managing your stress on a regular basis is another helpful strategy. Refer back to page 9 in the Introduction and Orientation Lesson to help remind yourself of why you started this program in the first place. Periodic reviews will reveal whether you have achieved your stress management goals and whether any additional benefits are worth the extra costs. Visualizing your life over the next few months and anticipating any potentially stressful events may also help to increase the *benefits* side of the ledger. Consider all of the possibilities. How confident you are in your ability to overcome and master the stressful events. Remember that you still have many more helpful stress management techniques to learn in this program.

Avoid Self-Criticism

It's easy to beat up on yourself when difficulties arise. Self-criticism, self-doubt, and negative self-talk are ineffective. This type of response to difficult situations often leads to abandoning all stress management efforts. Review your difficulties and see them for what they are—temporary setbacks—and make plans to address and overcome them. You can do it!

Define the Problem

When difficulties arise, identifying the exact nature of the problem is important. In Lesson Twelve, we will bring up the all-important topic of problem solving. Vague definitions of difficulties or problems are not likely to lead to effective solutions. For example, "I'm still feeling too stressed" or "I just don't have enough time to practice" are not specific enough to lead to possible solutions. Recording the specifics of a situation in which you felt too much stress will help you identify the specific problem. Understanding how you spend your time each day will help you understand why you believe that you don't have enough time to practice. Once you have identified a specific problem, then you can work on developing an effective plan to overcome the problem.

Develop a Plan of Action

Once you have identified a specific problem, you can set short-term objectives, goals, and strategies to overcome the problem. We like to think of *objectives* as something you would like to accomplish. An example of an objective would be, "Increase my physical activity to 45 minutes every day." Think of *goals* as something that you have absolute control over. For example, you may set the following goals to reach your objective of increasing your physical activity:

❶ Take three five-minute walks before noon each workday.

❷ Take three five-minute walks between noon and quitting time each workday.

❸ Go for a 15-minute walk immediately when I get home before I get involved in anything else.

Strategies will help insure that you reach your goals. Continuing our example, you may develop a strategy of getting up five minutes early each morning and taking a five-minute walk before getting ready for work. You may decide to park further away from work to get in your second five-minute walk each morning. And finally, you may decide to set an alarm for 10:00 a.m. each morning to remind yourself to go for a brief five-minute walk.

Developing a specific plan of action for any stress management problem that includes objectives, goals, and strategies can help you get past the temporary road blocks. Again, identifying the specific problem is the first step.

"Using strategies such as parking further away from work to get in an extra five-minute walk will help you increase your activity."

Plan for Contingencies

Inevitably, even the best conceived strategies may not always work as planned. For this reason, developing a back-up plan is a terrific idea—just in case! For instance, if you are unable to increase the time you devote to practicing deep muscle relaxation techniques, enlist the help and support of your family or friends. You may consider asking family members to give you time alone for your practice sessions. A close friend may be willing to practice deep muscle relaxation techniques with you. Backup plans are critical because they can help prevent the isolation and shame that often accompany slips in a stress management program. Asking for and seeking help is *not* a weakness—it is a strength.

Type III Procrastination—Not Knowing Where to Begin

This is the third and final lesson in which we discuss the topic of procrastination. In this lesson, we'll cover the third most common type of procrastination, that of not knowing where to begin a task. When faced with a difficult or challenging task, many people simply do not know where to begin. The more they think about the task, the longer they leave it untouched. The longer they leave it, the more overwhelming and stressful it becomes. The following strategies can help overcome this type of procrastination.

Divide the Task into Smaller Segments

We can divide most tasks into smaller, more manageable projects. Rather than trying to tackle a task as a single project, look for ways to divide it into smaller parcels. We can then undertake the much smaller pieces. Sit down and write out an overall plan instead of just trying to begin. In your plan, make sure that you list all of the project sections and subsections that need to be completed. Then, choose one section to begin and put the others aside. Here is a simple list for developing a project plan:

❶ Write an overall *mission* of the project to be completed.

❷ Develop at least five key *objectives* that, if they are accomplished, will fulfill the mission of the plan. Think of objectives as having the following characteristics:

- Specific
- Measurable
- Action oriented
- Achieve your mission

❸ For each objective, identify at least three goals. Goals should be thought of as time and action specific, and you should have absolute control over whether or not you achieve your goals. An example of a goal would be to spend 30 minutes from 7 to 7:30 p.m. next Tuesday, Wednesday, and Thursday working on an outline of your report.

❹ For each goal, identify a specific strategy that will help insure that you achieve the goal.

Set Deadlines for Ending and Beginning

Set a deadline for completing the task. This should be a realistic deadline that you are confident you can achieve. Then determine realistically how long it will take you to compete the task. From this information, you can set a beginning date. This may appear to be an excuse for delaying rather than starting a task immediately. But not every task can be started now, so deadlines are appropriate. Of course, you should also realize that you not only must lead yourself to water, but you must also *make* yourself drink!

"This project is extremely important, but it has no budget, no guidelines, no support staff and it's due tomorrow morning. At last, here's your chance to really impress everyone!"

Build Momentum

Some people are more alert and have more energy at the beginning of the day than at the end. For others, the opposite is true. Knowing the time of day that you are at your best is important in overcoming procrastination. Set aside time during your "peak" time of the day to work on your most difficult tasks. Simply taking the time to plan and think through difficult tasks can help you feel a sense of accomplishment and build momentum to continue.

Stimulus Control

Because your environment often has distractions, remove the distractions that keep you from working on the difficult projects. Make changes in your environment will help you to concentrate and focus on the task at hand.

Reward Yourself for Progress

As we discussed earlier, most large, complex tasks can be broken into smaller parts that are more easily completed. Small self-rewards like a coffee break, a trip to the mall, or an afternoon on the golf course are justified if they mark significant progress on a long, difficult project. Be completely honest with yourself. Make sure the rewards follow, but do not precede or replace the actual work on the project.

Include Others in Your Rewards

A sad reality of today's fast-paced, work environment is that it is void of family, friends, and other social interaction. Children, spouses, partners, and close friends may not know when you have accomplished something of great significance. Perhaps you could invite them out to a small dinner or other special outing to tell them of your project, objectives, goals, and strategies. Give them a small gift as a symbol of your appreciation for their understanding and support. Thank them for their implicit support of your project. After awhile, they may begin to share more with you and the exchange of small rewards may become mutual.

Procrastination is a major problem for many people, one that can easily lead to high levels of stress. Developing helpful strategies to overcome procrastination is a valuable stress management tool. Everyone procrastinates from time to time, so don't fall into the trap of trying to convince yourself that you are different. Admit it, confront it head-on, and develop your own strategies to help overcome procrastination. Below are some strategies that have been studied extensively at the Albert Ellis Institute and have been proven to be help-

Strategies for Overcoming Procrastination

1	**The Worst First Strategy** Do the most difficult part of the task first. This will make the rest of the task seem easier and will give you fewer reasons to procrastinate.
2	**The Knock-Out Strategy** If you know you need to do something, address it immediately so it doesn't weigh heavily on your mind. Focus on how good it will feel to get it off your to-do list.
3	**The Five-Minute Strategy** Invest a minimum of five minutes each day on a task you have been avoiding. After you have completed five minutes, assess whether or not you can invest another five minutes.
4	**The Step-by-Step Strategy** When you procrastinate about beginning a task, break it down into smaller, more manageable parts. Set the time aside as you would any other important engagement, and make yourself work on just one specific step at a time.
5	**The Swiss Cheese Strategy** Do anything at all that relates to the task you are avoiding. Gradually make large holes in the task until it becomes more manageable.

ful in reducing the tendency to procrastinate.

Imagery Review

Let's now turn our attention to the topic of imagery. In Lesson Ten, on page 241, we introduced imagery as a way to reduce stress. Changing the beliefs that lead to painful or uncomfortable emotions are key techniques to reducing stress. You were to first imagine a stressful event in great detail along with its associated negative feelings. Changing the negative feelings to less intense feelings was the next step. You were then asked to focus on the *thoughts* that allowed your feelings to change. "What did you tell yourself to reduce the emotion?"

How did the exercise go for you? Were you able to change the negative emotion to a less negative emotion? If you were, how did it feel when you gained control over the usually stressful situation? Did you feel a certain sense of mastery in not allowing the situation to stress you as much? If not, don't be alarmed. This technique of stress management takes much patience and practice. Perhaps you were trying too hard to make the negative emotion disappear completely. Remember, the goal is to make the negative emotions *less negative* and not necessarily eliminate them all together. We cannot expect the negative stressful situations we face in everyday life to suddenly disappear. But, by changing our thoughts, the stressful events become less stressful! Try again this week to reduce the negative emotions by asking yourself, "How can I reduce the intensity of this negative emotion." As you continue to practice this skill, you should find it much easier to do. With continued practice, you will be able to use imagery almost automatically to reduce stressful and negative feelings associated with particular events in your life.

More on Prediction Testing

In Lesson Ten, on page 235, we introduced prediction testing as a way for you to test your predictions about upcoming stressful events. Of course, prediction testing does not have to be restricted to formal or work situations. You can also use this technique to test your beliefs about everyday events. Imagine for a moment that you are hosting a dinner party. As you make the final preparations and the hour of the party draws near, you suddenly discover that you forgot to prepare dessert. Immediately, you get angry with yourself and become very stressed. This is a terrific opportunity to test the *predictions* that are contributing to your stress. Yes, you are making automatic predictions about not serving dessert. Let's review what some of these predictions may be.

First, think about why you are angry with yourself about forgetting the dessert. Identify the thoughts that make you feel angry. Thoughts such as "My guests will think I'm cheap," "The guests will not enjoy the

"You can use prediction testing to test your beliefs about everyday events such as forgetting to make dessert.

dinner," and "Everyone will comment on how poorly organized I am" are all possibilities. Now, have the dinner party without the dessert and see if your predictions come true. To do this, you could ask your guests how they liked everything. You could also ask your partner or a close friend to ask the other guests their opinions. If you want to be real devious, you could try eavesdropping on your guests' conversations during the evening to see if any negative comments are made. Examples like this may occur often in day-to-day life. Typically, if they turn out okay, you quickly forget them. But, if they end in disaster, you easily remember them. By turning the event into a prediction testing exercise, you force yourself to pay attention to your initial predictions and the final outcome. In doing this, you are more likely to remember it, whatever the outcome.

Being Creative

Most of our clients find the evidence they collect from prediction testing to be positive. However, testing your guesses is not always easy to do. For example, if you did not hear any negative comments about not serving dessert at your dinner party, how do you really know if the guests noticed? You have to be creative. You could ask your guests if they had enough to eat. You may also consider asking them if they would like anything else to eat. Certainly, you may encounter times when gathering objective evidence is simply not possible. In these situations, use your best judgement on the outcome. Ask yourself how you would have reacted if you were a guest at your dinner party. Would you have really minded not having dessert? Perhaps you would have considered it a clever way to eat a more healthy, balanced diet!

The Prediction Testing Worksheet

We hope that by now you have an appreciation for recording your practice sessions so that you can monitor how well you do. As with other techniques you have learned in the Mastering Stress Program, recording your prediction testing exercises is a powerful stress management tool. On page 261 is a Prediction Testing Worksheet sample. We provide you with a blank Prediction Testing Worksheet on page 273 for you to copy and use. Here is a brief explanation on how to use the Prediction Testing Worksheet.

❶ In the first column, record the upcoming event that increases your stress.

❷ In the second column, record your prediction (thought) or worry about this event that is causing you to feel

Prediction Testing Worksheet

(Dessert Example)

Today's Date:

Event	Prediction	Test	Outcome
Forgot to make dessert for tonight's dinner party.	My guests will think I'm cheap. My guests will not enjoy the dinner. The guests will think I'm poorly organized.	Ask the guests how they enjoyed dinner. Ask guests if they had enough to eat. Listened for comments about not serving des-sert.	Everyone said they had a great time. The guests said they had more than enough food to eat. I did not hear any nega-tive comments.

stress. Remember to clearly identify your specific thought.

❸ In the third column, record how you will test your guesses during and/or after the event.

❹ Finally, record the outcome of your prediction testing. Were your predictions accurate?

Prediction testing will help you evaluate past evidence more realistically so that you can more accurately predict future outcomes. This can become valuable proof that your worst fears do not always come true. Yet, you have to face the possibility that sometimes negative things do happen. What then? All of us must face the inevitable fact that at some time in our lives, something negative will happen. However, it is important that you do not allow the few negative events in life to obscure all of the wonderful things that happen. In other words, you must learn not to catastrophize every event that happens to you in life. Let's see how this works.

Conquering Catastrophizing Thoughts

When you catastrophize, you imagine the worst possible outcome. Equally important, you are underestimating your ability to cope with the *perceived* outcome. Let's assume that you have a performance review coming up at work. You may say something like, "If I get a bad review, I will lose my job. I will not be able to handle that." Assume that the first part of your statement does come true—you do get a bad review. Now, assume further that the second part also comes true—you loose your job. Telling yourself up front that you'll not be able to handle losing your job is the same as telling yourself that you have no coping skills.

Let's take a closer look at this now. Is it really true that you will not be able to handle losing your job? Would it be more correct to say something like, "If I lose my job, it will be difficult for me." Have you had upsetting things happen to you that you initially thought would be impossible to get through? Most of us have experienced such events in our lives. Yet, we were able to get through them, even though they seemed terrible at first. Haven't you also had experiences that seemed negative at first but turned out to be terrific opportunities?

What techniques have you learned to help you work through events that, at first, may appear to be catastrophic? How would you approach working through such a situation? Suppose you had a close friend who was catastrophizing about a particular event. Would you readily agree with the catastrophizing thought process your friend was going through? Of course not.

The next time you find yourself catastrophizing, first ask yourself, "What is

the probability that this will actually happen? Then ask yourself, "What will happen if it does? How bad will it really be?" Then remember to ask yourself, "Am I underestimating my ability to manage this situation? Reread Tim's counseling session in Lesson Eight, on page 184. You may recall that Tim used the Expanded Realistic Thinking Worksheet to help him work through a *perceived* catastrophic event. You too have learned the skills to help you more realistically view stressful events. We provide, on page 274, a blank Expanded Realistic Thinking Worksheet for you to use in such situations.

Frank believes that breakfast is the most important meal of the day.

Following a Balanced Diet

In Lesson Nine, on page 217, we introduced the importance of good nutrition and its role in stress management. When it comes to nutrition, common sense and rational eating are key components of following a balanced diet. This means following the Dietary Guidelines we outlined in Lesson Nine, on page 216. The important word here to remember is *balance.* This means eating a variety of food from the different food groups. Many people have heard this, but aren't sure what it means or how to go about achieving dietary balance. If you ordered *The LEARN Healthy Eating and Calorie Guide*, then you are well on your way to improving your diet. If you have not ordered this guide, we highly recommend that you do so at some point. Ordering information can be found on page 451, in the back of this manual. Providing a detailed guide to optimizing nutrition is beyond the scope of the Mastering Stress Program. Yet, we believe it is important to provide you with some information on good nutrition because we believe good nutrition is a key to good health.

Our bodies need a good balance of nutrients to be healthy and respond well to stressful events. They do not function well with too little of one nutrient and not enough of another. Some of our clients ask why nutrition is so important. The answer is very simple. What you eat helps determine how healthy you are. This, in turn, influences how you cope with stressful events, both physically and mentally. In Lesson Ten, on page 234, we had you rate your diet. How did you score on the Rate Your Diet Quiz in Appendix G, on page 234? Can you improve your diet? Let's look at a handy method that may help you to eat a more healthy and balanced diet.

The Food Guide Pyramid

The U.S. Department of Agriculture (USDA) and the Department of Health and Human Services (HHS) jointly developed a researched-based food and eating plan called the Food Guide Pyramid. The pyramid is a graphic illustration that incorporates the Dietary Guidelines we discussed in Lesson Nine, on page 216. The Food Guide Pyramid divides foods into five separate groups as shown in the graphic illustration below. At the top of the pyramid is a section fats, oils, and sugars—foods that should be eaten sparingly. This section represents the smallest section of the pyramid. As the food groups progress down toward the bottom of the pyramid, they make up a larger portion of your diet. As an example, the Bread, Cereal, Rice, & Pasta Group is the largest food group, and foods from this group should make up the largest portion of your daily diet.

Our purpose of introducing you to the Food Guide Pyramid is so that you have an idea of what makes up a healthy, balanced diet. This graphic is now illustrated on many food packages and should be well understood by individuals who want to improve their diet and nutrition. At this point in the program, we want you to be familiar with the different food groups. In upcoming lessons, we'll discuss in more detail the recommended servings from each food group and what makes up a serving within each group. The Food Guide Pyramid is a helpful guide to use to make sure that you get a balanced and nutritious diet.

More on Relaxation

You have been practicing deep muscle relaxation for several weeks. Are you finding it easier to relax your muscles while sitting in a comfortable chair, in a quiet room? If you are still somewhat uncomfortable with this, do not worry. This is not a contest; you are not competing for a gold medal in the Olympic Relaxation Marathon. In this lesson, we cover two advanced techniques of deep muscle relaxation: discrimination and portability.

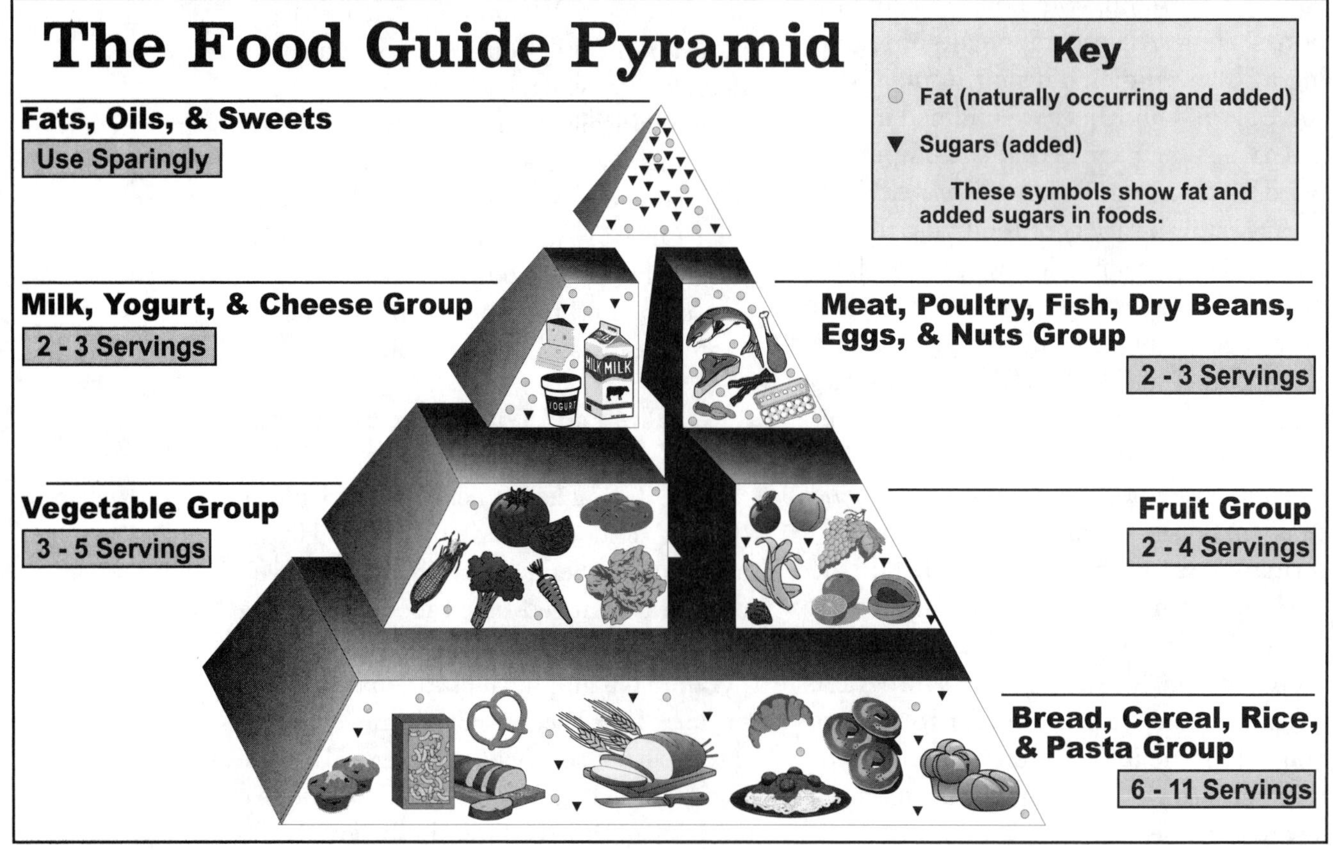

Discrimination

Learning relaxation techniques is important in stress management because it helps you identify tension in your muscles early. Think of relaxation techniques as your Doppler radar or early warning system. If you can detect the early signs of tense muscles before they become full-blown thunderstorms leading to headaches or other physical problems, you can take immediate action to calm the storm. Until now, your relaxation exercises have centered on big, obvious changes in tension. You have been tensing your muscles to three-quarters of their maximum, then flopping them down to zero tension. Most likely, you would agree that muscle tension in real life is rarely as obvious as three-quarters of the maximum. This is why learning to identify and reduce tension at lower and much more subtle levels is important. We refer to this as learning to *discriminate* muscle tension.

Having a muscle tension gauge that works like the fuel gauge in your car would be handy. Unfortunately, such a handy gadget does not exist—not yet, anyway. Therefore, you need to learn techniques that will help you gauge or estimate the tension in your muscles. Then, if you notice muscle tension in a particular muscle group increasing, you can take steps to reduce the tension. To help you learn to gauge the muscle tension in various muscle groups, we want you to begin using a new technique when you practice.

Beginning this week, when you practice relaxation, tense each muscle group three times instead of twice. The first time, tense the muscles to three-quarters, then release the tension (flop) to zero tension, just as you have been practicing. The second time, tense your muscles to only about one-half

"Think of relaxation techniques as your Doppler radar. If you can detect the early signs of tense muscles, you can take immediate action to calm the storm."

of your maximum (moderate tension) before releasing the tension to zero. Finally, on the third round, tense the muscles to only one-quarter of their maximum (mild tension) then release to zero tension. The chart on page 266 shows this advanced muscle relaxation technique more clearly.

As you practice holding your muscles at the one-quarter level and breathing normally, try to think about all the times during the day when you may feel this mild level of tension. The more you practice with these varying levels of tension, the sooner you will begin to notice when your muscles tense up as you go about your day. The sooner you notice tension, the sooner you can become proactive in reducing the tension. Let's now turn our attention to making deep muscle relaxation portable.

Portability

You have undoubtedly realized that a 20-minute relaxation practice session is not always practical. This is particularly true if you need to relax at work or in a traffic jam. Other relaxation techniques such as tapes and meditation are equally impractical when you have to keep your mind focused on something like driving a car. This is why

Advanced Deep Muscle Relaxation Techniques
Discriminating Muscle Tension

1. Close your eyes and breath slowly and evenly—in and out.
2. Breath in through your nose and out through your mouth.
3. As you breath out, relax your muscles.
4. When you are relaxed, begin with a specific muscle group.
5. Isolate the muscle group you're working on.
6. Check to make sure the rest of your body is relaxed.
7. As you breath in through your nose, tense the muscle group about three-quarters of its maximum.
8. Hold this tension as you breath slowly and normally—in and out.
9. As you exhale after the fourth breath (or after 10–15 seconds), relax the muscle group quickly (flopping).
10. Visualize all of the tension and stress leaving your body as you exhale.
11. Now as you breath in through your nose, tense the muscle group to about **one-half** of its maximum.
12. Hold this tension as you breath slowly and normally—in and out.
13. As you exhale after the fourth breath (about 10–15 seconds), relax the muscle group quickly to zero tension (flopping).
14. Visualize all of the tension and stress leaving your body as you exhale.
15. For the third time, breath in through your nose, tense the muscle group about **one-quarter** of its maximum.
16. Hold this tension as you breath slowly and normally—in and out.
17. As you exhale after the fourth breath (about 10–15 seconds), relax the muscle group quickly to zero tension (flopping).
18. Visualize all of the tension and stress leaving your body as you exhale.
19. Excellent! Repeat this exercise with the remaining muscle groups.

we teach and are proponents of the deep muscle relaxation technique; it's portable and you can carry it with you always.

You have been practicing relaxation for 20 minutes at a time. We had you begin this was so that you could learn to relax deeply in a more controlled environment. You are ready to make your relaxation more portable. To do so, you will make practice sessions shorter and work on fewer muscle groups at a time.

We will start by having you reduce the number of muscle groups you practice on at a time from 12 to 8, then to 4. Although you may choose any muscle group you like, it makes sense to concentrate on the ones in which you most often experience tension. The table below illustrates an example of Tyron's muscle group choices. On page 276, we provide tables for you to list your unique 8 and 4 muscle groups for portability practice.

Once you have mastered relaxation with the 12 muscle groups we discussed in Lesson Five, on page 110, try reducing the number to eight. Practice the cycles of tensing and relaxing following the chart on page 266 until you have completed all eight muscle groups. Keep practicing with these eight muscle groups until you feel completely comfortable; for most people, this takes about two weeks. Feel free to change the muscle groups if this fits your lifestyle better. Try not to rush yourself. When you feel as relaxed using 8 muscle groups as you did using 12, try reducing the number of muscle groups to 4. Some clients prefer to reduce the number of muscle groups by one each time. If this works best for you, that's perfectly fine. Once you become proficient at this, your relaxation could take as

Muscle Groups Portability Practice

Tyron's Example

My 12 Muscle Groups	My 8 Muscle Groups	My 4 Muscle Groups
1. Upper forehead	1. Forehead	1. Forehead
2. Lower forehead	2. Eyes	2. Upper & lower arms
3. Eyes	3. Back & neck	3. Neck & shoulders
4. Lips	4. Shoulders & neck	4. Chest & breathing
5. Back & neck	5. Chest & breathing	
6. Shoulders & neck	6. Upper arms	
7. Chest & breathing	7. Lower arms	
8. Upper arms	8. Abdomen	
9. Lower arms		
10. Abdomen		
11. Thighs		
12. Lower leg & foot		

little as five minutes. Even better, you can isolate particular muscles when you feel them tense and relax them on-the-go. Good luck with this weeks practice!

Dealing with Anger

In Lesson Two, on page 40, we listed anger as a common source of stress. Many people under stress can easily become angry and irritable for no logical reason. Often, they hold unconscious beliefs that others are stupid, incompetent, or nasty. They believe that they have to battle everyone else's ignorance. While this may be partly true, Dr. Albert Ellis asserts that people become angry when they believe and say that these things should not be so. For example, if you believe that *no one* should be inconsiderate, stupid, ignorant, or nasty, then you're setting yourself up to be angry when you encounter this perceived behavior. Certainly it's healthy to desire that everyone be nice, smart, and competent. But, when we *expect* and *demand* that they be, we're trying to control something we cannot control—another person's behavior. Remember, our choices are the only thing we have absolute control over.

When you find yourself getting angry, look for your "should" statement. More often than not, you'll find that you have a "should" statement about yourself, the world in general, or another person. For example, you may feel angry when you experience something you believe to be unfair in the world. Let's say that a credit card company refuses to give you a credit card. Your initial reaction is that this is unfair. After all, you have always paid your bills on time. Most of us desire the world to be fair (at least according to our standards). The reality is that the world is not fair. The reason for this may be that everyone has a different idea of what the term "fair" means.

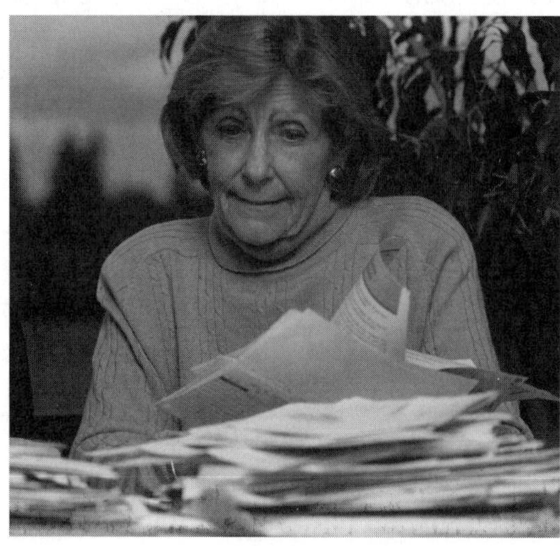

"When you feel angry, remember that you can ***choose*** *not to let the anger increase your stress."*

One of our clients once said that the world should be fair. She believed that she should not have to suffer the consequences of the damage to her home caused by a recent earthquake. Most of us would agree that it would be very disappointing to suffer such a loss. Yet, was it fair that she did not have any damage to her home during all the previous earthquakes when her neighbors' homes received much damage? She soon came to realization that fairness is desirable, but to expect and demand such fairness is stressful. Remember that disappointment varies with expectations. The more unrealistic our expectations, the greater our chances of experiencing disappointment. And disappointment can lead to much stress.

Another person's behavior easily angers some people. Too often, such anger is directed toward the person rather than the behavior. Separating a person's behavior from the person is an important first step in reducing your feelings of anger. Can you love someone and hate something he or she does? Of course you can. The next time you find yourself getting angry with someone, try separating the behavior from the person. Chances are the person is a terrific individual and may not be aware of how this particular behavior affects you.

Another way to handle anger is to put yourself in the other person's place. This is a good way to gain a new perspective on the situation and the resulting behavior that angers you. This also will help you better understand and forgive minor slips made by others. Let's look at an example.

Suppose that you're just getting onto the subway, and your hands are full. Suddenly, a much younger and seemingly healthy individual jumps in front of you and takes the only available seat. Many people would become intensely angry with this person. Why would someone become so angry? Your likely response is that he or she is rude and shouldn't behave that way. Can you identify the automatic "should" statement? What would you do? Being the star stress management student that you are, you might do some quick realistic thinking and probability assessment. Right?

Another strategy would be to put yourself in this person's shoes. Maybe this person is simply rude and inconsiderate of other people, and perhaps not. Try to imagine a scenario where you may behave the same way. Let's say that you just came from a doctor's visit where you had some minor surgery performed on the bottom of your foot, and the pain was unbearable. Might you behave the same way? You might also imagine that you had just been given a big project at work and your mind was working overtime trying to figure out how you were going to get it done. You need to sit down so you can write down your thoughts. You didn't even notice someone with their arms full heading for the same seat. What is the intensity of your anger now? Lower, we hope. What happened to your level of stress?

"My staff just left for a ten-day stress management retreat. I'm feeling more relaxed already!"

More on Job Stress

In Lesson Ten, on page 245, we introduced the topic of job-related stress. Too much stress can easily originate at work and affect all aspects of your life. After a while, stress can become so entangled in all aspects of your life that it's hard to identify its true origin. On page 270 is the Job Stress Questionnaire. We have put this simple questionnaire together to help you determine how much your job contributes to your overall level of stress. Take a few minutes now to complete the questionnaire. In the next lesson, we'll provide strategies for reducing job-related stress.

Taking Stock of Your Walking and Lifestyle Activity

Let's take a few moments now to review your progress with walking and increased physical activity. Look at your physical activity on your Physical Activity and Relaxation Worksheet in Appendix F, beginning on page 433. You are now in week 11 of the Stress Management Program. Have you increased your physical activity to where you are getting between 30 and 60 minutes of

Job Stress Questionnaire

Instructions: Rate each of the following items (scale from 0 to 4) in terms of how often the symptom was true for you during the past few months.

0=Almost always	2=Somewhat often	4=Never
1=Frequently	3=Occasionally	

____1. I feel enthusiastic about going to my job each d ay.
____2. I feel well rested when I rise in the morning.
____3. I am positively challenged by my work responsibilities.
____4. I am able to concentrate on the job.
____5. I am satisfied with the quality of my work.
____6. I am able to make decisions as well as ever.
____7. I enjoy the work I do.
____8. I communicate well with my co-workers.
____9. I am sensitive and receptive to the needs of others.
____10. I am able to manage my time at work well.
____11. I can assert my needs with others on the job.
____12. I can delegate responsibility when necessary.
____13. I am not overly bothered by small inconveniences or mini crises that arise on the job.
____14. I see job advancement in my future.
____15. I work for more than a paycheck each day.
____16. I enjoy talking about the work I do to friends and family.
____17. I feel competent at doing my job.
____18. I am able to remember as well as ever.
____19. I enjoy my co-workers.
____20. I get along with those in power at my job.

If you scored 0 to 25, most likely you are coping well with the stress at your job. If you scored 26 to 40, you are probably experiencing job stress that is beginning to interfere with your satisfaction and you should begin a plan to manage this stress more effectively. If you scored 41 to 55, you are definitely experiencing great job stress and a program is not only advisable, but necessary for healthier functioning. If you scored 56 to 80, your job stress is seriously interfering with your satisfaction and you need to address it immediately.

physical activity each day? If not, it may be a good time to look back at the benefits of exercise in Lesson Four, on page 86, and in Lesson Five, on page 104. Two of the most important benefits of regular physical activity at this point in your program is that exercise helps to reduce stress, and it can improve your mental attitude. Certainly, there are many ways to increase your physical activity. We are big proponents of walking. Walking is something practically anyone can do, and it can be done just about anywhere. If being physically active is difficult for you, let's look at some ways to increase the pleasure of walking.

Increasing the Pleasure of Walking

Walking can be a lot of fun, and even a short five-minute walk can help reduce stress. Best of all, you can take a short walk just about anytime. The more you enjoy walking and the more benefits you realize from being physically active, the more likely you will be to continue. Making regular physical activity a permanent lifestyle habit is a key to being successful in this program. Let's look at some ways to help make walking more enjoyable.

Make It Fun

Walking should be something you enjoy doing. The more enjoyable it is, the more likely you will want to do it again. Many clever ideas can help make walking fun. Asking someone you enjoy talking with to join you can increase the pleasure of walking. Walking in different places is a good way to change the scenery and make a walk more interesting. Many walkers enjoy taking a portable radio or one of the new MP-3 players along and listening to the news or their favorite music. If you have a place that is near water, the pleasure of walking can be increased. A river, stream, beach, or lake can make walking much more interesting and fun.

Take a Moderate Approach

Increasing your physical activity in moderate amounts is the key to making activity a permanent habit. Beginning at a level that is comfortable for you is much better than following a prescription in an exercise book or a video tape. Work your way up from there. This is the beauty of using a pedometer like the LEARN WalkMaster that we introduced you to in Lesson Four, on page 89. The pedometer will give you a base line or starting point. From there, you can increase your activity in moderate amounts.

Don't Overdo It

A sure way to sabotage an exercise program is to do too much too soon. Not only can you injure yourself, you may also become sore, uncomfortable, frustrated, and discouraged. Although you may be enthusiastic about increasing your physical activity, be careful not to over do it. Remember, you are developing lifelong habits that you can do the rest of your life.

Some people may stay at a comfortable activity level for a few weeks before moving ahead, while others may increase their activity levels more rapidly. Either way is fine.

Physical Activity Review

Week	Average Minutes/Day
5	
6	
7	
8	
9	
10	

The important message here is to make physical activity something you can live with for life. To see how your physical activity has increased since you began the program, complete the worksheet above. You will need to refer to your Physical Activity and Relaxation Record in Appendix F, on page 433, for weeks 5-10.

Lesson Review

We began this lesson with a discussion on motivation. You then reviewed your imagery and prediction testing assignments that you began in Lesson Ten. We completed our discussion on procrastination by talking about type III procrastination—not knowing where to begin. The topic of catastrophizing came up and we discussed ways of conquering these types of thoughts. We revisited the topic of relaxation and discussed ways to make your relaxation more portable, enabling you to "take it with you" wherever you go. We then looked at the relationship between stress and anger and explored ways to manage your anger more effectively. And finally, the topic of exercise came up again.

This is a good time in the program to take stock of your physical activity.

This Weeks Assignment

For the next week, continue with your imagery and prediction testing that you began in Lesson Ten. We include a blank Prediction Testing Worksheet on page 273 and a blank Visual Imagery Worksheet on page 275. We have also included a blank Expanded Realistic Thinking Worksheet on page 274, a Daily Stress Record on page 277, and a Time Investment Worksheet on page 278. Remember to complete your Stress Change Worksheet on page 227, the Average Stress Change Worksheet on page 430 in Appendix E, and the Physical Activity and Relaxation Worksheet in Appendix F, on page 433. Remember not to get stressed with all of the forms and worksheets we provide. These are here for your use if you find them helpful. Good luck with this week's lesson.

Knowledge Review

T F 86. Expecting and planning for difficulties in learning to master your stress is not a good idea because this means you plan to fail.

T F 87. Rewarding yourself for progress is justified when you are making significant progress in a long, difficult project.

T F 88. When testing your predictions, it is important to accept only objective evidence.

T F 89. When you catastrophize, you imagine the worst possible outcome and underestimate your ability to cope with the perceived outcome.

T F 90. Eating a balanced diet means eating equal amounts of protein and carbohydrate.

T F 91. Portability means being able to relax in shorter amounts of time by reducing the number of muscle groups tensed and relaxed.

T F 92. Regular physical activity such as walking is a helpful way to reduce your stress.

(Answers in Appendix C, page 415)

Prediction Testing Worksheet

Today's Date:

Event	Prediction	Test	Outcome

Expanded Realistic Thinking Worksheet

Today's Date:

(1) Event	(2) Initial Thought	(3) Evidence (How Do I Know?)	(4) Initial/Realistic Probability	(5) Initial/Revised Stress Level (0–8 Scale)	(6) Consequence

Visual Imagery Worksheet

Today's Date:

Event	Visualized Uncomfortable Emotions	Visualized Pleasant Emotions	What Changed?

Muscle Groups Portability Practice

My 12 Muscle Groups	My 8 Muscle Groups	My 4 Muscle Groups
1.	1.	1.
2.	2.	2.
3.	3.	3.
4.	4.	4.
5.	5.	
6.	6.	
7.	7.	
8.		
9.		
10.		
11.		
12.		

Daily Stress Record—Lesson Eleven

Name:______________________ Week of:____________

Date	Average Stress Level	Highest Stress Level	Time of Highest Stress Level	Stressful Event Associated with Highest Stress Level

My Physical Activity and Relaxation Record				
Day of the Week	Physical Activity Record		Relaxation Record[1]	
	Activity	Minutes	Time of Day	Minutes
Monday				
Tuesday				
Wednesday				
Thursday				
Friday				
Saturday				
Sunday				

1 **Remember to tense each muscle group three times—the first at ¾ of maximum tension; the second at ½ of maximum tension; and the third at ¼ of maximum tension.**

Time Investment Worksheet					
					Today's Date:
Time	**Activity**	**Urgent**	**Important**	**Stress Level (0–8)**	**Thoughts**
12:00–1:00 am					
1:00–2:00 am					
2:00–3:00 am					
3:00–4:00 am					
4:00–5:00 am					
5:00–6:00 am					
6:00–7:00 am					
7:00–8:00 am					
8:00–9:00 am					
9:00–10:00 am					
10:00–11:00 am					
11:00–11:59 am					
12:00–1:00 pm					
1:00–2:00 pm					
2:00–3:00 pm					
3:00–4:00 pm					
4:00–5:00 pm					
5:00–6:00 pm					
6:00–7:00 pm					
7:00–8:00 pm					
8:00–9:00 pm					
9:00–10:00 pm					
10:00–11:00 pm					
11:00–11:59 pm					

Lesson Twelve

This lesson begins some of the more advanced stress management techniques. We begin with an introduction to reality testing. You will find this technique a bit more difficult than other techniques, yet very effective in helping you manage your stress. We will introduce you to the stepladder approach to reality testing. This is a good introduction into a more in-depth discussion on setting reasonable goals. Our discussion then turns to relaxation by recall. This is an exciting extension of the deep muscle relaxation you have been practicing, and we hope you enjoy the discussion here. The topic of job-related stress comes up again followed by an important topic under the **A** (Attitudes) portion of the LEARN acronym. You will learn about an important attitude trap called imperatives. Frustration and stress is the next topic followed by more discussion about the **N** (Nutrition) component of LEARN. We conclude the lesson with a quality of life review. We hope that you are pleased with the progress you have made in the Mastering Stress Program and take credit for all the hard work you have put into the program.

Introducing Reality Testing

You have been using prediction testing to weigh the evidence and predict the outcome of stressful situations. This technique works on the *mental* component of stress by helping you evaluate all of the evidence more realistically. We now introduce you to a related technique that will help you work on the *behavioral* component of stress. We call this technique reality testing. In reality testing, you intentionally put yourself into situations that make you nervous or uncomfortable. This is done so that you can experience the related stress and discover if what you expect really happens. Try not to get stressed about the idea of reality testing! It is much easier to do that you may realize. We will not ask you to plunge right into the stressful situations that bother you most. You will learn how to do this gradually, taking one step at a time.

Learning comes about in many ways. One of the best ways to learn something new is to experience it firsthand. Many suc-

cessful people have learned by doing. Your parents may have told you that you have to learn from your own mistakes. Rather than learning from stressful situations, however, many of us avoid similar situations altogether—never learning how to deal with them. Avoidance is sometimes the best strategy, but too often, avoidance turns into faulty perceptions. In other words, avoidance can lead some people to avoid things they *perceive* to be stressful. Their thoughts and beliefs about certain situations are automatic and deeply ingrained. No amount of reading, writing, or talking will help them overcome these fears. The best way to overcome these stressful situations is to challenge them directly. You accomplish this by intentionally putting yourself in the stressful situation. Think of this as learning to swim—you can't learn to swim without getting in the water. Let's look at an example to help you understand this notion a little better.

Meet John

John is an accountant with a large pubic accounting firm in Seattle. He gets stressed at the slightest thought of being late for an appointment—personal or professional. The realistic thinking technique has help John considerably. Yet, he still gets stressed about the thought of being late to a client's office or being late for work. As a result, John tries hard to avoid the possibility of being late at all costs. He gets up early to avoid any traffic on the way to work. John arrives up to 30 minutes early for client appointments to avoid being late. Of course, this isn't an efficient use of his time, and it only adds to his stress. John doesn't have time to do things that are truly important to him, like exercise. Anything that makes John *think* he will be late, like heavy traffic, not knowing the directions, or not being sure of the time, increases his stress. Being on time is a good character quality. However, obsessively worrying and stressing over the notion of being late is not healthy. Reality testing helped John lower the stress he felt about being late. This, in turn, helped John reduce his overall level of stress throughout the day.

Reality testing is a widely used technique that was first used to treat phobias, such as fear of heights. The best way to overcome this fear is to approach heights gradually, in a step-by-step, controlled manner. Research at our clinics has also shown reality testing to be an effective stress management tool. This technique can help individuals overcome more general concerns, like being late for an appointment. Many people who experience high levels of stress also have phobias that increase their stress even more.

Let's consider another example. Imagine Alan, a young professional taking a public speaking course. When he first signs up for the course, he is very nervous. He lies awake the night before the first class, frightened at the thought of speaking before a group of strangers. When Alan finally falls asleep, he dreams about all the things that might go wrong in the class. The next morning, when he arrives at the first class, he is tired and feels very stressed. When the instructor asks him to stand up to introduce himself to the class, his stress level sores skyward.

After introducing himself and talking for a few moments about his work, Alan's stress level begins to fall. He then finishes the introduction, feeling a sense of relief and accomplishment. The following week, on the day before the next class, Alan's stress begins to increase again. Yet, he realizes that his stress level is not as high as it was a week earlier. His experience from the first class helps him realize that once he starts speaking, he feels better. Each class gets easier and less stressful for Alan. Before the last class, Alan experiences no stress at all. In fact, he anxiously awaits the last class.

Returning to the public speaking classes week after week, Alan learned an important lesson. He learned that there was really nothing to fear. Alan conquered his fear by taking one step at a time, learning that he could cope with his stressful feelings. Now imagine what would have happened if Alan had not returned to the class after the first day. He would have convinced himself that he was unable to speak before a group. Even worse, Alan would have convinced himself that he was unable to do anything about it. Instead, he decided to stay in the uncomfortable situation and conquer his fear. In other words, doing nothing raises concern, but avoidance makes the situation even more difficult.

The examples presented above illustrate the power of reality testing. This technique has helped many of our clients lower their stress. Reality testing can work with many situations that cause people stress, such as getting lost, being a little disorganized, speaking to people in authority, or making mistakes. Remember, people vary in what they consider to be stressful. Before you try reality testing, you need to carefully identify the areas where it will help you the most. Ask your friends and relatives whether they have noticed any situations that seem to make you particularly agitated. Then, review the stress management work you have been doing since you began this program. Are you encountering situations or events where your stress has not diminished to the level you would prefer? If so, reality testing may help you in these areas.

"Conquering fears such as public speaking can be achieved by repeating the uncomfortable situation over and over until you learn to cope."

A Word of Caution

Reality testing reminds us of an old story about two men walking down the street. Every time one man comes to a crack in the sidewalk he quickly steps over it. His friend eventually asks him why he keeps stepping over the cracks. To this he replies, "It keeps the tigers away." His friend quickly exclaims, "But I don't see any tigers in the middle of town!" "See, it works," came the reply.

This is a good illustration of how avoidance can work in our lives. Many of our activities and behaviors are unnecessary and may even be stressful or damaging. Yet, we believe we must do them to achieve certain ends. As long as we continue these activities, we never learn that the bad things we are trying to avoid either don't happen or are not as bad as we think.

A secretary, who was a client of ours, used to proof her letters several times for fear of making a mistake. Because she always checked her work so many times, she never learned that the chances of her making a mistake were actually very small or that if she did make a mistake, it would not be the end of the world. Reality testing helps you to stop avoiding certain activities or events. In doing this, you learn firsthand that what you fear is not as bad as you think. In other words, reality testing provides firsthand evidence for your realistic thinking. When the secretary stopped proofing her letters over and over again, she soon realized that she seldom made a mistake. When she did make a mistake, her boss didn't yell at her and she did not lose her job. She learned not to worry about absolute perfection, and she became much more efficient at doing her work. This tremendously reduced her daily stress level.

"We were way ahead of schedule, so we revised the schedule. Now we're way behind schedule because we lost too much time revising the schedule. What we need is a schedule to help us revise our schedules on schedule."

Thoroughly understanding reality testing before you begin experimenting with it is important. The first thing to realize is that it is somewhat difficult to do. Keep in mind that most new things we experience in life can be stressful. Do you remember learning how to swim? Putting your head under the water was probably a little stressful for you at first. Now you jump right in with little thought about your head being beneath the surface. Remember that short bouts of controlled short-term stress will help you reduce your overall stress in the long run.

Certainly, we do not want you to stress yourself too much. We will be discussing ways of doing reality testing in a gradual manner later. Here are some other points to remember about reality testing:

Stick with it. The key to reality testing is to stay in the situation until your stress level begins to come down. You may feel like running away, especially at first. Don't give in! If your stress becomes truly unbearable, it's okay to back off a little until you feel calmer. Try to return to the situation when you can. Think of the cliche about falling off a horse: the only way to learn how to ride is to get back on.

Keep practicing. The success of reality testing is like the success of any skill or technique you have learned—it depends upon practice. A stressful situation may become easier after a single session of reality testing, but it may still be difficult for you. You will need to do it again, and again, and again before it comes easy.

Remember the good days. Reality testing does not always go as smoothly as you would like. You are likely to encounter many ups and downs as you practice. You may have good days when you can stay in a stressful situation for a long time. You're also likely to experience bad days when the slightest exposure to the situation makes you want to scream. Don't let the bad days get you down. Everyone has them. Just do as much as you can, and get back into it again the next day. With repeated practice, your stress level will decrease.

Stay in control. Some of our clients do not believe that reality testing could possibly work for them. "I am in that situation a lot," they say, "and it still makes me stressed. So, what good will practice do?" Remember, in reality testing, you deliberately put yourself into a stressful situation. This is a gradual process of *planned* exposure. This process allows you to advance gradually and feel more in control than if you were unexpectedly placed in the same situation. You do this because you want to, not because you have to.

Be aware of avoidance. Running away from a stressful situation may not be the only way of avoiding it. Procrastination is a common way to avoid stressful situations. The more aware you are of the things you do to avoid stressful situations, the better your chances of stopping them. This is not to say that you should not use these techniques at all, but you should be aware of what you are doing so that eventually you can eliminate these behaviors.

Reality Testing

Points to Remember

- ✓Stick with it
- ✓Keep practicing
- ✓Remember the good days
- ✓Stay in control
- ✓Be aware of avoidance
- ✓Don't be distracted

Don't be distracted. Instead, focus on the situation and challenge your thoughts about it. Using the realistic thinking techniques and the skills you learned to overcome procrastination. Only you know what increases your stress and what makes it easier; only you know when you are being honest about reality testing. Remember, you have everything to gain from trying.

Making a Stepladder

In reality testing, your goal is to try things that make you nervous and uncomfortable, but they should not be too difficult. If you start by immediately throwing yourself into the most stressful situation you can imagine, you may not handle it very well. This may discourage you from trying again. We recommend you make your testing easier and more systematic by developing a step-by-step plan. We find the stepladder approach a simple and handy way to begin.

First, think of a stressful situation or event you want to master. To illustrate, we'll continue the example we started earlier. Let's say that you feel stress at the notion of giving a speech. Now think of 8 or 10 situations in which you might give a talk, each with varying degrees of difficulty. Arrange these situations in order of their difficulty, from the easiest to the hardest. The easiest step goes at the bottom of the ladder, with the hardest at the top. Real examples work best. If you can't think of an instance where giving a talk would be relatively easy to give, invent one. Giving a speech to yourself in front of a mirror, video camera, or to family or friends is an example. Make each of these steps just a bit harder than the last one. As you complete each step, you will gain the confidence to continue to the next rung of the ladder.

Once you have completed the stepladder, think about doing the first step. You should feel a little nervous, but not overwhelmed by the idea of beginning. If you do feel overwhelmed, break the first item down into smaller steps. If you feel overwhelmed by the idea of giving a speech to a partner or friend, consider putting it in writing first. Then you may consider reading the written speech into a tape recorder or your computer. Play it back and make any changes you feel necessary. When you are satisfied, ask your partner or friend to listen to the recording. Smaller, less-stressful steps can generally be taken toward achieving your larger goal. We have illustrated a sample stepladder for learning to be more comfortable about giving speeches on the left.

Stepladder Approach

(Example)

The first step, giving a speech to your spouse, is manageable—not too easy, but manageable. The next step, giving a speech to your family, is a little harder. It's important for you to set a time to do this next step—the sooner, the better. Don't let yourself fall into the avoidance trap. The longer you wait the more time you have to worry. Be sure to use the realistic thinking skills you have learned. They will help to reduce your stress as much as possible beforehand. Committing yourself to a date for beginning to practice and telling someone about it may be helpful. If not, at least write it down on your recording forms. You may ask, "How long does it take to test each step?" The answer is, "You should do each step until you become relatively comfortable (a stress level of one or two) doing it."

The stepladder approach is a strategy to help you practice the skill of coping with a stressful situation. You would not expect yourself to play a scale on the piano exactly right the first time you try. A week of practice may be necessary to play the scale correctly. Try not to expect more of yourself in this situation than you would if you were learning to play the piano for the first time. As you go along, you may find that the next step is too easy, or too hard. If you do not experience any stress at all the first time, then the step is too easy. You can move to the next step or change the step you are on to make it more challenging. The step is too hard if you find yourself dreading or postponing it. Consider breaking it down into easier steps. The key is to set *reasonable* goals.

Goal Setting

We have talked about setting reasonable goals in earlier lessons, and we will bring this topic up again in later lessons. Many people share the common attitude problem of setting unrealistic goals. Some may not realize that they are setting unattainable goals, but do so nonetheless. Suppose you were totally inactive before you started this program. Realizing the benefits of regular physical activity, you set a goal of running 45 minutes a day, five days a week. Is this reasonable? Of course not. This type of activity is possible, but not right away. Some individuals may set even more unrealistic goals when they do not meet their original goals. How realistic is this? Let's say that you do not meet your goal of running 45 minutes a day for five days a week. So, the next week you set a goal of running one hour a day for six days. Is this realistic? Setting unrealistic goals is a setup for failure and a failed program. You are a sensible person and can develop reasonable goals. Do you believe that your hidden or unconscious goals are unrealistic? If so, rethink your goals and test them for reasonableness.

Let's suppose that you reassess your activity goals. Instead of running for 45 minutes, five days a week, you set a goal of taking two five-minute walks on Monday, Wednesday, and Friday next week. Is this a more reasonable goal? Sure it is. Now, let's say that after the first week, you easily meet this activity goal. What do you think happens to your self-esteem, confidence, and overall mental attitude? Reality testing works much the same way. As you successfully complete each reasonable goal or step along the way, you will feel a mixture of challenge and accomplishment. The records you keep will show your progress and improvement.

"Working through the fear step-by-step will help you gain self confidence."

Relaxation by Recall

When you have truly mastered deep muscle relaxation, you can recognize the slightest tension in your muscles during the day. This allows you to immediately start reducing the tension. At this point, you are ready to advance to the next stage: relaxation by recall. This is different from the practice you have been doing. In your practices to this point, you were first tensing your muscles and concentrating on that feeling. In relaxation by recall, you do not tense your muscles. You simply try to recapture the feeling you had after you let your muscles flop. By now, this should be quite a familiar feeling for both your muscles and your mind. If you have difficulty, there is no shame in going back to the longer practices to become more proficient at this skill. Learning new skills is not always easy, but you can do it.

When you practice relaxation by recall, continue to use the same muscle groups on which you have been working. Begin the relaxation practice the same way that you normally would, but instead of tensing your muscles, simply let them flop. Try to think back to the relaxed feeling from earlier practices. Let the muscles you are focusing on feel warm, soft, and relaxed. Between muscle groups, you should still do the mental relaxation as you did before. Each time you breathe in, count to yourself "one, two, three . . ." When you exhale, picture the word "relax" in your mind, and try to feel the relaxation washing over your body, as if a gentle ocean wave has swept over you and is now retreating. Breathe slowly and evenly, in and out. Let your tension drift away, just as you did in the muscle relaxation exercise.

"Try to feel the relaxation washing over you, like a gentle ocean wave sweeping over your body."

Achieving a truly relaxed state simply by recall takes much practice. Once you master this technique, however, you will find yourself doing it often. Continue to practice deep muscle relaxation from time to time to ensure that you do not forget the feeling. Some of our clients practice deep muscle relaxation twice a week, some once a week, and others twice a month. Experiment to see what works best for you. Keep in mind that with relaxation by recall you can achieve a deep state of relaxation in a few seconds, but your relaxation skills have to be refined. Simply imagine the word "relax" and try to recall the feeling. You have come a long way from the 20-minute practices! Congratulate yourself. You have made much progress.

More on Job Stress

In Lesson Eleven, on page 270, you completed the Job Stress Questionnaire. We designed this questionnaire to help you identify some common job-related stress symptoms. Many of the stress management techniques you have already learned can be helpful in overcoming job-related stress. Let's look at some common job-related beliefs that contribute to stress. Then, we will show you how to challenge these beliefs to help lower your stress.

Belief—Perfectionism:

> "I must always perform perfectly at important things I do at work; I can never accept making mistakes."

Challenge:

> "Although I will try my best not to make mistakes, I'm human and will make them on occasion. Demanding that I must always be perfect may even increase the likelihood of making mistakes. Therefore, striving for excellence

instead of 'perfection' is a much better strategy."

Belief—Low Frustration Tolerance:

"I can't stand not getting what I want. My life should never be difficult; things should be easier for me than they are. I can't stand the day-to-day hassles. I can't stand being uptight, tense, and uncomfortable. I should have a more exciting and fun life, like everyone else."

Challenge:

"Although I'm unhappy not getting what I want, when I want it. I know I can stand it, because I have in the past! Sometimes life is just difficult. Nobody ever said life would always be easy, fun, and exciting. When I tell myself that I can't stand something, I am probably underestimating my ability to cope with a difficult situation. I have many wonderful things in my life, and I have developed some terrific coping skills."

Belief—Approval-Seeking:

"I must always have the approval of my co-workers. I can't stand it when I believe they are thinking bad things about me and my work."

Challenge:

"Although it's normal to want the approval of others, I don't really need it. It is always nice to get approval, but not getting it is not the end of the world. I can always seek input on my performance at work and strive to do the best job I can. And, even if I don't get approving comments, I will know that at least I have done my best. This will make me more pleased with myself."

Belief—Awfulizing:

"I feel terrible when I don't succeed at something. I hate getting criticized or treated unfairly. It is just awful when I fail."

Challenge:

"Few things in life are truly awful. When I constantly tell myself that something is awful, I'm most likely catastrophizing, and it's really not very bad. Is it terrible and awful when I don't succeed, or is it just unfortunate and disappointing? I think the latter. When I try to tell myself that something is awful, perhaps I should ask myself if it will matter as much in a week, a month, or a year. This may help give me a better perspective on what seems awful to me at the time."

Belief—Personalizing:

"When I make mistakes or don't always do an excellent job on something at work, I'm a failure. When this happens, I feel hopeless."

Challenge:

"How does making a mistake at work or not always achieving excellence make me a failure? I know it's important to take responsibility for my mistakes and learn from them. Still, making mistakes from time to time is part of being hu-

"Challenging common beliefs can reduce your job-related stress."

man. At times I will do well, and at other times I may not do so well. However, if I continue to strive for excellence, then I will know I have done the best I can."

Belief—Self-Blaming:

"It's always my fault when something goes wrong."

Challenge:

"Is it accurate to say that it's always my fault when something goes wrong? Most things, other than my choices, are beyond my control."

Belief—Self-Generalizing:

"Not performing well at something proves that I'm not good at doing anything."

Challenge:

"It is an overgeneralization to say that not doing well at one thing means I'm not good at doing anything. We all have strengths and weaknesses. Doing poorly in one area does not necessarily affect other areas. I'm actually good at doing many things."

Belief—Inaccurate Forecasting:

"I'll never be successful at anything. Things will never turn out the way I want."

Challenge:

"How do I know I will never be successful at anything? Although I don't think I've been successful at anything yet, maybe I'm being too hard on myself. If everybody gave up the first time they failed at something, they might never succeed at anything. I should view my failures as opportunities to learn how to do better the next time."

Belief—Demanding:

"People should treat me fairly, considerately, professionally, and respectfully. I cannot accept unfair and inconsiderate treatment from others."

Challenge:

"Everyone would like to be treated fairly, considerately, professionally, and respectfully. However, demanding that this always happens is not realistic and certainly no guarantee that it will. I will assert myself in an appropriate way if I believe I am not being treated fairly. But, it is more realistic to expect and accept that others may behave in unfair and inconsiderate ways. Realizing the only

thing over which I have control is my choice of how I *respond* is important."

Belief—Condemning:

"People who behave unfairly and inconsiderately are totally bad. Someone should punish them."

Challenge:

"I should apply the same standard to other people that I apply to myself. An inconsiderate act does not make someone a *bad* person. I'm sure that I sometimes appear inconsiderate to others. We are all human, and we all behave in unfair or inconsiderate ways at certain times. This does not make us totally bad."

We have said many times before in this program that most of our thoughts and beliefs are *automatic*. Can you see how your automatic beliefs contribute to your stress? Can you also see how challenging your beliefs can help to reduce your stress and make you feel better as a person? Realizing that you have the power to review and challenge your stressful automatic beliefs is important. Being aware of the attitude trap of *imperatives* is another way to reduce your stress. Let's explore this a little further.

Imperatives— An Attitude Trap

From the previous discussion, you may have picked up on the many imperatives automatic beliefs often include. Imperatives are words and phrases that imply perfection, urgency, or allow no room for error. Examples of imperative words include, *never, must,* and *always*. The thoughts and beliefs of most people are saturated with imperative words and phrases. Let's review the example beliefs above and see how many we can find. Here are a few:

- "I must *always* perform perfectly."
- "I can *never* accept making mistakes."
- "My life should *never* be so difficult."
- "I need to *always* have the approval of my co-workers."
- "It's *always* my fault when something goes wrong."

Imperative thoughts can hide in the recesses of your mind, waiting to leap out when you least expect them. They can ravage your self-esteem and sense of control. You can easily recover from making a mistake, doing a particular job poorly, or not getting a long-awaited approval from someone you admire. However, imperatives can torpedo everything about and around you with thoughts like, "I never do anything right. I'm such a failure." When this happens, you and the world around you can be devastated with a single imperative torpedo blast.

"Imperatives are like a torpedo blast, devastating you and the world around you. But they can be changed."

Individuals who believe that they should never make a mistake, must always receive recognition for everything they do, or must succeed in everything they attempt to do

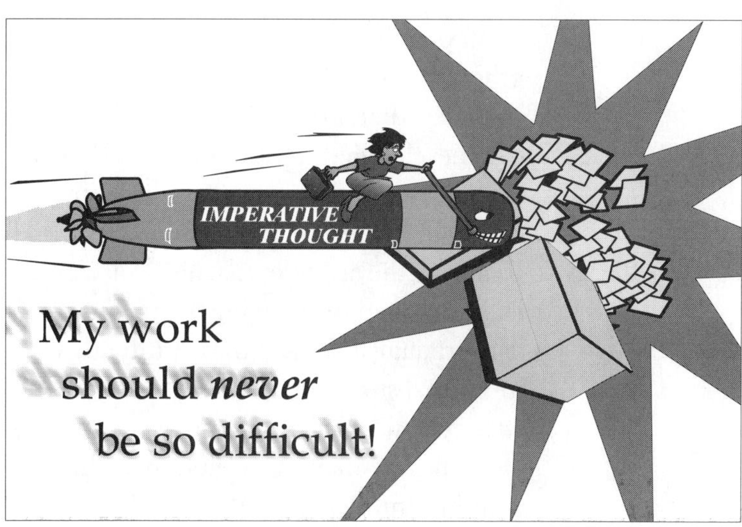
IMPERATIVE THOUGHT
My work should *never* be so difficult!

Imperative Statements and Their Counter Statements	
Imperative Statement	**Counter Statement**

fall prey to the attitude trap of imperatives. To deny yourself the right to make a simple mistake may work well for a week or so. Yet, inevitably a mistake or imperfection will surface. When this happens, you are likely to feel like a failure and your sense of control can wane even more.

Search for imperatives in your self-talk. On the worksheet above write down at least five imperative statements that are a regular part of your vocabulary. Then, to the right of each statement, write out a counter statement.

Imperative statements are just like any other lifelong habits that develop over time. But, like other attitudes and behaviors, they can be changed—with practice. Practice thinking a different way may seem strange or silly to you at first, but it really does work! Realizing the attitudes that give you trouble is the first step to changing them. Then you can gradually replace these attitudes with more realistic and positive approaches to stressful situations. Eventually, you will weaken and may even eliminate the unhealthy attitudes altogether.

Frustration and Stress

Imagine for a moment that you are standing in line at the grocery store. You're in a hurry because the dinner you are preparing is cooking on the stove. You needed a few items to finish this masterpiece of a meal, so here you are in the express lane with only three people ahead of you. The person at the checkout has two items that do not have a bar code. So, the checker calls for a price check. A minute goes buy, then two and three. Finally, someone comes to the counter to help. Another three minutes pass before the clerk returns with the right pricing. "Finally," you think, "Now the line will move along." Just then, you notice the customer is having trouble with her credit card. After another few minutes, she decides that the credit card simply will not work. She doesn't have enough cash so she tells the clerk she will have to run to her car and get her checkbook. She asks the clerk to wait "one second" while she gets her checkbook. By now, your blood is boiling, and you're totally frustrated.

The frustrations we experience in life directly affect the stress we feel. Our ability to learn, practice, and apply appropriate coping skills is paramount to managing the stress associated with frustrations. Overall, we know that some individuals can handle frustration quite well, while others find the slightest hassle intolerable. Tolerating frustration and its related stress does not mean you have to welcome or passively accept everything in life with open arms. It simply means accepting those things that we cannot control or change and realizing the power of what we can control and change—our thoughts. Below are some more realistic and rational beliefs that can help you tolerate the day-to-day frustrations and hassles in life:

- "Although I do not like frustration, I have the skills and abilities to deal with it. To say that I can't is an underestimation of my coping abilities."
- "That woman has held up the express lane for more than 10 minutes now. I may be inconvenienced, but she may also be feeling very embarrassed. Her situation could be worse than mine."
- "In the long run, the easier and less disciplined approach to pleasure and enjoyment is usually less rewarding than the more difficult or uncomfortable route. The shortest route is not necessarily the best one to follow."
- "I'm happiest when I accomplish something that I worked hard for and that took a long time to achieve. The sensation of achievement lasts a long time. Short-term achievements are fine, but the gratification is also short lived."
- "While some things I have to do may be difficult, unpleasant, and even boring, they are generally manageable."
- "Yes, it's a hassle to do this now. But, putting it off will only make matters worse, not to mention all of the additional stress I'll feel. Waiting won't make it any easier."
- "While it may be unfair that I have to work so hard, my life does not have to be easy."
- "In order to achieve pleasing results, I may have to do unpleasant things."

Are you easily frustrated over the slightest inconvenience? If so, you can learn to build your frustration tolerance and reduce your stress. You have already learned many skills for handling frustration. On the worksheet on page 292, list five of the most common frustrations you experience in life. Then, to the right of each one, list the stress management skills and techniques you

Five Common Frustrations	
Frustration	**Stress Management Skill**

have learned that will help minimize the stress you feel when you encounter the situation. Let's look at an example.

Meet Joe

Joe had a difficult project assigned to him at work. The more he thought about the project, the more frustrated and stressed he became. Joe procrastinated about beginning the project for many weeks. In Joe's words, "This assignment is difficult, dull, and serves no purpose." Yet, Joe realized that the firm's client viewed the project as a necessary step in improving efficiency. Joe's frustration resulted from his belief that his supervisor unfairly assigned him the project. After all, this was not *his* client.

"Our company lost 900 million dollars last quarter. Your job is to make this look like the best thing that ever happened to us."

Joe soon realized that this project was not going away. He was running out of time to complete the assignment, so he began to challenge his beliefs about the situation. This is what Joe said to himself to build his frustration tolerance and reduce his stress:

- "Why must I always have projects that are interesting, easy and useful? Couldn't I do a good job even though it's not what I enjoy doing?"
- "Haven't there been times when others got stuck doing the bad projects and I lucked out with something good?"
- "How does putting it off make it better? I know that it will be worse if I put it off so long that I run out of time and produce an inferior product."
- "Although I may not see the value of this project, I can respect the fact that someone else does."
- "Although doing unpleasant things is undesirable at times, it is part of life. I can handle it!"

Joe used his realistic thinking and probability analysis to more clearly understand why he had been given the difficult assignment. He soon realized that he was the most skilled employee to handle the project. He then used the skills he had learned to overcome procrastination, along with appropriate time management skills, to get the project moving along. In no time at all, the once frustrating and seemingly worthless project became Joe's favorite assignment. Joe did an outstanding job on the project. He not only received a promotion, but also was assigned permanently to one of the firm's largest clients!

Revisiting the Food Guide Pyramid

In Lesson Eleven, on page 263, we introduced you to the Food Guide Pyramid. We promised to discuss servings and serving sizes in more detail. This is a good time in the program to continue with this discussion. Let's begin with the number of servings from each of the five food groups.

Servings from the Five Food Groups

The five food groups of the Food Guide Pyramid are shown in the illustration on page 263. Keep in mind that it is important to eat daily servings from each of the five food groups. Even if you are a vegetarian or vegan, the pyramid can easily be adapted to help you eat a balanced and healthy diet. The number of servings you eat from each of the five food groups is dependent upon the number of daily calories in your diet. Once you know your target calorie level, you can use the table to determine the recommended number of servings from each of the five food groups. This is relatively simple for most people to do. The more difficult task is understanding and estimating the serving sizes.

We have borrowed two helpful illustrations from *The LEARN Program for Weight Management 2000*, by Kelly D. Brownell at Yale University, to help you better understand a serving sizes. On page 294, is an illustration titled, "What Counts as a Pyramid Serving?" We like this illustration because it is easy to visualize serving sizes from each of the five food groups. If you would like even more information on serving sizes you may want to consider getting a copy of *The LEARN Healthy Eating and Calo-*

Food Pyramid Servings and Calorie Guide*

Food Group	1200 calories (number of servings)	1400 calories (number of servings)	1500 calories (number of servings)	1800 calories (number of servings)	2000 calories (number of servings)
Bread, Cereal, Rices, & Pasta Group	6	6	7	8	9
Fruit Group	3	3	3	4	4
Vegetable Group	4	4	5	6	6
Milk, Yogurt, & Cheese Group	2 (non-fat)	2 (low-fat)	2 (low-fat)	2 (low-fat)	3 (low-fat)
Meat, Poultry, Fish, Dry Beans, Eggs, & Nut Group	5 oz lean meat (or equivalent)	5 oz medium-fat meat (or equivalent)	5 oz medium-fat meat (or equivalent)	7 oz medium-fat meat (or equivalent)	7 oz medium-fat meat (or equivalent)

* This plan does not leave room for added fat. If you choose lower fat meats and dairy products, you can add some items from the Fats, Oils & Sweets Group.

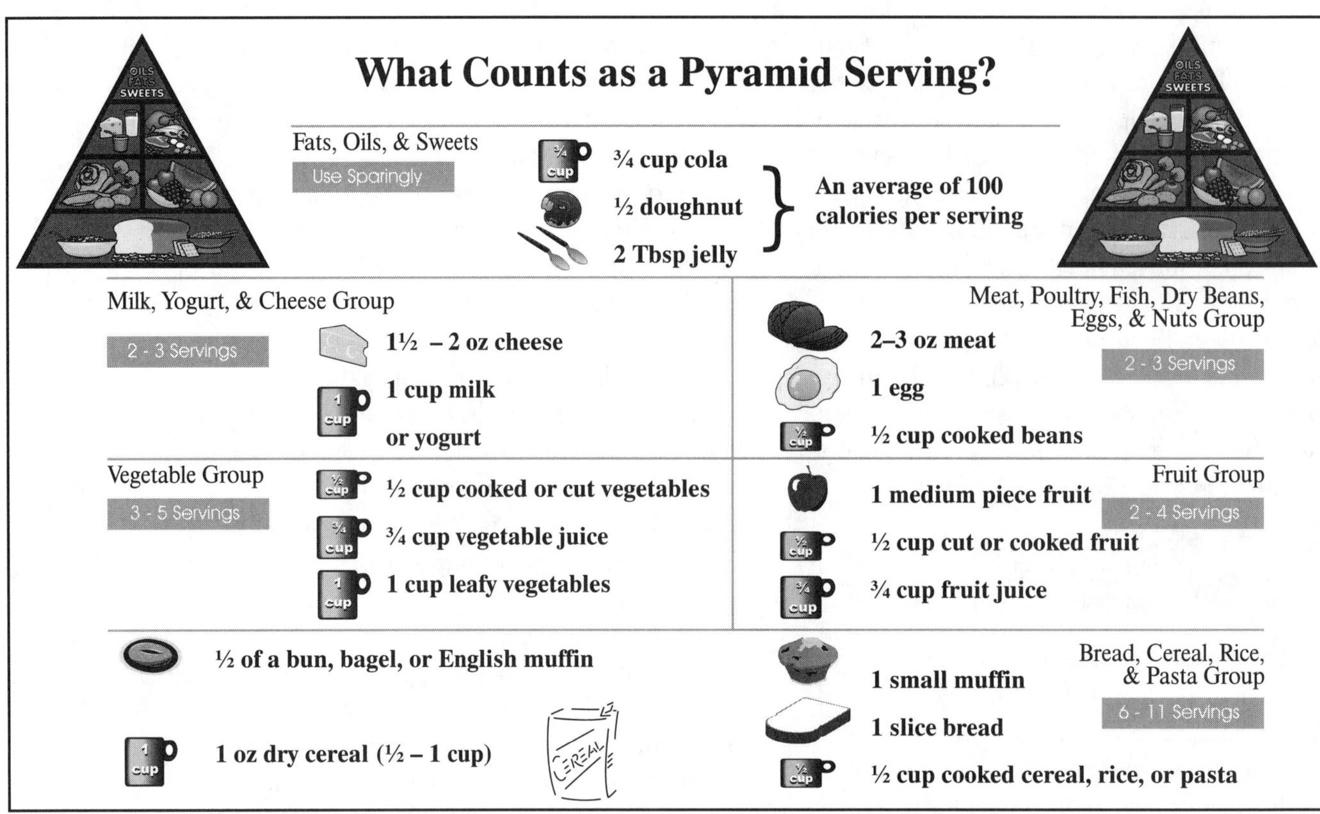

rie Guide, discussed on page 451 in the back of this book.

Foods from the second tier of the pyramid (see illustration above) are primarily from animal sources. Foods in the third and last tier of the pyramid come primarily from plant sources. This is important to know because animal and plant sources of food provide different nutrients for our bodies.

The Food Guide Pyramid arranges food groups by the nutrients they provide. This is why eating a variety of food items from within each food group is important. For instance, food choices from the Meat, Poultry, Fish, Dry Beans, Eggs, and Nuts Group are high in protein, B vitamins, iron, and zinc. The Milk, Yogurt, and Cheese Group includes foods high in protein and provides other key nutrients such as calcium and vitamin D. Fruits, vegetables, cereals, rice, and other grains are all excellent sources of dietary fiber and other important vitamins and minerals. Choosing the right number of servings from the different food groups each day helps you achieve a healthy and balanced diet. This is important in stress management because your diet directly affects how your physical response system responds to stress.

A Visual Guide

Another helpful guide is the Visual Portion Guide illustrated on page 295. If you are concerned about your weight and calories, accurately measuring your food portions is key. You can accurately measure portion sizes using measuring cups, food scales, and measuring spoons. However, carrying these measuring devices around with you is not always easy.

The Visual Portion Guide is a handy tool to use when more accurate measuring is not possible. Review this guide carefully so that you can more accurately estimate the portion sizes of the foods you eat. You may want to make a copy of this and carry it with you.

In Lesson Ten, we had you rate your diet. We'll have you do this again in Lesson Fourteen to see if your diet has improved. Use the Food Guide Pyramid to help improve your diet. You may be surprised how easy it is to improve your eating habits and your overall health with a well-balanced diet.

Time Management Checkup

In Lesson Seven, on page 171, we introduced you to the Time Investment Worksheet. If you have been keeping a daily Time Investment Worksheet, that's terrific. If not, we would like you to keep this record four or five days during the next week. In the next lesson, you will be referring to these worksheets as we forge ahead with time management skills and techniques. We have included a blank Time Investment Worksheet on page 299 for you to use. Make as many copies as you need.

Quality of Life Review

The time has come to once again review your quality of life. Why? Your life, how you feel about your life, and your ability to control your choices may be the most important measures of stress management of all. Yet, all to often, people tend to overlook many of the important changes they have made while going through the Mastering Stress Program. Consider confidence, self-assurance, and comfort level in social situations. If you are feeling less stressed and have more confidence in your ability to handle stressful situations and events, you have made tremendous progress. Unlike

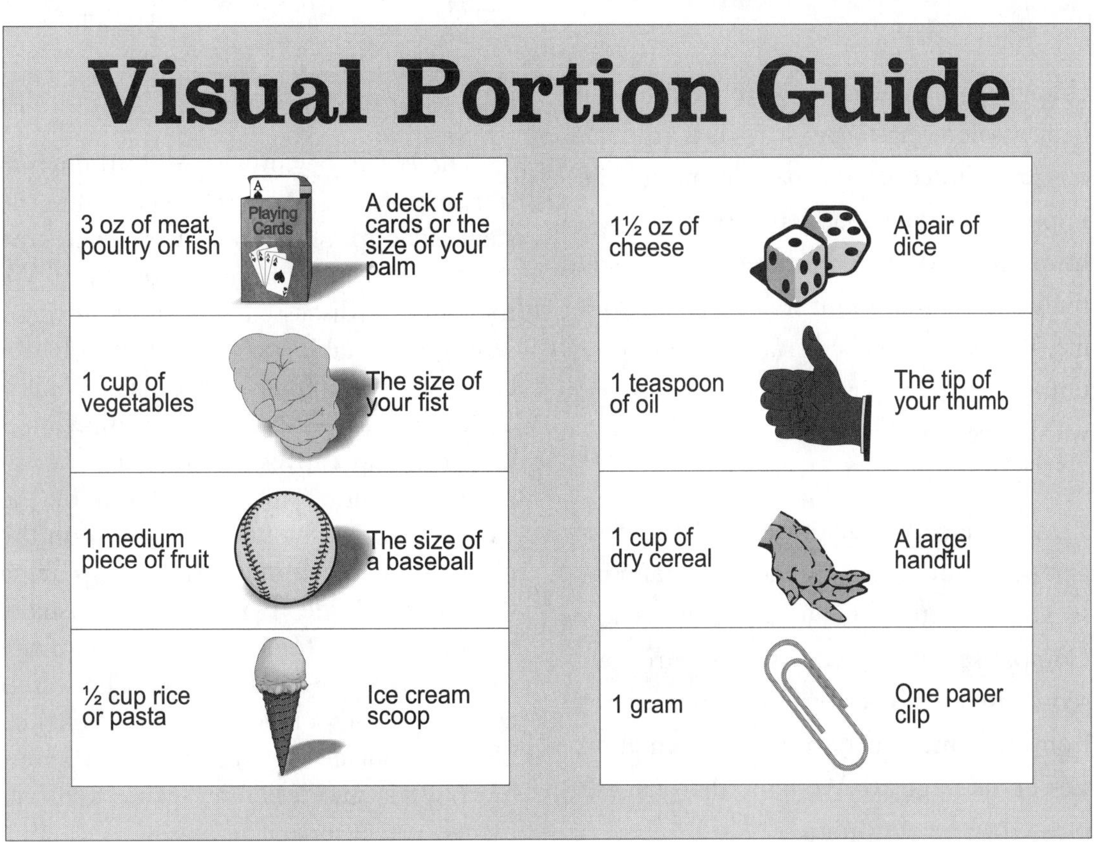

Visual Portion Guide
3 oz of meat, poultry or fish
Playing Cards
A deck of cards or the size of your palm
1 cup of vegetables
The size of your fist
1 medium piece of fruit
The size of a baseball
½ cup rice or pasta
Ice cream scoop
1½ oz of cheese
A pair of dice
1 teaspoon of oil
The tip of your thumb
1 cup of dry cereal
A large handful
1 gram
One paper clip

Quality of Life Review

Please use the following scale to rate how satisfied you feel now about different aspects of your daily life. Choose any number from this list (1 to 9) and indicate your choice next to each numbered item below.

1 = Extremely Dissatisfied
2 = Very Dissatisfied
3 = Moderately Dissatisfied
4 = Somewhat Dissatisfied
5 = Neutral
6 = Somewhat Satisfied
7 = Moderately Satisfied
8 = Very Satisfied
9 = Extremely Satisfied

____ 1. Overall mood (feelings of sadness, anxiety, happiness, etc.)

____ 2. Sense of self-esteem

____ 3. Confidence, comfort in social situations

____ 4. Internal dialog (self-talk)

____ 5. Energy level

____ 6. Focus and concentration

____ 7. Ability to manage time

____ 8. Relationships

____ 9. General health

____ 10. Exercise and recreation

____ 11. Assertiveness skills

____ 12. Eating habits

____ 13. Overall quality of life

changing the color of your hair at the beauty salon, mastering stress is a gradual, on-going process. You may not notice the important changes and the progress you have made. We are delighted to help you realize these important milestones in your life. We want to make certain these important occasions don't slip by unnoticed and without celebration.

Complete the Quality of Life Review above. By now, this form should be familiar to you. Use the Quality of Life Review Comparison on page 297 to compare your scores from this lesson with your scores from the Introduction and Orientation Lesson on page 10. We hope that you are pleased with your progress.

Lesson Review

The lesson began with an introduction to reality testing. We introduced you to the stepladder approach to help you overcome stressful and uncomfortable situations. We then briefly discussed the importance of setting reasonable goals. Relaxation by recall was the next topic of discussion. This is a more advanced form of deep muscle relaxation. Imperatives were discussed as important attitude traps to watch out for. We gave you some helpful information on the number of recommended servings from the Food Guide Pyramid and visually showed you what makes up a serving from each of the five food groups. The lesson concluded with a review of your quality of life. Pat yourself on the back for all your hard work and celebrate your achievements. You deserve it!

This Week's Assignment

Try the reality testing technique this week with a problem that has been bothering you lately. If can't think of one, practice the technique by using your imagination and inventing a problem or by applying the technique to a past problem. Continue to use the Daily Stress Record and the Expanded Realistic Thinking Worksheets if you find them helpful. Blank copies are included at the end of the lesson. Check your physical activity. Are you becoming more physically active? If not, why not? Finally, remember to complete the Stress Change Worksheet on page 227, the Average Stress Change Worksheet on page 430 in Appendix E, and the Physical Activity and Relaxation Worksheet in Appendix F, on page 433. Keep up the good work and good luck with this week's lesson.

Knowledge Review

T F 93. Reality testing helps you deal primarily with the mental component of stress.

T F 94. Reality testing is best learned by reading about it in this manual.

T F 95. The best way to overcome stressful situations is to challenge them directly.

T F 96. Making a stepladder is helpful because it allows you to visualize the steps you can take to overcome and master stressful situations.

T F 97. Relaxation isn't very helpful in overcoming job-related stress.

T F 98. Learning to tolerate everyday frustration and hassles can be improved with practice.

T F 99. Perfectionistic beliefs on the job will only increase productivity and performance.

T F 100. Learning to avoid using imperatives is an important stress management technique.

T F 101. Eating the recommended number of servings from the Food Guide Pyramid can help you achieve a healthy and balanced diet.

(*Answers in Appendix C, page 415*)

Quality of Life Review Comparison

(a) Category	(b) Score from Introduction and Orientation Lesson	(c) Score from Lesson Twelve	(d) Change in Scores (column c minus column b)
1. **Overall mood (feelings of sadness, anxiety, happiness, etc.)**			
2. **Sense of self**			
3. **Confidence, comfort in social situations**			
4. **Internal dialog (self-talk)**			
5. **Energy level**			
6. **Focus and concentration**			
7. **Ability to manage time**			
8. **Relationships**			
9. **General health**			
10. **Exercise and recreation**			
11. **Assertiveness skills**			
12. **Eating habits**			
13. **Overall quality of life**			

STEPLADDER APPROACH

GOAL

Step 8

Step 7

Step 6

Step 5

Step 4

Step 3

Step 2

Step 1

Time Investment Worksheet

Today's Date:

Time	Activity	Urgent	Important	Stress Level (0–8)	Thoughts
12:00–1:00 am					
1:00–2:00 am					
2:00–3:00 am					
3:00–4:00 am					
4:00–5:00 am					
5:00–6:00 am					
6:00–7:00 am					
7:00–8:00 am					
8:00–9:00 am					
9:00–10:00 am					
10:00–11:00 am					
11:00–11:59 am					
12:00–1:00 pm					
1:00–2:00 pm					
2:00–3:00 pm					
3:00–4:00 pm					
4:00–5:00 pm					
5:00–6:00 pm					
6:00–7:00 pm					
7:00–8:00 pm					
8:00–9:00 pm					
9:00–10:00 pm					
10:00–11:00 pm					
11:00–11:59 pm					

Average Level of Stress Today		
Highest Stress Level Today		
Physical Activity Today		
Relaxation Practice Today		

Daily Stress Record—Lesson Twelve

Name:____________________________________ **Week of:**______________

Date	Average Stress Level	Highest Stress Level	Time of Highest Stress Level	Stressful Event Associated with Highest Stress Level

My Physical Activity and Relaxation Record				
Day of the Week	Physical Activity Record		Relaxation by Recall	
	Activity	Minutes	Time of Day	Minutes
Monday				
Tuesday				
Wednesday				
Thursday				
Friday				
Saturday				
Sunday				

1 **Do not tense your muscles, simply try to recapture the feeling you had after you let your muscles relax (flop).**

Expanded Realistic Thinking Worksheet

Today's Date:

(1) Event	(2) Initial Thought	(3) Evidence (How Do I Know?)	(4) Initial/Realistic Probability	(5) Initial/Revised Stress Level (0–8 Scale)	(6) Consequence

"I believe that every employee should be rewarded for good work. Push the red button whenever you deserve a pat on the back."

Lesson Thirteen

This lesson marks another milestone in your stress management program as you begin the last four weeks. We begin the lesson with an expanded discussion on the **E** (exercise) component of LEARN. You will learn techniques to help increase your daily physical activity. We then continue the discussion from Lesson Twelve on reality testing by reviewing the stepladder approach. You will have an opportunity to review several stepladder examples. Our clients find that reviewing examples helps them better understand the process. We discuss another attitude trap, external validation, and follow this topic with a discussion on demanding attitudes and frustrations. We then dive into the interesting topic of problem solving. The lesson concludes with additional material on time management.

Increasing Your Physical Activity

We have talked much about the importance of physical activity and its role in stress management throughout this program. We cannot overstate the importance of being physically active. Researchers in recent years have found many important health-related reasons to be active, including decreased risk for heart disease, diabetes, and certain cancers. The many benefits of being physically active are impressive. Moderate amounts of regular physical activity are perhaps the most powerful means readily available to you for improving both your body and your mind. Some of the more current studies suggest that exercise may even improve learning abilities and increase the number of cells in the brain. Regular activity in moderate amounts literally puts more life into every step; improves your mood, well-being, and quality of life; gives you more energy; and makes you feel good!

Review your completed Physical Activity and Relaxation Worksheet in Appendix F, on page 434. Are you more active now than you were a few weeks ago? Is your activity increasing steadily? Take a few moments now to reread The Benefits of Being Active, on page 86, in Lesson Four.

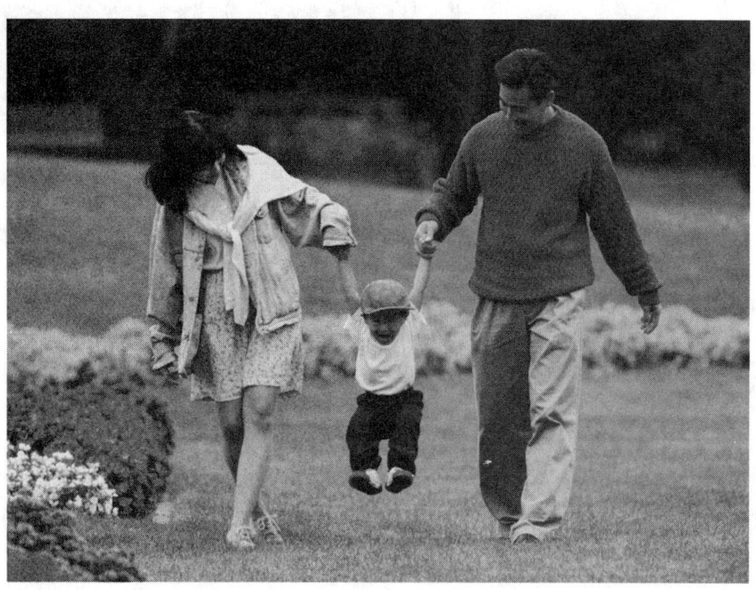

"Walking can be done almost anywhere and is a terrific way to relieve stress."

In almost all surveys on the topic of exercise and activity, most of us know that regular physical activity is good for us. The research certainly confirms this. If you believe that activity is good for you, then it is important for you to continually look for ways to stay active and make exercise fun. Too often, we allow other things (the urgent) to get in the way of exercise (the important). Some people may be embarrassed about exercise or think they cannot possibly do enough to get any benefits. We have given you many ways to challenge these thoughts and overcome the barriers to being active. Now is a good time to bring up the topic of programmed activity.

Programmed Physical Activity

Until now, we have focused our attention on lifestyle activity, with particular emphasis on walking. Walking is perhaps one of the best activities for beginning exercisers. It is also a terrific way to relieve stress because it can be done almost anywhere. More important, walking doesn't require any special exercise equipment. By now, you should feel very comfortable about being physically active. You may be ready to do even more than you are now, so consider trying regular programmed activity.

Many of our clients who use the Mastering Stress Program are ready for more rigorous physical activity. Others prefer to stick with walking. If you fall into the latter category, read the information about programmed activity that follows. This way, when you're ready to increase your activity, you will have some ideas on how to do so. Until then, continue increasing your walking by adding time or by increasing the speed at which you walk. Before long, you'll feel like trying out for the Olympics!

Programmed activities include aerobics, jogging, cycling, bowling, swimming, golf, or other regular activities that require some skill and specialized equipment. Selecting the right activity can sometimes be tricky, so let's look at some important things for you to consider.

Don't be afraid to begin. Many people become embarrassed at the thought of starting a new programmed activity. Don't let this stop you. Programmed activities require more skill than walking, but everyone begins at the same place. Put thoughts about embarrassment out of your mind, take a deep breath, and get started. By now, you have learned many techniques to help you overcome your thoughts about feeling embarrassed. Remember, embarrassment is something you choose to feel!

Choose something you can do. When choosing a programmed activity, you need to consider your current physical condition. Tennis can be an exciting activity, but also can be somewhat strenuous. Choose an activity that allows you to go at your own pace. Bowling, beginning aerobics, and weight training are examples.

Choose something you enjoy doing. Selecting an activity that you enjoy is very important. You may have an activity in mind that you have always thought would be fun, but never considered doing. Go ahead, give it a try. We once had a 60-year-old client who had always been intrigued with scuba diving. After a little encouragement, Margaret decided to try it. He son, Kevin, was a certified dive instructor, so Margaret asked him to give her lessons. She completed the first course, but Kevin didn't believe her skills were adequate for certification. This made Margaret even more determined. A few weeks later, she took the course again and passed with flying colors. Today, Margaret travels all over the world on scuba diving trips.

Decide whether you enjoy solo or social activities. We discussed the notion of being a solo or social changer in Lesson Three, on page 54. When you are considering an activity, think about whether you would rather be alone or with other people. If you prefer being alone, you have many solo activities to choose from. If you are more of a social person, having others around can be both inspirational and motivational. You may find team or partner activities more appealing than solo activities.

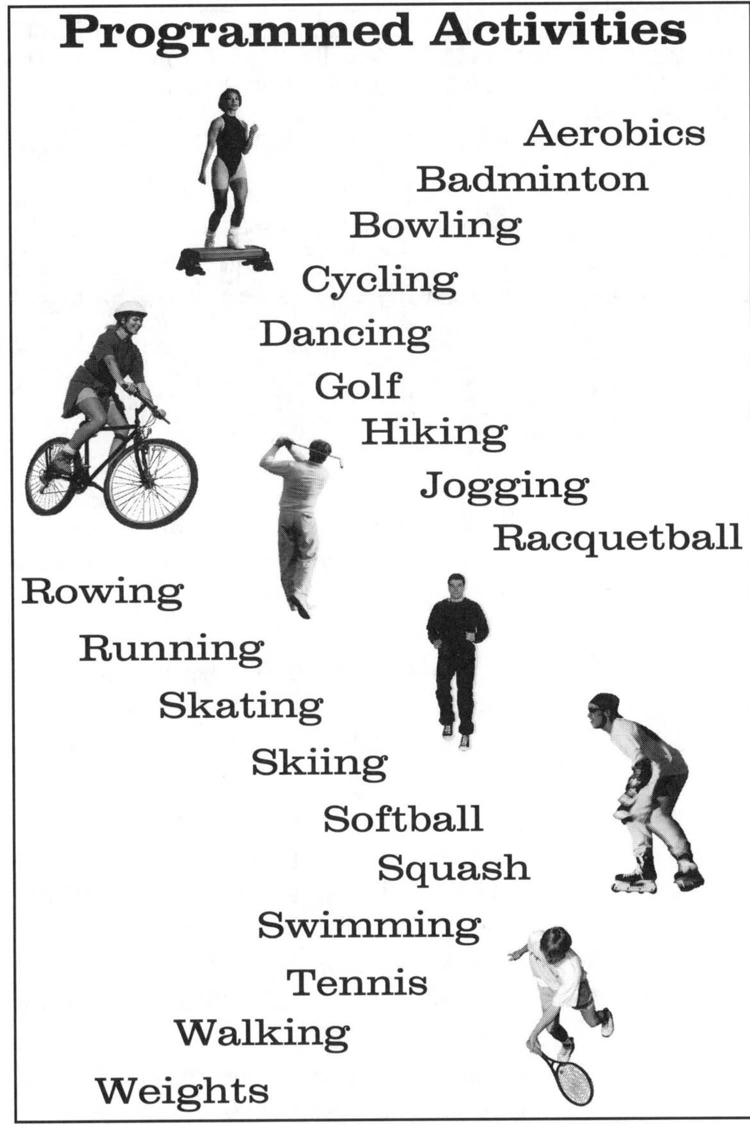

Programmed Activities
Aerobics
Badminton
Bowling
Cycling
Dancing
Golf
Hiking
Jogging
Racquetball
Rowing
Running
Skating
Skiing
Softball
Squash
Swimming
Tennis
Walking
Weights

The Exercise Threshold Belief

Many inactive people hold an exercise threshold belief. They believe that in order to get *any* benefit at all from exercise, they must do a magical amount. This notion of an exercise threshold has its origin in cardiovascular training. If you hold this belief, banish it from your mind right now. Remember this: **Any exercise you do is better than no exercise at all.** Walking a block is better than not walking at all. Walking two blocks is better than one. Do anything to be active, even if you have only a minute or two. Remember the new activity formula: 30 minutes of cumulative activity on most days (preferably all). Small amounts of cumulative activity add up to a lot of exercise over the course of a day, a week, a month, a year, and a lifetime.

The Stepladder Review

In Lesson Twelve, on page 283, we introduced you to the stepladder approach to stress management. This technique is used to help you deal with a stressful situation or one that you find yourself avoiding. To use

this handy technique, you first identified the stressful event or situation. You then came up with 8 to 10 ways you might go about overcoming this stressor and ranked them in order, from the easiest to the most difficult. The easiest task went on the bottom step and the most difficult on the top.

In dealing with the stressor, you were to attempt the first step, even if you felt a little nervous. When you could do the step with little difficulty, you were ready to move on to the next step on the ladder. This step was to be more difficult than the first one. If this step was too difficult to do, you were to come up with one that was less difficult. If your stressor was a difficult situation, it's unlikely that you progressed very far up the ladder in just one week. Nevertheless, were you able to come up with a stepladder for a stressful situation you are facing? If not, did you make a stepladder for a stressor you had faced in the past? If you are having trouble identifying the steps or understanding how to proceed, the examples that follow should help.

Meet Julie

Julie is a 29-year-old attorney. She is married and has a three-year-old son, Josh. Julie tries so hard to live a healthy life that her desire began causing much stress in her life. She constantly worried about getting sick. Since the birth of her son, the thought of becoming ill began to stress her even more. Because of this worry, Julie went to an exercise class three times a week, tried to eat a balanced diet every day, and got a full eight hours of sleep each night. If she missed a single exercise session, didn't eat exactly right, or wasn't able to sleep through the night without waking up, Julie became highly stressed and irritable. She would even leave parties early so that she could get to bed on time. She refused to take one step in a restaurant she considered "unhealthy." She became angry when the demands of her family or work made her miss an exercise class.

Gradually, Julie began to realize that she was also avoiding other situations she considered to be unhealthy. Visiting a friend in the hospital, going into a smoky bar to meet a client, or even using a public restroom are a few examples. What started out as a desire to stay healthy had become a phobia that was running Julie's life and increasing her stress. Julie used realistic thinking techniques to reduce her worries about getting sick. This helped her realize that the probability of becoming ill was low if she missed an aerobics class or two. Still, she was having trouble completely believing this, and her stress level was still moderately high.

Julie also tried prediction testing when she missed an exercise class one evening. She didn't become ill because she missed the class. This helped, but she continued to feel upset and angry about missing the class.

Julie then tried the stepladder approach. First, she wrote down seven things that would make her nervous or stressed when it came to staying healthy. She realized that changing these would improve her overall quality of life. This would also free up her time and allow more time for friends. Next, Julie ranked her list in order of difficulty, from the easiest to the hardest, based on how stressed each item on her list made her feel. Julies stepladder is shown on the right.

On the first rung of Julie's stepladder, she listed, "Skip one aerobics class." As the time of the class grew near, she felt more and more stressed, but less than she had expected. Once the time for the class had passed, she was surprised to find that she felt a little relieved. She then decided to try missing the class again.

The following week, Julie's stress level again rose as the time of the class approached. Still, her stress level was not as high as it was the first time she deliberately missed the class. By the third week, Julie felt very little stress at all when class time rolled around. She then knew that she was ready to try the next step on her ladder.

As a reward for completing the first step, Julie used the time she would have spent in aerobics to play with her son. She was confident that she was not just distracting herself from her stress now.

Next, Julie planned to stay up two hours beyond her bedtime. She allowed herself to experience the worry she felt about getting sick as a result. The second time she tried this, she became so involved reading a book that she decided to stay up again. The third time, she felt a moderate amount of discomfort, and knew she should practice this step again.

The fourth time Julie decided to stay up, she was amazed to discover that her stress was gone. She felt in charge of making the

Stepladder Approach

(Julie's Example)

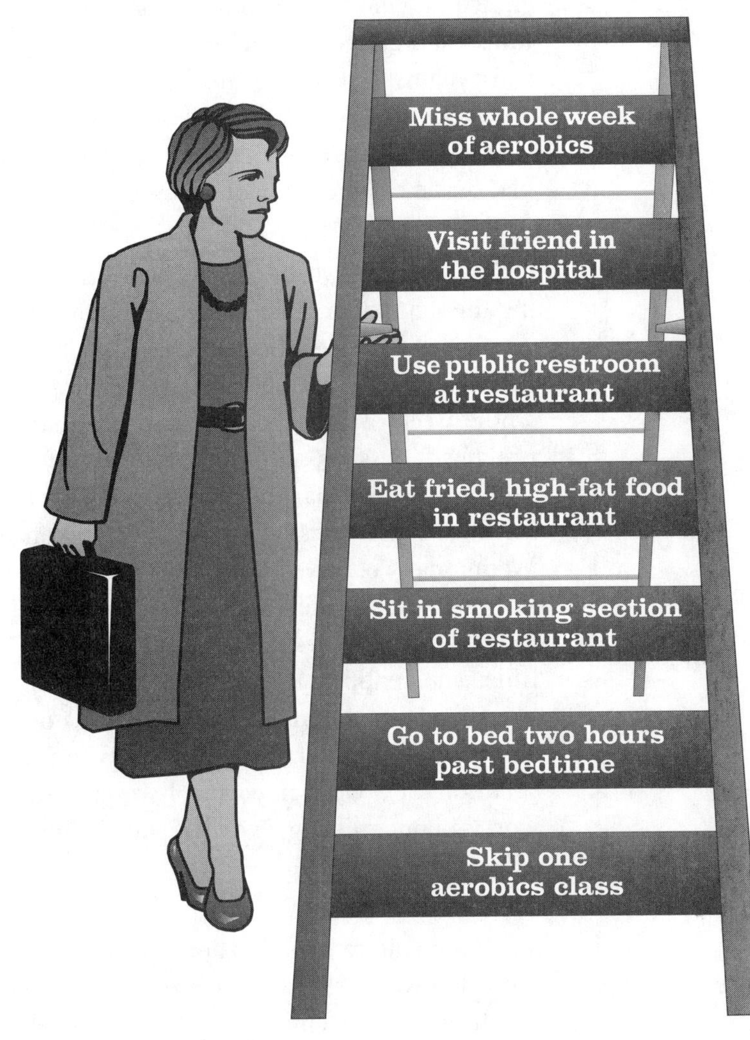

choice of when she wanted to go to bed. Julie still preferred to get plenty of sleep on work nights, but she became more flexible on weekends. From that point on, when circumstances prevented her from going to bed on time, Julie was not stressed.

After several weeks of reality testing using the stepladder, Julie discovered that she no longer worried about her health. She then tried the hardest test of all—missing a whole week of aerobics. Because she had practiced missing aerobics on Mondays, she did not feel particularly stressed over missing Monday's class. But, when Wednesday came, her stress level increased, and she felt agitated. The same thing happened on Friday, but at the same time, she realized that it had been four years since she had missed a whole week of aerobics. She felt terrific! "We can go on a vacation for a week now, and I won't even worry about missing exercise class," Julie thought to herself.

When Julie returned to aerobic class the following week, she was surprised by how much she really enjoyed it. She realized that forcing herself to go every week, three days a week, had taken much of the fun out of her exercise classes. Her attitude about attending the class had changed. She even found herself thinking of other types of programmed activities she could try to help make exercising fun and exciting. Julie still prefers a healthy lifestyle and continues to exercise regularly. Learning to conquer her worry about living healthy, however, improved her health and also improved her quality of life.

Tracking Your Reality Testing Progress

Reality testing is one of the more difficult stress management techniques. Yet, it is also a powerful way to lower your stress. If you haven't taken the opportunity to try it, we encourage you to do so. If you have tried this technique and found it difficult, be patient. Many of our clients have difficulty at first. Keeping a record of your practice sessions may be helpful.

On page 309 is an example of Julie's sample Reality Testing Practice Record. Review this example and see how a completed form might look. In the first column, list the stepladder task from the stepladder you completed. Then record the date and time of your planned activity, listing the activity in the fourth column. Before you do the activity, be sure to record the stress you expect to experience as you do the activity. After you have finished the activity, record in the last column the actual stress that you experienced while doing the activity. Notice that in Julie's example, as she did the various activities, she always expected her stress to be higher than it actually was.

Continue to practice each step of your ladder until the stress level in the last column is as low as you think it can go. Then,

Reality Testing Practice Record

(Julie's Example)

Stepladder Task	Date	Time	Activity	Expected Stress (0–8 Scale)	Actual Stress (0–8 Scale)
Skip one aerobics class	2/10	6 pm	Missed Monday evening class	7	5
✓	2/17	6 pm	Skipped another Monday class	5	4
✓	2/24	6 pm	Skipped another Monday class	4	1
✓	2/26	6 pm	Skipped Wednesday class	5	2
✓	2/28	6 pm	Skipped Friday aerobics class	6	2
Go to bed two hours late	3/1	10 pm	Stayed up two hours late	5	3
✓	3/3	10 pm	Stayed up reading book	4	3
✓	3/4	10 pm	Stayed up reading again	3	0
Sit in smoking section of restuarant	3/7	7 pm	Went to Lucille's with Rod and sat in smoking section	7	4
Eat fried, high-fat food in restuarant	3/14	5 pm	Went to Joey's and ate a medium serving of french fries	6	3

move on to the next step of your stepladder. You may want to make a new form as you begin each step, and keep repeating the step until you can do it with little or no stress. On page 326, we give you a blank Reality Testing Practice Record for you to use. Make as many copies as you need. Good luck with your practice!

Before we move on to the next topic, let's review a few more examples. Our clients often find that reviewing examples helps them to become more proficient with their reality testing practice sessions.

Stepladder Approach

(Peter's Example)

Meet Peter

Peter, a 53-year-old retail store manager, constantly experienced stress over the thought of being on time for every appointment. If there was even the slightest chance he would be late for something, Peter's stress level increased and he became irritable. As a result, he often arrived early for appointments. Of course, Peter wasted much time waiting for his scheduled appointments. If his family or co-workers were late for anything, he became very angry with them. Peter realized that his obsession with punctuality made him unhappy and stressed. More important, it was damaging his relationships with other people, people he deeply cared about.

We have illustrated Peter's stepladder on the left. At first, even hitting his snooze button and staying in bed an extra 10 minutes in the morning was stressful for him. Then, taking a longer, more scenic route to work in the morning was almost impossible for Peter. He was so nervous about arriving late for work that he could barely pay attention to the road. Gradually, Peter realized that he usually arrived at work on time without even thinking about it. He could stay in bed an extra 10 minutes and take the longer, more relaxing, scenic route and still arrive on time. He also realized that when this new route caused him to be late, nothing happened—the world did not stop! No one said anything, he got all of his work done, and he did not waste time fuming while he waited for his co-workers to arrive.

Peter gradually completed all of the steps on his ladder. He learned to master his stress when he could not avoid being late. We knew Peter had made great progress when he showed up smiling for his session one day—10 minutes late!

Meet Janice

Janice is a 32-year-old secretary to the president of a large manufacturing company. When Janice first got married, she worried a lot about keeping the house perfectly clean, just in case guests dropped by. When she came home from a stressful day at work, she could not relax. If anything looked even slightly out of place or messy, she hurried around to tidy it up immediately. She would wash a dish as soon as it was used, no matter how late it was. She made the bed every morning, even if she were running late for work. If Janice didn't have time to clean something before she left for work, she worried about it for the rest of the day. Soon, Janice began to get upset and yell at her husband every time he left something lying around the house.

Part of Janice's stepladder for dealing with this stress in her life is shown on the right. As Janice worked though the reality testing, she did not change the fact that she preferred to keep the house neat and clean. This stress management skill simply helped Janice feel less stressed when circumstances kept her from cleaning something right away.

Meet Sam

Sam is a 32-year-old chef in a nice restaurant in Los Angeles. Sam is single and prefers to work in restaurants where he is the only chef on staff. This preference comes from not wanting to supervise or rely on anyone else. Sam is quiet and has trouble asking people to do anything for him. He also has difficulty refusing to do favors for anyone who asks. As a result, Sam often finds himself doing things for others that he doesn't want or have time to do. This became particularly difficult for Sam because he couldn't bring himself to ask anyone else for help. These things continually stressed and frustrated Sam.

Sam realized that his lack of assertiveness came from a basic fear of asking others to do something. He feared that if they said no, they would not like him or would be angry with him for asking. We worked with Sam and helped him to develop a steplad-

Stepladder Approach

(Janice's Example)

Stepladder Approach

(Sam's Example)

der approach to this problem. His ladder is illustrated above.

Sam made tremendous progress using this technique to lower his stress and become more assertive. He soon found himself less stressed, his quality of life improving, and eventually went to work as the head chef in a much larger restaurant.

Revisiting Stress at Work

In Lesson Twelve, on page 286, we looked at the specific beliefs associated with stress on the job. For example, individuals who are perfectionistic, self-blaming, or demanding are likely to experience more stress at work than those who are not. Which beliefs do you have? Are you overly concerned with getting the approval of others? How does this add to your stress at work? Let's take a look at Connie and see how her thoughts and beliefs added to her stress at work.

Meet Connie

Connie is a 33-year-old paralegal who works in a large New York City law firm. She has a lot of responsibility. As you already know, having much responsibility at work does not cause stress. Connie has many thoughts and beliefs that make her work far more stressful than it needs to be. For example, she believes that her work must always be perfect and that there is *never* any room for error. Striving for excellence is an admirable character trait. However, *always* insisting on perfection and *never* accepting an error is unrealistic. Do you remember the imperative attitude traps we discussed in Lesson Twelve, on page 289? Connie's beliefs deny the reality that she is human and will occasionally make mistakes. Her perfectionism gets in the way of her performance. Because Connie knows she can never do a perfect job, she often procrastinates, fearing the end. Does this type of procrastination sound familiar?

Connie's perfectionism was keeping her from beginning many projects. She believed that even working drafts of documents should be perfect. She would tell herself that the first draft must be flawless. In addition, Connie believed that she had to have the approval of everyone in the office. Underlying this desire for approval, Connie also believed that by doing everything perfectly, her colleagues would respect and like her. Connie's need for approval created additional stressful feelings. For example, if a co-worker did not approve of her work or thought that she wasn't smart, Connie began to believe this about herself—even if it was not what her co-worker thought. These thoughts made Connie feel bad about herself. Connie used reality testing and the stepladder approach to overcome her perfectionistic beliefs. This process greatly reduced the stress she was experiencing at work.

Another Attitude Trap—External Validation

Many people fall into the attitude trap of allowing their *perceptions* of what others *might* be thinking to validate their self-worth. Connie did this by giving others the power to validate her. She also personalized criticisms and suggestions about how to improve her work. If a co-worker criticized her *work*, Connie believed the person was criticizing *her*, not her work.

If you find yourself falling into this trap, we have some suggestions that may help. The first step, however, is for you to recognize that you do this. Once you are aware of this, you can take steps to overcome this dangerous attitude trap.

Validate yourself. Self-validation is an important stress management skill. You may not do everything as well as you would like. Still, this does not make *you* a bad person or worth any less. *Choose* not to allow others to validate your self-worth. Instead, choose to validate yourself.

Uncouple who you are from what you do. Everyone has times when they do not do a task as well as they could. In fact, you may even do a *bad* job on something. Does this mean you are a *bad* person? Does this mean that *everything* you do is *bad*? Certainly not! Uncouple yourself as an individual from the work that you do. You are a unique person, and your work is only one aspect of your life. You and your work are *not* the same thing.

Genuinely seek input from others. At the beginning of this program, we talked about the power we each have to control our choices. You may recall our discussion about self-awareness. The more genuine self-awareness we have, the better our choices will be. Consider Connie's example again. Suppose her co-workers respected and liked Connie very much. Yet, they knew that any criticism of her work would send her self-esteem into a tailspin. They may decide to never criticize her work, though she could make improvements. Over time, what do you think would happen to the quality of Connie's work? If Connie is unaware of the quality of her work, she will likely make poor choices in future projects. Seeking honest input from others will help Connie become more self-aware of her work and how her work is perceived by others. In turn, this will provide her with valuable information on how

"The bad news is, you do less work than anyone in this office. The good news is, you make the fewest mistakes."

her work can be improved, even if it is terrific already.

The Demanding Attitude

Have you ever felt that someone didn't treat you fairly or wasn't as nice and courteous as you would have been in a similar situation? Most of us have had experiences like this. When events like this happen, we can easily fall into the trap of demanding that others treat us a certain way. If we are not treated as we would like, we can easily become angry and blow up at the person or the circumstances. You can probably guess what else goes up—our stress level.

Connie also had some demanding thoughts and beliefs that increased her stress. For example, when Connie would get on the subway with her hands full and someone who was not carrying anything refused to offer her the seat, she got very angry. She never said anything, but she could not understand how someone could be so rude and inconsiderate.

Expecting others to treat you fairly is a reasonable expectation. Yet, you will encounter situations when this doesn't happen. Connie was more than happy to give up her seat on the subway to others who had more to carry than she did. Expecting others to always do the same for her was unrealistic. People do not always behave the way they should and certainly not the way you may expect them to. It is fine for Connie to expect fairness, but she should not demand it. To do so is unhealthy and increases stress. When we demand that others behave a certain way, we are trying to control them.

Beliefs Associated with Frustration

In Lesson Twelve, on page 290, we discussed the issue of frustration and how this contributes to increased stress. Similar to other thoughts and beliefs that cause stress, many people hold beliefs that make stress management more difficult. Last week, we asked you to list your frustrations on the worksheet on page 292. In addition, you were to list the stress management skill you have learned to overcome each particular frustration. Some people find it difficult to handle even the smallest amount of frustration. They may believe that a particular incident is so small that it does not warrant the use of an important stress management skill. "I can handle this without any special skills," is often the response we hear from our clients. If the person is unable to handle a frustrating situation, his or her stress level can outrun a space shuttle being

launched into orbit. During the past week, were you able to recognize the thoughts and beliefs that contributed to your frustrations in life? If so, were you able to lower your frustration level by challenging and disputing these thoughts and beliefs? Let's look at Cory and see how he conquered some of his frustrations.

Meet Cory

Cory is a 29-year-old high school teacher in Cleveland Ohio. He works in a very challenging classroom. Toward the end of the fall semester, Cory began to have difficulty in his classroom. He became increasingly frustrated and intolerant of his students' behavior. Not only was his job extremely difficult, Cory told himself it was "too difficult." He soon convinced himself that he was having no effect in the classroom, and it was impossible for him to have an impact on his students' lives, so he stopped trying.

Undoubtedly, frustrating situations can take a toll in our daily lives. When these events happen, we have three choices available to us:

- Avoid them
- Let them frustrate us
- Learn how to deal with them

Cory knew he could not avoid or ignore what was going on in the classroom. Teaching was his livelihood, but perhaps more important, he truly enjoyed helping others learn. Allowing his students' behavior to continue to frustrate him was not an option. This increased frustration meant increased stress for Cory, and it affected every aspect of his life. Working through these options, Cory soon realized he had to

face the situation head-on and learn how to deal with it.

"As Cory's thoughts and beliefs about his job and the difficult students began to change, his stress decreased."

Cory's self-talk, "This situation is too difficult for me to handle," was in reality a statement to himself that he did not have the skills to be in the classroom. Once he realized this, Cory's response was, "Nonsense." Cory was an excellent teacher and extremely skilled in making learning in the classroom entertaining and exciting. True, his students were the most difficult in the school, but not *impossible* to teach. Cory also considered the possibility that he had been given these students because he was the best teacher in the school.

As Cory's thoughts and beliefs about his job and the difficult students began to change, so did his confidence. Cory soon found himself deeply involved in learning more about his students. He learned about his students' lives and their families and what interests they had as individuals. This knowledge allowed him to individualize his teaching style to more closely match the interests and culture of his students. Soon, Cory's students were staying after the bell and coming by his room after school hours. They were eager to learn more.

From Cory's example, we can easily see how questioning his beliefs and thoughts was the key to developing strategies to handle his students. Frustrating situations can easily get out of hand and send our stress level skyward. The next time you feel frustrated and your stress meter begins to rise, pause for a few minutes. Identify the thoughts and beliefs you have that are contributing to your frustration. Write them down if it's helpful, unless you're driving along a busy freeway! Challenge each thought by asking yourself these questions: "How realistic is this thought?" "What is the probability that this thought is true?" "What are some alternative thoughts?"

Problem Solving

"Problems are often like books. What is on the inside may be nothing at all like the cover."

Now is a good time to bring up the interesting and often challenging topic of problem solving. Realistic thinking and reality testing are helpful techniques to help you master many stressful situations. Yet, you are likely to encounter difficult problems where a solution or appropriate course of action is not clear. These can be very trying and stressful times. You may lie awake at night thinking about how you are going to solve the problem. Your concentration at work may wane as you try to come up with a solution. This is where the skill of problem solving can be very helpful and effective.

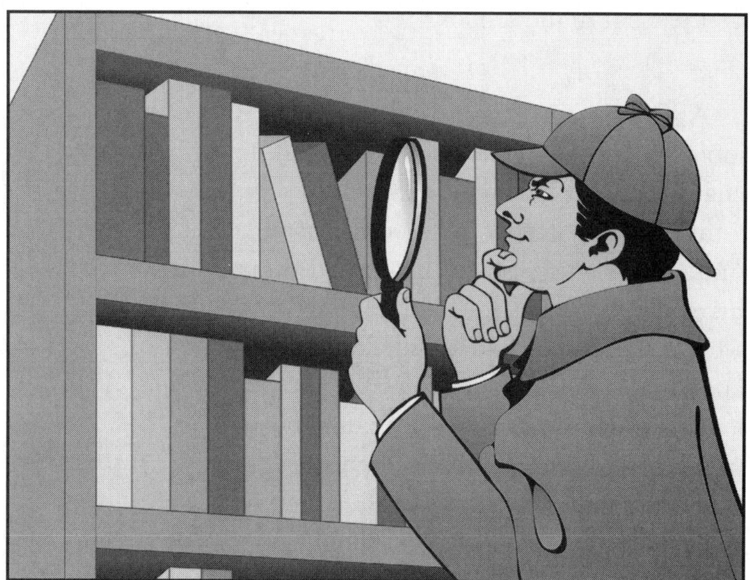

Problem solving is a more advanced form of realistic thinking. By now, we hope that you are a master at realistic thinking. We often find our clients work feverishly on a solution to a phantom problem. That's right, a *phantom problem*. Sure, a problem exists, but it's not clear exactly what it is. So, the first stop in problem solving is to define the problem. Once you have identified the problem, you can then go to work on finding a solution. Remember that to get the right answer, you must ask the right question!

Defining the Problem

Problems are often like books. What is on the inside may be nothing at all like what is on the outside. Think of yourself as Sherlock Holmes. Your job is to gather as much evidence as possible about the situation. Then, look closely at the clues so that you clearly understand and identify the problem. Where do you begin? You begin by writing down your initial thoughts about the problem.

Let's say, for example, that you are having trouble with employees not showing up regularly for work. You may define the problem as, "Employees are not showing up for work." Still, this is vague. You may then think, "The stupid employees don't care about their jobs." Obviously, this is a bit emotional! You may also be catastrophizing by applying the behavior of a few employees to *all* of your employees. Or, perhaps, you may be assuming the worst possible motive. Let's say you have a staff of 12 employees, and 2 of them did not come to work this week. A more realistic definition of the problem may be something like, "Two employees (Mark and Jan) did not come in to work on two days this week." Do you see how the problem is becoming more clearly defined?

As we said before, problems are not always what they seem on the surface. You cannot solve them until you find out what they really are. In other words, you must find the cause or root of the problem. As you put on your Sherlock Holmes cap and trench coat, you discover that Mark didn't come to work one day this week because his wife had emergency surgery the day he was out. As you continue to investigate, you discover that Jan missed work on Tuesday because she had requested a personal day off three months ago to volunteer for a local charity's fund raiser. Your initial thought about *all* of your employees not showing up for work wasn't really the problem at all. Nor are *all* of your employees *stupid* and *uncaring* about their jobs! So, what was the problem?

In Mark's case, his wife had a medical emergency. Situations like this are going to happen, and there's nothing you can do about them except learn not to become frustrated when they happen. In Jan's case, you forgot to write her request on your calendar. You can see from this example how real problems can be nothing like your initial definition.

Specifically defining a problem is crucial to finding an appropriate solution. Similar to writing your thoughts down on your Realistic Thinking Worksheet, writing down your thoughts about specific problems is also very helpful. This helps you to "see" the problem in your own words. Many of our clients tell us that as they begin to write a problem on a piece of paper, they suddenly realize how silly it sounds. This often happens after they have spent days trying to solve the problem in their heads. This illustrates again that record keeping is the hallmark of mastering stress. Let's look at another example.

"My boss treats us like we're a bunch of children. We'd like to complain, but we're afraid he won't bring us candy anymore."

Assume that your child, Johnny, is not doing well in school. Many solutions are available, depending upon the specific problem. Simply saying that the problem is that Johnny is not doing well in school doesn't lend itself to finding a possible solution. However, if Johnny is not doing well because he is bored, the problem starts to come into focus. If Johnny is bored because he already knows the material, you now know specifically what the problem is. A number of solutions to this problem can now be considered. If, on the other hand, Johnny is not doing well in school because he is being teased, the possible solutions are much different from his being bored.

On page 318, we have included an example of these two problems. You can see how alternative thoughts about what the problem is can lead to more investigation and discovery. In turn, this information can clue you in to what the real problem is. Once you clearly define the problem, you are ready to find the solution.

Finding a Solution

From the discussion above, you can see how not clearly defining a problem can leave a person floundering for possible solutions. Similarly, not identifying the *real* problem can lead to the wrong solution. Using a form like the Problem Solving Worksheet can help you identify a problem along with a possible solution. We provide you with a blank Problem Solving Worksheet on page 324 to use in solving problems you come across. Feel free to design your own form if you prefer.

Just as people often have trouble defining a problem, they sometimes have trouble believing that any possible solution exists. In reality, however, every problem has a solution. The question is, will you be proactive in determining the solution or react to the solution that surfaces? Possible solutions are much easier to see if you have clearly defined the problem. This is when you can try what we call *brainstorming* to come up with alternative thoughts. Brainstorming means letting your mind go and writing down every possible definition of the problem. This is what we did in Johnny's example. We brainstormed for the possible reasons why Johnny may not be doing well in school. Solutions work the same way. Once you define the problem, you can brainstorm many possible solu-

Problem Solving Worksheet

(Johnny's Example)

Initial Thought	Alternative Thoughts	Possible Solutions
Johnny isn't doing well in school	1. Johnny is bored 2. Johnny is bored because he already knows the material	1. Find out why he is bored 2. Change teachers 3. Change grades 4. Change schools
Johnny isn't doing well in school	1. Johnny dislikes school because other kids tease him 2. Other kids tease Johnny because of his weight	1. Why do the other kids tease him 2. Talk to the teacher and have her educate the other kids about weight problems 3. Talk to the kids who tease Johnny with their parents present about the problem

tions and the consequences of each one. The idea here is simply to get your mind working. When you do, you may find solutions that otherwise would not have occurred to you. Therefore, anything you think of, no matter how dumb it sounds, can help lead you to other possibilities.

Another way to help you define a problem and find possible solutions is to involve others. Viewing a set of circumstances through the eyes of another person can be very helpful. Have you ever had a friend or co-worker present you with a set of circumstances and ask your opinion? Most of us have. In giving this friend or co-worker feedback, he or she may have said something like, "Wow, I never thought of that!" or "I didn't look at it that way!" Let's look at some other examples.

The Barking Dog

Assume that your neighbor's barking dog is keeping you awake at night. Write your initial thought about what the problem is in the first column. Let's say you come up with "I can't sleep at night because my neighbor's dog is barking." Now, brainstorm and consider any other reasons that may be keeping you from sleeping. Why is the dog's barking keeping you awake at night? Perhaps your neighbor just got a new dog or just let the old dog start sleeping outside. Both possibilities will help you more clearly define the exact problem. Write these ideas in the second column.

Having a better idea of what the problem is, you can now begin to brainstorm possible solutions to the problem. Write these ideas in the third column. In our example here, you may consider any of the following solutions: talk to your neighbors and ask them what they are willing to do, ask them to keep the dog inside at night, ask them to get rid of the dog, file a complaint with the local authorities, sleep in another part of your house, or move. Once you have written down every possible solution you can think of, decide which ones are the most practical. Then rank them in order of practicality. Similar to the stepladder approach, you then try your first and most practical solution. If that doesn't work, move on to the next one.

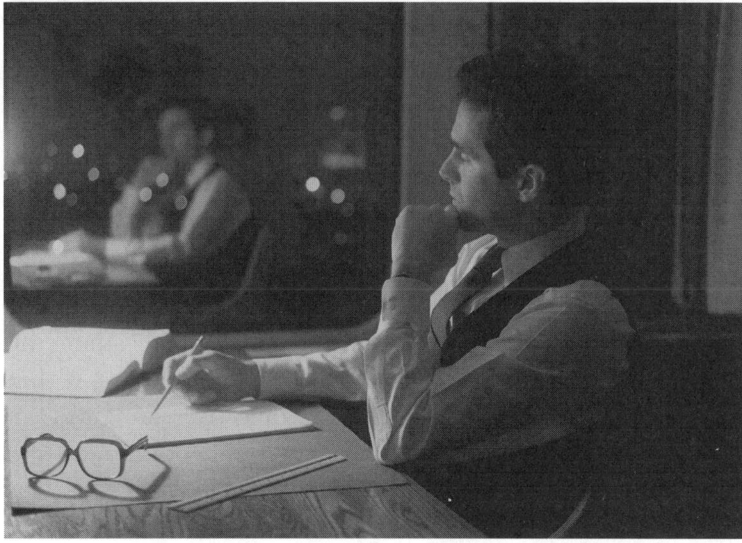

"Brainstorming means letting your mind go and writing down every possible definition of the problem."

Meet Julia

Julia is a 25-year-old homemaker in Mt. Pleasant, Iowa. Her husband, Don, is a farmer and farms almost 1600 acres of land. Julia moved to Iowa from Illinois to marry Don a few months ago. As Julia became acquainted with other people in town, she soon became good friends with Mary. When Don met Mary for the first time, Julia immediately sensed he did not like her. She noticed a similar reaction when she talked about Mary. Julia decided to talk with Don and find out why he behaved the way he did when she talked about Mary. After talking with Don, she discovered that Mary reminded him of an ex-girlfriend who had treated him very badly. With this additional information,

Julia now knew more specifically what the problem was. From here, she developed alternative solutions to the problem. We have reproduced Julie's sample Problem Solving Worksheet below.

The solution that most appealed to Julia was going out with both Don and Mary so that they could get to know each other. She listed that next in her plan of action. If that did not work, she would try talking to Don about all of Mary's good points and explaining why her friendship with Mary was important to her. And if that did not work, she would talk with her husband and see if they could set up an acceptable amount of time for her to spend with Mary. Finally, Julia applied her realistic thinking skills to the problem and asked herself what would happen if Don never learned to like Mary.

Julia realized that she was afraid that if Don continued to dislike Mary, he would eventually hate her (Julia). Looking at that thought realistically, she quickly concluded that the probability of her husband hating her was close to zero. She realized that while she would prefer her husband to like her best friend. If he did not, it wouldn't be the end of the world.

Clearly defining a problem is an important first step to finding a solution. Too often, people spend too much time trying to find a solution to a *phantom* problem. Take the time to clearly define problems in your life. You may be surprised how quickly you can find a solution that will lower your stress.

Problem Solving Worksheet

(Julia's Example)

Initial Thought	Alternative Thoughts	Possible Solutions
Don doesn't like Mary	1. Don may not like something Mary does 2. Mary reminds Don of an ex-girlfriend who treated him badly	1. Talk to Don and find out if he does not like Mary 2. Arrange a night out with Don and Mary 3. Talk with Don about what a wonderful person Mary is 4. Plan separate time with Don and Mary 5. Don't talk about Mary with Don 6. Stop seeing Mary 7. Tell Don off 8. Divorce Don

Scheduling the Important

In earlier lessons of the Mastering Stress Program, we talked about how many people spend so much time doing the urgent things, that they never seem to have time for the important things. You have been keeping track of how you spend your time over the past few weeks. Are you spending more of your time on the urgent than the important? If so, that's terrific. If not, you may need to work on additional time management skills. Let's look at Carol, the "wonder mom."

Meet Carol

Carol is a 43-year-old mother of three. She once held a part-time sales job at a local retail store but decided to quit so that she could enjoy life a little more. Carol wanted to learn more about computers, attend exercise classes at the neighborhood gym, and take some gourmet cooking classes. After quitting her job, Carol was busier than ever and still was not finding time to do the things she had quit her job to do. She couldn't understand why. Carol was frustrated and stressed. "This is not why I quit my job," Carol kept saying to herself.

To help Carol, we had her keep the Time Investment Worksheet for three consecutive days, including one weekend day. As she studied the worksheets, Carol was surprised at what she discovered. She was spending many hours doing things she didn't really need to do. Her worksheets showed that she spent nearly four hours each day preparing and serving food—far more than she would have ever guessed. She spent over an hour each day driving her children to various activities. Carol was amazed at this because they had managed quite well when she was working. Her husband had even started asking her to run more errands since she quit her job. She was spending about two hours running his errands.

If you can identify with Carol's example, review at least three days of your Time Investment Worksheets from last week. If you didn't keep the worksheets, try to keep them for at least three days over the coming week. Review the activities that you checked in the *urgent* column first. Which of these activities could you have spent less time doing? What activities could be delegated to other people? Realistically, what activities could you have skipped altogether? Were you able to do everything each day that is truly important to you? If not, how could you have scheduled your time differently to do these important things?

Over the next week, try to reschedule your time so that it includes more time for your important tasks. In Lesson Fourteen, we'll give you some suggestions on how to go about doing this. But, try it on your own this week and see how it goes.

"When we spend our time on urgent matters we have little time left for the important things, making our lives unbalanced."

"As soon as I get organized, I promise to make room in my schedule to attend last week's time management seminar."

A New Stress Change Worksheet

On page 328, we provide you with a new Stress Change Worksheet for weeks 13 through 16. The worksheet in Lesson Nine, on page 227, should now be completed. How has you stress level changed over the past four weeks? We hope that you have lowered your stress and that you are pleased with your progress.

Lesson Review

We covered a lot of material in this lesson. We talked about ways to increase your physical activity and provided many examples on how to refine your reality testing skills using the stepladder approach. We covered some common attitude traps and talked a bit about thoughts and beliefs that are often associated with frustration and stress. Problem solving was the next topic of discussion, and we concluded the lesson with a note on time management. We hope you enjoyed this lesson and that you are well on your way to effectively using the advanced stress management techniques discussed. If so, pat yourself on the back—you're doing a terrific job. If not, continue to practice. Your hard work and practice will pay off in the long run.

This Week's Assignment

Continue to use the Daily Stress Record if you find it helpful. At this point in the program, many of our clients carry the form with them and complete it on particularly stressful days. Experiment with the form and use it as you see fit. A blank form is provided on page 327. Continue to use the stepladder approach to reality testing. We provide a blank form on page 325 and a blank Reality Testing Practice Record on page 326 to help you track your progress. On page 329, we include a blank Time Investment Worksheet for you to use as you begin to focus more on setting time aside to do things that are truly important to you. Use the Problem Solving Worksheet on page 324 to help you begin to use the technique to solve problems. Make as many copies of the worksheets as you need.

Finally, complete the new Stress Change Worksheet for week 13 at the end of this lesson, on page 328, along with the Physical Activity and Relaxation Worksheet in Appendix F, on page 434, and the Average Stress Change Worksheet in Appendix E, on page 430. Keep up the hard work, and good luck with this week's assignment.

Knowledge Review

T F 102. If you have been relatively inactive, you should not consider programmed activity.

T F 103. The stepladder technique is a helpful tool to use in reality testing.

T F 104. Allowing others to validate your self-worth is a common attitude trap some people fall into that increases stress and lowers self-esteem.

T F 105. It is perfectly fine to be demanding of others if it helps you keep your stress under control.

T F 106. Frustration and the accompanying stress is most often directly related to our thoughts and beliefs about a particular situation or event.

T F 107. The first thing to do when problem solving is to define the problem as specifically as possible.

T F 108. Brainstorming refers to the idea of thinking hard for a long time for one good idea to use as a solution to a problem.

T F 109. Problem solving is an effective stress management technique.

T F 110. Coming up with a single solution to a complex problem and then working hard on that solution is the best approach to problem solving.

(***Answers in Appendix C, page 415***)

Problem Solving Worksheet

Today's Date: ______________

Initial Thought	Alternative Thoughts	Possible Solutions

STEPLADDER APPROACH

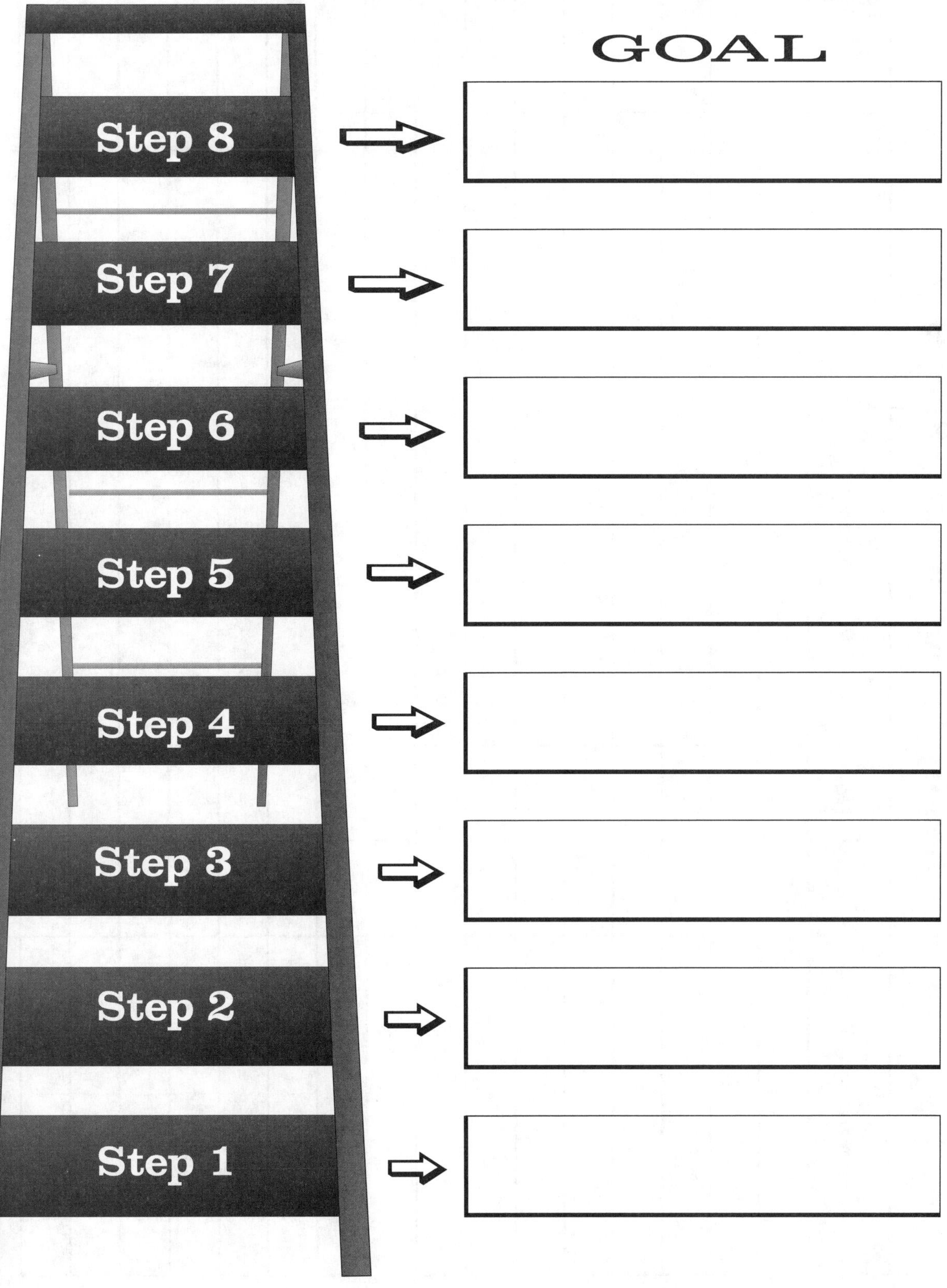

Reality Testing Practice Record

Stepladder Task	Date	Time	Activity	Expected Stress (0–8 Scale)	Actual Stress (0–8 Scale)

Daily Stress Record—Lesson Thirteen

Name:______________________________ **Week of:**____________

Date	Average Stress Level	Highest Stress Level	Time of Highest Stress Level	Stressful Event Associated with Highest Stress Level

My Physical Activity and Relaxation Record				
Day of the Week	Physical Activity Record		Relaxation by Recall	
	Activity	Minutes	Time of Day	Minutes
Monday				
Tuesday				
Wednesday				
Thursday				
Friday				
Saturday				
Sunday				

Stress Change Worksheet

(Weeks 13 – 16)

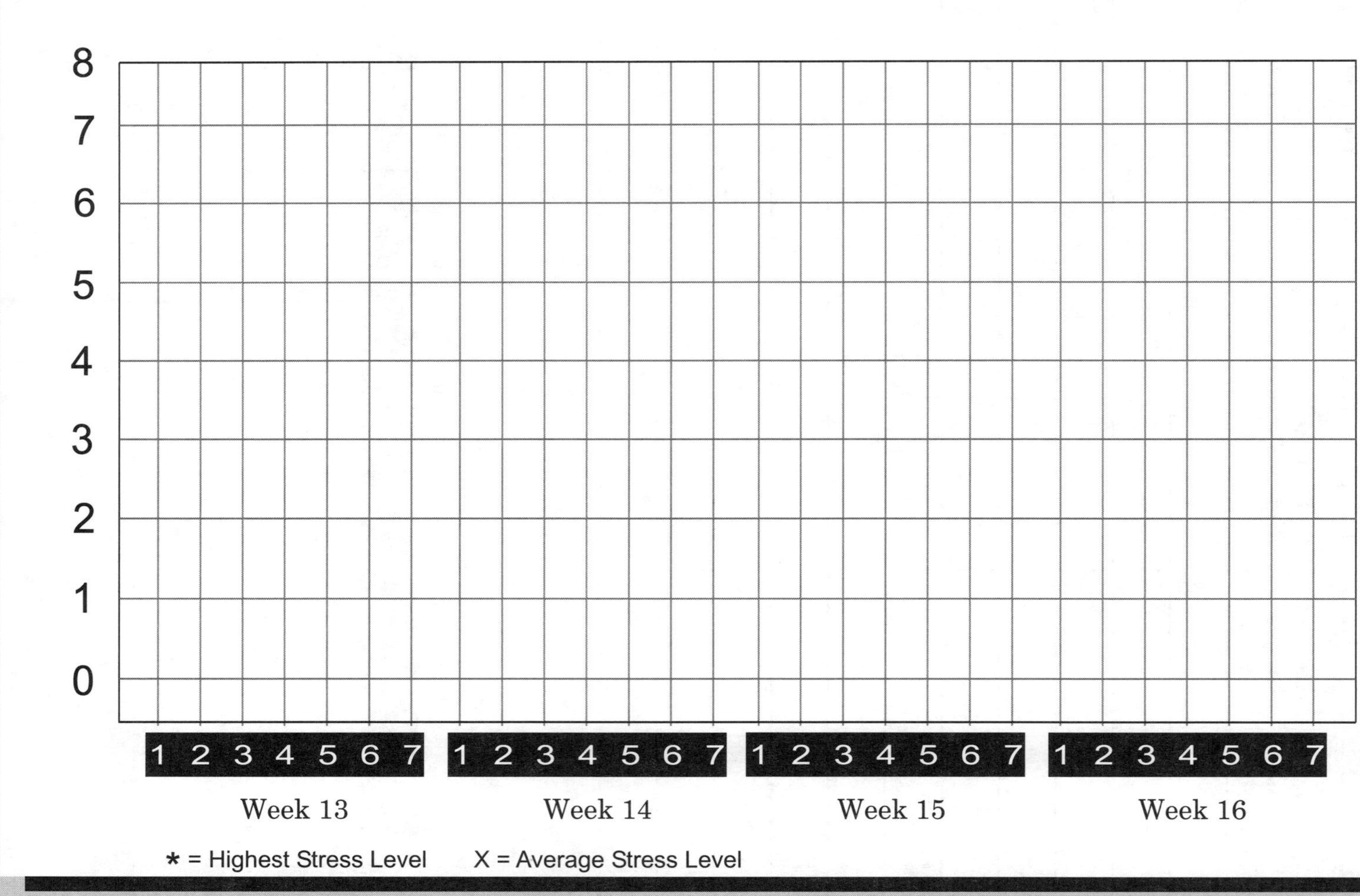

* = Highest Stress Level X = Average Stress Level

Time Investment Worksheet

Today's Date:

Time	Activity	Urgent	Important	Stress Level (0–8)	Thoughts
12:00–1:00 am					
1:00–2:00 am					
2:00–3:00 am					
3:00–4:00 am					
4:00–5:00 am					
5:00–6:00 am					
6:00–7:00 am					
7:00–8:00 am					
8:00–9:00 am					
9:00–10:00 am					
10:00–11:00 am					
11:00–11:59 am					
12:00–1:00 pm					
1:00–2:00 pm					
2:00–3:00 pm					
3:00–4:00 pm					
4:00–5:00 pm					
5:00–6:00 pm					
6:00–7:00 pm					
7:00–8:00 pm					
8:00–9:00 pm					
9:00–10:00 pm					
10:00–11:00 pm					
11:00–11:59 pm					

Average Level of Stress Today		
Highest Stress Level Today		
Physical Activity Today		
Relaxation Practice Today		

ROWWRF! GROWFF!
SNARL SNARL
WOOF!
JIM DAVIS

BARK! BARK!
ROWRFF!
SNORT SNORT
WOOF!

ROOF! ROOF! ROWF!
HAVE YOU HAD YOUR BLOOD PRESSURE CHECKED LATELY?
3-19

Lesson Fourteen

You now have only three lessons to go in the Mastering Stress Program. In this lesson, we'll help tie everything together by introducing you to the Behavior Chain. This is a helpful way for you to put everything you have learned so far into a simple illustration. We discuss the importance of roles and help you set reasonable goals for each role. The important topic of relapse comes up in this lesson, and we conclude the lesson with an advanced relaxation technique. Let's begin this important lesson.

Putting it All Together—Stress as a Chain

We now need to organize the information you have learned in this program into a logical format so that you can see how it all fits together. We have talked about ways to identify stressful situations and your individual stress triggers. Along with these topics, we have introduced to you many techniques (more than 100 now) to help you master your stress. Yet, you are still left with an important challenge: which technique or tool to pull out of your stress management tool box in a given stressful situation.

Let's say, for example, that you are waiting at the airport to meet your partner or a close friend. Outside, a blizzard is raging, and mounds of snow are piling up, yet some flights continue to takeoff and land. The flight you are waiting for is now more than two hours late. The airline has provided no information about the status of the flight. You recognize this as a high-risk situation for experiencing stress.

Imagine that you could log onto a computer and click an icon that says "high-risk situations." You could then pull down a file that says something like "Late arrival of my partner or friend." The file would list different scenarios of the situation that would help you determine your risk of becoming overly stressed. One scenario might be the mode of transportation, who is late, how late the person is, what other things you have to do, how balanced your diet is, how active you are, and so forth. When all of the aspects of a stressful situation or event merge, a number of possible responses are revealed.

I HAVEN'T READ ENOUGH BOOKS FOR FUN... HAVEN'T LISTENED TO ENOUGH MUSIC...

HAVEN'T SEEN THE WORLD... HAVEN'T DANCED... HAVEN'T LEARNED TO PAINT... HAVEN'T TAKEN UP GARDENING...

HAVEN'T TAUGHT MY DOG TO PLAY FRISBEE... HAVEN'T STUDIED PHOTOGRAPHY OR COOKING... HAVEN'T NAPPED OUTSIDE...

RELAXATION STRESS TAKES OVER WHERE JOB STRESS LEAVES OFF.
I'VE WASTED MY WHOLE LIFE TRYING TO ACCOMPLISH SOMETHING!
TAKE ONE
TRAVEL

"A chain is only as strong as its weakest link. Your job is to break the links."

Dr. Kelly Brownell uses a Behavior Chain to help illustrate this process. This is a clever method for breaking stressful events into discrete, smaller parts. As you examine each part independently, you can more easily identify strategies and techniques for stopping stress in its tracks. Like the other techniques we discuss in this program, becoming proficient at this skill requires much practice. When you master the technique, you will have made significant strides in mastering your stress.

The Behavior Chain and Its Links

Think of high levels of stress as a chain of events, with each event linked to another. We can use the familiar phrase: *A chain is only as strong as its weakest link.* Your challenge is to find as many weak links as you can to break the chain.

If we return to our example of the late flight, becoming angry and frustrated in a crowded airport terminal is at the end of a long chain of events. Preceding this were many other links that all contributed to the high stress level experienced at the airport. The chain can be broken at any of these links.

Each stressful event can be viewed with the Behavior Chain in mind. Once you identify the links in your chain, you can spot the best link to break and take action. The earlier in the chain you break the links and the more links you break, the easier it is to master your stress.

A Sample Chain—Meet Kevin

To illustrate the Behavior Chain, we introduce you to Kevin, an engineer with a large architectural firm in downtown Chicago. His wife, Rhonda, is a flight attendant for a large airline with a major hub at Chicago's O'Hare Airport. Kevin finds himself waiting for Rhonda's flight, which is now over two hours late. The crowded airport is filled with noisy people on the evening before a four-day Thanksgiving weekend. Kevin's muscles are tied up in knots, he is angry with everyone around him, including Rhonda for being a flight attendant, and he is extremely irritable. Kevin's stress occurred in a long chain that included many links before and after he arrived at the airport. By looking closely at Kevin's chain, we can identify ways to help him control his stress. Keep in mind, this is only an illustration to highlight the *principle* of a Behavior Chain. As you read the following example, think of how this principle applies to a stressful situation you have experienced.

Kevin's chain began at work. His example Behavior Chain is illustrated on page 333. Here are the 12 links in the chain that led to Kevin's high level of stress. Kevin skipped breakfast that morning and worked through lunch so that he could

Behavior Chain

(Kevin's Example)

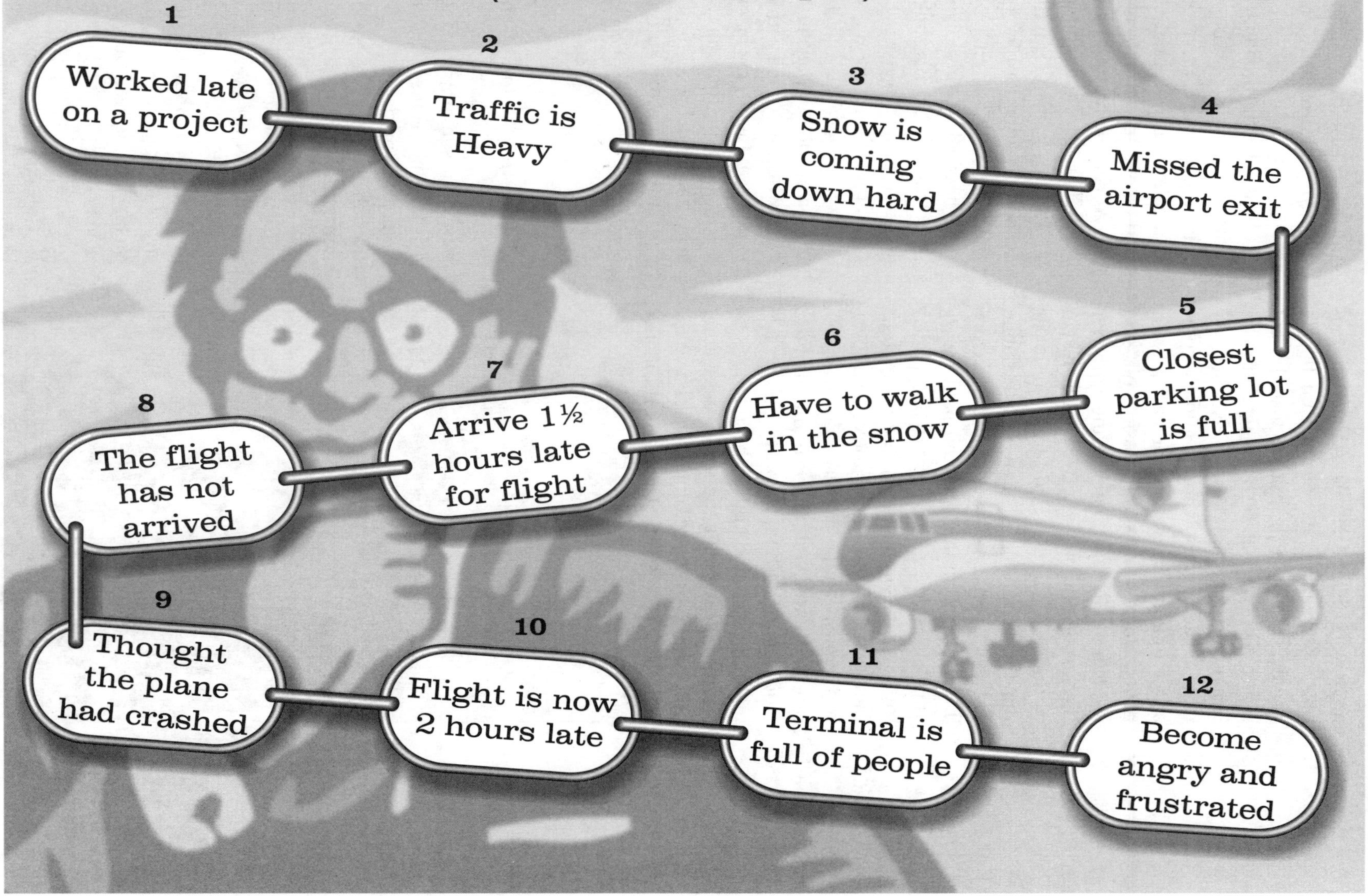

1. Worked late on a project
2. Traffic is Heavy
3. Snow is coming down hard
4. Missed the airport exit
5. Closest parking lot is full
6. Have to walk in the snow
7. Arrive 1½ hours late for flight
8. The flight has not arrived
9. Thought the plane had crashed
10. Flight is now 2 hours late
11. Terminal is full of people
12. Become angry and frustrated

leave work on time. He also skipped his regular 30-minute walk during lunch. He worked late on a project because he got sidetracked by helping a co-worker with her project that same day (1). Kevin knew that he had to meet Rhonda at the airport at 6:00 p.m. The evening forecast was for heavy, blowing snow and possible blizzard conditions. Rather than leaving early for the airport, he chose to work late. Kevin could have called the airline to discover that the flight would be arriving late, but he did not. Because it was the day before Thanksgiving, traffic was unusually heavy and congested (2). The blizzard only added to the traffic problems (3); the normal 45 minute trip to the airport took Kevin over two hours. Traffic crawled along, sometimes not moving at all for many minutes. Not wanting to be late to meet Rhonda's flight, Kevin found himself becoming frustrated and angry at the snow, the traffic, and everyone around him. He was so frustrated and stressed that he missed the airport exit (4), adding another 30 minutes to his trip to the airport.

When Kevin finally arrived at the airport, the closest parking lot was full (5). Kevin's stress level increased even more because he hadn't brought his snow boots, and he had to walk a long way in the snow (6). Kevin finally reached the gate an hour and a half after the scheduled arrival time of Rhonda's flight (7). He expected to see Rhonda waiting for him, but he discovered the flight had not yet landed (8). He was convinced that the plane had crashed somewhere in the blinding snow storm (9). Rhonda's flight was now over two hours late (10).

Kevin tried to pace in the crowded airport, which was filled with holiday travelers waiting for flights. He began to think about the possibility that he would never see Rhonda again (11). This weakened Kevin's restraint even more and he found himself becoming very angry and frustrated with the entire situation (12). His stress level spiked to an 8.

Is Kevin a victim of an unfortunate set of uncontrollable circumstances? Could he have done something to interrupt the chain of stressful events? Kevin had many options and opportunities to break the chain over the day. Before we discuss these options, think of your own examples. Can you think back over a series of stressful events you have experienced? What are the links that connect the events in the chain?

Take a few minutes now to think of a stressful experience you have had. Form a picture of this event in your mind. Use the blank chain provided on page 349 to fill in the details of your particular situation. Use Kevin's chain as an example to follow, but make the circumstances apply to you. Se-

"Stress often occurs in a long chain of events that has many links. You can use your stress management tools to break the links."

lect an event that really increases your stress.

Your chain may contain more or fewer links than the blank chain provides, but try to include all of the important details. Once you have completed this exercise, you will begin to see how your stress level increases with each additional link in the chain. Think of this as runaway train, without any brakes, running out of control down a steep mountain—once it gets started, it's hard to stop. You have learned many stress management techniques that will help you derail this runaway train. The more proficient you are at using these techniques and skills, the better you will be able to master the stress in your life.

Breaking the Chain

Your mind was probably racing with ideas as we were discussing Kevin's example. We can use his example to show how a chain might be broken. Some of the techniques and tools Kevin could have used to interrupt the chain are shown in the table on page 336.

The Behavior Chain idea can become a key part of your stress management program. The Behavior Chain method allows you to review stressful events and situations more clearly and helps you identify ways you can begin using your stress management tools to gain control. Compare this with the more common approach that relies on a person's ability to recognize a stressful situation, apply the right technique, and then depends upon willpower to derail stressful feelings.

Reviewing Your Behavior Chain

Let's now look more closely at the chain you completed on page 349. Look carefully at each link in the chain. For each link,

"First my ball rolled under the sofa, then my water dish was too warm, then the squeaker broke on my squeaky rubber pork chop. I've had a horrible day and I'm completely stressed out!!!"

write at least two ways you could have broken the link. This may take you a while, but it is truly an important step in mastering your stress. Think back on all the techniques you have learned in this program. Use these tools to begin thinking of *chain-breaking techniques* you can use to master stress. You may want to refer to the Master List of Stress Management Techniques in Appendix B, on page 413. You may be thinking that you do not need to complete this exercise. You may even be correct. Keep in mind that writing things down will help you see events much more clearly. You can see your high-risk situations and behaviors as you never have before.

Rating Your Diet

We have talked much about the importance of eating a healthy diet and its role in stress management. In Lesson Ten, on page 234, we had you rate your diet. We then introduced you to the Food Guide Pyramid and discussed the components of a balanced, healthy diet. We also suggested that you order a copy of *The LEARN Healthy Eating and Calorie Guide* to help you improve your diet even more. How have you done? Have your eating habits improved? Is your diet more balanced? Do you have more energy?

Breaking the Links in the Behavior Chain

(Kevin's Example)

Link	Link-Breaking Techniques
Worked late on a project	Take a 15-minute walk and reduce my tension Master my thoughts—I got an important project finished
Traffic is heavy	Apply relaxation skills Control my anger—I may be late, but I'll drive safely
Snow is coming down hard	Master my thoughts—it's okay if I'm a little late Reshape my attitude—the snow really is beautiful
Missed the airport exit	Challenge the belief that it will be awful to be late Stop worry—I'll just take the next exit
Close-in parking lot is full	View this as a terrific opportunity to exercise A short walk will give me time to relax and reduce tension
Have to walk in the snow	I love the snow, and this is a good excuse to walk in it Think realistically—a few more minutes won't make a difference
Arrive 1½ hours late for flight	Conquer catastrophizing—so, I'm a little late! Use realistic thinking
The flight has not arrived	Relaxation skills—this is a great time to relax Increase activity—walk around the terminal
Thought the plane had crashed	Use realistic thinking to think of the alternatives Seek more information from airport staff
Flight is now 2 hours late	Time management—use the time to return some calls Relax—buy a magazine at the gift shop
Terminal is full of people	Deal with anger—I'm sure everyone else is as tired as I am Cope with frustration—I could still be on the freeway!

EARLIER TODAY YOU TURNED DOWN A 15¢ DONUT, A 35¢ COOKIE, AND A 50¢ CUPCAKE...

... AND NOW YOU'RE DIVING INTO A $10.00 BOX OF GOURMET CHOCOLATES.

CATHY, HOW COULD YOU DO THIS TO YOURSELF ??!

I WAS HOPING THE MORE EXPENSIVE FAT WOULD LOOK BETTER ON ME.

It's time again to rate your diet. Take the Rating Your Diet Quiz in Appendix G, beginning on page 439. When you have completed this quiz, compare your score at the bottom of page 442, with your score on the first quiz at the bottom of page 438. Write your scores down in the spaces below.

Your Diet Score on page 442	______
Your Diet Score on page 438 –	______
Change in Diet Score	**= ______**

Now, subtract the bottom number from the top number to get your change in Diet Score. If you Diet Score shows a positive change, congratulations! Keep up the good work. If your score has decreased or remained the same, and your total score is less than 30, there is still room to improve your diet. Try making dietary improvement an important part of your overall lifestyle change. You may be surprised at how a healthy diet will help improve your overall quality of life.

Schedule Your Priorities

In Lesson Thirteen, on page 321, we talked about doing things that are truly important to you. We introduced you to Carol, who had quit her part-time job so that she would have time to do things that were important to her. Carol's example typifies many people living in today's fast-paced world. Most people constantly try to find time for the important activities in an already overflowing schedule. They move activities around, delegate some, cancel others, and postpone what they don't have time to do—all in the hope of finding time for the important things in their lives. The problem is that most people spend their time *prioritizing* their schedules. The key, however, is to *schedule* their priorities. A colleague once shared this experience:

I once attended a class on time management. One day, at the end of a session, the instructor said, "It's time for a quiz." He reached under the table and pulled out a one-gallon glass jar. He then reached under the table, pulled out a platter of large rocks, and set it next to the jar. "How many of these rocks do you think we can get into the jar?" he asked.

After everyone in the class made their guess, the instructor said, "Okay, let's find out." He carefully began putting the large rocks in the jar. After about a dozen or so, the jar appeared full. Then the instructor asked, "Is the jar full?"

Unanimously the class said, "Yes." "Ahhh," the instructor said, as he reached under the table and pulled out a bucket of fine gravel. Then he began dumping the gravel into the jar, shaking the jar until the gravel filled the small spaces between the large

"When scheduling priorities, you must identify the 'big rocks' and put them in first, or you won't have room for them."

rocks. The instructor grinned, looked around the room, and asked once more, "Is the jar full?"

Being a smart group of MBA students, we said, "Probably not." "Good!" he replied, as he reached under the table and brought out a bucket of sand. He started pouring the sand into the jar, and it quickly filled the small spaces left by the rocks and the gravel. Once more, he looked around the room and said to us, "Is the jar full now?" "No," came the resounding response.

"Very good!" he said, as he reached under the table and brought out a pitcher of water and began pouring it in. He poured about a quart of water into the jar before it reached the top. "What's the point?" he ask, looking around the room.

One of the students said, "Well, there are gaps, and if you really work at it, you can always fit more into your life." "No," said the instructor, "that's not the point. The point is that if you had not put the big rocks in first, you would never have gotten them in."

Most people think that more is better. They work hard to squeeze more and more activities into their day. Carol found herself doing this after quitting her part-time job. But what is more important, how *much* we do or *what* we do? Carol was filling her day with other activities—the gravel, sand, and the water—first, then she tried to fit in the big rocks. Not only did they not fit, she was miserable and stressed in the process.

We titled this section "Scheduling Your Priorities" because if you know what the big rocks are and put them in first, you'll be amazed how many of them you can get in. In addition, you'll find there's plenty of room for the gravel, sand, and water. Irrespective of what else fits in, you will have at least included the big rocks.

The Importance of Roles

Our lives consist of multiple roles. These are not roles in the context of role playing, but are the genuine roles we have each chosen for our lives. You may have multiple roles at work, as a partner or spouse, a parent, a member of your community, and in other areas of life. Roles embody relationships, responsibilities, identity, meaning, and contributions.

In Lesson Seven, on page 161, we illustrated these roles as a wheel. Too often, stress results when we devote too much time to one role at the expense of another. You may be successful and terrific at your job, but may not be a good parent or spouse. You may be like Carol and meet the needs of your family. Yet, you may fail at meeting your own needs for health, growth, and personal development.

Clearly defining your roles is an important first step in balancing your life. Once you define your roles, you can set goals that you want to accomplish in each role. These goals become the big rocks! Balance in your life does not mean that you spend the same amount of time in each role. You achieve balance when all of your roles work in harmony to accomplish the important things in your life.

On page 350, is the My Personal Roles and Goals worksheet. List the roles in your life that come to mind in whatever way seems appropriate to you. Don't worry about getting them "exactly" right the first time. This is a process that you should do over and over again. Over time, your roles in life will change. On page 343, we illustrate an example of Carol's worksheet.

Studies show that managing more than seven categories at any one time is difficult. So, we recommend that you keep your roles to seven or fewer. You may want to combine some roles to that you can keep the maximum number to seven. Also, don't feel like you have to come with seven roles. If you only identify five or six, that's fine.

The Power of Goal Setting

Perhaps the most common component of self-help and lifestyle-change literature is the notion of goal setting. Throughout this program, we have talked much about setting goals, particularly setting reasonable goals. Goal setting is obviously a powerful stress management tool. It allows us to focus our energy into putting the *right* "big rocks" into our glass jars. Goal setting is the expression of two of our gifts of human ability that affect our power to choose: our

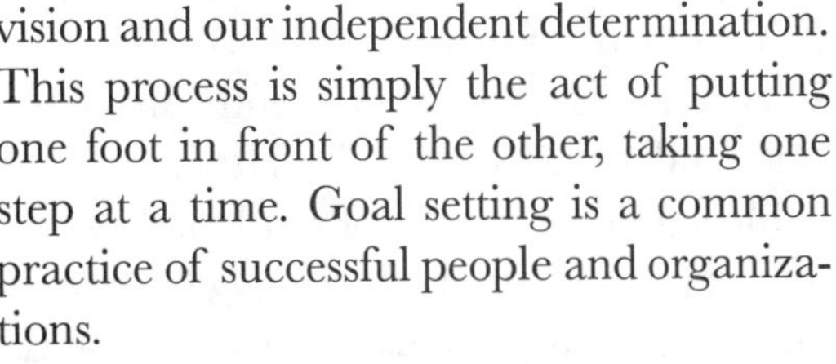
vision and our independent determination. This process is simply the act of putting one foot in front of the other, taking one step at a time. Goal setting is a common practice of successful people and organizations.

"Clearly defining your roles is an important first step in balancing your life."

Our experience with hundreds of clients over the years has revealed mixed feelings about goals. Some of our clients set heroic goals, exercise tenacious discipline, and pay a hefty price for incredible achievements. Others can't seem to keep a New Year's resolution for even a week. Some people view goals as vital to shaping the destiny of individuals, nations, and the world. Others see goals as superficial idealism that plays no role in the *real* world.

Setting realistic goals in each of the roles in your life can add balance and help align the minute and the map (see page 160), which reduces stress and improves quality of life. In setting goals, asking *what?*, *why?*,

and *how?* is important. Let's look at these important questions.

What?

In each of your roles, what do you truly want to accomplish? What contributions do you want to make? What is the result you visualize? Principle-based goals focus on growth, contribution, and personal achievement. Creating quality-of-life results requires much more than simply setting and achieving goals. Hitler set and achieved goals. So did President Reagan. The difference is on what they chose to focus. When you set goals that are compatible with who you really are (self-awareness) and your true principles, you will achieve the best possible quality of life. What you seek, you will generally find.

Why?

Why do you want to do it? Is your goal an extension of your needs and principles? Does your goal allow you to contribute and grow in your various roles?

Goals and commitments made in the moment of passion or enthusiasm lack staying power. They often end in failure. Motivation is the key to success. Your motive for beginning this program and staying with it for 14 weeks was based upon a well-planned goal that included a deep commitment to master your stress. Motivation is "why" we do something. Some people have motives that are in harmony with their roles and principles, and others do not. Motivation provides the inner strength to continue when times are difficult. It gives you the strength to say, "Yes, I will to continue this program," when life's daily struggles tempt you to give up.

How?

How are you going to accomplish the goal? What are the key beliefs that will help you achieve your purpose? What strategies can you implement to help you succeed? After you align the "what" and the "why," you're ready to look at the "how." How you accomplish a goal is a matter of choice. And, as you know, your choices are based upon the four human gifts of ability we discussed in Lesson Six, on page 133: self-awareness, vision, principles, and independent determination.

Aligning the minute and the map is important in deciding how you achieve your goals. Doing the right thing, for the right reason, in the right way, is the key to optimizing your quality of life. Again, this is a matter of choice.

Goal Setting and Roles

You are now ready to set goals for each of your roles. We suggest that you try to set at least three goals for each of the roles you listed on the My Personal Roles and Goals worksheet on page 350. These should be goals that you can accomplish over the next week. As you set your goals for the coming week, keep in mind that goals should have the following characteristics:

- Goals should be *time* specific
- Goals should be *action* specific
- Goals should be *within your control*

As you set goals, keep in mind that they are a matter of choice. You choose whether or not to do them. For example, a goal to "loose two pounds next week" is not really a goal because you do not have direct control of your weight. You cannot *choose* what you weigh. A better goal would be to "limit my calories to no more than 1500 calories each day and exercise 30 minutes every day next week." Whether or not you accomplish each of these goals is within your power, your power to choose.

Take a few minutes now to list your goals for next week on the worksheet on page 350. It may be helpful for you to review Carol's worksheet on page 343. Good luck!

Handling Relapse

You are now in your fourteenth week of the Stress Management Program. Most of our clients have experienced at least some minor setbacks during this program. This is natural, and you should expect some setbacks as you continue polishing your stress management skills. All too often, however, one minor slip can send an otherwise successful program into a tailspin. You may have experienced a stressful event and allowed your stress level to soar for a day or more before you took a proactive role to master the situation. The guilt people often feel when this happens can make them even more vulnerable to slips. Ultimately, they may believe that they have no control over stressful situations. This may paint a hopeless picture, but there is good news! You can learn skills to overcome and recover from the inevitable slips that will occur with any lifestyle-change program. The key is to be prepared to respond in a positive and constructive way when slips occur. Remember, it's not the slip that will knock you down, it's your response to the slip.

Slips will happen. Some people use slips as opportunities to learn, and they respond with an even stronger sense of motivation and mastery. Yet, others may experience negative reactions such as guilt or despair. This, in turn, weakens their sense of mastery until they are in a tailspin.

"When people believe they have no control over stressful situations, they become even more vulnerable to slips."

Two separate routes can lead to success. We believe both are important for you to learn. The first is to avoid or prevent slips from occurring to begin with. The second

is to learn coping skills that will help you regain control of the situation. We will cover both routes separately. In this lesson, we'll work on the prevention and avoidance strategy. In the next lesson, we'll work on recovery strategies.

Our discussion here and in the next lesson is based on the work of two psychologists from the University of Washington, Drs. G. Alan Marlatt and Judith Gordon. These researchers have devoted much time to studying circumstances associated with relapse in compulsive gamblers, alcoholics, drug addicts, smokers, and overweight people. In their work, they have developed helpful strategies for preventing relapses. First, distinguishing between a lapse, relapse, and collapse is important.

"When slips occur, your coping skills will help you regain control of the situation."

A lapse is a small slip or mistake. This is the *first* instance of feeling a loss of control. A lapse is a single, discrete event, like worrying excessively when your partner or spouse is late, when your boss asks to have a meeting with you at 4:30 p.m. on Friday afternoon, or when you overcommit yourself and lie awake at night worrying about how you're going to get everything done.

A relapse occurs when many slips occur in a series. Relapse puts a person back to where he or she was before beginning the Mastering Stress Program. When this happens, a negative trend of backsliding has begun.

A collapse occurs when the relapse has completely run its course. At this point, there is little chance of reversing the negative trend, and the individual may even slide further back than where he or she began.

Three important points to remember are:

❶ A slip does not have to become a lapse.

❷ A lapse does not have to become a relapse.

❸ A relapse does not have to become collapse.

Identifying High-Risk Situations

We have talked much about identifying your stress triggers and your high-risk situations. Think back over what you have learned over the last several weeks. You now have many stress management tools to identify your high-risk situations and to help you cope with stressful situations. Let's review a few.

Keeping Records

We have emphasized the importance of keeping records throughout this program. Awareness is perhaps the most valuable stress management tool that emerges from keeping good records. Many of our responses to stressful situations and events are often automatic. Awareness is the key to learning about our reactions and how we

My Personal Roles and Goals

(Carol's Example)

Roles		Goals
Role #1	Individual, personal, physical, social, mental	1. Go to the gym for exercise classes M-F from 3-4
		2. Enroll in cooking class on Wednesday
		3. Work on the computer from 10-11 on Tuesday and Thursday
Role #2	Wife	1. Spend an evening out with Jim on Saturday
		2. Prepare Jim's favorite meal on Wednesday
		3. Get Jim a small gift and give it to him on Friday
Role #3	Mother and caretaker	1. Be home every afternoon when the kids arrive
		2. Talk to each child every evening along about his/her day
		3. Take the kids swimming on Saturday
Role #4	Church member	1. Attend choir practice Thursday evening
		2. Attend church on Sunday
		3. Bake a cake for bake sale on Saturday
Role #5	Daughter	1. Call parents Sunday afternoon
		2. Send mom my new baked chicken recipe
		3. Send dad an e-mail about the football game tickets
Role #6	Sister	1. Get Mary a birthday card and present on Thursday
		2. Send Martin the water rafting brochure
		3. Call Amy to see how her vacation to Europe was
Role #7	Friend	1. Call Betty to go with me to the gym this week
		2. Visit Edna in the hospital on Monday
		3. Pick up Betty on Sunday for church

can *respond* more proactively to stressful events.

Avoidance

Avoiding certain events and situations may, at times, be the best strategy. Certainly, we cannot avoid all stress-producing situations, but we can avoid some. As we said in Lesson Seven, on page 151, some relationships may need to be reevaluated, terminated, or avoided all together.

Realistic Thinking

Realistic thinking is a terrific strategy for confronting a stressful situation head-on. Some stressful situations may repeat themselves and cannot be avoided altogether. Realistic thinking can help you change your thoughts and beliefs about the situation. Remember the key question, "What would happen if . . .?"

Assertiveness

Overcommitment and not standing up for one's rights is a common stressor. Learning how to be assertive is a key coping strategy for not becoming overcommitted. You can use the stepladder approach to reality testing to identify your thoughts about what you think might happen when you're assertive.

We have listed only a few of the many skills and techniques you have learned to use in high-risk situations. Yet, even the best planning cannot *guarantee* your stress level will remain under control. Slips can still happen. In Lesson Fifteen, we'll discuss how your can cope with lapses and relapses.

Sleep to De-Stress

Lack of sleep is a problem for many people in our fast-paced, high-tech world. The more we accomplish, the more we want to do. Too often, we don't seem to have enough time to get everything done. When this happens, many people shortchange getting a good night's sleep. Lack of sleep can be a contributor to and a result of stress. Adequate sleep gives you the recovery time you need for your busy life. It allows your body and your mind to recharge. Getting enough sleep is something everyone can do—even if you're not getting enough now!

Everyone's sleep needs differ. What is adequate sleep for one person may not be enough for another. How do you know if you're getting enough sleep? Below are some signs of a *good* night's sleep:

- You awake in the morning feeling refreshed, not fatigued.

- You have energy throughout the entire day.
- You are not agitated easily by small things that pop-up during the day.
- You don't fall asleep while driving.
- You are still interested in having sex.

Good sleeping habits are something everyone can learn. If you are having trouble getting enough sleep, here are some helpful suggestions:

- Avoid strenuous exercise before sleep, it may be too stimulating.
- Make sure your mattress is comfortable and provides adequate support.
- Keep your room dark and cool.
- Avoid caffeine at least six hours before going to sleep.
- Avoid alcohol entirely before bedtime.
- Go to sleep when you feel tired.
- Use your bed for sleeping, not for working or studying.

If you still have trouble sleeping, see your physician or a mental-health professional who specializes in sleeping disorders. You will find that mastering stress is much easier after you have had a good night's sleep.

Technology—Friend or Foe?

Have you thought much about all of the advances in technology over the past 40 years? During this period of time, more technology has been introduced into our society than in the entire history of humans. Technologies have advanced to make our lives easier, but have they?

"In many ways, technology has increased the stress in daily life."

Technology is a wonderful thing. Many view technology as an important contribution to the advancement of our society and culture. In many respects this is true. Yet, in other ways, technology may be a leading contributor to stress. Most people would agree that we live in a face-paced world. Most people say they don't have enough hours in the day to accomplish everything they would like—even with all the advances in technology. Couple this with the massive amounts of information we have readily available to us at the touch of a button. Forty years ago, we read or listened to a radio broadcast about stressful events after the fact. Today, we have a front-row seat and can witness stressful events, such as war or natural disasters, as they unfold. In many ways, technology has increased the possibility of adding much stress to our daily lives.

Meet Joe

Joe is a 50-year-old attorney who works in a large law firm in downtown Kansas

City, Kansas. Joe has been practicing law for about 25 years. He claims that his practice is much more stressful now than it was 20 years ago. Joe admits that he is much more experienced, credentialed, and supported than he was 20 years ago. Yet, he is also a slave to technology.

Joe's day begins with a pager and a cell phone clipped to his belt, a phone and fax machine in his car, and e-mail and Internet access on his portable, hand-held computer. Joe's associates and certain clients can reach him anytime of the day or night, virtually anywhere in the world. Joe never really leaves work or takes a break from it. He is accessible during evenings, weekends, holidays, vacations, and even at night, during intimate times with his wife! Would you agree that technology adds much stress to Joe's life?

"Technology plays an important role in our lives, but it can add to our stress when we allow it to dominate."

The real problem experienced by Joe is not technology itself. The problem is how Joe has allowed the technology designed for work to interfere with and infiltrate into every role of his life. We worked with Joe and helped him clearly define the important roles in life. Then, Joe set out to set realistic and attainable goals for each role. Soon, Joe put technology in its proper place. The technology then began to serve Joe and make his life easier, as it was designed to. He learned the key was not to allow himself to become the servant of the technology.

Technology can play an important role in our lives, but technology can easily add much stress to our lives. As you go through the next week, make a list of all the technologies you use and the related stress they cause. Then, plan strategies to reduce the stress each technology contributes to your daily life. You have learned many skills to do this, so good luck!

Advanced Relaxation

Over the last few weeks, you have been practicing relaxation techniques. Although some of your practice sessions may have been shorter than others, you have been practicing in a setting with as few distractions as possible. During this time, your concentration has been getting stronger. Now, you are ready to learn more advanced relaxation techniques. We begin with generalization.

Generalization

We now want your relaxation practices to be a little more difficult. This will allow you to *generalize* and apply your relaxation skills to different and more difficult situations. Let's face it, your relaxation skills are more likely to be needed in situations other than a quiet room, where no one is present. You will be learning to deal with increased distractions in much the same way that a weight lifter learns to lift heavier weights and a runner learns to run longer distances. Gradually increasing the difficulty is important. Move on to harder situations only after you have learned to relax and feel comfortable with the less difficult ones. Proceed at your own pace, we won't be behind you keeping score!

Think of ways to make your relaxation more difficult. Begin with the easiest, and gradually work your way up to the more difficult practices. In the More Difficult Relaxation Practice example on the right, you will find a list of practices we use with our clients. Modify this list to fit your needs. Practice at home this week with a variety of distractions. In Lesson Fifteen, you will learn to apply these techniques directly to stressful situations as they happen.

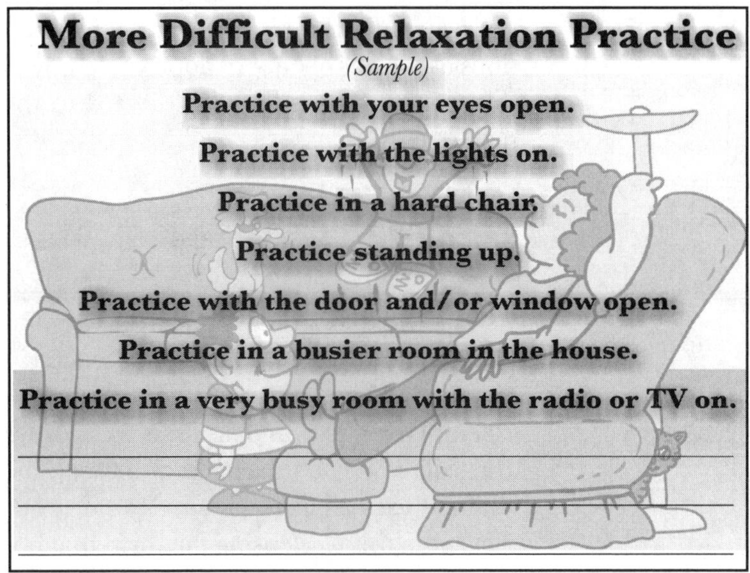

More Difficult Relaxation Practice
(Sample)
Practice with your eyes open.
Practice with the lights on.
Practice in a hard chair.
Practice standing up.
Practice with the door and/or window open.
Practice in a busier room in the house.
Practice in a very busy room with the radio or TV on.

Program Review

You now have three weeks remaining in the Mastering Stress Program. The time has come again to review your progress and set goals for the remainder of the program. This is a similar review to the one you completed in Lesson Nine. We provide you with the My Stress Management Program Review worksheet on page 351. Review your Stress Change Worksheets on page 227 and 328 for weeks 9–13. In the second column, list your review comments and any patterns that you uncovered. Look back on your worksheet in Lesson Nine, on page 223. Did you reach the goals you set for weeks 9–12? If so, that's terrific. If not, try to assess why you did not meet your goals. Were the goals unreasonable? Did your motivation wane? Whatever the reasons, try to learn as much as possible about why your goals were not met. With this information in mind, set new goals for weeks 14–16 and beyond the last lesson. Write these goals in the third column of the worksheet.

Now, review your Physical Activity and Relaxation Practice Worksheet in Appendix F, on page 434. Continue to complete the worksheet for your physical activity and relaxation as you did with the Stress Change Worksheet review. This is an important step, so complete your review before continuing.

Lesson Review

At the beginning of this lesson, you were introduced to the Behavior Chain and we asked you to make a chain of your own to review. This is a terrific technique to help show you that stress is often the result of a chain of events. Your goal is to break the weakest link in the chain at the earliest possible point. Next, we had you rate your diet again. Has your diet improved in the last four weeks? We hope you are on your way to eating a more healthy diet. Schedules and priorities were the next topics, followed by the importance of roles. We revisited the topic of goal setting, and followed this discussion with information about relapses. You were then asked to think about the role that technology plays in your life and whether it increases or decreases your stress. Finally, you learned the advanced technique of generalizing your relaxation practices. This is important because, in the next lesson, you will be learning how to apply relaxation techniques to stressful situations as they happen. We hope you enjoyed this lesson and are looking forward to the next one.

This Week's Assignment

Practice developing a behavior chain to a stressful situation you have experienced in the past. Then, complete your Behavior Chain Worksheet and list the techniques and skills you could have used to break the chain at various links. Be sure to rate your diet again this week using the form that begins on page 439, in Appendix G. Define your various roles on My Roles and Goals Worksheet on page 350, then set goals for each role for the coming week. Remember to complete your Daily Stress Record, on page 352, along with your Stress Change Worksheet for week 14, on page 328, and the Average Stress Change Worksheet in Appendix E, on page 430. Also, record your physical activity and relaxation practice on the worksheet in Appendix F, on page 434. Good luck with this lesson—you have only three more to go!

Knowledge Review

T F 111. Caffeine and alcohol will help you sleep better at night.

T F 112. Technology has helped to reduce everyone's stress level.

T F 113. Identifying the various roles you have chosen in life is an important first step in identifying the things in life that are truly important to you.

T F 114. Learning to identify and avoiding lapses is critical in mastering your stress.

T F 115. Everyone needs eight hours of sleep each night.

T F 116. The idea behind building a Behavior Chain is to help you identify techniques and strategies to break the various links in the chain.

T F 117. It is better and less stressful to prioritize your schedule rather than trying to schedule your priorities.

T F 118. Learning to generalize your relaxation skills is an important step before applying these skills to real situations in the real world.

(Answers in Appendix C, page 415)

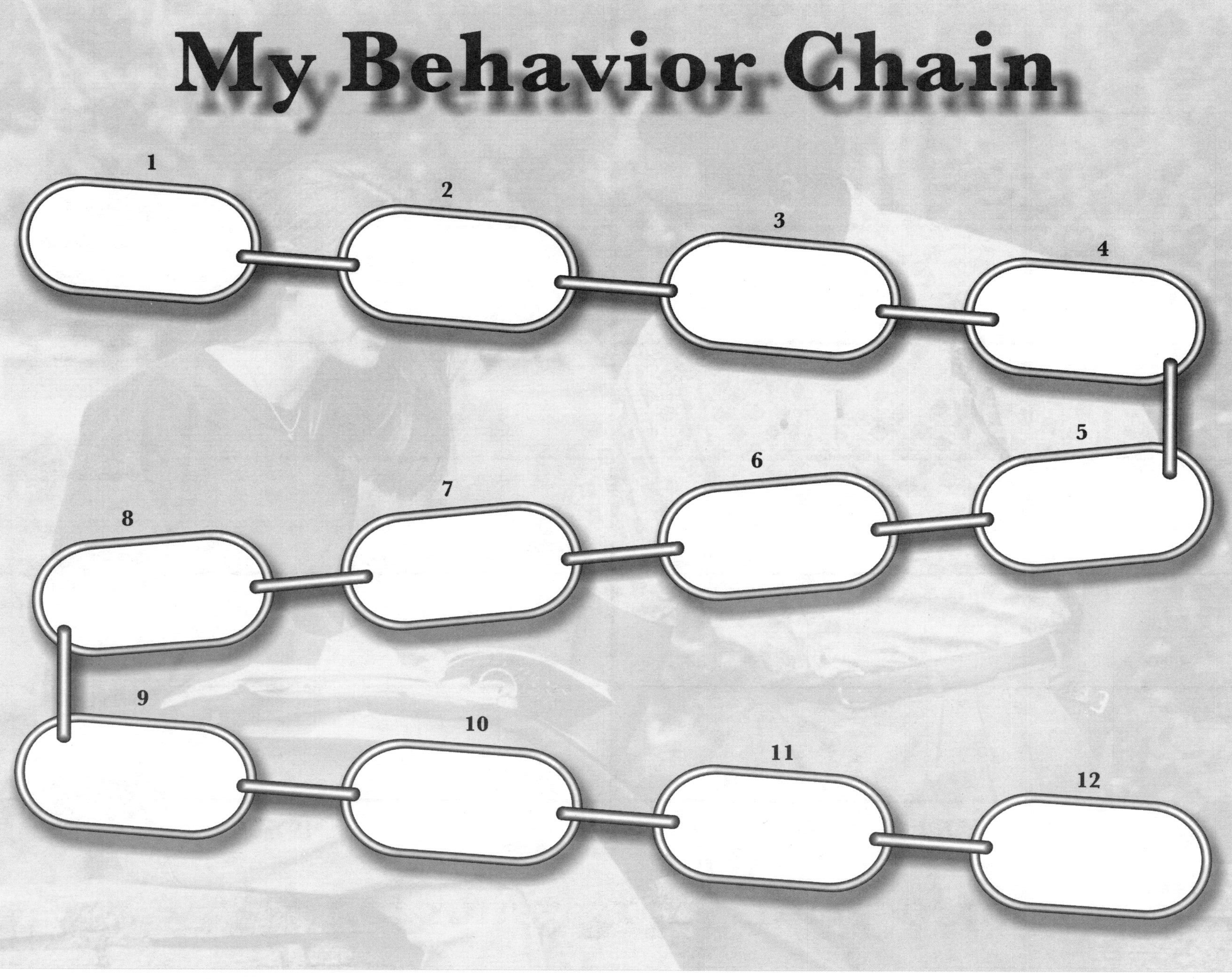
My Behavior Chain
1
2
3
4
5
6
7
8
9
10
11
12

My Personal Roles and Goals

Roles	Goals
Role #1	
Role #2	
Role #3	
Role #4	
Role #5	
Role #6	
Role #7	

My Stress Management Program Review

Worksheet/Activity	Weeks 9–13	My Goals for Weeks 14–16
Stress Change Worksheet	**Review comments:** **Patterns uncovered:**	**Goals for week 14:** **Goals for week 15:** **Goals for week 16:** **Goals after the program:**
Physical Activity	**Review comments:** **Patterns uncovered:**	**Goals for week 14:** **Goals for week 15:** **Goals for week 16:** **Goals after the program:**
Relaxation	**Review comments:** **Patterns uncovered:**	**Goals for week 14:** **Goals for week 15:** **Goals for week 16:** **Goals after the program:**

Daily Stress Record—Lesson Fourteen

Name:______________________________________ **Week of:**______________

Date	Average Stress Level	Highest Stress Level	Time of Highest Stress Level	Stressful Event Associated with Highest Stress Level

My Physical Activity and Relaxation Record

Day of the Week	Physical Activity Record		Relaxation by Recall	
	Activity	Minutes	Time of Day	Minutes
Monday				
Tuesday				
Wednesday				
Thursday				
Friday				
Saturday				
Sunday				

Lesson Fifteen

We hope you had a terrific week. Only two lessons (Lesson Sixteen and the Commencement Lesson) remain in the Mastering Stress Program, and we have important information to share with you. Most of the program thus far has been designed to help you learn skills and techniques to change the way you respond to the environment around you. We begin this lesson with some techniques designed to help you change your environment to make it less stressful. Our discussion then turns to the important role of medications in stress management. We continue our discussions on relapse prevention, relaxation, assertiveness, and time management. This lesson continues to bring together, in an advanced way, many of the stress management skills and techniques you have learned in this program. So, with these things in mind, let's move on.

Bracing Yourself Against a Stressful Environment

We discussed early in this program that stress comes from two sources: the world around you or your environment is an *external* source, and the way in which you choose to respond is an *internal* source. For the past 14 weeks, you have been learning skills and techniques that will help you proactively respond to your environment in a less stressful way. We hope that at this point, you have learned to make choices that result in much less stress. You don't have to change everything about yourself, nor would you want to. But, if you have been practicing and using the techniques properly, a small part of your "self" should be much different by now. You should be calmer, more relaxed, and more in control of how you respond to stressors.

We now turn our discussion to the other side of stress—changing our stressful environment. Sometimes we face situations and events that are truly stressful. They would be stressful for just about anyone. No matter how much we change our thoughts and beliefs about these events, we're still going to experience stress. In these situations, you may need to make changes in your environment to lower your stress. In other instances, you may be able to take control and master your stress, even in a continu-

THIS SOOTHING TAPE WILL HELP YOU LEARN TO MAXIMIZE DRIVE TIME BY CHANNELING STRESS INTO PRODUCTIVITY.

TRAFFIC PILE UP ? HAVE A MINI GOAL-SETTING SESSION!
... STUCK IN THE SLOW LANE ? DICTATE THOSE OVERDUE LETTERS!
... GET TRAPPED BEHIND A FLAT TIRE ON THE FREEWAY AND YOU COULD MENTALLY OUTLINE YOUR BUSINESS STRATEGY FOR THE.....

EEEYAAH

... NOT THAT PRODUCTIVE, BUT WELL WORTH THE $12.95.

ally stressful environment. For example, let's say that you lack assertiveness skills, and you find yourself taking on more than you can handle. Your environment may be *directly* responsible for your high levels of stress by giving you more than you can do. Yet, your lack of assertiveness is what led you to taking on too much in the first place. Learning and using stress management skills and techniques can, therefore, help you respond to your environment in a less stressful way.

Life's Challenging Events

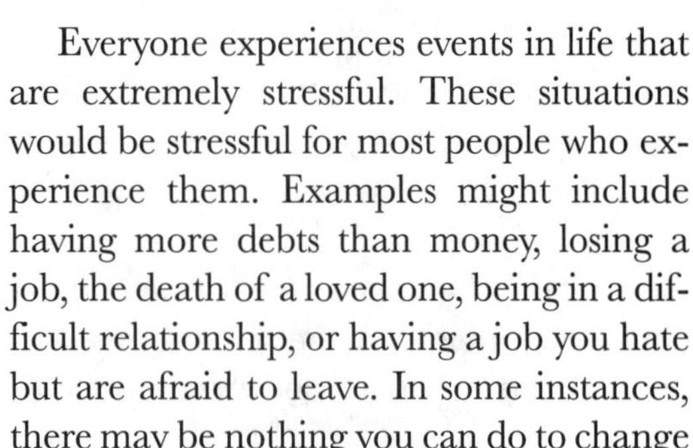

"Your environment and events in life may be directly responsible for your high level of stress."

Everyone experiences events in life that are extremely stressful. These situations would be stressful for most people who experience them. Examples might include having more debts than money, losing a job, the death of a loved one, being in a difficult relationship, or having a job you hate but are afraid to leave. In some instances, there may be nothing you can do to change the environment. An example would be the death of a loved one.

You may use some of the skills and techniques you learned in this program to help you cope, but you may continue to experience stress. In these cases, you may simply have to accept the stress and use your skills to minimize it. Simply accepting the stress by understanding that it is realistic to experience stress in these circumstances may be the most effective stress management technique available to you. Understanding that a high level of stress is only temporary can often help you feel more comfortable and less stressed.

You may experience some situations, however, that you do have the power to change. Being in a job that you hate is an example. After all, you can *choose* to leave the job! Your immediate response may be something like, "Yes, but I have a family to support and bills to pay. There is no way I can quit my job!" You should recognize this type of thinking by now as unrealistic and catastrophic thinking. You have the power to leave your job. Doing so may not be easy, but you *can* do it. The point to remember is that you do have options. The options may not seem pleasant, or even possible to live with, but they still exist. One of the most stressful feelings we experience is the feeling of having no control in a situation. Feeling a lack of control is often the result of believing that you have no choice in a matter. Realistically, however, you always have the power to choose less-stressful thoughts and, more often than not, less-stressful environments.

Much research shows that people who believe they have no control and no alternative choices are actually *choosing* not to make those choices when the opportunity arises. Alternatively, those who realize they have the power to choose are more likely to make less stressful choices when they are available. The take-home message here is that simply realizing that you do have the *power to choose* can, by itself, lower your stress.

We can think of stress as a "mental fever." When a harmful bacteria or virus invades your body, your body responds. The resulting fever tells you that something is wrong. We can say the same about stress. When stressful situations invade your life, your body and mind respond. The resulting stress tells you that something is wrong. It may be telling you that life is not a bed of roses at the moment, and that you may want to consider making some changes in your environment. On the other hand, the stress may be telling you that you need to employ some stress management techniques, and you may need to choose to respond to the event in a different, less stressful way. In either instance, the stress you experience lets you know something is wrong—with your environment or your thoughts and beliefs!

Revisiting Job-Related Stress

We have talked much about job-related stress. Stress on the job is the most common source of stress for most people. This can happen for many reasons. In some cases, stress may result from having too much to do or the lack of being assertive. A more common reason, however, is feeling a lack of control or a lack of choice in one's job. If you feel this way, introducing some changes to the work environment may help lower your stress.

You may work in a stressful position where you can do little to change the environment, except leave. You may work for a supervisor who is unlikely to change the way he or she interacts with you or treats you. You may try some coping strategies you learned in this program to help lower your job-related stress, or you may need to change jobs. Alternatively, you may want to address the situation directly with your supervisor. If you approach your supervisor with some practical, concrete suggestions on how you think you might lower your job-related stress, the results may surprise you.

"I want the public to think of us as 'The Company With A Heart'. But I want *you* to think of us as the company that will chew you up, spit you out and smear you into the carpet if you screw up."

Coping with Change

We live in a rapidly changing world. Advances in information, medicine, technology, and many other things in our world seem to change in a flash. Some people embrace the notion of change, yet others experience increased stress when things change too fast.

What can you do to cope with the stress of rapid change? Realistically, you can do little to alter the course of change. Change is all around and is constant. You can, however, learn how to better cope with change. Understanding that fear and frustration in the face of rapid change and uncertainty are perfectly natural and understandable is important. You are not alone in the chal-

lenge of coping with change. Everyone faces the same challenge. Some people cope better with change than others. Viewing change itself as the stressor may also be helpful. You can then apply many of the techniques you have learned in this program to help you master the associated stress.

"Realistic thinking can help you examine your thoughts and beliefs about change, such as rapid changes in computer technology at work."

Realistic thinking can help you examine your thoughts and beliefs about change. For example, if the rapid changes in computer technology increase your stress at work, try to define the specific stressor. Could the stressor be the fear that you will lose your job because you can't master the new technology? You may be feeling angry that your employer has introduced something new to your job that you don't fully understand. Perhaps you feel that other people may now be able to do your job better than you can. Challenge your thoughts and beliefs with the evidence. You may need to talk with your supervisor, other colleagues, read additional information, or change perspectives.

Reality testing can also help you cope with change. If, in our example, you are stressed over new computer technology, break your exposure to the change into small steps. Then you can build your stepladder, starting with the first step. You may be surprised by the many resources that are available to you to help you better understand the new technology.

Discussing your concerns about change in the workplace with your supervisor may be a helpful strategy. Most organizations have many wonderful resources available to help their employees cope with change. Use these resources to help you cope with change and lower your stress. If the thought of having a discussion with your supervisor is too stressful, have a discussion with a co-worker, a friend, or family member. This may be an ideal time to call upon your social support network to help. Chances are that you're not the only person having difficulty coping with change. Also, you may know other people who have struggled through similar changes. They may have some helpful suggestions. The important thing to remember is that you do have choices. You can *choose* to take control of the situation rather than allowing the situation to control you.

Other Techniques

You have learned other skills and techniques in this program that can help you better change the world around you. Assertiveness skills can be used to keep you from taking on too much and help you get more of the things you want out of life. Time management skills are certainly important in helping you organize your time more efficiently and focus on things that are truly important to you. Finally, problem-solving skills can help generate a host of possible solutions and action plans for practical problems in your environment.

You will realize the greatest benefit from using these techniques after you have mastered the basic skills of realistic thinking, relaxation, and reality testing. Try not to underestimate the importance of these basic skills. You should continue to practice to remain proficient at using these important stress management techniques. These basic skills are paramount in learning and effectively using the more advanced techniques you have learned.

The Role of Medication in Stress Management

If you were taking prescription medication for stress before you started this program, you may be ready to stop, or you may have already stopped taking medication. If so, congratulations! You deserve much credit for your hard work. If you are considering stopping, be sure to discuss this with your physician before you stop taking your medication. About one-half of the people who use this program and who are taking medication for stress will be ready to stop taking the medication at about this point in the program. Many others stop within a year. Remember, you should always work with your doctor when making any change involving the use or dosage of prescription medication.

Common Medications for Stress

The medications most commonly prescribed for short-term relief of stress include tranquilizers, most of which are part of a class of medications known as benzodiazepines. This group includes dozens of types and brand names, among them diazepam (Valium®) and alprazolam (Xanax®).

Generally, these medications are prescribed for short periods because individuals can develop tolerances for them. After a few weeks, the medications become less effective, and a higher dose may be necessary to achieve the same effect. Increasing the dose of these medications increases the risk for addiction and dependency. For this reason, most physicians only prescribe these tranquilizers to help patients through difficult, short-term situations.

Physicians also prescribe antidepressant medications for stress and anxiety. Some of the more common antidepressants are in the tricyclic category. These include imipramine (Tofranil®) and amitriptyline (Laroxyl®). Another category, the monoamine-oxidase (MAO) inhibitors, include phenelzine (Nardil®).

The tyicyclic antidepressants often have side effects that appear to increase stress early in the treatment cycle, but typically subside with time. For example, the MAO inhibitors often require dietary restrictions to prevent an increase in blood pressure. Antidepressants generally can be used for a longer time than tranquilizers. Dependency and addiction are less of a problem with these drugs.

"You should always work with your doctor when making any change involving the use or dosage of prescription medication."

The newer antidepressants, the SSRI's (Selective Serotonin Reuptake Inhibitors) are also used to treat stress and anxiety related disorders. The SSRI's increase the amount of serotonin, a feel-good chemical produced in the brain, and therefore have a positive effect on mood. These newer med-

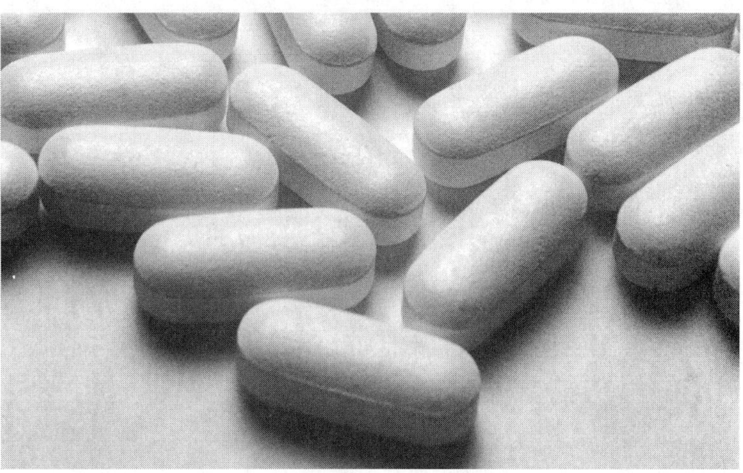

ications have fewer side effects than the older ones and are more easily tolerated. Examples of the SSRI medications include fluoxetine (Prozac®), paroxetine (Paxil®), sertraline (Zoloft®), fluvoxamine (Luvox®), and citalopram (Celexa®).

Stopping Your Medication

You now have 14 weeks of the Mastering Stress Program behind you. During this time, you have learned many skills and techniques to help you master the stress in your life. You may now feel that you are ready to stop taking medication. If so, be sure to discuss this with your physician before making any changes, because only he or she knows whether you should stop taking the medication and the best way to do so. Working closely with your physician, following the guidelines below, and using your stress management skills and techniques should help when you are ready to stop using stress medications.

"Working with your physician, following the guidelines, and using your stress management skills will help you stop using stress medications."

Withdraw Slowly

Despite what you may have seen on television or in the movies, stopping "cold turkey" is not the way to go. Ask your physician to help you work out a schedule for slowly decreasing the medication dosage.

Set a Target Date

Work with your physician and pick a date by which you hope to be completely off the medication. This date should be far enough away to allow gradual withdrawal from the medication, but the date should not be so far away that your goal seems unrealistic and unreachable.

Use Your Stress Management Techniques

Eliminating your medication is nothing to get stressed about! Most people cope very well with a gradual decrease in medication dosage. Still, others may experience temporary increases in stress as they begin decreasing their medication. This is more likely to happen if the individual has been taking one of the benzodiazepines. However, this slight increase in stress goes away after a week or two as the medication clears your system. If you experience this "outbreak" of stress, remember that it is only temporary. Combine the deep muscle relaxation techniques with other techniques you have been using all along. You may have to put up with a little discomfort as you body adjusts to the change of not having the medication. At some point, you may feel as though you are relapsing and that your stressful feelings will *never* go away. How likely is that, really?

If you did the reality testing exercises while taking medication, you may need to repeat some of the tasks after you stop taking medication. You may have told yourself that the only way you got through the tasks was with the help of the medication. Learning to do the same things without the medication will give you a far greater sense of accomplishment and control. Without the medication, you will know that you did it yourself!

Relapse Prevention

In the last lesson, we introduced the notion of handling relapses. You may recall that we discussed two paths to relapse prevention: avoiding them and learning to cope with them. On page 342, we discussed strategies to help you plan for high-risk situations. This can help you avoid many stressful situations, but not all of them.

The second path to success is learning how to cope with lapses and prevent relapses. Slips and lapses are an unfortunate reality. Most of our clients using this program have experienced times of great joy when they went for days without experiencing increased stress. They have also experienced setbacks. Rarely do we encounter clients who do not occasionally allow a crowded freeway or subway or an important deadline to increase their stress. The important issue is not *whether* a lapse occurs, but the person's reaction when it occurs.

Regaining Control

Dr. G. Alan Marlatt, mentioned in Lesson Fourteen, has developed specific steps a person can take to regain control when a lapse occurs. Remember, the idea is to not allow a lapse to turn into a relapse. The six steps that follow have been adapted from Dr. Marlatt's work.

Step 1—Stop, look, and listen. A lapse is like a road sign. It signals possible danger ahead. Stop what you are doing, particularly if the lapse has already begun.

"Whenever you're feeling overworked, I want you to stop and smell the roses we've programmed into your screensaver."

Examine the situation. What is happening? Why is the lapse happening at this moment? Try to relax and remove yourself from the stressful situation to a safe place where you can be alone. A short walk may help you think more clearly about what is happening.

Step 2—Stay calm and relaxed. If you become highly stressed and begin blaming yourself for the lapse, the situation will only get worse. You may conclude that you are a hopeless case and that you will *never* learn to master your stress. Thinking like this will only add to the stress you may already be feeling. Separate yourself from the situation and view it objectively, as an outside observer would. Would you tell a friend that a single lapse makes him or her a total failure? Staying calm and relaxed makes the next step easier to follow.

Step 3—Renew your commitment to mastering your stress. Take a minute to remind yourself of all the hard work you have done and the tremendous progress you have made. Visualize your Stress Change Worksheets and the progress they illustrate. Think of how sad it would be to throw away all this hard work. Would you

"Program partners, family, and friends can be a great source of support during a lapse."

tell a child or close friend to drop out of school during the last week just because the work was difficult? Of course not. Now is a good time to renew your commitment to mastering your stress for a lifetime.

Step 4—Review the lapse event. Rather than laying blame at your doorstep and giving up as a complete failure, use the lapse as an opportunity to learn. Experiencing a lapse can provide you with valuable information. Use this knowledge to learn what places you at increased risk. Do certain events increase the risk? Do you have specific thoughts and beliefs that are increasing your stressful feelings? Did you recognize this earlier as a high-risk situation? If so, did you do anything to plan for it in advance? If so, did it work? If not, why not? What thoughts do you have? Write down your thoughts and look at them objectively, weighing the evidence for and against each one.

Step 5—Choose to take charge. When a lapse occurs, plan in advance to leap into action and take control of the situation. Go for a walk, find a safe place where you can be alone, or call a close friend. Do whatever works for you. Don't wait. Be proactive and decisive. Waiting around for things to get better means losing even more control and is a setup for more lapses. Jump in and take control.

Step 6—Ask for help. Program partners, friends, family members, and others can be a great source of support during a lapse. Now is a great time to ask others for help and input. Don't be shy about asking for help when you need it most. Not asking for help is asking for trouble!

These six steps to gain control of a lapse are simple and easy to follow. Jot them down on a small piece of paper and carry them with you. When you find yourself beginning a lapse, take out the paper and follow these six steps.

Applied Relaxation

In the last lesson, we discussed ways to generalize and make your relaxation practice sessions more difficult. We are doing this to help you more easily apply relaxation to stressful situations, anywhere and anytime. Once you can practice efficiently at home with a variety of distractions, you are ready for the ultimate relaxation challenge. Your mini-practices have begun to prepare you for this, just as practice prepares a runner or weight lifter for competition. Like every athlete, however, you should not expect to *win* every time. You cannot beat stress in every situation. Some situations will always be more difficult than others. With continued practice, you can learn to master your stress in most situations and keep it at the lowest possible level.

This technique works much the same way as the stepladder approach. Think of an event or situation that makes you feel tense. Then, strange as it may seem, we want you to deliberately put yourself into the situation. Your objective is to try to stay as relaxed as possible. This is the only way to practice your relaxation skills when and where you need them most—in circumstances that make you tense. You may want to try visualizing the situation first, feeling the tension building in your muscles, then try to keep the muscles relaxed.

You are likely to encounter many situations that require your attention. In these situations, you will not be able to totally concentrate on relaxing your muscles. By now, however, the relaxed feeling should be very familiar to you so it should not require all of your attention. As we have said often throughout this manual, practice is essential.

The table on the right, titled "Situations That Make Me Tense," is a sample from one of our clients. Take time now to think about what your own list would look like. What are some of the situations where you are the most tense? If you have trouble coming up with a list, try looking back at some of your old Realistic Thinking Records and your Stressful Events Records. Going into any stressful situation and just trying to relax can be helpful, you do not have to choose only those situations that are a problem for you.

On page 370, we provide you with a blank "Situations That Make Me Tense" worksheet. Make your list now and arrange the list from the easiest to the hardest. Begin this week by working on the first item on your list.

Situations That Make Me Tense

Watching a suspenseful move
Standing in the longest line at the bank
Standing in the longest line at the supermarket
Doing that frustrating task I have been putting
off at work
Making that phone call I have been avoiding
Driving behind the slowest car on the road

More on Being Assertive

Learning to be more assertive is not terribly difficult. The key is to keep reminding yourself of the description of assertiveness we discussed in Lesson Eight, on page 191. It is surprising how many people try to assert themselves in awkward ways. Some people have trouble getting their message across clearly, and others may come across as being too strong or aggressive. Do you recall the section in Lesson Seven, on page 155, about changing perspectives? This is a very useful technique to use. When you want to be assertive with someone, try mentally swapping places with them. Then, ask yourself, "If I were in his or her place, how would I respond to what I am about to say?" If you answer is "I would feel angry" or "I would ignore it," you are not expressing yourself well. Try to think of different ways to express yourself. Then, concentrate on the one that you believe would produce the best results. This is another opportunity to use your social support network. Try your suggestion out on friends or family members. Ask them for their honest reaction to the situation and your assertive statements.

"The idea is not to score the most points or enter a battlefield. You want to create a win-win situation for both you and the other person."

When asserting yourself, keep in mind that if you make the other person angry, they are likely to become defensive. If this happens, you are not likely to get your way! The idea is not to score the most points or enter a battlefield. You want to create a win-win situation for both you and the other person.

Using common sense to assert yourself is important. Think about how you can most effectively get your message across. People are much more likely to listen if you are clear, confident, and express yourself appropriately. They are more likely to help if they clearly understand your feelings and perspective. On the other hand, they are not likely to be helpful if they feel threatened or believe that you are being antagonistic toward them. The following guidelines may be helpful:

Timing Is Important

Timing is very important in being assertive. Make sure the other person has set aside time to listen to you and that you have his or her full attention. This sets the stage for the best possible communication. Your thoughts and ideas are much more likely to be heard if the other person is not distracted by other things.

Watch Out for the Nonverbal Cues

You want your message to be heard, so deliver it clearly and confidently. Good eye contact, upright posture, and a clear voice give the image of someone who knows what they want and is confident of getting it. When you look at the ground or ceiling, shuffle your feel, mumble, or speak with a weak voice, you give the impression that you are not sure about what you want. By the same token, you do not want to come across as being arrogant or overbearing. Be sure not to stand too close to the other person, don't stare, and keep your voice calm and level. Yelling makes people respond defensively.

Be Empathetic

Being assertive requires you to acknowledge that the other person also has rights in the situation. These rights are important. Acknowledge the other person's position. Steven Covey highlights this point very clearly: "Seek first to understand before trying to be understood." If the other person recognizes that you clearly understand his or her position, your position is more likely to be understood. Consider these two examples:

Poor: "I want you to stay here as long as it takes tonight and finish this paperwork."

Better: "I realize that you want to get home and spend time with your family. It's very important that this paperwork is finished tonight. Please stay and finish it so that I will have it first thing in the morning for my meeting."

In the second statement, you acknowledge that your request is an inconvenience. You also acknowledge that you realize the importance of the other person's family time. You are sharing your compassion and empathy. Yet, you are communicating that your needs are more urgent at this time.

Use "I" Statements

"I" statements personalize your comments. This allows the other person to know how you feel, not how other people may feel in a similar situation. This is particularly important when you are expressing negative feelings. Consider the following statements:

Poor: "People don't like it when you smoke in here."

Better: "I have trouble breathing when you smoke in here."

The first statement leaves you open to arguments and resentment. After all, what do you know about what other people like or dislike? With the second statement, no possibility for argument exists. This gives the impression that you are being open and honest.

Describe the Causes and Effects

Explaining the entire situation clearly rather than simply making demands is an important assertiveness technique. This is more likely to convince the other person that your rights and desires are important. When you want someone to change something, telling them exactly what it is you want changed and why is often effective. Consider the following two statements:

Poor: "Stop talking."

Better: "When you talk, it is difficult for me to hear what is being said in the movie. I would appreciate it if you would not talk to me right now."

The second statement clearly explains the behavior you are not happy with and its effect on you. It also suggests how the other person can be helpful. This request will be more likely give you the desired results without sounding offensive.

Suggest Alternatives

Making suggestions about acceptable alternative behavior can often further diffuse the situation. You may consider adding a second statement in the previous exchange:

Poor: "Stop talking."

Better: "When you talk, it is difficult for me to hear what is being said in the movie. I would appreciate it if you would not talk to me right now. *Perhaps we could discuss the movie when it is over.*"

TALKING WITH YOUR MOUTH FULL . . . BAD!
TALKING WITH YOUR BRAIN FULL . . . GOOD!

Making a reasonable request lets the other people in the situation know that you accept their right to do whatever it is they are doing. Your suggestion is an attempt to find a mutually satisfactory solution.

Being assertive can help you stand up for your rights and keep your stress level down. At times, however, you may encounter aggression from the other person. In the next lesson, we'll give you guidelines for handling aggression.

Delegating Responsibility

The inability to delegate tasks and responsibility can significantly increase stress for many people. Delegating tasks and asking others for help has been shown to reduce stress significantly. Our clients tell us many reasons why they do not delegate. We would like to share a few of the most common ones with you.

- "Nobody can do this as well as I can."
- "My way is the only right way."
- "It takes more time for me to explain what I need to have done than it takes to do it myself."
- "I feel bad about asking someone to do my work because they may get mad at me."
- "What if they do a better job?"

As you have learned, you have the power to choose new thoughts and beliefs that can help you delegate. Below are some examples:

- "Maybe someone else can do it as well as I can. If they can't, they can learn."
- "Maybe there are other good ways to do things. My way does not always have to be the only way."
- "It may take more time to explain, but in the long run, I'll have less to do."
- "Why should I feel bad about asking for help? I would be happy to help my co-workers."
- "Chances are that they won't be mad at me for asking. If they are, I'll survive."
- "What if they do a better job? This may be an opportunity for me to improve my skills."

"I want you to cut everyone's salary by 15% — but make it look like a reward."

Scheduling Your Weekly Priorities

In the last lesson, you made a list of your roles and set weekly goals for each role on the My Personal Roles and Goals worksheet on page 350. Did you meet each

MONDAY:
VOWED TO SLOW DOWN MY CRAZY PACE AND RECONNECT WITH THE SIMPLE JOYS OF LIFE.
SUN TEA
POETRY

TUESDAY:
SPENT DAY TRYING TO CLEAN OFF THE PATIO TO MAKE ROOM FOR A CHAIR.

WEDNESDAY:
SPENT DAY TRYING TO CLEAN OUT THE GARAGE TO MAKE ROOM FOR THE JUNK FROM THE PATIO.
THURSDAY:
SPENT DAY TRYING TO CLEAN THE BASEMENT TO MAKE ROOM FOR THE JUNK FROM THE GARAGE.

96 HOURS INTO MY NEW SIMPLE LIFE, AND THE ONLY ACTIVITY I'VE ELIMINATED IS SITTING DOWN.
E-Z BUILD SHELVES
PAINT
PUT SOMEPLACE
MOTOR OIL

goal? If so, that's terrific. If not, do you know why you didn't?

Once you establish weekly goals for each of your roles, the next step is to schedule your priorities so the important tasks get completed. You can easily accomplish this by planning one day at a time. The Personal Roles and Goals worksheet contains the most important goals you have set for each role. You will likely prepare another list of other things you need to accomplish over the next week, but this list will be the *urgent* not necessarily the *important*. Look again at Carol's example Personal Roles and Goals Worksheet from the last lesson, on page 343. On page 366, we have provided an example of Carol's Weekly Tasks List that includes the other tasks that she needs to accomplish over the next week. We have provided a blank copies of the Weekly Tasks List (on page 372) and the Daily Planner (on page 373) for you to copy and use this week. Once you list all of your tasks, you can then prioritize them by ranking them in order of importance, such as with the ranking that follows:

I-level priorities are the *important* weekly goals you established from your Personal Roles and Goals worksheet. Schedule the "I" tasks first on your Daily Planner, directly from your Roles and Goals Worksheet. These *important* goals are the ones most often leftover at the end of the day! Don't fall into this trap. These important tasks should not appear on your Weekly Task List.

A-level tasks are the next level priority. Give an "A" only to the tasks on your Weekly Tasks List that absolutely, positively have to be done that day. On some days you may have many "A" tasks and on other days, none. Be careful with your ratings. Ask yourself, "Do I really have to do this today?" If not, the task does not get an "A" rating. Remember our discussions on setting reasonable goals. Do not schedule so many "A" tasks that you will be stressed trying to get them all done in one day. Consider this question, "What will 'really' happen if this doesn't get done today." Too often we believe that *everything* has to get done today, but, in reality, *everything* does not have to be done!

B-level tasks are the most common type of task. These tasks need to be done, but they don't necessarily have to be done immediately or by a specific time. If "B" tasks go uncompleted for very long, they may eventually become "A" tasks. Don't get stressed if you do not get to a "B" task im-

Weekly Task List

(Carol's Example)

Week of: August 6, 2001

Scheduled Day/Time	Task	Priority Rating	Done
M-F/ 6:30 p.m.	Dinner each evening	A	
M & Th / 8:00 a.m.	Go to the Market	A	
Sat a.m.	Laundry	A	
Sat 3:00 p.m.	Take Michael shopping for shoes	B	
Sat / day	Clean house	C	
Wed / 1 p.m.	Go to the dry cleaner	B	

mediately. This is a priority task, but not your most important priority. At about the B-level tasks, most people begin to see the power of scheduling the "I" priorities first. You may recall that you spent a lot of time defining the important roles you have choosen and developing weekly goals for each role. Don't let all of the other tasks overpower or diminish these truly important priorities. Remember, these are the *large* rocks that go inside your weekly "jar." Think of the "A" tasks as the fine gravel and the "B" tasks as the sand that can be worked in and around the big rocks!

C-level tasks are those that will need to be done someday, but at the moment they are not all that urgent or pressing. Some "C" tasks may stay "C" tasks indefinitely, while others may eventually become "B" or "A" tasks. You may even discover that some don't really have to be done and you scratch them off entirely.

D-level tasks can usually be delegated to someone else. Often, these tasks will come from one of the other categories on your task list.

A Word of Caution! Carefully review tasks that remain in any single category for more than a couple of weeks. This may be a sign that you are procrastinating starting the task. If you are procrastinating, reread the sections in this program about overcoming procrastination. If you truly are not procrastinating, the task may not really be all that important and you may need to delete it from your task list altogether.

Now, look at Carol's example Daily Planner for Monday, on page 368, to see how Carol's personal goals and tasks have been scheduled into her day on Monday. Carol uses the Reminder column to rate her goals and tasks. We have provided a blank Weekly Task List on page 372, along with a blank Daily Planner on page 373 for you to use this next week. Make as many copies of these forms as you need.

Many time management strategies exist for ranking tasks and scheduling priorities. The one we present here is just one of many. If you have another method that works better for you, use it. If you are not currently using a planning program, we strongly encourage you to give this one a try. Our clients often tell us that they don't have time to plan their schedule. What they are really telling us, is that they don't have time to define and schedule their truly important tasks. If you have similar feelings, you will benefit the most from this exercise.

Lesson Review

We hope you enjoyed this lesson. At this point in the program, most of our clients feel like they have come a long way in just a few short weeks. They truly begin to believe that they have the knowledge and ability to master their stress. We hope you share these feelings.

We began the lesson with a discussion on how to change your environment to a less stressful one. You now have many stress management tools in your tool chest to help you make the changes you believe are important for you. If you are currently taking mediation to help you manage your stress, we gave you some guidelines for decreasing or withdrawing from these. Remember to always consult your physician before making changes in your prescription medications. Relapse prevention was our next topic of discussion followed by the section on applied relaxation. This technique is an advanced technique that will help you take your relaxation skills with you anywhere so that they can be used at a moment's notice.

Today's Date: Monday (Carol's Example)

Daily Planner

Reminders	Time	Schedules Tasks	Comments
	7		
A	8	Go to the market	
	9		
I	10	Call Betty to join me at the gym	
I		Visit Edna in the hospital	
	11		
	12		
I	1	Write mom a letter and send her	
		new baked chicken	
	2		
I	3	Exercise at the gym	
	4		
I		Be home for the kids	
	5		
	6		
A		Dinner at 6:30	
	7		
	8		
	9		

		Other Priorities	Other Priorities

We provided helpful information on becoming more assertive. We hope that by now you are more confident about being assertive at the right times and in the right way. The lesson concluded with more information on time management. Specifically, we present you with a method for scheduling your priorities and tasks. You should now be well on your way to becoming a time-management whiz!

This Week's Assignment

This week, you begin to apply your relaxation skills to "real life" stressful situations. Try to put yourself in at least one stressful situation in which you must apply your relaxation skills. Remember to complete My Personal Roles and Goals Worksheet and the Weekly Tasks List *before* you complete you Daily Planner for the week. If you have trouble with this exercise, go back and reread the section titled "Scheduling Your Weekly Priorities." After you have identified the "I" (important) tasks for this next week, and you have prioritized the tasks (A, B, C, or D) on the Weekly Tasks List, you are ready to complete the Daily Planner. A blank copy of the Daily Planner is on page 373, so you can make as many copies as you need. Enter the "I" tasks first on your Daily Planner, then add the items from the Weekly Tasks List. Remember to complete your Daily Stress Record, on page 374, along with your Stress Change Worksheet on page 328, the Average Stress Change Worksheet in Appendix E, on page 430, and the Physical Activity and Relaxation Practice Worksheet in Appendix F, on page 434. Good luck on this week's assignment—you have one more weekly lesson to go!

Knowledge Review

T F 119. Changing how you respond to the environment around you is always a better stress management strategy than trying to change the environment.

T F 120. Stress on the job is the most common source of stress for most people.

T F 121. Most people who are taking medication for stress reduction, continue to take the medication after they complete this program.

T F 122. Applied relaxation techniques are more advanced that the earlier relaxation practices you have been doing.

T F 123. Learning to be assertive can be accomplished with practice.

T F 124. Delegating responsibilities is a good way to help reduce your stress in the long run.

T F 125. Time management skills like scheduling priorities is more useful to busy executives than to other people.

(Answers in Appendix C, page 415)

Situations That Make Me Tense

My Personal Roles and Goals

Roles	Goals
Role #1	
Role #2	
Role #3	
Role #4	
Role #5	
Role #6	
Role #7	

Week of:

Weekly Task List

Scheduled Day/Time	Task	Priority Rating	Done

Today's Date: Monday

Daily Planner

Reminders	Time	Schedules Tasks	Comments
	7		
	8		
	9		
	10		
	11		
	12		
	1		
	2		
	3		
	4		
	5		
	6		
	7		
	8		
	9		

		Other Priorities	Other Priorities

Daily Stress Record—Lesson Fifteen

Name:____________________________________ **Week of:**______________

Date	Average Stress Level	Highest Stress Level	Time of Highest Stress Level	Stressful Event Associated with Highest Stress Level

My Physical Activity and Relaxation Record

Day of the Week	Physical Activity Record		Relaxation by Recall	
	Activity	Minutes	Time of Day	Minutes
Monday				
Tuesday				
Wednesday				
Thursday				
Friday				
Saturday				
Sunday				

Lesson Sixteen

Here we are, starting the last lesson in the Mastering Stress Program. Only the Commencement (graduation) Lesson follows. We have covered much information over the past 15 weeks, yet we still have several important topics to cover. In this lesson, we discuss more on attitudes, exercise, nutrition, and much more. So, let's continue our journey!

Dichotomous Thinking

This is a classic attitude problem that stifles progress for many people in stress management programs. We also know it as *Light Bulb Thinking.* This common attitude trap involves viewing everything as either right of wrong, perfect or terrible, good or bad, friend or foe, legal or illegal. We see this type of thinking in almost every client we see. Let's look at an example of dichotomous thinking.

Michael practiced his relaxation exercises for seven days in a row. He missed the next two days or practice, and during these two days, experienced a stressful situation at work. Michael's dichotomous response was "I've really blown it now. I am off my program, and my stress is back."

Notice Michael's use of the phrase "off my program." This is the view that you are either perfect or terrible or that you are either on or off a program. This is where the term *Light Bulb Thinking* was born, because a light bulb is either *on* or *off.*

Michael believes he has made an unforgivable mistake, although missing two days of relaxation practice is trivial over a week, a month, or a year. The problem is *not* that Michael experienced a stressful situation or missed two days of practice. These experiences are inevitable, and should be expected. The danger lies in Michael's *reaction* to these skipped practice sessions, which could be devastating and lead to relapse and eventual collapse.

Another example of dichotomous thinking is the tendency for people to rank their reactions to stressful situations. Even the most practiced stress manager may not always apply the appropriate stress management technique in every stressful situation. Instead of *responding* with an appropriate technique, a person may *react* with auto-

"is your thinking like a light bulb—either on or off?"

matic dichotomous thinking that increases stress. When this happens, a typical reaction is to rank the behavior as good or bad, acceptable or unacceptable. Whether a specific behavior is good or bad varies from person to person. For you, skipping one relaxation practice may be a bad behavior. For someone else, a bad behavior may be losing his or her temper in traffic. Dichotomous thinking occurs when a small, insignificant slip makes you feel as though you have "blown your program."

Being aware of your thoughts is important, especially if you have thoughts about good or bad responses or reactions to certain stressful situations? Do you believe that you must always respond to stressful situations with the right technique to keep you stress level in check? Have you established stress management *rules* that you believe you *must always* follow? If you violate these rules, do you experience *negative* feelings?

You will soon realize how illogical it is for you to feel terrible about one slip. If you have made internal rules about certain stress responses that you must maintain in order to stay "on your program," you're setting yourself up for failure.

Attitudes are habits that can be changed, but simply reading this material and knowing that attitudes may be hindering your progress is not enough. You must actively search for these attitude traps and be ready to counter them when they occur.

Countering Dichotomous (Light Bulb) Thinking

My Stress Thoughts	My Counter Statements
1.	
2.	
3.	
4.	
5.	
6.	
7.	

You can counter dichotomous thoughts by talking back to yourself. On the worksheet provided on page 376, write down your most common dichotomous thoughts and write a counter statement for each one. Then, you will be prepared when these thoughts occur.

Negative Self-Talk

Negative self-talk can also plague your progress in the Stress Management Program. One of our clients named John had a lot of self-doubt during his program. He became discouraged when he wasn't making the progress he believed he should be making in the program. When this happened, he began to question whether he should continue. He was on the verge of giving up. We asked John to list some negative thoughts he was having about the program and his progress. John's list appears in the illustration on the right.

We suggested that John challenge each of his negative thoughts. After some thought, John came up with more positive ways of looking at things. He took the time to look back over all the progress he had made in the program. This helped him get back on track and take credit for his hard work. More important, John realized that he had made tremendous progress and that he was much less stressed than when he began the program. John's sample Progress in My Program worksheet is reproduced on page 378. Take a moment now to evaluate your progress using the blank Progress in My Program worksheet on page 393. This will help you realize your progress since you began this program.

Think of stress as a train moving down the tracks. Mastering stress is like the train. Wouldn't it be nice if stress management were like the train, always moving forward and never stopping or going backwards? With the right tools and continued practice to keep those tools polished and sharpened, your stress management train can continue moving forward. Sure, you will encounter hills when progress may seem slow, but you now have the skills to ascend those hills. We also hope that you have confidence in yourself to keep moving forward as well.

John's Negative Self-Talk

"I knew I could not learn to control my stress."

"I'm just not smart enough to do this."

"This program isn't working for me. What good is it for me to learn these techniques if I still can't master all my stress?"

"I'll never make it after this program ends."

"I'm never going to be able to control my stress."

Expecting a train to continually move along the tracks at the same speed is unrealistic. No one can maintain perfect stress management, so expect some hills and valleys. Just as the geography of a train track changes, you will experience highs and lows in your stress level. Your challenge is to use the tools you have learned in this program to manage the inevitable changes you will experience. Try to keep the train moving in one direction, expecting slowdowns and occasional stops. You may even go backward from time to time. The key is to keep the train moving and be ready to apply the brakes to stop the train from going backward!

Progress in My Program

(John's Example)

Progress I've Made	Positive Things I've Changed	Reasons to Continue and Maintain the Changes
I am much less stressed today than before I started the program	I challenge my thoughts I do not always react automatically	My quality of life has improved I'm more physically active now My relationship with my wife has improved a lot
I sleep better at night now	I'm more assertive at work My coworkers respect my work more now	I enjoy work more now that I did before I'm much more productive at work
I don't feel rushed now	I plan my days in advance now I work hard to avoid time wasters	I get more accomplished I feel in control of my time

The Rating Game

We discussed the attitude trap of *external validation*, in LessonThirteen on page 313, that gives others the power to validate your self-worth. A habit closely related to the problem of external validation is the practice of *chronic comparison*. Continually rating yourself against an ideal standard leads to discouragement and increased stress because you can never attain the "ideal." Although it's healthy to rate and judge your behaviors, rating yourself as good or bad based on a single behavior is risky business. To better understand this problem, let's look at an example.

Meet Linda

Linda is a 35-year-old mother of two. She works as a dental assistant and lectures to colleagues on advances in dental treatment. Linda believes that she *is what she does.* If, for example, she has a good day at work, then she is a good person. If she has a bad day, she feels as though she is "bad" person and a failure.

Linda listens carefully to thoughts and opinions from her clients and her children about her performance on various tasks. She uses these observations as evidence of her worth. One day, for example, a colleague suggested to Linda that wasn't her usual persuasive self in a weekly lecture. Upon hearing this, Linda withdrew and began to criticize herself. She felt like a total failure, telling herself, "The feedback I just received is proof that I will never be a good lecturer." A more appropriate response for Linda would have been to ask her colleague, "What do you think made me less effective?" Listening to feedback from others is important. Yet, allowing this input to establish self-worth is not realistic.

Linda also made the same mistake with her children. One day, her oldest daughter said, "I would rather walk to school than have you drive me." When Linda heard this, she assumed the worst. Linda made the faulty assumption that her daughter was embarrassed to be seen with her. "I'm a bad mother for not being 'cool,'" Linda thought to herself.

When Linda asked her daughter why she preferred to walk to school, she said, "All my friends walk to school and it's a great way for me to get more exercise." Even if Linda's daughter had said that she was embarrassed to have her mother drive her to school, this wouldn't mean that Linda was a bad mother. Using realistic thinking, Linda came to the conclusion that most girls her daughter's age felt the same way. Linda even admitted that she had felt that way about her mother, although she loved her very much. Linda also came to the realization that she may not be a model mother, but she does not have to rate herself as a *bad* person because she isn't perfect. Realistically, the *perfect* mom doesn't really exist!

A Final Word on Time Management

One of the most common discoveries that overcommitted people make is the large number of tasks they do in a day that could easily be done by someone else. This can happen for many reasons. Some people lack assertiveness skills. Some believe that doing the task themselves is easier than trying to explain it to someone else, while others may think no one else can do the task as well as they can.

Do you remember Harvey from Lesson Five, on page 119? He managed the family clothing company that employed 30 people. Harvey realized that he was wasting valuable time by answering all the phone calls from customers who wanted to check on their orders. His secretary, Mary, could easily handle these calls. If necessary, she could transfer the more difficult calls to him.

When Harvey tried to delegate this responsibility to Mary, he discovered it was easier said than done. Harvey suddenly realized his reluctance to delegate this responsibility was a fear that Mary would pass along misinformation. Using realistic thinking and probability analysis, Harvey began to challenge this thought. He asked himself, "What is the probability Mary will give customers inaccurate information?" Harvey realized that Mary understood the status of orders as well as he did. It was highly unlikely she would make an error. Even if she did, Harvey asked himself, "How bad would that *really* be?" He realized that his customers would be understanding if she made a mistake. After all, he sometimes made mistakes too! If there were any problems, he would be there to

"By being more assertive and using time management skills, overcommitted people can reduce their workload."

"I hate to criticize, but you've only been employed here for two days and you're already three weeks behind in your work."

step in and help. By combining realistic thinking and time management techniques, Harvey significantly reduced his workload.

Can you identify with the problem of overcommitment? If so, breaking the cycle of overcommitment is important. Let's look at some ways to do this.

Setting Role Goals

In Lesson Fifteen, on page 364, we discussed the importance of identifying the roles you have chosen in your life. For each role, identifying weekly goals is similarly important. We emphasize the importance of doing this *weekly*. Weekly planning is a key to insuring that you set aside time each day to do those things that are truly important to you. This process allows you to cultivate both personal and professional relationships. Perhaps more importantly, it empowers you to become the master of your schedule rather than allowing your schedule to become your master.

Just Say "No"

We have all heard the anti-drug slogan, "Just say no." The same slogan is equally appropriate to time management. Many people run out of time because they spend too much of time doing things they should not be doing in the first place. These are typically the *urgent* instead of the *important* tasks in life. Being assertive is very important in limiting how much you do in a day. If saying no is difficult for you, you may want to review the assertiveness techniques we discussed in Lesson Fourteen, on page 344, and in Lesson Fifteen, on page 361. You may also practice realistic thinking, reminding yourself that people will not be angry with you or hate you because you do not have time to do something for them. Just saying "no" can help you find the valuable time to do the important tasks in your life. This will go a long way to helping you master your stress.

In our example from Lesson Thirteen, on page 321, Carol found she had more time for her important tasks by not automatically agreeing to take her children everywhere they wanted to go. They were somewhat annoyed at first, but within a few weeks, they didn't notice the change. They didn't ask for rides unless it was absolutely necessary, and they still found ways to get around. Similarly, Carol asked her husband to do some of his own errands. After a few weeks, Carol asked her family how they felt about these changes. To her surprise, they said they realized they had been making too many demands of her time. They didn't mind the changes at all.

Dealing with Interruptions

Many of our clients tell us that dealing with interruptions is the most stressful part of their day. Learning to handle interruptions at work and at home is important to managing stress. Many people who have trouble handling interruptions share some common beliefs. Here are a few of those beliefs:

❶ "I am the expert at this skill, and if someone needs my help, I must drop what I am doing and be ready to help immediately."

❷ "This person will be mad at me if I don't help them now, and that would be horrible."

❸ "Most interruptions require only a short amount of my time."

❹ "I would rather be doing what is being asked of me (the interruption) than the work I need to do for myself."

❺ "Any interruption (phone, e-mail, fax, etc.) must be handled immediately."

If some of these beliefs sound familiar, challenging them can be helpful. Realistic thinking and reality testing using the step-ladder can be very helpful techniques to help you deal more effectively with interruptions.

Sticking to Agendas

Sticking to an agenda is difficult for some people. This can easily increase stress when agendas never seem to be completed. Let's say, for example, that you are in the habit of going out to lunch with a colleague every time you have an issue to discuss. If you want to go to lunch because it is fun and relaxing, that's fine. But if you're doing it simply to discuss business, then it may be far more efficient to write a memo or talk on the phone. Brainstorming can often help you break old, inefficient habits and find ways to complete your agendas.

Assess Your Priorities Weekly

"Setting weekly goals will help you stay focused so that you can more clearly identify the urgent from the important."

Assessing your roles and goals weekly is the first step to scheduling your *important* priorities. Let's face it, all of us could prepare a "to do" list so long that it would never be completed. So, how do you decide what to do and what not to do? You start by setting your goals for each role. Getting into the habit of doing this on a weekly basis is a good idea. This process will help you stay focused and more clearly identify the *urgent* from the *important.*

One of our clients, for example, was working three jobs and trying to raise two children. As a result, she felt very stressed because she did not think she was giving the children enough attention. She reassessed

"Learning to handle interruptions at work and at home is important to managing stress."

her roles and established goals for each one. This helped her to realize that the extra money she earned from her third job was less important than spending more time with her children, so she decided to quit her third job.

For some people, giving something up can increase stress. This typically happens when a person has not clearly identified or set goals for his or her roles. If you go through this process and still feel stress, try realistic thinking to challenge your beliefs about giving up tasks.

Meet Robert

Robert is an accountant in a small firm. He finds it very difficult to deal with interruptions during the work week. Robert prefers to work on weekends because he is not interrupted and, therefore, gets a lot accomplished.

Because Robert considered himself an expert in many areas of accounting, his associates with far less experience relied on and asked for his assistance daily. Robert eventually realized that, when he helped a co-worker, he basically did the work himself and reduced the likelihood that they would ever learn how to do a similar task on their own. He was, in essence, almost guaranteeing that he would always be interrupted. This does not mean that he shouldn't help out a co-worker in need, but Robert realized that he needed to teach his colleagues how to help themselves.

Robert was concerned that if he said no to someone, that person would be angry with him. Although this may be true for some people, it is not true for everyone. Perhaps that person would understand that he didn't have the time at that particular moment to help them, but he could help them at another time. Robert learned that he could say, "I can't give you 10 minutes now, but I can give you 60 minutes at lunch." Robert also learned that he could deal with someone's anger or disapproval, and that someone's negative judgement did not make him a bad person.

Robert discovered that every interruption does not need to be handled immediately. He found that when he was working on a project, it was helpful to let his phone ring into voice mail and to take only emergency phone calls. Faxes and e-mails were checked hourly by his secretary, who would alert him to any urgent issues. After modifying his behaviors, Robert was amazed at the time he was able to save.

Robert also became aware that, at times, he welcomed the interruptions because they distracted him from the less appealing work he had to do. Although some distractions are pleasant, sometimes they are not an effective use of time. Robert tried to become more conscious of whether he was using distractions as a way of avoiding something he did not want to do.

Plan Your Schedule and Follow Your Plan

Once you have clearly identified your important roles and set goals for each one, you are ready to plan your weekly schedule. In Lesson Fifteen, on page 368, we provided you with an example of how this is done. First, schedule your goals on a personal planner. Remember, these are the things in life that are *important* to you. Next, schedule your weekly tasks. Look again at Harvey's example in Lesson Five, on page 119. The tasks on this list are Harvey's *urgent* tasks. By ranking your urgent tasks in order, you can schedule them into your weekly plan.

We recommend you do this more detailed planning each week. Then, you will need about 5 to 10 minutes each morning to review your daily schedule. Avoid scheduling too many tasks in one day. It is much better to have more time at the end of the day than uncompleted tasks. If you consistently schedule too many tasks in one day, work hard to reduce the number of scheduled tasks. You'll find this both motivational and inspirational.

We have observed clients developing terrific plans for their lives. They painstakingly identify their various roles then develop important goals for each one. Each goal and task is then meticulously scheduled in the weekly planner. But, before they realize it, their schedule falls by the wayside when distractions and interruption arise. This is like spending $90,000 on a new Mercedes and keeping it parked in the garage. Developing priorities in your life and then scheduling them is certainly important. Yet, this planning does little good if you don't follow your plan.

Plan to Plan Again

Many of our clients find a planning process of some kind to be very helpful. They use it for a while and tell us they see a noticeable improvement in getting the *important* things accomplished. Then, over time, the planning begins to slip. Why? Often, the reason is that they simply fail to schedule time to plan again. Yet, this is a crucial stress management skill.

Think of planning as breathing. If you stop breathing, what happens? You're right, you stop living. When you stop planning, you stop doing the *important*. We cannot emphasize enough the importance of *planning to plan*. Plan for it, schedule it, and by all means, stick to it!

A Final Word on Being Assertive

As we discussed in Lesson Eight, on page 191, the reason most people do not assert themselves is not because they don't know how to express themselves, but because they worry about the effects of assertive behavior on others. In particular, they worry that others may think they are pushy, aggressive, or demanding. They fear others will get angry or not like them. To deal with these concerns, the stress management techniques that you have learned in this program will be helpful. In particular, you can use realistic thinking and reality testing to convince yourself that being assertive does not mean that other people won't like you or will think you are pushy.

Realistic thinking can help you understand your reluctance to assert yourself. Clearly, a person who goes around demanding his or her own way all the time will not be popular. But, if you use assertiveness appropriately, after weighing the pros and cons in a given situation, people will respect you for standing up for your rights. When using realistic thinking, ask yourself, "How likely is it that this person will be angry with me?" "What is the worst that can happen if I ask this person for something?" The best form of evidence often comes from putting yourself in the other person's place. "If this person were to ask the same favor of me, would I be angry?" In most cases, you will find that the answer is no.

You might also want to look at assertiveness as a kind of avoidance. You can overcome this by using reality testing, as we discussed earlier in this lesson. Now that you know how to make a stepladder, you can make one for situations in which you find assertiveness difficult. At the bottom of the ladder, you could begin with something easy, such as asking your partner for a favor. Then, at the top, you could write something more difficult, like saying no to your boss. You could then brainstorm a number of other assertive behaviors and place them in their appropriate places on the ladder. Set a time to try the first situation and keep practicing until you feel comfortable doing it, then move on to the next step of the ladder, and so on. Do not forget to use you realistic thinking skills during your practices.

You learned about prediction testing in Lesson Ten, on page 235. This technique can be particularly useful with this sort of stepladder. Before you try each step, record your predictions about what you think might happen, how you think you will feel, and how the other person will respond. Then, when you have completed the step, make a note of whether your predictions came true. Applying familiar techniques to assertiveness in this way can help reduce one more source of stress in your life.

Assertiveness, like the other stress management techniques, improves with practice. The more you assert yourself, the easier it will become. You will find you have fewer unnecessary tasks and are less frequently loaded down with work you shouldn't have to do. Of course, when you are practicing, you need to make sure that you don't become too demanding of the same group of people. But, if you remember to consider their rights as you think about your own, this should not become a problem.

Meet Matt

Matt is as a nurse in a large hospital in Phoenix, Arizona. Although he liked his job, Matt knew that he was not assertive enough at work. As a result, he often got the worst shifts. He ended up doing extra work and got stuck with the unpleasant jobs that others refused to do. The more this happened, the more stress Matt felt. He used the stepladder approach to become more assertive. We have reproduced Matt's stepladder in the illustration on the right.

Before trying each step of the ladder, he used his realistic thinking techniques and looked carefully at the realistic evidence. For example, the first step was making a small request from a patient. He expected the patient to think it was unfair of him to ask patients to do anything. Matt's main source of evidence came from reversing positions and thinking about how he would feel if he were the patient and a nurse made a request of him. He realized that he would think the nurse had every right to make such a request. He also realized that this was logical, after all, it was his job—another source of evidence.

Matt then went on to predict what would happen if the patient did think his request was unfair. His next three expectations were that the patient would get angry, he would complain to Matts' supervisor, and Matt would be fired. When Matt looked at the evidence for the first two consequences, he realized they were only moderately likely to happen. The third consequence was even more unlikely. Matt realized that making requests of patients is

Stepladder Approach

(Matt's Example)

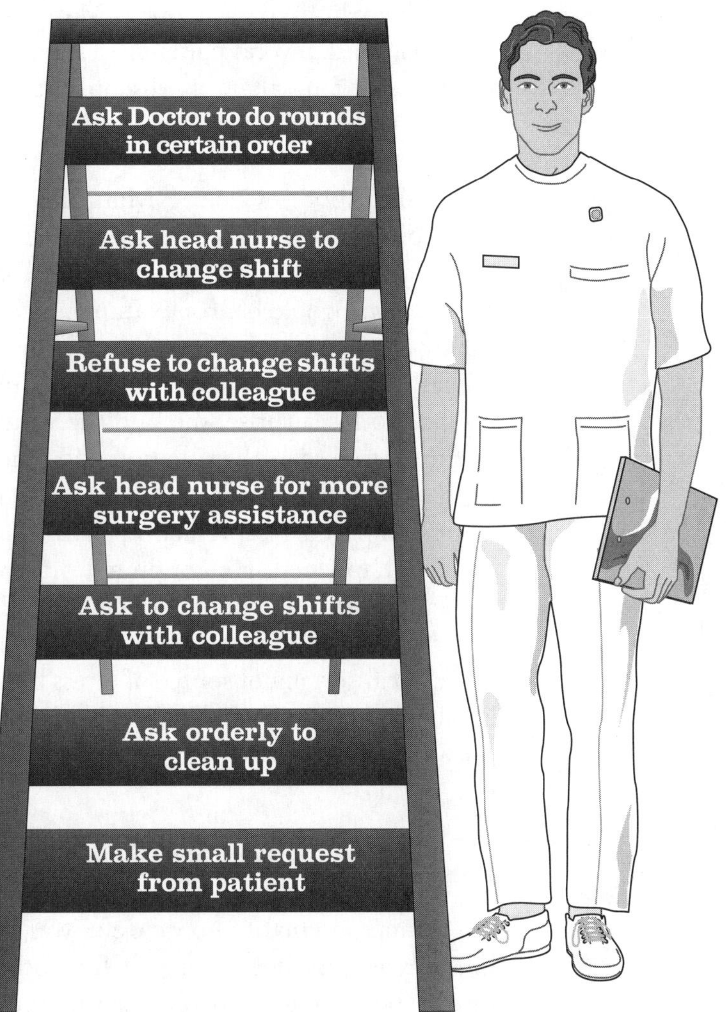

Prediction Testing Record *(Matt's Example)*			
Event	**Guess**	**Test**	**Outcome**
Ask Mr. Willis in Room 212 to turn down the volume.	1. He will refuse. 2. He will tell my supervisor.	1. Asked him to turn down volume on TV. 2. See is complains to supervisor.	1. He agreed. 2. He didn't complain to anyone.
Ask the orderly to tidy up the supply room.	1. He will be angry. 2. He will do a poor job.	1. Watch his face. 2. Check supply room when he is finished.	1. He looked annoyed, but was friendly later in the day. 2. The supply room looked fine, even better than usual.

part of a nurse's job and that his supervisor would back him up all the way. Matt then went on to ask several patients a variety of requests, finding that his discomfort decreased with practice.

To find more evidence, Matt also did some prediction testing with each step on the ladder. For each task, he predicted what the outcome would be. For example, before asking the head nurse to assign him to an earlier shift, Matt predicted that she would say no. To his surprise, she said she would be happy to discuss the situation and reach a compromise. As he finished each step, Matt compared his prediction with what actually happened. He continued practicing each task until he could do it easily. Over time, Matt began to enjoy his job more because a major source of stress in his life had been reduced. The table above shows the first few steps in Matt's prediction testing.

Dealing with Aggression

At times, no matter how careful you are in your assertiveness, you will find other people becoming aggressive toward you. This can be a source of intense stress—no one likes to be abused. Here are a couple of suggestions for trying to reduce or combat aggression without becoming too stressed.

Don't buy in. The main rule with aggression is not to buy into it and start being aggressive in return. When you are aggressive to someone who is angry, this will only serve to increase her or his anger. Then, the whole interaction can spiral out of control. Back off and try again later. Don't add fuel to the fire!

Stay calm. The best way to diffuse someone's anger is for you to stay calm and in control. If you have a few spare seconds, try using your realistic thinking to help you control your own feelings. Is the other person really better than you? Is the other person really going to hit you? Is the other person going to get his or her way? Does it matter if the other person doesn't like you? Once you can calm your feelings, try to back this up with your manner. It is very hard for someone to get carried away with aggression if you are looking them confidently in the eye; speaking in a gentle, quiet manner; and standing in a relaxed, nonaggressive stance.

Use "I" statements. As above, it is much harder for someone to argue with you and get angrier if you own your own feelings. Try not to make broad sweeping statements about the situation or the other person.

Be empathetic. Similarly, it is hard to be angry with someone who seems to understand your side of the story. Rather than trying to force your view on the other person, try acknowledging their perspective first. You are then much more likely to get your message across successfully. Remember, try to understand *before* you try to be understood!

Point out assumptions. Sometimes a person's anger is based on unstated assumptions or misunderstandings. Rather than simply hearing what the person is saying to you at a superficial level, try to mentally step back a little to see the situation from their side. Try to understand the underlying assumptions behind the person's anger. You may realize that there is a misunderstanding. If so, you can point this out calmly. If, on the other hand, you are at a crossroad, simply agree to disagree.

Stick to your point. In some instances, it is just not possible to diffuse an aggressive situation. In this case, it is often useful to repeat your message. Each time you speak, you should begin by acknowledging what the other person is saying, then simply repeat your message. For example, "I would like to see the manager, please," "Yes, I realize that it is very late, but I really do need to see the manager," "I know you would like to get home, but it is important for me to see the manager," and so on. Obviously, if the situation looks as though it might become violent, or you are getting nowhere, it may be better to back off and try again at a later time when everyone has calmed down.

Dealing with Aggression

Don't buy in
Stay calm
Use "I" statements
Be empathetic
Point out assumptions
Stick to your point

The Stress of Dealing with Illness

Prolonged illness of a family member or close friend can easily increase stress. An illness in the family, often requires role adjustments. This can be upsetting to the entire family. Too often, when a family member becomes ill, the family's focus turns to the illness. The day-to-day ordinary routine may become disrupted. This is a perfectly natural response. It can become a more serious problem, however, when the illness remains the focus for an extended period of time.

Meet Robin

Robin is a stay-at-home mom with three children. She and her a husband, Joe, have been married 17 years. Robin and Joe have a healthy, supportive relationship and have dealt effectively with conflict in the past. Robin handles most of the daily responsibilities involving the children. Joe works full time in his own business. Because finances were limited and a housekeeper is not an option, the children were responsible for helping out with the daily chores.

When Robin suffered a serious back injury, the family experienced a significant amount of stress. The defined roles in the family had to change because of Robin's physical limitations. For example, Robin was no longer able to drive the car pool each day for the children, so Joe had to rearrange his work schedule to drive in her place. The kids offered to give up one activity for the week to help out during the difficult time. Robin did not want her children's daily lives to be affected for too long, so she arranged for some assistance from friends who were happy to offer their support.

"A lapse in managing stress is like a forest fire. Whether you recover or lose the forest, depends on your stress management skills."

Joe also helped out with the daily chores to relieve the children's workload. He also decided to work on Saturdays for a short time to help pay for a weekly housekeeper. This meant that Joe was not able to spend as much time with his children during weekends. During their crisis, conversations around the dinner table often focused on Robin's physical limitations, which disturbed Robin. She made a concerted effort to refocus attention on the children's accomplishments and Joe's daily needs.

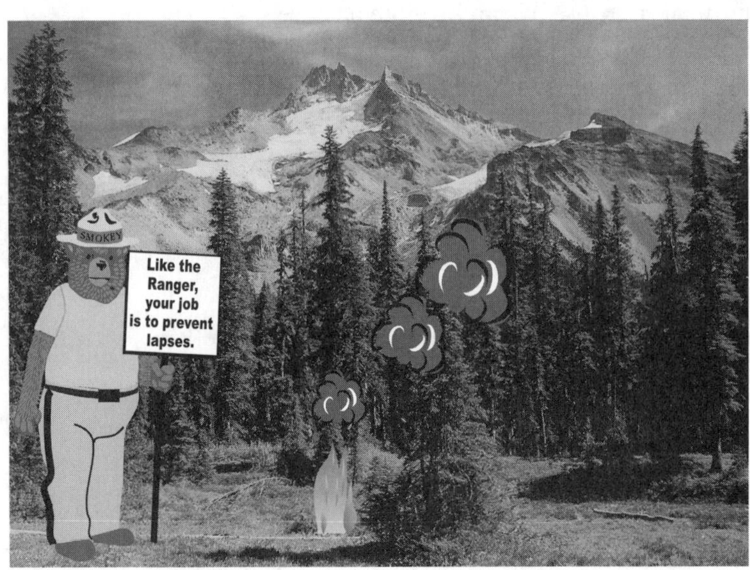

As you can see, Robin's illness and each family member's role change became the family focus for a few months. Fortunately, this was a family who worked together in a supportive way to get through the crisis. Many families don't respond as well to changing roles in their families when illness strikes. Robin and her family did not panic when the crisis hit, instead, they mobilized their efforts and worked as a team. They also did not catastrophize or project too much into the future. Instead, they tried their best to make it through each day and to focus on what was most important.

Become a Forest Ranger

Dr. Kelly Brownell of Yale University has developed an excellent metaphor for dealing with relapse. We are grateful to him for allowing us to use the following illustration.

Consider yourself a forest ranger. Your job is to be constantly on the lookout for fires. Your first priority is to prevent fires from breaking out. If one does break out, you are to put it out quickly. Think of your lapses as the small fires in the forest. You will try to prevent them, but when they do flare up, you extinguish them immediately. Occasionally, a fire may get out of control, but you don't have to lose the forest!

Let's develop this notion of the forest ranger a bit further. Your job is to take control over you stress. The ranger's job is to keep control over the forest. The ranger must do everything possible to prevent fires from breaking out. Because fires may be difficult to control once they start, the ranger believes in "an ounce of prevention." Prevention is also important for you. You have learned dozens of ways to take control of your stress so that lapses will not occur. As you know, the key is to be prepared for high-risk situations, to plan in advance, and to keep the right attitude.

The forest ranger's second task is to stop the spread of fires when they do occur. The ranger's ability to do this will determine whether the forest is spared or destroyed. A lapse in managing your stress is like the fire that breaks out. Whether you bounce back and continue your progress or let the mistake destroy your hard work (lapse, relapse, then collapse) depends on your skill in using your stress management techniques.

Please remember the dual tasks that confront both you and the forest ranger. You are concerned with both prevention *and* crisis management. Identify the situations where you are most likely to confront problems. Then plan to use both your prevention techniques and the stress management techniques you have learned to deal with lapses. These are the ways to prevent lapses and to stop lapses dead in their tracks. This dual approach of preventing problems and coping with problems when they do arise allows you to hit temptation from two angles.

Using the Master List of Techniques

Appendix B, on page 413, contains a summary list of all the techniques used throughout this program. You will notice that this list of techniques is arranged around the LEARN acronym: **L**ifestyle, **E**xercise, **A**ttitudes, **R**elationships, and **N**utrition. Use this list to review your progress and to decide which techniques are important to you. They may be the techniques you struggled with most, which is one sign that the habits they targeted are difficult to change.

Go through the list in Appendix B, on page 413, and circle the techniques that are most important in your attempts to master your stress. These are not necessarily the behaviors that are easiest for you. They should be the ones that are the keys to your future success. Circle any behavior you feel fits the bill. Think back carefully over your

Techniques That Are Important to My Stress Management
1.
2.
3.
4.
5.
6.
7.
8.
9.
10.

experience with this program and consider other programs you may have used in the past. Circle the behaviors that help you manage your stress.

Now that you have circled the important behaviors, it is time to narrow the list. You should end up with 5 to 10 behaviors. Having too few techniques can make you miss opportunities to change your habits and having too many makes record keeping too complex. Write these down on the worksheet on page 389. You can modify the list as your habits change, but for now, this list should be your marching orders to yourself.

"Now you can change the focus of your efforts from trying to master your stress to enjoying the benefits of less stress and improved health, well-being, and quality of life."

Keep in mind that your list of techniques will change from time to time. We suggest that you review this list and rewrite your own list at the beginning of every month for a while. This will help you focus on the techniques that work best for you as your life circumstances change.

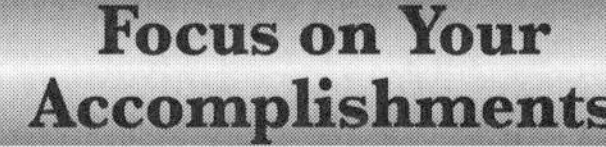

Focus on Your Accomplishments

At this point in the program, we hope you are able to change the focus of your efforts from trying to master your stress to recognizing and enjoying all that you have accomplished. You have worked hard to decrease your stress and improve your health, well-being, and quality of life. Look at all the things that you can do now that you could not do a few months ago. These are the true measures of your success. Your ability to celebrate your success is a sign of your improved well-being. The alternative is to remain fixed on reaching an unrealistic goal of total mastery of your stress. This is a classic recipe for frustration and failure.

Keep up Your Effort

Focusing on what you have achieved, rather than focusing on what you have not yet achieved, will keep you inspired and motivated. Feeling proud that you have learned the necessary skills to master your stress will help you continue moving forward. The new, less stressful habits you have learned will help you maintain your improved quality of life.

Does this mean that you can not make any more progress? No, not at all. Many clients continue to make progress in managing their stress long after the program has ended. The best approach is to continue to practice your new habits to maintain your less stressful lifestyle.

A Final Word on Activity and Good Nutrition

Throughout this program, we have discussed the importance of physical activity and good nutrition. We have not intended these discussions to be exhaustive dissertations on these important topics. Rather, our intent is to highlight their importance in stress management and to your overall health and well-being. As you continue to improve your stress management skills, we encourage you to also continue to improve your diet and increase your physical activity. Exercise and nutrition impact all three of your stress response systems: physical, mental, and behavioral.

A Tribute to You

We designed the Mastering Stress Program to include 16 weekly lessons plus the Commencement Lesson that follows this lesson. If you have been following the program as it was designed, you should now be in your sixteenth week. This may sound like a long time, but let's put this into perspective. Some people begin programs and give up the same day. Others continue for a few days, a few weeks, and on rare occasions, even a few months. Why is this?

Some programs are faddish. They try to convince you that they have found a "magic" bullet or a "quick fix" for stress management. Others tell you what to do, but don't provide directions on how to do it. And still others simply do not work. Realistically, sticking to any program for a long time is difficult. Yet, you now know that changing lifelong habits takes time, practice, and skill. For this reason, many people get off the train before it reaches its destination. And as we said at the beginning of this program, the journey itself is the destination! While you may now be completing the Mastering Stress Program, you are just beginning your lifelong journey to mastering your stress.

We salute you for staying with the program. Reaching this point in the program is a VERY GOOD sign that you are serious about mastering your stress and that you are well on your way to doing so. We wish there were a easier way, even a magic pill, but no such "cure" exists. The only answer to permanent stress management is per-

"Congratulations! You deserve much credit for your achievement. If we could be there with you, we would give you a standing ovation."

sonal choice and effort. We are delighted that you made this choice and have continued your efforts. Congratulations! You deserve much credit for your progress. If we could be there with you, we would give you a standing ovation! You deserve it!

Lesson Review

We covered many important topics in this lesson. We started by discussing three common attitude traps that can derail even the most serious stress manager. Our discussion then turned to more on time management, followed with additional insight on being more assertive. We dealt with the topic of dealing with aggression and how to deal with the stress associated with the illness of a family member or a close friend. The lesson concluded with a metaphor on how your job as a stress manager is like being a forest ranger. We hope you enjoyed the lesson and that you are indeed, pleased with all your hard work and progress.

This Week's Assignment

Now is the time for you to begin making decisions on what forms and techniques are helpful for you. Keep in mind that these forms and worksheets may change from time to time, depending upon your unique life circumstances. Make as many copies of the worksheets you have used throughout this program as you need to continue your progress. Feel free to develop your own worksheets if you like.

Complete your Stress Change Worksheet for Lesson Sixteen on page 328, along with your Average Stress change Worksheet in Appendix E, on page 430, and the Physical Activity and Relaxation Practice Worksheet in Appendix F, on page 434. These worksheets should now be completed. Take a few minutes to review your worksheets. Are you satisfied with your progress?

Knowledge Review

T F 126. Dichotomous thinking is referred to as "light bulb thinking" because it is on or off.

T F 127. Reading this material and being aware that some attitudes may hinder your progress is the best way to counter negative thoughts.

T F 128. Constantly comparing yourself to others or to an idea or labeling yourself as good or bad, will help you stay motivated and will keep your standards high.

T F 129. To reduce the number of interruptions in your day, you should handle all interruptions immediately.

T F 130. A key strategy to reducing stress is to be prepared for high-risk situations though advanced planning and keeping the right attitude.

T F 131. Over time, planning may begin to slip because people fail to schedule time to plan again.

T F 132. The best way to overcome aggression is to stick it out until you win the argument.

T F 133. Like the forest ranger, mastering stress involves both prevention and crisis management.

(Answers in Appendix C, page 415)

Progress in My Program

Progress I've Made	Positive Things I've Changed	Reasons to Continue and Maintain the Changes

"I'm sending you to a seminar to help you work harder and be more productive."

Commencement Lesson

Here we are at the final lesson of the Mastering Stress Program. Congratulations on a job well done! We hope you have enjoyed your journey. Throughout this program, you have acquired many stress management tools that will be invaluable in the future as you continue to practice and develop your stress management skills. In this lesson, we will examine your progress and will help you identify areas that need more work so that your progress will continue. It is also fitting that in this lesson we will ask you to complete your last Quality of Life Review. This will help you realize just how much progress you've made in this program and will help you establish goals for the future.

Our Congratulations to You!

If you have followed this stress management program as designed, it should be about four months since you started the program. Let's place this time frame in context. Many people start a stress management program, but give up in the first weeks or even days. Why is this so common?

Many people find programs hard to follow. They may get frustrated with a program if they are not encouraged to view small changes as meaningful. On a similar note, some people may feel stressed and overwhelmed to begin with, and when they put a lot of effort into a program and don't see immediate results, they get discouraged. Also, they may not believe it is possible to manage their stress. They may hold the erroneous belief that all stress in their lives should be eliminated. In many cases, these belief systems are a set up for failure and lead many people to give up on their stress management programs before they've really started.

Congratulations for beating the odds and staying with the program! Even if this means you took a break from the program and came back later—congratulations for coming back and getting back on track. You have already demonstrated that you understand that managing stress is a process that requires persistence and dedication.

As you have learned, the management process is not always an easy one; there were times when it would have been easier to abandon the program. We are so pleased that you have made the effort, and we hope that the rewards have been, and will continue to be, worth it all.

At this stage in the program, individuals have had different experiences in stress management. Some have done well and attained their goals, and others still have a ways to go. Some struggled at times, succeeded at others, and are now on their way to a positive outcome. Let's reflect on your progress.

Interpreting Your Progress

"If you do well on this program, you should take responsibility for your achievement, and your progress will continue."

Are you pleased with your progress and the goals you have achieved? Are you able to see your achievements, or are you criticizing yourself because you believe you still have changes to make? Some people are not used to giving themselves credit for their success. When they do well on this program, they credit the program for their success, but if they don't do well, they blame themselves. Failing to give yourself credit can lead to doubt about your ability to handle more stressful "real life" situations.

Self-blame also has negative consequences. Taking responsibility for not making certain changes may be appropriate, but blame is a different matter. Blame is judgmental, not motivational. Self-blame is a setup for failure because the individual starts to believe that failure is the *only* possibility. As we have discussed, thoughts about an event determine our feelings, which, in turn, influence our behavior.

Realistically, if you do well on a program, the credit is yours. The program only provides a structure for ideas and techniques to be taught—you are the one responsible for implementing them. Whatever you have achieved is your own accomplishment, and you should feel good about it. If you take responsibility for your progress and achievements in stress management, your progress will continue.

If you are not pleased with your progress in the program, it is important to consider a few things.

First, make certain that you are accurately assessing your progress. Very often people are unable to see accomplishments because they have perfectionistic beliefs that everything in their lives should be completely changed. This keeps them from seeing even small changes as positive. If you are prone to this tendency, make a list of all the changes that you made or look at your monitoring forms from the earliest lessons. Look at your Quality of Life Review Comparisons in Lessons Four (page 94), Eight (page 194), and Twelve (page 297). In the face of all the evidence, you should be able to see the progress you've made.

What if, after assessing your progress, you determine that you have achieved less than you expected, what can you conclude? Don't despair and blame yourself—this will only make matters worse. See if you can figure out why you did not achieve the results you desired. For example, perhaps it was a difficult time for you to be in a program, and your success was limited because the timing wasn't ideal. Now, we know that there is never a perfect time in life when we are free of difficulty, but some times are more difficult than others. You also may want to consider whether this program was right for you. There may be a different program that better fits your stress management needs.

The Beginning—Not the End

Although these lessons have come to an end, your stress management skills should continue to develop. A primary goal of this stress management program is to learn new behaviors and habits that will become permanent. Continued practice will help these new habits become a permanent part of your life. Now is the time to reinforce those habits so that they become second nature to you.

This is a good time to identify which techniques were most helpful for you. Which ones can you begin to integrate into your daily routine? Were any techniques more difficult for you to master? Consider going back to those lessons in the manual and rereading the sections that gave you trouble.

Setting Reasonable Maintenance Goals

In Lesson Fourteen, on page 339, we discussed the concept of setting realistic goals. As you learned, keeping expectations realistic helps maintain motivation and commitment. When goals are realistic and attainable, achieving them increases self-confidence. As a result of this increased confidence, additional goals can be set and met.

"If you keep your stress management tools sharp and ready to use you will be able to recover from minor setbacks and reach your goals."

Although you have finished the stress management program, setting realistic goals is still important. There is no reason to expect perfection from yourself. For example, there will be times when you indulge in some irrational or unrealistic thinking. Instead of losing confidence in your ability to maintain your stress management goals, see these thoughts for what they are, a minor slip rather than a total failure of your stress management ability.

Also understand that you may experience more slips after the program ends because the program helped you focus on daily goal setting. Without this daily structure, you may find yourself forgetting to monitor your stress level or not using your stress management tools. Use this as a cue to refocus daily! Remember, your stress management muscles are strong and developed, and they will bounce back even if you forget to use them once in awhile.

A great deal of research has been done on goal setting. You should not be surprised to hear that people get frustrated, disappointed, and even depressed when they do not reach their goals. Goals, therefore, must be challenging but not impossible to reach. By setting realistic goals and rewarding yourself for reaching them, your self-confidence will increase, and you will be in a much better position to sustain the changes you have made.

Making Your Habits Permanent

There are several keys to developing permanent habits. *Practice* is just one of these tools. The 16 lessons in this program may not have given you enough opportunity to change all of your habits. Because habits develop over many years, you must be patient when they don't change as quickly as you would like them to.

Awareness is another tool for developing permanent habits. Throughout this program, you were challenged to be aware of your thoughts, behaviors, and emotions. By doing this, you made yourself accountable for your actions and were prepared to face your stressors head on. During maintenance, it will be just as important to maintain this level of awareness. You may even find that it is easier to maintain your awareness because you have been practicing it for the past few months. Now you can see how your mastering stress tools, practice, and awareness work together to help make habits permanent!

"Practice is an important key to developing permanent lifestyle habits such as increased physical activity."

Maintain Record Keeping

To help you practice and maintain awareness, you will need to continue your record keeping. As we said in earlier lessons, record keeping reminds you to practice your stress management techniques and gives you positive feedback about the changes you have made. Record keeping also is a way to maintain accountability because the record is filled out every day.

Look back at your records for the entire program. Your records will show what worked and what didn't, and provide valuable cues and warning signs that you may be heading toward a difficult situation. Your records will change and may not be as detailed as they once were, but they will continue to be effective if you commit to keeping them on a regular basis.

A blank Daily Stress Record form is provided on page 404. Make as many copies as you need. We recommend you continue to complete this form for at least eight more weeks, or longer if you want to.

Where to Go From Here

As we discussed in the Introduction and Orientation Lesson, on page 4, having a plan will help you maintain your stress management goals. Here are a few things to consider as you put your maintenance plan into action:

Use the Mastering Stress Program Again

You may want to start at the beginning of the program and follow it as though you were doing it for the first time. Remember, practice makes habits permanent. Or, you may decide to use certain sections in the manual that may be more helpful to you at particular times. For example, the section on assertiveness may be helpful if you find yourself stressed because you are taking on too many projects and you have trouble saying "no."

Find a Support Team

As we discussed earlier, seeking support from friends, family, and colleagues can be helpful in your efforts to manage stress. Also take a look at why you may be reluctant to seek support—what negative things are you telling yourself? You may want to remind those close to you that you still need to practice your stress management techniques. You may ask a friend or family member if they will practice these skills with you. If this is not a possibility, you may find it helpful to join a stress management group. Working together with others on a common goal, can make maintenance more rewarding and even more fun!

Try Another Program

Many self-help and commercial programs are available, each with its own unique approach. Find a program that works for you, that offers the "best-fit" between the program and your lifestyle. Try to identify the features that are most important for you (e.g., structure, cost, convenience, etc.). Some people find other programs very helpful when they are having an especially difficult time managing their stress.

Seek Professional Help

You may have learned a great deal from this program and are practicing techniques regularly, but you may still find yourself requiring more assistance. You may be experiencing symptoms of anxiety, depression, or anger and may need to focus your efforts on dealing directly with these issues. At this point, seeing a psychologist or other health professional could be beneficial. You also may discover that prescription medication may be helpful. Realizing that you may require additional help is a great first step to feeling better!

Facing Your Future

Kick off your shoes, relax, and think how far you've come in managing your stress since you started this program. Did stress seem like a big obstacle or an ugly dragon you had to battle every day to stay in control of your life? Now think about your situation today, after months of practicing stress management techniques. Do you feel calmer and more in control of your life? When you feel the symptoms of stress coming on, do you know what to do about it?" If so, you should give yourself credit for your hard work. None of us feel calm every day of our lives, but you have come a long way from the person who filled out those first forms. If you don't believe it, just look back at the forms and see for yourself. Keeping your expectations realistic is important—after all, you don't want the process of mastering stress to create more

"Think how far you've come in managing your stress since beginning this program. You should feel calmer and more in control of your life."

stress! You cannot expect every one of your records to show zero stress.

As we have emphasized throughout this book, having some stress in your life is not only natural, but healthy. Stress also helps keep you motivated and makes your life challenging and interesting. Remember that the skills you have been learning are designed to last beyond the end of this program—for a lifetime. They will never be perfect, but they will become more effective the more you practice them. By now, for example, you probably can do your relaxation at will, wherever you happen to be. Just think how different this is from the first time you tried to do your deep muscle relaxation exercises.

As we have repeated throughout the program, the problem is not that you experience stress, but your response to stress. By now, stress should no longer control your life, and your feelings of anxiety, anger, frustration, and so on should be within manageable levels.

Before we send you out to a lifetime of mastering stress, we need to make one last point. No matter how skilled you become at practicing your relaxation techniques, you will have times in your life when circumstances leave you feeling extremely stressed. Everyone faces major upheavals—a loved one dying, a business failing, a family crisis. When you face such situations, remind yourself that feeling stress in trying times is natural and can be expected. Your response is perfectly rational—it's part of being human. Everyone's life is punctuated with crises, but these things pass. No matter how bad you feel, you are better able to manage stress than you were before. You now possess specific skills to help keep your stress from becoming excessive or going on longer than it should.

When you come up against a major life event that leaves you feeling highly stressed and out of control, remind yourself that you now have the skills to quickly regain control. Don't be embarrassed to go back to basics and work through the techniques in this program again. This is not an admission of defeat. For all of us, life's events sometimes become more than we can handle. When this happens, going back and practicing the basic stress management techniques should help you sharpen the skills you've already learned—and it won't take you as long to go through this program the second time!

Remember the basic message throughout our program: The more you practice, the more successful you will be in mastering your stress. If you incorporate realistic thinking and the other techniques into your daily life, they will become so automatic that you won't even notice you are using them—except that you will feel less stressed. With your stress under control, you should be able to get excited about things again and actually enjoy your job and spending time with your family and friends.

Your Quality of Life Review

Now it's time to take your final Quality of Life Review. In the Introduction and Orientation Lesson, on page 11, we introduced the Quality of Life Review. As we described, taking this Quality of Life Review at different times throughout the program will help you measure your progress in each area. Take a few moments now to complete the Quality of Life Review below.

Analyzing Your Quality of Life Review

We want you to compare your responses at the beginning of the program to your responses in this lesson. First, turn back to the Quality of Life Review in the Introduction and Orientation Lesson, on page 11. Then turn to your Quality of Life Review below and compare your responses.

To help you in your review, turn to the Quality of Life Review Comparison, on page 402. In column (b) record the scores from the Introduction and Orientation Lesson and in column (c) record your scores from this lesson. Column (d) reflects the change in your responses; either positive (+) or negative (-). The positive (+) numbers in column (d) reflect increased quality of life in the related category, whereas a nega-

Quality of Life Review

Please use the following scale to rate how satisfied you feel now about different aspects of your daily life. Choose any number from this list (1 to 9) and indicate your choice next to each numbered item below.

1 = Extremely Dissatisfied
2 = Very Dissatisfied
3 = Moderately Dissatisfied
4 = Somewhat Dissatisfied
5 = Neutral
6 = Somewhat Satisfied
7 = Moderately Satisfied
8 = Very Satisfied
9 = Extremely Satisfied

____ 1. Overall mood (feelings of sadness, anxiety, happiness, etc.)

____ 2. Sense of self-esteem

____ 3. Confidence, comfort in social situations

____ 4. Internal dialog (self-talk)

____ 5. Energy level

____ 6. Focus and concentration

____ 7. Ability to manage time

____ 8. Relationships

____ 9. General health

____ 10. Exercise and recreation

____ 11. Assertiveness skills

____ 12. Eating habits

____ 13. Overall quality of life

Quality of Life Review Comparison

(a) Category	(b) Score from Introduction and Orientation Lesson	(c) Score from Commencement Lesson	(d) Change in Scores (column c minus column b)
1. Overall mood (feelings of sadness, anxiety, happiness, etc.)			
2. Sense of self			
3. Confidence, comfort in social situations			
4. Internal dialog (self-talk)			
5. Energy level			
6. Focus and concentration			
7. Ability to manage time			
8. Relationships			
9. General health			
10. Exercise and recreation			
11. Assertiveness skills			
12. Eating habits			
13. Overall quality of life			

tive (-) number represents decreased quality of life. If you have negatives (-) in any of the categories, this may represent areas you may want to spend more time on in the future. The positives (+) in the categories indicate your relative strengths. Remember, this is a journey—don't be hard on yourself if you still have some work to do!

Looking at the results of your review comparison, what areas are you most satisfied with now? Has your confidence and self-assurance improved? Are you more active, and do you have more energy? Think about how remarkable this is. In just four months, you have achieved some impressive benefits. The comparison you just completed is proof of your accomplishment.

How can you improve those areas in which you are not more satisfied? For starters, you can identify one area and start there. For instance, you are not satisfied with your leisure and recreational activities, identify a concrete goal that you would like to achieve. It should be something specific, such as walking more. Make a specific plan concerning what you will do, when, and with whom. That's the best way to get new behaviors going. Use the worksheet titled Quality of Life Improvement Worksheet, on page 403, to help identify specific areas that need work and develop a specific plan of action for each area.

If you need ideas, the Master List of Techniques, in Appendix B, on page 413, lists the techniques used in the program, such as visual imagery, time management, and assessing relationships. You may also use this list for future reference when you want to focus on a certain area. Continued practice will improve the areas you have trouble with and will help you further develop your stress management tools.

Believe in Yourself

Throughout this book, we stressed the importance of believing in yourself and your ability—believing that with the right amount of motivation and perseverance, you too can succeed. The people most likely to make successful, long-term changes are those with the skills and confidence to do so. You have learned many skills. These skills will help you manage difficult situations, handle setbacks, and will enable you to live a more balanced, fulfilling life.

Quality of Life Improvement Worksheet

Area to Improve	How to Improve	When to Improve
1. ______	______	______
2. ______	______	______
3. ______	______	______
4. ______	______	______
5. ______	______	______
6. ______	______	______

You can be secure in your ability, without being perfectionistic. There will be road blocks and difficult paths along the way that may make achieving your goals more difficult. Keeping your perspective is important, especially when it comes to slips in using your stress management tools. Think of slips as bumps along the road, or reminders of what you need to do. Your recovery from a slip is more important than the slip itself.

There will be times when you will have to give yourself a pep talk to get your motivation going again. Think about what works best for you. What are the most powerful things you can say to yourself when you need encouragement? How have you inspired yourself in the past when you felt less secure? Anticipate that there will be times when a pep talk is necessary, make a list of all the things you want to say to yourself and keep the list handy—be your own best friend.

Saying Goodbye and Good Luck!

We hope that you have found this program enjoyable as well as helpful in attaining your stress management goals. The new skills and habits you have developed will guide you through the challenges ahead. You are now ready to continue the journey, as a stronger, wiser, and more practiced stress manager.

Finally, please feel free to contact us with your ideas and comments about this program. We welcome all your success stories as well as suggestions for improvement. Your feedback is important to us. You may send your comments to us at the address below:

American Health Publishing Company
P.O. Box 610430, Dept. 70
Dallas, Texas 75261-0430

You may also fax or e-mail your comments and suggestions to us at the numbers listed in the very beginning of the book.

Best of Luck!

Daily Stress Record

Name:______________________ **Week of:**__________

Date	Average Stress Level	Highest Stress Level	Time of Highest Stress Level	Stressful Event Associated with Highest Stress Level

My Physical Activity and Relaxation Record

Day of the Week	Physical Activity Record		Relaxation by Recall	
	Activity	Minutes	Time of Day	Minutes
Monday				
Tuesday				
Wednesday				
Thursday				
Friday				
Saturday				
Sunday				

Appendix A

Stress Management Readiness

Readiness is important to assess before beginning any journey. Are you prepared to take on the responsibilities of a stress management program? Are your expectations realistic? Recall our example of the balloonist on page 6 in the Introduction and Orientation Lesson. Is the weather clear for you to begin your stress management journey or is a storm brewing? To help you answer these important questions, let's begin by looking more closely at the notion of readiness.

What Is Readiness?

As we said, people begin stress management programs for a variety of reasons. For some, they have had enough of the negative effects of too much stress. These individuals are ready to commit the time and do the work it takes to manage their stress—their motivation is high. Others may feel pressured into the decision by family members, friends, or co-workers. For these individuals, motivation may not be as high. The decision to begin the program is not their choice, but the choice of others. As you can see from these examples, there are many reasons to begin a program.

Readiness refers to a person's reasons for wanting to start a program. Personal readiness includes, motivation; commitment to make a sustained effort; ability to take on the added stress of starting a program; realistic expectations; and ability to change behaviors, thoughts, and activities that contribute to stressful patterns.

The Consequences of Not Being Ready

Individuals often begin a stress management program feeling motivated, but soon their motivation fades. They may fall into some of their old behavior patterns, become frustrated, and question their ability or desire to make lasting changes. For some, this can lead to feelings of negative self-worth caused by repeated "failures" in managing their stress. This highlights the importance of assessing readiness from the start.

"Is the weather clear for you to begin your journey, or is a storm brewing?"

Assessing Readiness

You are more likely to succeed in a stress management program when your readiness is high. Therefore, it is important to properly assess your level of readiness.

First you must recognize how readiness is linked to success. The time to begin a stress management program may never be convenient or perfect, but some times are better than others. This also means that you need not feel discouraged if you are not ready. Readiness can change with life circumstances. Just because a person isn't ready to begin a program today, doesn't mean he or she will not be ready next month or two months from now.

We have developed a tool that may help you assess your readiness to begin a program. We call this tool the Stress Management Assessment and Readiness Test (SMART). The SMART has 24 items designed to help you assess your current stress management abilities and your readiness to begin a stress management program. The SMART is divided into six sections with a scoring key at the end of each section. Section 1 addresses readiness and sections 2–6 address your current stress management abilities. The sections include:

1. Goals and Attitudes
2. Realistic Thinking
3. Assertion and Time Management
4. Stress-Busting Behaviors
5. Coping
6. Flexible Response to Daily Demands

The SMART tool will help you consider some important factors when assessing your stress management skills and readiness. However, it does have some limitations based on its newness. When an

"Assessing readiness is an important step."

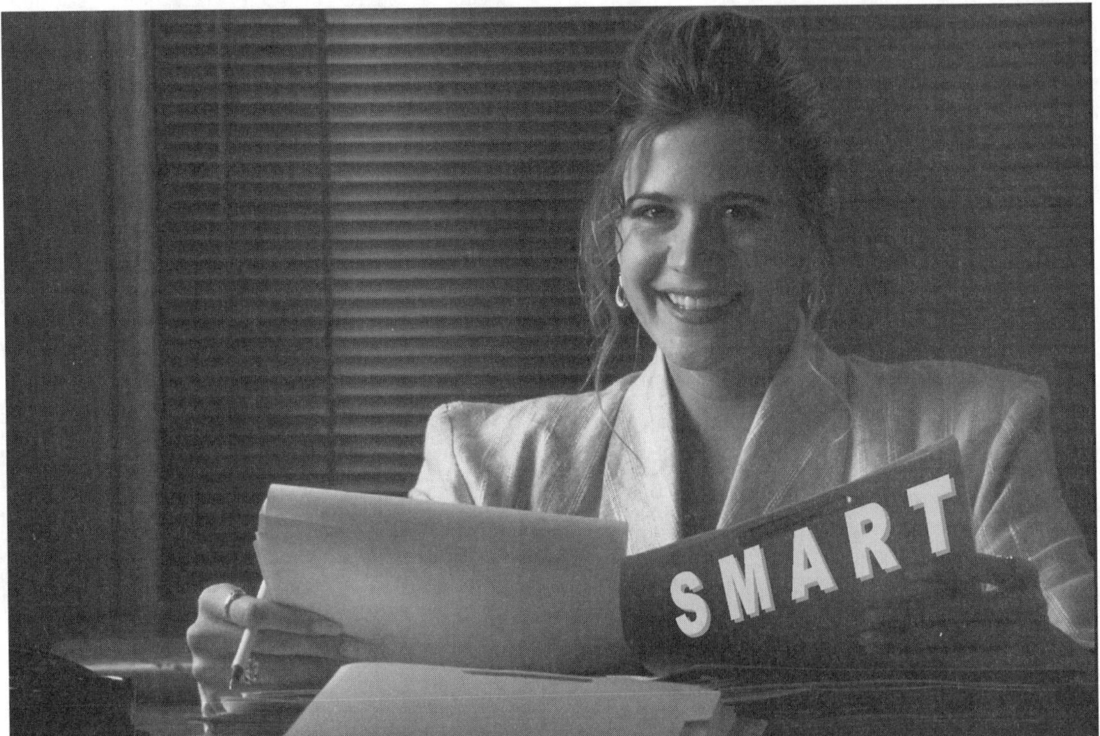

assessment tool is first developed, it must be used over and over to determine whether it is correctly measuring what it is intended to measure. The SMART tool is in the early stages of use and is being revised based upon feedback. Therefore, it should not be used as the only measure to assess your stress management skills or whether you are ready to begin a program. It is only one of many tools available to help you assess your readiness to make changes in your life. The SMART tool does not yield a single score. Instead, the scores for each section are provided to help you assess your readiness (section 1) and abilities in each area (sections 2–6).

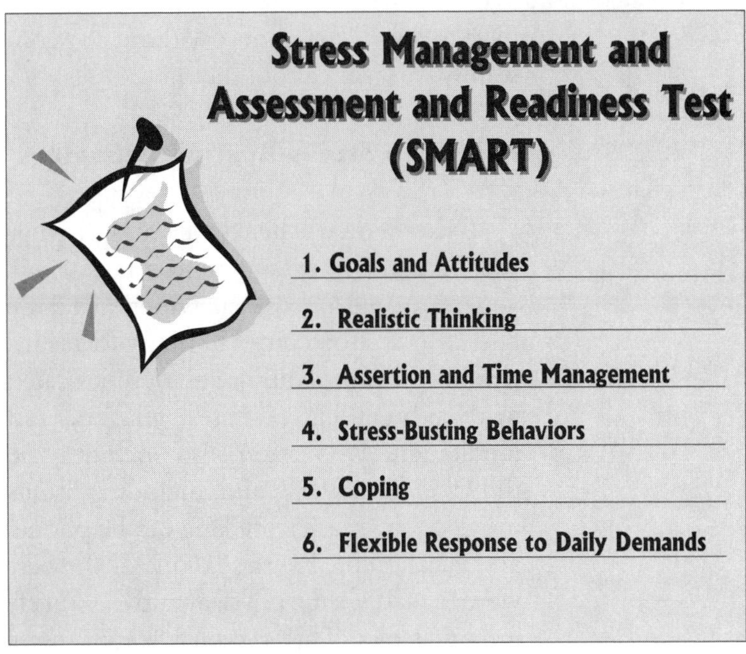

The Stress Management Assessment and Readiness Test (SMART) Categories

We have divided the SMART tool into six separate categories. Let's look at each category carefully.

Section 1: Goals and Attitudes

The questions in this section are designed to help you evaluate how motivated you are to do the work needed for change, how realistic your expectations are, your belief that you can stay motivated, and your willingness to include stress management in your lifestyle. This section also deals with setting realistic goals. When expectations are realistic, you are less likely to be disappointed.

Section 2: Realistic Thinking

This section will help you decide whether your self-talk is helping or hurting you. Specifically, we are looking for thoughts that increase stress. Our thoughts prepare us to deal with stressors or threats in our environment. More often than not, our thoughts cause us to worry unnecessarily—even when we are not being threatened. For example, thoughts that are overly demanding, rigid, and negative, will lead to more stressful feelings and behaviors. Thoughts that are flexible, forgiving, and positive will help reduce stress.

Section 3: Assertion and Time Management

This section of the test is designed to help you determine your skills in expressing your desires and thoughts to others. A significant part of the stress in our lives can come from the inability to assertively express our desires to others. Thus, learning to assert yourself can be very helpful in managing stress.

This section also deals with your ability to manage your time. Effect time management includes setting priorities and limits. When we are able to manage our time, we are more productive and less stressed. This gives us the confidence that everything we have to do will get done—without our constantly worrying about them.

Section 4: Stress-Busting Behaviors

This section will help you assess whether you find time to exercise and relax, and if you make time for these activities on a daily basis. Relaxation comes in many forms including the more traditional methods, such as deep-breathing exercises, imagery, and meditation. Relaxation also includes the things we do to feel calm, including listening to music, reading, talking on the phone, and vacationing. Exercise is one of the best ways to manage the physical and mental effects of stress. This section also addresses whether or not you follow a healthful eating plan.

Section 5: Coping

This section will address how you cope with stress. For example, when you are feeling stressed do you turn to drugs and/or alcohol in order to "cope"? Are you more likely to overeat when stressed? Do you use avoidance to "deal" with your stress? You will find that these strategies, although seemingly helpful in the short term, create even greater problems in the long term.

Section 6: Flexible Response to Daily Demands

Feeling a sense of control over one's environment is likely to reduce stress. On the other hand, demanding too much control over your environment increases stress. The balance of control over your environment is one key to mastering stress. This section will help you determine if you are overly responsive to the distractions and external demands placed on you by the environment.

Just a Reminder

As we discussed earlier in this section, the SMART tool should not be used as the only basis for determining your readiness to start a program. It is a guide to help you decide if "now" is a good time for you to begin a program. Remember, your readiness and abilities assessment should be based on your score in *each* of the six sections, not general readiness. High scores in one section suggest strength or readiness in that area. Low scores in another section are cues that weaknesses may be lurking about.

By assessing your skills and readiness, you are considering the issues of commitment, motivation, and timing related to starting a program. Remember that a low score in one area means that you need to spend more time on problems within that area. The SMART tool measures readiness at a single point in time. Readiness is constantly changing and evolving. This means that even if you determine the time is not right for you to begin a stress management program at this time, your readiness could change in the future.

Sections 2–6 of the SMART can help you assess your current stress management skills. What are your strongest skills? Are you able to assert yourself in appropriate situations? How are you at managing your time? Turn to the SMART tool on page 409. Take as much time as you need to answer each question completely and honestly. Good luck!

Stress Management Assessment and Readiness Test (SMART)

Answer the questions below to assess your readiness to begin a stress management program. For each question, circle the answer that best describes your attitude. At the end of the section, add the numbers of your answers and compare them with the scoring guide at the end of each section.

Section 1: Goals and Attitudes

_____ 1. How motivated are you to begin a stress management program at this time? (Compare this to your motivation in the past.)

1. Not at all motivated
2. Slightly motivated
3. Somewhat motivated
4. Quite motivated
5. Extremely motivated

_____ 2. How confident are you that you will stay committed to a stress management program for the time it will take to reach your stress management goals?

1. Not at all confident
2. Slightly confident
3. Somewhat confident
4. Quite confident
5. Extremely confident

_____ 3. At first, incorporating a stress management program into your lifestyle may seem to increase your level of stress. How willing are you to make this a priority for the next few months?

1. Not at all willing
2. Slightly willing
3. Somewhat willing
4. Quite willing
5. Extremely willing

_____ 4. In order to fully master the techniques you will learn, how committed are you to completing homework assignments each week?

1. Not at all committed
2. Slightly committed
3. Somewhat committed
4. Quite committed
5. Extremely committed

_____ 5. Stress management programs can't eliminate all your stress or make your life perfect. It is more realistic to expect that they can help you cope better with your stress and improve the overall quality of your life. How realistic are your expectations?

1. Very unrealistic
2. Somewhat unrealistic
3. Moderately realistic
4. Somewhat realistic
5. Very realistic

_____ 6. If you see yourself slipping or you get temporarily derailed while on a stress management program, how likely are you to quit or abandon your goals?

1. Very likely
2. Somewhat likely
3. Slightly likely
4. Somewhat unlikely
5. Very unlikely

_____ **Section 1- Total Score**

If you scored:

24 to 30 Your goals and attitudes indicate that you are ready to start a program.

17 to 23 Your attitudes indicate that you may need to increase your motivation and commitment a bit more before you are ready to begin a program, but you are not far off!

6 to 16 This may not be the best time for you to start a stress management program. Low levels of motivation, lack of commitment, and goals that are not realistic can impede progress. Before starting a program, it will be important for you to think about how you can improve these areas.

Section 2: Realistic Thinking

_____ 7. When your performance falls short of perfect, or you don't meet your self-determined expectations, what are your beliefs?
1. I believe I am a failure
2. I believe I have failed
3. I believe I need to figure out how I can do better in the future

_____ 8. To what extent can you tolerate others not behaving the way you believe they should behave?
1. Cannot tolerate
2. Moderately tolerate
3. Easily tolerate

_____ 9. When anticipating an upcoming event that has traditionally been stressful for you, how likely are you to expect a negative outcome?
1. Extremely likely
2. Somewhat likely
3. Slightly unlikely
4. Somewhat unlikely
5. Extremely unlikely

_____ 10. How comfortable are you in dealing with uncertainty in your life?
1. Very uncomfortable
2. Somewhat uncomfortable
3. Somewhat comfortable
4. Very comfortable

_____ 11. How important is it to you to have the approval of others?
1. Extremely important
2. Very important
3. Somewhat important
4. Slightly important
5. Not at all important

_____ **Section 2- Total Score**

If you scored:

16 to 20 Your self talk appears to be realistic and helpful. Keep up the good work!

10 to 15 At times your inner dialog may get in the way of you achieving happiness and well-being. Challenging these thoughts and replacing them with more rational thoughts will help you achieve your goals.

5 to 9 Your self talk or inner dialog is probably contributing greatly to your stress. Learning how to change these stress-producing thoughts (perfectionism, need for approval, overly demanding) is critical to you managing your stress more effectively.

Section 3: Assertion and Time Management

_____ 12. How effective are you in communicating your desires and needs to others?
1. Not at all effective
2. Slightly effective
3. Somewhat effective
4. Quite effective
5. Extremely effective

_____ 13. When faced with a difficult project, how often do you procrastinate?
1. Always
2. Frequently
3. Occasionally
4. Rarely
5. Never

_____ 14. When you are asked if you would like to help with a project and you know you are already at your limit, how often do you take it on?
1. Always
2. Frequently
3. Occasionally
4. Rarely
5. Never

_____ 15. When you have multiple tasks to accomplish, how likely are you to prioritize tasks and come up with a structured plan of action?
1. Extremely unlikely
2. Somewhat unlikely
3. Slightly likely
4. Somewhat likely
5. Extremely likely

_____ **Section 3- Total Score**

If you scored:

16 to 20 You seem to be quite skilled at communicating your needs to others and at managing your time effectively.

10 to 15 Although you have some effective assertion and time management skills, you may find it difficult at times to employ them.

4 to 9 You may often find yourself feeling overwhelmed because it is hard for you to say no to others or disappoint them. In addition, you may find it hard to prioritize your tasks or stick to a schedule. To more effectively reduce your stress, these areas will need to be addressed.

Section 4: Stress-Busting Behaviors

_____ 16. How often do you eat a healthful, well-balanced diet?

1. Never
2. Rarely
3. Occasionally
4. Frequently
5. Always

_____ 17. During a busy or stressful day, how often do you take time out for some type of relaxation (walking, deep breathing, taking a nap, listening to music, etc)?

1. Never
2. Rarely
3. Occasionally
4. Frequently
5. Always

_____ 18. How often do you exercise?

1. Never
2. Rarely
3. Occasionally
4. Frequently
5. Always

_____ **Section 4- Total Score**

If you scored:

12 to 15 You appear to have a healthy approach to diet, exercise, and relaxation.

7 to 11 Although you have developed some healthful habits, you seem to have difficulty making them a priority in your schedule as much as you would like. To manage your stress more effectively, it will be important to figure out what keeps you motivated to include these healthful habits into your routine.

3 to 6 Your diet and lack of exercise are most likely contributing to your overall level of stress. Recognizing how your eating habits affect your level of stress will encourage you to maintain a more balanced diet. Also, understanding the importance of relaxation and exercise and making an effort to include them in your schedule, will help you manage your stress more effectively.

Section 5: Coping

_____ 19. When you are feeling stressed, how often do you turn to drugs and/or alcohol (or any other addictive substance) for comfort?

1. Always
2. Frequently
3. Occasionally
4. Rarely
5. Never

_____ 20. How often do you avoid dealing with difficult situations that need to be addressed?

1. Always
2. Frequently
3. Occasionally
4. Rarely
5. Never

_____ 21. After a stressful day or experience, how likely are you to overeat?

1. Extremely likely
2. Somewhat likely
3. Slightly unlikely
4. Somewhat unlikely
5. Extremely unlikely

_____ **Section 5- Total Score**

If you scored:

12 to 15 You appear to manage your stress with healthful coping mechanisms most of the time.

7 to 11 Although you have developed some healthful habits, you sometimes turn to less healthful means to manage your stress. Monitor these behaviors to learn why and when they occur, so you can then employ more effective coping strategies.

3 to 6 You often rely on less healthful coping techniques to manage your stress. These techniques are not only unhelpful in managing stress, but they eventually increase your stress level. Learning more healthful strategies for managing your stress is essential.

Section 6: Flexible Response to Daily Demands

_____ 22. How effective are you in taking the unexpected stressors in everyday life in stride (traffic, long lines, slow or inefficient sales clerks)?

1. Not at all effective
2. Slightly effective
3. Somewhat effective
4. Quite effective
5. Extremely effective

_____ 23. When you are surprised by an additional stressor in an already stressful day, how confident are you that you will be able to handle the situation?

1. Not at all confident
2. Slightly confident
3. Somewhat confident
4. Quite confident
5. Extremely confident

_____ 24. If you have planned in advance how you are going to handle your day (filled with things that need to be accomplished) and a friend unexpectedly asks you to spend the day "relaxing together," how likely are you to abandon your original work plan?

1. Extremely likely
2. Somewhat likely
3. Slightly unlikely
4. Somewhat unlikely
5. Extremely unlikely

_____ **Section 6- Total Score**

If you scored:

12 to 15 You appear to be flexible with what the environment sends your way.

7 to 11 You are sometimes affected negatively by situations that are not planned. It will be important for you to figure out why and when you are better able to handle environmental influences.

3 to 6 You need to work more on not allowing your environment to affect you negatively or derail you in achieving your goals. You can learn to feel more in control even when forces outside of you appear to pushing you in the wrong direction.

Appendix B

Master List of Techniques

Lifestyle Techniques

Exercise Techniques

Attitude Techniques

Relationship Techniques

Nutrition Techniques

Appendix C

Answers for Knowledge Review Questions

Lesson One

1. ***False***. A lifestyle approach to stress management focuses on all aspects of living. It is the interaction of our thoughts, feelings, behaviors, attitudes, goals, and personal values.

2. ***True***. Cooperation and team work are an important part of group membership and will help you get the most out of your experience.

3. ***True***. The Daily Stress Record is a self-monitoring form designed to track your highest levels of daily stress.

4. ***True***. Self-monitoring has many benefits. By keeping accurate records, you can give yourself credit for what you accomplish, and this can help motivate you to continue to work hard.

5. ***False***. It is important to establish techniques to help improve your motivation *before* you have trouble.

6. ***False***. Choosing to involve your friends and family members in your stress management efforts can be very helpful because they will see the changes you are making.

7. ***True***. Visualization is a powerful tool that uses your creative imagination to help you see into your future—a future with less stress.

8. ***True***. Social techniques involve enlisting the help of others, such as asking your friends to exercise regularly with you. Material techniques may involve setting up a reward system.

Lesson Two

9. ***False***. Even if you diligently complete your Daily Stress Records, reviewing your records is necessary so you can recognize stress patterns more effectively.

10. ***False***. Patterns should be analyzed because they provide important information about your stress experiences. Understanding patterns will help you anticipate and prepare for recurring stressors.

11. ***False***. We cannot and do not want to eliminate all of our stress. Low levels of stress are a normal part of life.

12. ***False***. Stress that has an impact on us can be anything that causes us to adapt, including positive events.

13. ***True***. Many people develop excessive and addictive behaviors as a way of reacting to or coping with stress. These behaviors cause even more stress in the long term.

14. ***True***. Low self-esteem often results from rating yourself. The healthiest approach is to rate your behavior and take responsibility for it.

15. ***False***. Shaping refers to making behavior and attitude changes gradually, in a step-by-step fashion.

Lesson Three

16. ***False***. A good program partnership can be motivational, but it does not have to be formed with someone who is going through the program.

17. ***False***. Everyone, no matter what their genetic makeup, can learn to manage their stress if they appropriately apply the stress management techniques.

18. ***True***. Feeling a loss of control over the negatives in one's life can be a major source of stress.

19. ***True***. Danger does not have to be real; anything you perceive as a threat or challenge can trigger your mind and body to react.

20. ***True***. When responding to challenging situations, you may vacillate between stress and anxiety because they are next to each other on the continuum of feelings.

21. ***False***. Feelings come primarily from thoughts, not from events.

Lesson Four

22. ***False***. Developing a good program partnership can be a powerful source of motivation and inspiration, but you do not have to work with a partner to use this program.

23. ***True***. The physical response system includes all of the changes that take place in your body when you feel stressed.

24. ***False***. The three response systems have unique purposes and closely interact with each other. Any one system can affect the other, starting the entire stress-response cycle.

25. ***False***. The benefits of being physically active are important to overall health and stress management.

26. ***True***. Experts say that laughter provides a total inner body workout and helps to relieve stress by improving our perspective.

27. ***True***. Stress-producing thoughts focus more on the likelihood that something negative will happen, even in the face of positive evidence.

28. ***True***. Stress-producing thoughts may seem automatic because we have practiced them regularly over the years.

29. ***False***. Thinking patterns are learned in early life, and we practice them over time, which makes them difficult, but not impossible, to change.

Lesson Five

30. ***True***. Regularly reviewing your progress helps keep motivation high and helps you identify areas that may need more work.

31. ***True***. It is realistic to expect a gradual decrease in your levels of stress each week of the program. Remember that lasting changes do not happen quickly.

32. ***True***. Studies show that regular, moderate-intensity physical activity can provide substantial physical and mental benefits.

33. ***False***. The new exercise guidelines recommend 30 minutes of cumulative, moderate-intensity physical activity on most days of the week, preferably every day.

34. ***True***. The more specific your requests for help, the easier it will be for your partner to respond.

35. ***False***. Although people enjoy many forms of passive relaxation, few practice the more active forms of relaxation that are effective in reducing stress.

36. ***True***. Because deep muscle relaxation is very portable and does not require equipment, you can use it in almost any stressful situation and at any time.

37. ***False***. Deep muscle relaxation is a form of active relaxation.

38. ***False***. When practicing deep muscle relaxation, keep breathing evenly as you tense and relax each muscle group.

39. ***True***. These three typical problems are common for people who have rouble managing their time.

Lesson Six

40. ***False***. The *beliefs* we have about activating events, *not* the activating events themselves, cause stress.

41. ***True***. The ABC approach to emotion and behavior change is based on the premise that our beliefs lead to our emotions and behaviors. Our beliefs about the activating events determine our consequences.

42. ***True***. Unlike positive thinking, realistic thinking asks you to look at situations rationally and objectively, accepting that negative consequences might occur.

43. ***True***. These four uniquely human gifts converge when we make choices in life.

44. ***True***. Learning the skills and techniques to choose thoughts that are less stressful is critical to mastering stress.

45. ***False***. Generally, the lower the realistic estimate, the less intense your emotion will be.

46. ***True***. The event is not causing the stress, your thoughts about the event are causing the stress.

47. ***False***. Consequences, both emotions and behaviors, are the direct result of our thoughts, not the result of events beyond our control.

48. ***True***. Even in the harshest of circumstances, this independence gives us the power to choose our response.

Lesson Seven

49. ***False***. Relaxation practice is even more important if you are very busy each day. Learning how to take time to relax is an important part of stress management.

50. ***True***. Problems with concentration are common for individuals who are just beginning to practice relaxation. This should improve with practice.

51. ***True***. A good night's sleep is important. Adequate sleep enables your body to recover from the stressors you experience each day.

52. ***False***. Although relationships can be a great source of stress relief, this is not always the case. There are many times where our relationships, and our reactions to them, increase our stress.

53. ***True***. Examining your past experiences, both good and bad, is a good way to challenge your estimates.

54. ***True***. Changing perspectives, or putting yourself in the other person's place, is a good strategy for viewing evidence related to social situations.

55. ***True***. After you have considered all the evidence, revising your estimate should reduce the intensity of the stress response.

56. ***False***. Investing your time in the important items, rather than just the urgent, is a good way to lower your stress.

57. ***True***. Learning time management skills can help reduce much stress. Simply increasing responsibility and working longer hours does not increase efficiency, it increases stress.

Lesson Eight

58. ***False***. Even if you are a quick thinker, you still may not be thinking realistically. Realistic thinking takes dedication and a lot of practice before it becomes "automatic."

59. ***True***. When looking at your initial thoughts related to a stressful event, the four types of evidence will help you determine the probability of your initial thought.

60. ***False***. When you spend most of your day on the urgent matters, the truly important things in your life get left behind, which will increase your stress.

61. ***False***. You can't avoid all stressful situations, but you can learn to identify them early and use your stress management skills to manage your stress.

62. True. People who catastrophize tend to blow things out of proportion by overestimating the possibility of a negative outcome.

63. ***True***. Although we would prefer not to, our minds can cope with amazing amount of difficulty, including tragedies and catastrophes.

64. ***True***. Assertive people believe that they are entitled to an opinion, and that other people are entitled to one as well.

65. ***False***. In addition to helping you feel better, assertive behavior can significantly reduce stress because you are communicating your needs to others in a healthy way.

66. ***True***. New research has shown that you can improve your overall fitness by incorporating at least 30 minutes of incremental lifestyle activity each day.

Lesson Nine

67. ***False***. Use this opportunity to review your progress and focus more on areas of difficulty. Use this as a learning experience and continue to work on reducing your stress.

68. ***False***. Reviewing your progress is important because it makes you more aware of your accomplishments. This review also may reveal areas that need additional work.

69. ***True***. Your thoughts and behaviors have developed over your lifetime and changing them takes time and practice.

70. ***True***. Procrastination is a common behavior that increases stress. Everyone procrastinates, but when it becomes a habit, it can be a serious problem.

71. ***True***. Procrastinators often believe that life should be easy and as a result, they avoid difficult tasks. By avoiding difficult tasks however, they make their stress worse.

72. ***True***. An important step in overcoming procrastination is to challenge the thoughts that lead to putting things off.

73. ***False***. Nutrition is a key component of good health, and good health is a key ingredient of stress management. A healthy body responds better to the inevitable stressors in our lives.

74. ***False***. Families can be a terrific source of help and support for your stress management program.

75. ***False***. Learning to identify low muscle tension is very important because it allows you to identify stress early, before it gets out of control.

Lesson Ten

76. ***True***. Type II procrastinators put things off because they fear the outcome, not because they mind doing the task itself.

77. ***False***. Although the exact relationship between stress and eating may not be clear, one thing is certain: Eating a healthy and balanced diet, without overeating, is a powerful stress management tool.

78. ***True***. It is important to include all predictions, both positive and negative, when you are doing prediction testing.

79. ***True***. Feeling upset, sad, or even angry about a negative event is natural. Your thoughts and the way you choose to respond to the event will directly affect your level of stress.

80. ***False***. Realistic thinking takes into account all of the evidence, good and bad. Too often, we remember only the negative and forget all our accomplishments.

81. ***False***. Very often, perfectionism leads to decreased performance or even avoidance.

82. ***False.*** Rational Emotive Imagery (REI) is based on the notion that our thoughts about events, not events alone, cause stress in our lives. REI helps people change their stressful feelings by changing their stress-producing thoughts.

83. ***True***. With imagery, you first imagine yourself in a very stressful situation, then you imagine yourself reducing the stressful emotions by changing your thoughts about the situation.

84. ***False***. Imagery is a helpful technique for reducing (not eliminating) the intense emotions associated with stressful events.

85. ***False***. Stress at home and stress at work are closely related. The sad reality of job stress is that it doesn't stay there—it follows you home. This, in turn, can lead to increased stress at home.

Lesson Eleven

86. ***False***. By planning ahead, you will not be caught off guard, and you will be equipped with strategies for getting back on track.

87. ***True***. In order to help you stay motivated, rewarding yourself for progress along the way is very important. Rewards can serve as self-acknowledgments of progress.

88. ***False***. You may encounter times when gathering objective evidence is simply not possible. In these situations, use your best judgement.

89. ***True***. Catastrophizers not only expect that the worst will happen, but also believe they do not have the ability to deal with the outcome.

90. ***False***. Eating a balanced diet means eating a variety of food from the different food groups of the Food Guide Pyramid.

91. ***True***. A 20-minute relaxation practice session is not always practical. Making your relaxation more portable, allows you to use this technique during stressful situations.

92. ***True***. Walking is one example of the many ways to increase your physical activity and reduce your stress.

Lesson Twelve

93. ***False***. Although there is some overlap between the stress response systems, Reality Testing helps you work primarily on the behavioral component of stress.

94. ***False.*** You should thoroughly understand reality testing before you begin using it. Then you can gradually increase your exposure to stressful situations as you practice this technique.

95. ***True.*** You can directly challenge stressful situations by intentionally putting yourself in stressful situations.

96. ***True***. Making a stepladder can help you approach a stressful situation gradually, in a step-by step fashion.

97. ***False***. Relaxation and the many other stress management techniques are helpful in overcoming job-related stress.

98. ***True***. Although we may never like hassles and frustrations, we can learn to tolerate them with practice.

99. ***False***. Perfectionism is unrealistic and the added pressure it creates often leads to decreased productivity and performance.

100. ***True***. Imperatives are words and phrases that imply perfection, urgency, or allow no room for error. Using these statements in your self-talk will increase your stress.

101. ***True***. This is important in stress management because your diet directly affects how well your physical response system responds to stress.

Lesson Thirteen

102. ***False***. Programmed activities include aerobics, jogging, and swimming and may require more skill than lifestyle activities. You should consider your current physical condition when choosing an activity.

103. ***True.*** The stepladder approach is an effective stress-reduction technique that can be used for situations that are stressful or that you find yourself avoiding.

104. ***True.*** Choose *not* to allow others to validate your self-worth. Instead, choose to validate yourself.

105. ***False***. Demanding that others treat us a certain way increases stress.

106. ***True***. Once again, the event does not cause our stress and frustration, although it may contribute to it. We make ourselves frustrated and stressed by our thoughts about a particular event.

107. ***True***. Because problems are not always what they seem on the surface, specifically defining a problem is a crucial first step in finding an appropriate solution.

108. ***False***. Brainstorming means letting your mind go and writing down every possible solution to a problem, rather than focusing on one idea.

109. ***True***. Problem solving is a more advanced form of realistic thinking that is especially helpful for problems that do not have clear solutions.

110. ***False***. Brainstorming to come up with several possible solutions is an effective way to solve difficult problems. You can then pick the most practical solutions and try them out.

Lesson Fourteen

111. ***False***. Both alcohol and caffeine will interfere with a good night's sleep.

112. ***False***. Although technology has been very helpful to us and has enabled us to do more things than we could have ever imagined, it has increased stress for almost everyone.

113. ***True***. Clearly defining your roles is an important first step in balancing your life.

114. ***True***. Learning to identify high-risk situations will help you to avoid lapses and master your stress more effectively.

115. ***False***. Everyone's sleep needs differ. What is adequate sleep for one person may not be enough for another.

116. ***True***. The Behavior Chain method allows you to review stressful events and find ways to use your stress management tools to gain control.

117. ***False***. When people have trouble finding time for the important things the problem is often that they are trying to prioritize their schedules, rather than scheduling their priorities.

118. ***True***. Generalizing your relaxation skills in increasingly difficult situations will help prepare you to use these skills in more stressful situations.

Lesson Fifteen

119. ***False***. Some situations are stressful, no matter how much we try to change our response. These situations require a change in the environment to lower stress.

120. ***True***. When polled, most people ranked job-related stress (e.g., having too much to do, feeling a lack of control, etc.) as the most common source of stress.

121. ***False***. About one-half of the people who use this program will be ready to stop taking their stress medication at about this point in the program.

122. ***True***. Applied relaxation helps you apply your relaxation skills to stressful situations.

123. ***True***. Building your assertion skills is like developing muscles, it can be accomplished with practice.

124. ***True***. One of the best ways to manage time and reduce your stress is to delegate responsibility. Delegation may require some work initially because you have to explain the task you are requesting. In the long run, it can greatly reduce your stress.

125. ***False***. Time-management skills can be useful to anyone who is interested in managing their time more effectively.

Lesson Sixteen

126. ***True***. Also called *Light Bulb Thinking*, this classic attitude problem involves viewing everything as either right or wrong, good or bad.

127. ***False***. Being aware of negative attitudes and taking action to counter them is the best way to overcome negative attitude traps.

128. ***False***. Chronic comparison, or continually rating yourself against an ideal standard, leads to discouragement and increased stress because you can never attain the "ideal."

129. ***False***. Not all interruptions need to be handled immediately. It is important to distinguish between what has to get done immediately and what can wait.

130. ***True***. Preparing for high-risk situations by planning and maintaining a healthy attitude are key elements to stress reduction.

131. ***True***. Planning often slips because individuals fail to schedule time to plan again. This is a crucial stress management skill.

132. ***False***. Sometimes it is best to back off and try again later—especially if you see the interaction is spiraling out of control.

133. ***True***. Like the forest ranger, your job as a stress manager is to be concerned with both prevention and crisis management.

Appendix D

Guidelines for Being a Good Group Member

Many health professionals offer stress management programs in a group setting. This is done for several reasons. One important reason is that members of the group can be a tremendous help to each other. This help may come in the form of encouraging words, a pat on the back, or ideas to solve a specific problem. Also, just knowing that others who have difficulty managing their stress care about you can be an important source of help and motivation.

Importance of the Group

From a problem-solving perspective, a group provides a shared experience that can help you develop your stress management techniques and skills. Yet beyond providing information, group members can provide support and encouragement. Most people in a stress management program experience motivational peaks and valleys. When you take a detour from your program, the group can help the motivation return. When you are highly motivated yourself, you can encourage someone else in the group who may be having trouble.

Good Chemistry and Teamwork

When a group has the right chemistry, it functions like a well-oiled machine. The meetings are enjoyable, informative, and motivational. Each group member receives as much as he or she gives, and all are better off for the effort.

The analogy of a sports team is especially appropriate. Let's take a basketball team, for example. We all know of teams with great individual players, but the team won't get anywhere if the players do not work together. One player may have an opportunity to take a shot, but passing to a teammate who has a better shot will help the team. Teams with far less talent win championships by working together and helping each other. This intangible *team spirit* motivates everyone to work harder. Each player receives and gives, and all benefit in the process.

Being a good group member is a ***responsibility*** of anyone entering a group. Yet more than duty, it is the best way to learn to manage stress. Entering a group with a spirit of cooperation and the willing-

"A good group is like a sports team. Each player receives and gives, and all benefit in the process."

ness to help others will insure that the help comes back to you. In the long run, you emerge the winner.

Being a good group member requires following specific guidelines. There are things to do, things to say, and ways to act. The guidelines that follow can make this happen.

Guidelines and Responsibilities

Attend Meetings

People in a group are responsible for attending meetings, not only for themselves but for others. When a group member misses a meeting, others in the group may worry about the person, may wonder if the absence is a sign of trouble, or may have other thoughts about the absence.

Undoubtedly, at times you may question whether you should attend a meeting. You may have forgotten to keep your Daily Stress Record, it may be rainy and miserable outside, or you may have had a difficult time with work or with the kids. These are the times when your program might be most in jeopardy, so attending the meeting is important. The times when you feel like missing a meeting may be the times when you need the support and encouragement of the group the most. In addition, the group functions best when all attend. So remember that by joining a group you are agreeing to do your level best to make the meetings.

Be Punctual

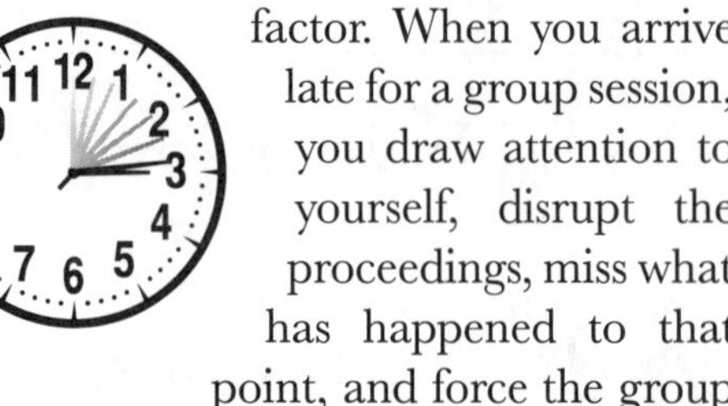

Being on time is another key factor. When you arrive late for a group session, you draw attention to yourself, disrupt the proceedings, miss what has happened to that point, and force the group leader to either ignore what you have missed or cover it again. Showing up late, especially if it occurs chronically, is a sign of disrespect for other members of the group.

Sometimes, of course, being late is inevitable. You might have just arrived in town on the flight from Tokyo where you were thinking of buying SONY or Toyota. If you live in the mountains, the Abominable Snow Man might have attacked you. Or, you might have some more common reason like a traffic jam, late baby-sitter, or deadlines at the office. These things are fine, but when you're late and the lateness can be helped, we start to worry.

Being late can be a sign of many things. Some people are always late because they fall into the Type A behavior pattern. They are always rushing and want to get in every last bit of activity before leaving for their stress management group meeting. Such a person would cringe at sitting around for a few minutes with nothing to do. Our advice is to go ahead and cringe, *but be on time.*

Sometimes group members are late because they have done poorly and want to avoid speaking with the group leader. Others might be angry with the group leader or dissatisfied with the program or their progress. These things are usually not done on a conscious level. But, if you look closely at your reasons for being late, these things may be the driving factors. If you find yourself being late, or wanting to be late, think carefully about the reasons.

Really Listen

Sure, we all listen in a group, but do we ***really*** listen? Are you tuned in to what is happening? Do you hear the emotions behind the words of another group member? Are you listening to what the other group members are saying, not just the words that they speak?

It is quite apparent when someone in the group is not listening. Yawning, rolling the eyes, looking out the window, and daydreaming are all dead giveaways. It's easy to get distracted, especially if the discussion is not relevant to you or if you're thinking about something else that is important. It takes a real effort to listen carefully.

Being a good listener involves watching the person who is speaking. Does the person speaking look like he or she is expressing some strong emotions? Is the topic a sensitive one? Have you experienced a similar situation or feeling? Have you found some approach helpful with the problem? It is fine to ask questions if you don't understand what the person is trying to say. Also, it's fine to respond with supportive statements or suggestions. It will be pleasing when others in the group do this for you, so start by really listening.

Be Non-judgmental

This may sound like psychological jargon, but here is what it means to be non-judgmental. Sometimes you may feel that what another group member says or does is wrong, silly, or even stupid. Some people tend to come down on individuals like this or to point out the folly in their ways. The risk lies in being too negative. This can antagonize the person on the other end and make the remaining group members mad at you for being critical.

This does not mean that you are in a group where *everything is wonderful* and no negative emotions can be expressed. Yet, remembering that there are different ways of saying things is important. What others

"A non-judgmental statements are supportive and understanding and open the door for further discussion."

Being Non-judgmental

One Person Says	Judgmental Response	Non-judgmental Response
I just couldn't exercise this week.	You must be getting lazy.	It's hard to keep motivated to exercise.
I don't think this group is helping.	You are just making excuses.	Can we do something to help?
Others here don't understand me.	You talk too much.	I would like to. What can I do?

say can be used as an opportunity for growth or an occasion to create bad feelings. The basic notion is for group members to accept each other as they are. In such a climate, people in the group feel free to say things they might otherwise hide for fear of being criticized.

The chart provided on page 425 gives some examples of judgmental and non-judgmental statements. As you can see, the non-judgmental statements are supportive and understanding and open the door for further discussion. They show others that you care about them and are willing to help.

Be an Active Participant

In any group, some people are more active than others. This is fine, and can reflect differences in personalities. Not everyone has to be talkative to benefit from the group. However, opening up to be an active participant can help both you and the other members of the group.

Being silent in a group sometimes reflects being shy or reserved. In other cases, it shows that a person is angry, resentful, or bored. When you have something worth saying, don't be afraid to share your insight. If you would like to share some of your own experiences, ask if anyone has a solution to a particular problem you face, or provide ideas of your own about an issue, speak up. Many times, what you have to say will be listened to with all the attention given to a group leader, and you might have ideas that the leader or others in the group do not have.

If you are the silent type, don't feel pressured to be exceptionally talkative. Not everyone will participate equally or will speak the same amount. When you do have something to offer, please share it with the others.

Share the Air Space

Think of the air in the group room as the territory around a hot-air balloon festival. If too many balloons enter the air space, the situation becomes dangerously confusing. If one balloon occupies more than its share of the air space by following an erratic pattern, it would be tough going for the others.

In a group, the air space is limited. Only so many voices can be heard during the course of a group meeting. For members of the group who are particularly verbal, there can be a tendency to monopolize the

"Think of group space as air space in a hot-air balloon festival. The air space is limited. Only so many voices can be heard during the course of a

conversation and to crowd others from the air space.

Again, not everyone speaks the same amount. So, if some people are naturally more vocal in the group, there is no need to pull in the reins. But if such a person interrupts or always speaks first, there may be a problem with sharing the air space. If the person takes a long time to make a point or has to say something during every discussion, it may be time to open the air space to others. Think about the way you speak in the group, and see if any of these apply to you. If so, try to pull back and think before speaking. By all means, speak up when you have something important to say. Say what you feel, but try not to speak just because there is an opportunity.

Be Supportive

One of the fundamental reasons there are groups is for group members to support each other. This can be motivating and encouraging. In fact, sometimes a kind word or a supportive gesture will mean more coming from a fellow group member than the exact same word or gesture coming from the group leader.

Group members should try to be pleasant, helpful, and understanding. When something troubles another group member, do what you can to show that you understand. You can offer moral support by showing that you understand that the person faces a difficult situation. Share similar experiences you might have had, and most of all, give some constructive suggestions if you can think of ways to help.

In Summary

When you enter a group, you enter a situation in which you can reap impressive rewards. You have the opportunity to not only learn the facts and techniques of the program, but to support and be supported, learn and teach, and help and be helped. This does not happen automatically, so people must be serious about their responsibilities as group members. In so doing, they will benefit from you and you will benefit from them. All will be better off, and the long-term result can be that you learn to master your stress.

[***Note***: These Guidelines for Being a Good Group Member were adapted with permission from Brownell, KD, *The LEARN Program for Management 2000,* 2000, American Health Publishing Company, Dallas, Texas. All rights reserved.]

"I want everyone at the meeting to dress up like Lego blocks. Then we can see exactly how each team member interlocks with the other team members in the project."

Appendix E

The Average Stress Change Worksheet

The Average Stress Change worksheet helps you track your average stress level from week to week. On the sample worksheet in Lesson Two, on page 48, you can see two lines. The straight line represents what your average weekly stress would look like if you reduced the level of stress in your life by exactly the same amount every week. Certainly, change doesn't happen in a straight line. The jagged line is more realistic and has ups and downs. You will experience some weeks where your stress level will decline and, at other times, your stress may increase. To obtain your average stress change number for each week, refer to your Daily Stress Record for that particular week.

To help you stay on track, you can set goals for how much you would like to reduce your stress by certain landmark dates. For example, your anniversary may be at week 6, your daughter's birthday at week 11, and New Year's at week 15, as shown on the sample worksheet. When you reach the dates you select, you can see if you are accomplishing your goals and whether you need to work harder.

Take a few minutes to pencil in some landmark dates on the Average Stress Change Worksheet on page 430. Remember, this is each week's *average* stress level, so you will be making one entry on this worksheet each week. When your landmark dates come around, compare them with your actual stress level to see if you are achieving your goals.

A Word About Goal Setting

Setting realistic goals is the best way to assure your success in learning to master your stress. Many people begin stress management programs with a specific goal in mind. Some people expect to significantly reduce their stress by reading a book or attending a one-day seminar, but their hopes quickly fade when their stress returns.

These examples highlight the importance of setting reasonable goals. Many people set themselves up for failure by setting unrealistic goals for learning to manage their stress. If you set reasonable goals, you will enjoy a sense of accomplishment when you achieve them. This, in turn, will boost your self-esteem, increase self-confidence, and will help motivate you to do more.

The process of change is slow, and there will be weeks when your stress level may rise a bit. Don't panic! Instead, look for patterns and trends and try to figure out what you did differently that week. Use the less-than-perfect weeks as opportunities to reassess your weaker points and work on them. Use your strengths to help improve the areas that need more work. Remember to set reasonable goals and don't get discouraged with slow progress—many worthwhile changes take time and effort to realize positive results.

Average Stress Change Worksheet

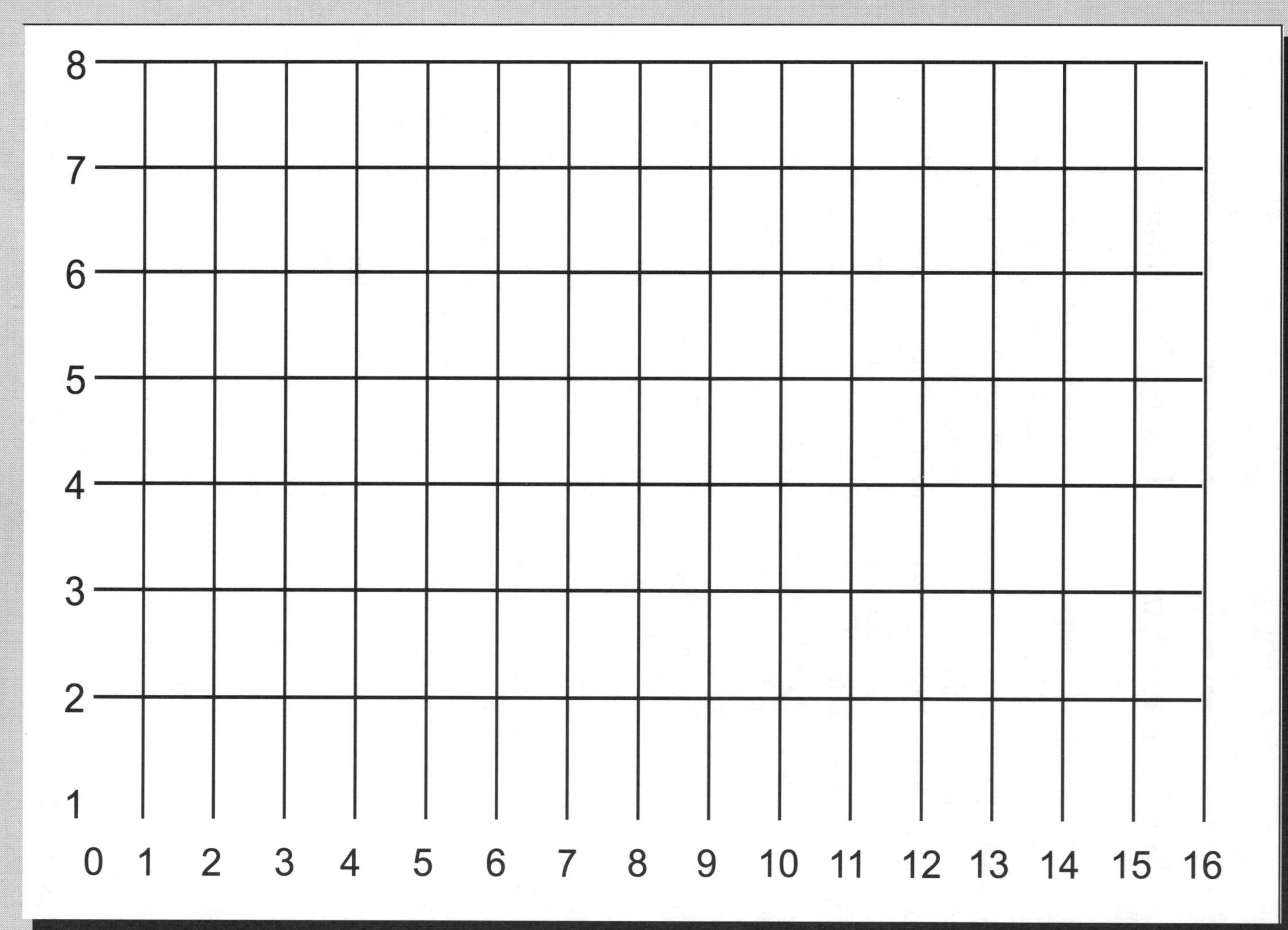

Week

Appendix F

Physical Activity and Relaxation Worksheet

The Physical Activity and Relaxation Worksheet will help you track your progress. At the end of each week, record the number of minutes you were active and the number of minutes you practiced relaxation techniques. You can complete this record by taking the information from your Daily Stress Record. After you complete the first worksheet for weeks 5–8, on page 432, go to the second worksheet for weeks 9–12, on page 433, and then go to the third worksheet for weeks 13–16, on page 434. Good luck keeping this important worksheet.

Physical Activity

The current exercise guidelines recommend 30 minutes of cumulative physical activity. Don't feel overwhelmed by the idea of exercising 30 minutes each day—all activity counts. Physical activity is not limited to a two-hour workout at the local gym. Several five-minute walks taken throughout the day also count. If you park your car in the faraway spots where the people with new cars park, count the extra steps as exercise. Household chores like vacuuming, raking leaves, and walking the dog also count as exercise. Be sure you include programmed activity, such as playing tennis, cycling, jogging, or dancing, in your daily total.

Relaxation Practice

Deep muscle relaxation is a skill that requires a great deal of practice. We recommend that you practice this technique at least twice a day for 20 minutes each time. This exercise practice should become a regular part of your daily routine and is an important step in stress management.

Look at the consistency of your practice sessions. You may become bored or find that practicing twice a day was awkward. If so, don't despair. This is common among individuals learning this skill. Practice is the key to mastering this technique.

Physical Activity and Relaxation Worksheet

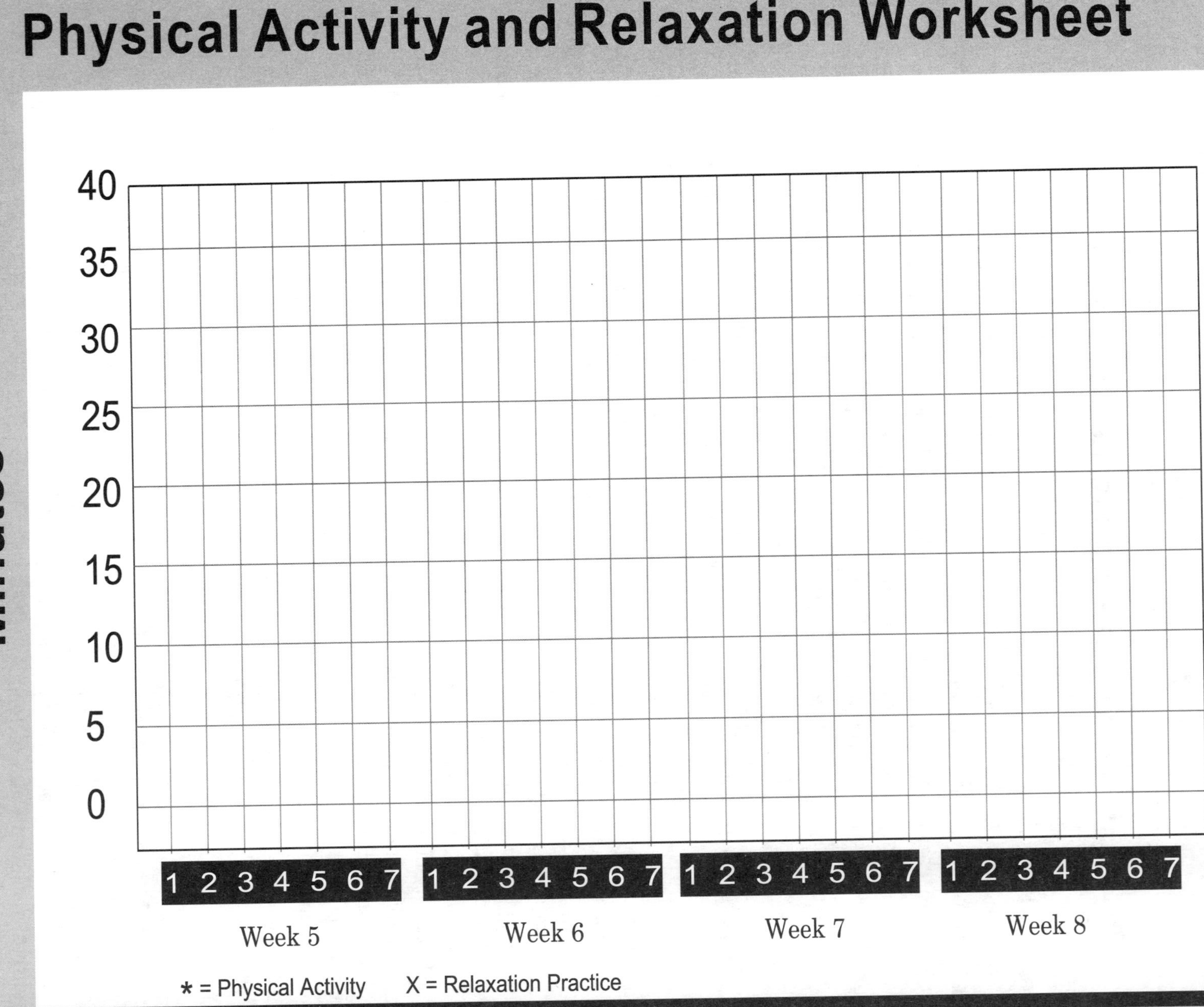

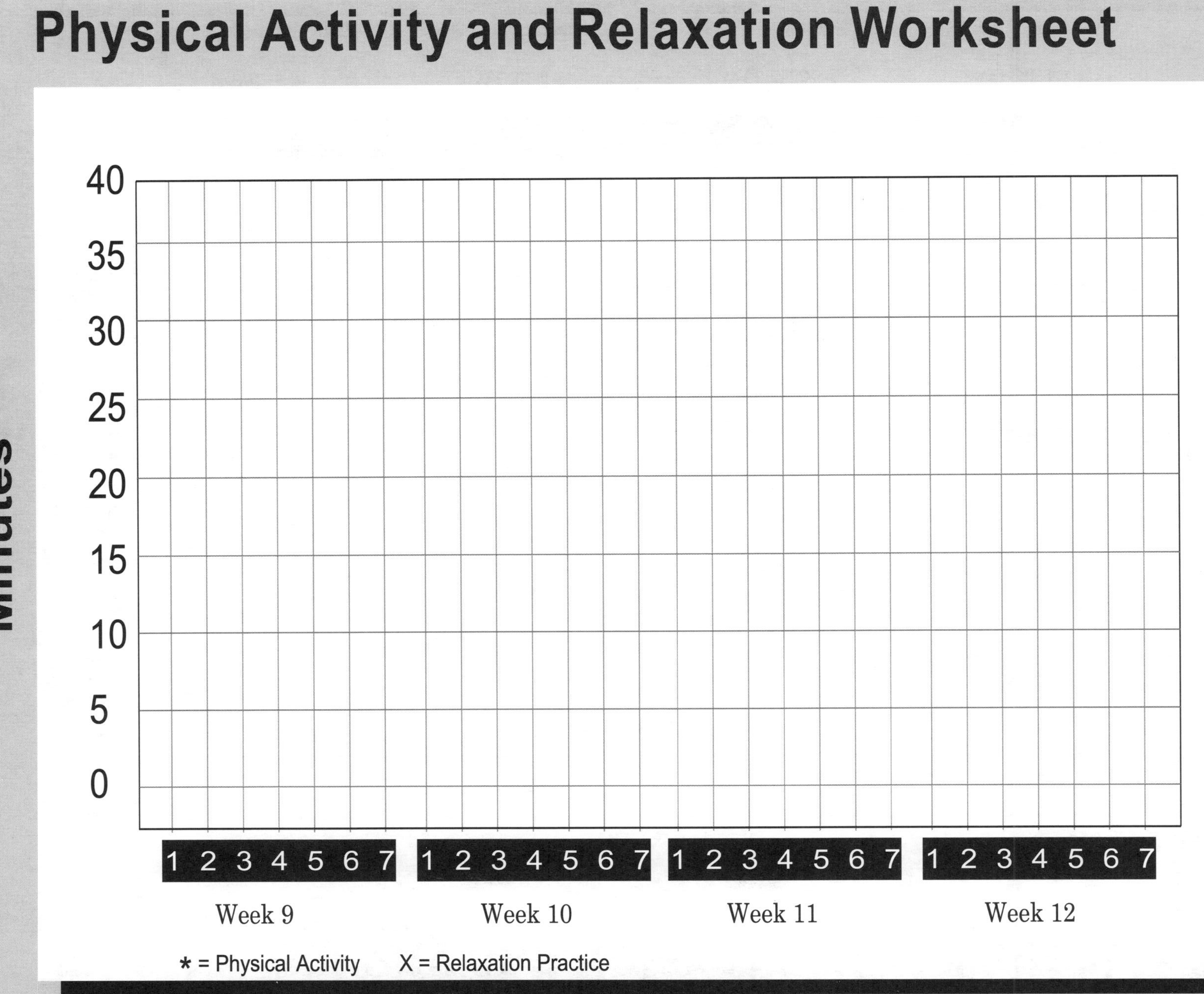
Physical Activity and Relaxation Worksheet
Minutes
40
35
30
25
20
15
10
5
0
1 2 3 4 5 6 7
1 2 3 4 5 6 7
1 2 3 4 5 6 7
1 2 3 4 5 6 7
Week 9
Week 10
Week 11
Week 12
* = Physical Activity
X = Relaxation Practice

Physical Activity and Relaxation Worksheet

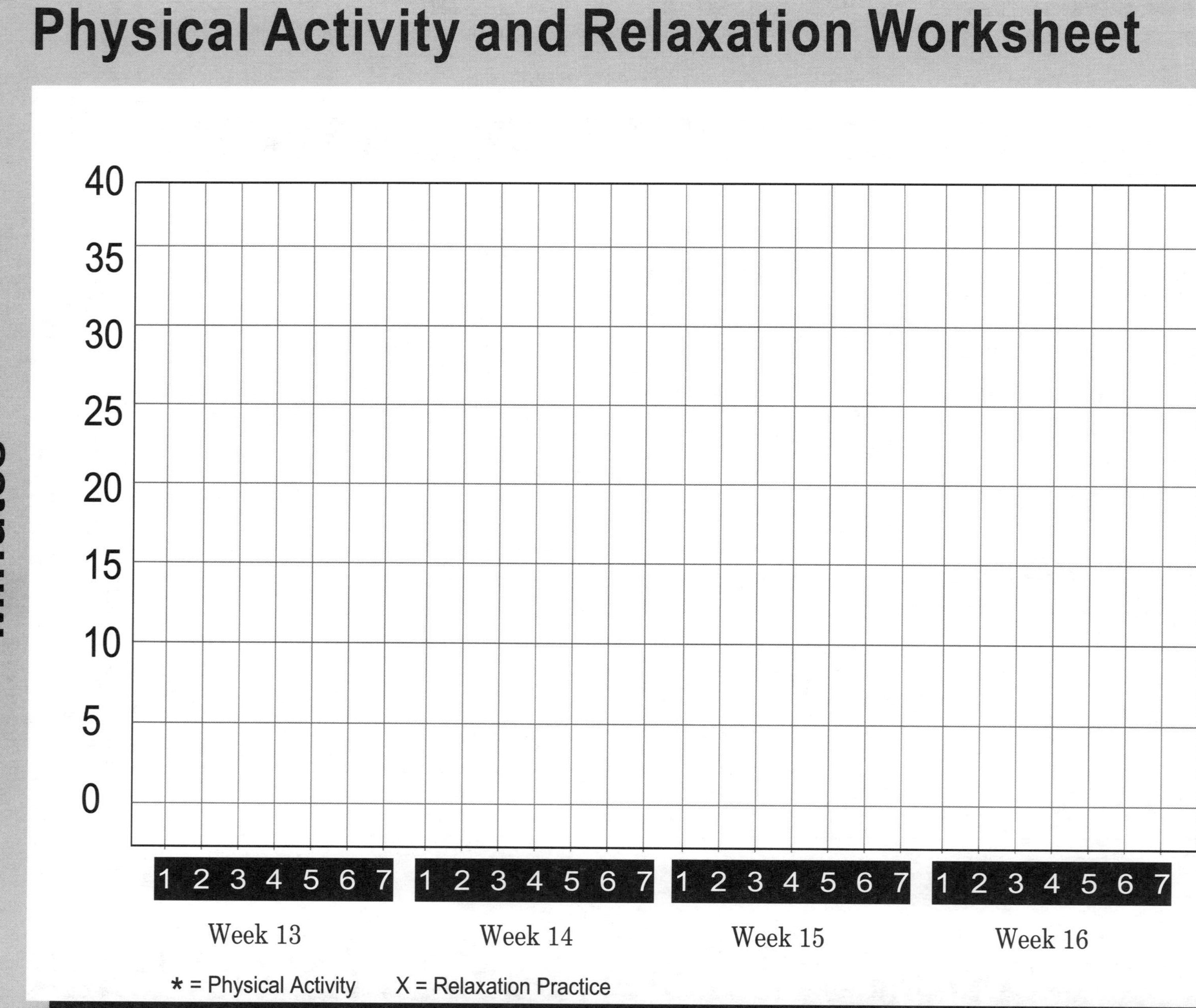

* = Physical Activity X = Relaxation Practice

Rate Your Diet Quiz—Lesson Ten

The following questions will give you a rough sketch of your typical eating habits. The (+) or (-) number for each answer instantly pats you on the back for good eating habits or alerts you to problems you didn't even know you had. The quiz focuses on fat, saturated fat, cholesterol, sodium, sugar, fiber, and fruits and vegetables. It doesn't attempt to cover everything in your diet. Also, it doesn't try to measure precisely how much of the key nutrients you eat. Next to each answer is a number with a + or - sign in front of it. Circle the number that corresponds to the answer you choose and write that score (e.g., +1) in the space provided in front of each question. That's your score for the question. If two or more answers apply, circle each one. Then average them to get your score for the question.

How to average. In answering question 19, for example, if your sandwich-eating is equally divided among tuna salad (-2), roast beef (+1), and turkey breast (+3), add the three scores (which gives you +2) and then divide by three. That gives you a score of +⅔ for the question. Round it to +1. Pay attention to serving sizes, which are given when needed. For example, a serving of vegetables is ½ cup. If you usually eat one cup of vegetables at a time, count it as two servings. If you're ready, let's start.

Fruits, Vegetables, Grains, and Beans

____ 1. How many servings of fruit or 100% fruit juice do you eat per day? *(OMIT fruit snacks like Fruit Roll-Ups and fruit-on-the-bottom yogurt. One serving = one piece or ½ cup of fruit or 6 oz of fruit juice.)*

- -3 None
- -2 Less than 1 serving
- 0 1 serving
- +1 2 serving
- +2 3 serving
- +3 4 or more servings

____ 2. How many servings of non-fried vegetables do you eat per day? *(One serving = ½ cup. Include potatoes.)*

- -3 None
- -2 Less than 1 serving
- 0 1 serving
- +1 2 serving
- +2 3 serving
- +3 4 or more servings

____ 3. How many servings of vitamin-rich vegetables do you eat per week? *(One serving = ½ cup. Only count broccoli, Brussels sprouts, carrots, collards, kale, red pepper, spinach, sweet potatoes, or winter squash.)*

- -3 None
- +1 1 to 3 servings
- +2 4 to 6 servings
- +3 7 or more servings

____ 4. How many servings of leafy green vegetables do you eat per week? *(One serving = ½ cup cooked or 1 cup raw. Only count collards, kale, mustard greens, romaine lettuce, spinach, or Swiss chard.)*

- -3 None
- -2 Less than 1 serving
- +1 1 to 2 servings
- +2 3 to 4 servings
- +3 5 or more servings

____ 5. How many times per week does your lunch or dinner contain grains, vegetables, or beans, but little or no meat, poultry, fish, eggs, or cheese?

- -1 None
- +1 1 to 2 times
- +2 3 to 4 times
- +3 5 or more times

____ 6. How many times per week do you eat beans, split peas, or lentils? *(Omit green beans.)*

- -3 None
- -1 Less than 1 time
- 0 1 times
- +1 2 times
- +2 3 times
- +3 4 or more times

____ 7. How many servings of grains do you eat per day? *(One serving = 1 slice of bread, 1 oz of crackers, 1 large pancake, 1 cup pasta or cold cereal, or ½ cup granola, cooked cereal, rice, or bulgur. Omit heavily sweetened cold cereals.)*

- -3 None
- 0 1 to 2 servings
- +1 3 to 4 servings
- +2 5 to 7 servings
- +3 8 or more servings

____ 8. What type of bread, rolls, etc., do you eat?

- +3 100% whole wheat as the only flour
- +2 Whole-wheat flour as 1st or 2nd flour
- +1 Rye, pumpernickel, or oatmeal
- 0 White, French, or Italian

____ 9. What kind of breakfast do you eat?

- +3 Whole-grain (like oatmeal or Wheaties)
- 0 Low-fiber (like Cream of Wheat or Corn Flakes)
- -1 Sugary low-fiber (like Frosted Flakes or low-fat granola)
- -2 Regular granola

Meat, Poultry, and Seafood

____ 10. How many times per week do you eat high-fat red meats *(hamburgers, pork chops, ribs, hot dogs, pot roast, sausage, bologna, steaks other than round steak, etc.)*?

+3 None
+2 Less than 1 time
-1 1 time
-2 2 times
-3 3 times
-4 4 times

____ 11. How many times per week do you eat lean red meats *(hot dogs or luncheon meats with no more than 2 grams of fat per serving, round steak, or pork tenderloin)*?

+3 None
+1 Less than 1 time
0 1 time
-1 2 to 3 times
-2 4 to 5 times
-3 6 or more times

____ 12. After cooking, how large is the serving of red meat you eat? *(To convert from raw to cooked, reduce by 25 percent. For example, 4 oz of raw meat shrinks to 3 oz after cooking. There are 16 oz in a pound).*

-3 6 oz or more
-2 4 to 5 oz
0 3 oz or less
+3 Don't eat red meat

____ 13. If you eat red meat, do you trim the visible fat when you cook or eat it?

+1 Yes
-3 No

____ 14. What kind of ground meat or poultry do you eat?

-4 Regular ground beef
-3 Ground beef that's 11 to 25% fat
-2 Ground chicken or 10% fat ground beef
-1 Ground turkey
+3 Ground turkey breast
+3 Don't eat ground meat or poultry

____ 15. What chicken parts do you eat?

+3 Breast
+1 Drumstick
-1 Thigh
-2 Wing
+3 Don't eat poultry

____ 16. If you eat poultry, do you remove the skin before eating?

+2 Yes
-3 No

____ 17. If you eat seafood, how many times per week? *(Omit deep-fried foods, tuna packed in oil, and mayonnaise-laden tuna salad—low-fat mayo is okay.)*

0 Less than 1 time
+1 1 time
+2 2 times
+3 3 or more times

Mixed Foods

____ 18. What is your most typical breakfast? *(Subtract an extra 3 points if you also eat sausage.)*

-4 Biscuit sandwich or croissant sandwich
-3 Croissant, Danish, or doughnut
-3 Eggs
-1 Pancakes, French toast, or waffles
+3 Cereal, toast, or bagel (no cream cheese)
+3 Low-fat yogurt or low-fat cottage cheese
0 Don't eat breakfast

____ 19. What sandwich fillings do you eat?

-3 Regular luncheon meat, cheese, or egg salad
-2 Tuna or chicken salad or ham
0 Peanut butter
+1 Roast beef
+1 Low-fat luncheon meat
+3 Tuna or chicken salad made with fat-free mayo
+3 Turkey breast or humus

____ 20. What do you order on your pizza? *(Subtract 1 point if you order extra cheese, cheese-filled crust, or more than one meat topping).*

+3 No cheese with at least one vegetable topping
-1 Cheese with at least one vegetable topping
-2 Cheese
-3 Cheese with one meat topping
+3 Don't eat pizza

____ 21. What do you put on your pasta? *(Add one point if you also add sautéed vegetables.)*

+3 Tomato sauce or red clam sauce
-1 Meat sauce or meat balls
-3 Pesto or another oily sauce
-4 Alfredo or another creamy sauce

____22. How many times per week do you eat deep-fried foods *(fish, chicken, French fries, potato chips, etc.)?*

+3 None
0 1 time
-1 2 times
-2 3 times
-3 4 or more times

____23. At a salad bar, what do you choose?

+3 Nothing, lemon, or vinegar
+2 Fat-free dressing
+1 Low- or reduced-calorie dressing
-1 Oil and vinegar
-2 Regular dressing
-2 Cole slaw, pasta salad, or potato salad
-3 Cheese or eggs

____24. How many times per week do you eat canned or dried soups or frozen dinners? *(Omit lower-sodium, low-fat ones.)*

+3 None
0 1 time
-1 2 times
-2 3 to 4 times
-3 5 or more times

____25. How many servings of low-fat calcium-rich foods do you eat per day? *(One serving = ⅔ cup low-fat or nonfat milk or yogurt, 1 oz low-fat cheese, 1½ oz sardines, 3½ oz canned salmon with bones, 1 oz tofu made with calcium sulfate, 1 cup collards or kale, or 200 mg of a calcium supplement.)*

-3 None
-1 Less than 1 serving
+1 1 serving
+2 2 servings
+3 3 or more servings

____26. How many times per week do you eat cheese? *(Include pizza, cheeseburgers, lasagna, tacos or nachos with cheese, etc. Omit foods made with low-fat cheese.)*

+3 None
+1 1 time
-1 2 times
-2 3 times
-3 4 or more times

____27. How many egg yolks do you eat per week? *(Add 1 yolk for every slice of quiche you eat.)*

+3 None
+1 1 yolk
0 2 yolks
-1 3 yolks
-2 4 yolks
-3 5 or more yolks

Fats & Oils

____28. What do you put on your bread, toast, bagel, or English muffin?

-4 Stick butter or cream cheese
-3 Stick margarine or whipped butter
-2 Regular tub margarine
-1 Light tub margarine or whipped light butter
0 Jam, fat-free margarine, or fat-free cream cheese
+3 Nothing

____29. What do you spread on your sandwiches?

-2 Mayonnaise
-1 Light mayonnaise
+1 Catsup, mustard, or fat-free mayonnaise
+2 Nothing

____30. With what do you make tuna salad, pasta salad, chicken salad, etc.?

-2 Mayonnaise
-1 Light mayonnaise
0 Fat-free mayonnaise
+2 Nothing

____31. What do you use to saute vegetables or other food? *(Vegetable oil includes safflower, corn, sunflower, and soybean.)*

-3 Butter or lard
-2 Margarine
-1 Vegetable oil or light margarine
+1 Olive or canola oil
+2 Broth
+3 Cooking spray

Beverages

____32. What do you drink on a typical day?

+3 Water or club soda
0 Caffeine-free coffee or tea
-1 Diet soda
-1 Coffee or tea (up to 4 a day)
-2 Regular soda (up to 2 a day)
-3 Regular soda (3 or more a day)
-3 Coffee or tea (5 or more a day)

____33. What kind of "fruit" beverage do you drink?

+3 Orange, grapefruit, prune, or pineapple juice
+1 Apple, grape, or pear juice
0 Cranberry juice blend or cocktail
-3 Fruit "drink," "ade," or "punch"

Rate Your Diet Quiz—Lesson Ten (continued)

____ 34. What kind of milk do you drink?

- -3 Whole
- -1 2% fat
- +2 1% low-fat
- +3 skim

____ 35. What do you eat as a snack?

- +3 Fruits or vegetables
- +2 Low-fat yogurt
- +1 Low-fat crackers
- -2 Cookies or fried chips
- -2 Nuts or granola bar
- -3 Candy bar or pastry

____ 36. Which of the following "salty" snacks do you eat?

- -3 Potato chips, corn chips, or popcorn
- -2 Tortilla chips
- -1 Salted pretzels or light microwave popcorn
- +2 Unsalted pretzels
- +3 Baked tortilla or potato chips or homemade air-popped popcorn
- +3 Don't eat salty snacks

____ 37. What kind of cookies do you eat?

- +2 Fat-free cookies
- +1 Graham crackers or reduced-fat cookies
- -1 Oatmeal cookies
- -2 Sandwich cookies (like Oreos)
- -3 Chocolate coated, chocolate chip, or peanut butter cookies
- +3 Don't eat cookies

____ 38. What kind of cake or pastry do you eat?

- -4 Cheesecake
- -3 Pie or doughnuts
- -2 Cake with frosting
- -1 Cake without frosting
- 0 Muffins
- +1 Angle food, fat-free cake, or fat-free pastry
- +3 Don't eat cakes or pastries

____ 39. What kind of frozen dessert do you eat? *(Subtract 1 point for each of the following toppings: hot fudge, nuts, or chocolate candy bars or pieces.)*

- -4 Gourmet ice cream
- -3 Regular ice cream
- -1 Frozen yogurt or light ice cream
- -1 Sorbet, sherbet, or ices
- +1 Nonfat frozen yogurt or fat-free ice cream
- +3 Don't eat frozen desserts

____ **Total Score**

Add up your score for each question and write it in the total score line above. **If your score is:**

1 to 29	Don't be discouraged. Eating healthy is tough, but you can learn to eat healthier.
30 to 59	Congratulations. Your are doing just fine. Pin your quiz to the nearest wall.
60 or above	Excellent. You're a nutrition superstar. Give yourself a big pat on the back.

Source: Adapted with permission from *Nutrition Action Healthletter*, May 1996, V23/N4. (*Nutrition Action Healthletter*, 1875 Connecticut Ave., N.W., Suite 300, Washington DC 20009-5728. $24 for 10 issues.)

Rate Your Diet Quiz—Lesson Fourteen

The following questions will give you a rough sketch of your typical eating habits. The (+) or (-) number for each answer instantly pats you on the back for good eating habits or alerts you to problems you didn't even know you had. The quiz focuses on fat, saturated fat, cholesterol, sodium, sugar, fiber, and fruits and vegetables. It doesn't attempt to cover everything in your diet. Also, it doesn't try to measure precisely how much of the key nutrients you eat. Next to each answer is a number with a + or - sign in front of it. Circle the number that corresponds to the answer you choose and write that score (e.g., +1) in the space provided in front of each question. That's your score for the question. If two or more answers apply, circle each one. Then average them to get your score for the question.

How to average. In answering question 19, for example, if your sandwich-eating is equally divided among tuna salad (-2), roast beef (+1), and turkey breast (+3), add the three scores (which gives you +2) and then divide by three. That gives you a score of +⅔ for the question. Round it to +1. Pay attention to serving sizes, which are given when needed. For example, a serving of vegetables is ½ cup. If you usually eat one cup of vegetables at a time, count it as two servings. If you're ready, let's start.

Fruits, Vegetables, Grains, and Beans

____ 1. How many servings of fruit or 100% fruit juice do you eat per day? *(OMIT fruit snacks like Fruit Roll-Ups and fruit-on-the-bottom yogurt. One serving = one piece or ½ cup of fruit or 6 oz of fruit juice.)*

- -3 None
- -2 Less than 1 serving
- 0 1 serving
- +1 2 serving
- +2 3 serving
- +3 4 or more servings

____ 2. How many servings of non-fried vegetables do you eat per day? *(One serving = ½ cup. Include potatoes.)*

- -3 None
- -2 Less than 1 serving
- 0 1 serving
- +1 2 serving
- +2 3 serving
- +3 4 or more servings

____ 3. How many servings of vitamin-rich vegetables do you eat per week? *(One serving = ½ cup. Only count broccoli, Brussels sprouts, carrots, collards, kale, red pepper, spinach, sweet potatoes, or winter squash.)*

- -3 None
- +1 1 to 3 servings
- +2 4 to 6 servings
- +3 7 or more servings

____ 4. How many servings of leafy green vegetables do you eat per week? *(One serving = ½ cup cooked or 1 cup raw. Only count collards, kale, mustard greens, romaine lettuce, spinach, or Swiss chard.)*

- -3 None
- -2 Less than 1 serving
- +1 1 to 2 servings
- +2 3 to 4 servings
- +3 5 or more servings

____ 5. How many times per week does your lunch or dinner contain grains, vegetables, or beans, but little or no meat, poultry, fish, eggs, or cheese?

- -1 None
- +1 1 to 2 times
- +2 3 to 4 times
- +3 5 or more times

____ 6. How many times per week do you eat beans, split peas, or lentils? *(Omit green beans.)*

- -3 None
- -1 Less than 1 time
- 0 1 times
- +1 2 times
- +2 3 times
- +3 4 or more times

____ 7. How many servings of grains do you eat per day? *(One serving = 1 slice of bread, 1 oz of crackers, 1 large pancake, 1 cup pasta or cold cereal, or ½ cup granola, cooked cereal, rice, or bulgur. Omit heavily sweetened cold cereals.)*

- -3 None
- 0 1 to 2 servings
- +1 3 to 4 servings
- +2 5 to 7 servings
- +3 8 or more servings

____ 8. What type of bread, rolls, etc., do you eat?

- +3 100% whole wheat as the only flour
- +2 Whole-wheat flour as 1st or 2nd flour
- +1 Rye, pumpernickel, or oatmeal
- 0 White, French, or Italian

____ 9. What kind of breakfast do you eat?

- +3 Whole-grain (like oatmeal or Wheaties)
- 0 Low-fiber (like Cream of Wheat or Corn Flakes)
- -1 Sugary low-fiber (like Frosted Flakes or low-fat granola)
- -2 Regular granola

Meat, Poultry, and Seafood

____ 10. How many times per week do you eat high-fat red meats *(hamburgers, pork chops, ribs, hot dogs, pot roast, sausage, bologna, steaks other than round steak, etc.)*?

+3 None
+2 Less than 1 time
-1 1 time
-2 2 times
-3 3 times
-4 4 times

____ 11. How many times per week do you eat lean red meats *(hot dogs or luncheon meats with no more than 2 grams of fat per serving, round steak, or pork tenderloin)*?

+3 None
+1 Less than 1 time
0 1 time
-1 2 to 3 times
-2 4 to 5 times
-3 6 or more times

____ 12. After cooking, how large is the serving of red meat you eat? *(To convert from raw to cooked, reduce by 25 percent. For example, 4 oz of raw meat shrinks to 3 oz after cooking. There are 16 oz in a pound).*

-3 6 oz or more
-2 4 to 5 oz
0 3 oz or less
+3 Don't eat red meat

____ 13. If you eat red meat, do you trim the visible fat when you cook or eat it?

+1 Yes
-3 No

____ 14. What kind of ground meat or poultry do you eat?

-4 Regular ground beef
-3 Ground beef that's 11 to 25% fat
-2 Ground chicken or 10% fat ground beef
-1 Ground turkey
+3 Ground turkey breast
+3 Don't eat ground meat or poultry

____ 15. What chicken parts do you eat?

+3 Breast
+1 Drumstick
-1 Thigh
-2 Wing
+3 Don't eat poultry

____ 16. If you eat poultry, do you remove the skin before eating?

+2 Yes
-3 No

____ 17. If you eat seafood, how many times per week? *(Omit deep-fried foods, tuna packed in oil, and mayonnaise-laden tuna salad—low-fat mayo is okay.)*

0 Less than 1 time
+1 1 time
+2 2 times
+3 3 or more times

Mixed Foods

____ 18. What is your most typical breakfast? *(Subtract an extra 3 points if you also eat sausage.)*

-4 Biscuit sandwich or croissant sandwich
-3 Croissant, Danish, or doughnut
-3 Eggs
-1 Pancakes, French toast, or waffles
+3 Cereal, toast, or bagel (no cream cheese)
+3 Low-fat yogurt or low-fat cottage cheese
0 Don't eat breakfast

____ 19. What sandwich fillings do you eat?

-3 Regular luncheon meat, cheese, or egg salad
-2 Tuna or chicken salad or ham
0 Peanut butter
+1 Roast beef
+1 Low-fat luncheon meat
+3 Tuna or chicken salad made with fat-free mayo
+3 Turkey breast or humus

____ 20. What do you order on your pizza? *(Subtract 1 point if you order extra cheese, cheese-filled crust, or more than one meat topping).*

+3 No cheese with at least one vegetable topping
-1 Cheese with at least one vegetable topping
-2 Cheese
-3 Cheese with one meat topping
+3 Don't eat pizza

____ 21. What do you put on your pasta? *(Add one point if you also add sautéed vegetables.)*

+3 Tomato sauce or red clam sauce
-1 Meat sauce or meat balls
-3 Pesto or another oily sauce
-4 Alfredo or another creamy sauce

____22. How many times per week do you eat deep-fried foods (*fish, chicken, French fries, potato chips, etc.*)?

+3	None
0	1 time
-1	2 times
-2	3 times
-3	4 or more times

____ 23. At a salad bar, what do you choose?

+3	Nothing, lemon, or vinegar
+2	Fat-free dressing
+1	Low- or reduced-calorie dressing
-1	Oil and vinegar
-2	Regular dressing
-2	Cole slaw, pasta salad, or potato salad
-3	Cheese or eggs

____ 24. How many times per week do you eat canned or dried soups or frozen dinners? *(Omit lower-sodium, low-fat ones.)*

+3	None
0	1 time
-1	2 times
-2	3 to 4 times
-3	5 or more times

____ 25. How many servings of low-fat calcium-rich foods do you eat per day? (*One serving = ⅔ cup low-fat or nonfat milk or yogurt, 1 oz low-fat cheese, 1½ oz sardines, 3½ oz canned salmon with bones, 1 oz tofu made with calcium sulfate, 1 cup collards or kale, or 200 mg of a calcium supplement.)*

-3	None
-1	Less than 1 serving
+1	1 serving
+2	2 servings
+3	3 or more servings

____ 26. How many times per week do you eat cheese? *(Include pizza, cheeseburgers, lasagna, tacos or nachos with cheese, etc. Omit foods made with low-fat cheese.)*

+3	None
+1	1 time
-1	2 times
-2	3 times
-3	4 or more times

____ 27. How many egg yolks do you eat per week? *(Add 1 yolk for every slice of quiche you eat.)*

+3	None
+1	1 yolk
0	2 yolks
-1	3 yolks
-2	4 yolks
-3	5 or more yolks

Fats & Oils

____28. What do you put on your bread, toast, bagel, or English muffin?

-4	Stick butter or cream cheese
-3	Stick margarine or whipped butter
-2	Regular tub margarine
-1	Light tub margarine or whipped light butter
0	Jam, fat-free margarine, or fat-free cream cheese
+3	Nothing

____ 29. What do you spread on your sandwiches?

-2	Mayonnaise
-1	Light mayonnaise
+1	Catsup, mustard, or fat-free mayonnaise
+2	Nothing

____ 30. With what do you make tuna salad, pasta salad, chicken salad, etc.?

-2	Mayonnaise
-1	Light mayonnaise
0	Fat-free mayonnaise
+2	Nothing

____ 31. What do you use to saute vegetables or other food? *(Vegetable oil includes safflower, corn, sunflower, and soybean.)*

-3	Butter or lard
-2	Margarine
-1	Vegetable oil or light margarine
+1	Olive or canola oil
+2	Broth
+3	Cooking spray

Beverages

____ 32. What do you drink on a typical day?

+3	Water or club soda
0	Caffeine-free coffee or tea
-1	Diet soda
-1	Coffee or tea (up to 4 a day)
-2	Regular soda (up to 2 a day)
-3	Regular soda (3 or more a day)
-3	Coffee or tea (5 or more a day)

____ 33. What kind of "fruit" beverage do you drink?

+3	Orange, grapefruit, prune, or pineapple juice
+1	Apple, grape, or pear juice
0	Cranberry juice blend or cocktail
-3	Fruit "drink," "ade," or "punch"

Rate Your Diet Quiz—Lesson Fourteen (continued)

____ 34. What kind of milk do you drink?

-3	Whole
-1	2% fat
+2	1% low-fat
+3	skim

____35. What do you eat as a snack?

+3	Fruits or vegetables
+2	Low-fat yogurt
+1	Low-fat crackers
-2	Cookies or fried chips
-2	Nuts or granola bar
-3	Candy bar or pastry

____ 36. Which of the following "salty" snacks do you eat?

-3	Potato chips, corn chips, or popcorn
-2	Tortilla chips
-1	Salted pretzels or light microwave popcorn
+2	Unsalted pretzels
+3	Baked tortilla or potato chips or homemade air-popped popcorn
+3	Don't eat salty snacks

____ 37. What kind of cookies do you eat?

+2	Fat-free cookies
+1	Graham crackers or reduced-fat cookies
-1	Oatmeal cookies
-2	Sandwich cookies (like Oreos)
-3	Chocolate coated, chocolate chip, or peanut butter cookies
+3	Don't eat cookies

____ 38. What kind of cake or pastry do you eat?

-4	Cheesecake
-3	Pie or doughnuts
-2	Cake with frosting
-1	Cake without frosting
0	Muffins
+1	Angle food, fat-free cake, or fat-free pastry
+3	Don't eat cakes or pastries

____ 39. What kind of frozen dessert do you eat? *(Subtract 1 point for each of the following toppings: hot fudge, nuts, or chocolate candy bars or pieces.)*

-4	Gourmet ice cream
-3	Regular ice cream
-1	Frozen yogurt or light ice cream
-1	Sorbet, sherbet, or ices
+1	Nonfat frozen yogurt or fat-free ice cream
+3	Don't eat frozen desserts

_____ **Total Score**

Add up your score for each question and write it in the total score line above. **If your score is:**

1 to 29	Don't be discouraged. Eating healthy is tough, but you can learn to eat healthier.
30 to 59	Congratulations. Your are doing just fine. Pin your quiz to the nearest wall.
60 or above	Excellent. You're a nutrition superstar. Give yourself a big pat on the back.

Source: Adapted with permission from *Nutrition Action Healthletter*, May 1996, V23/N4. (*Nutrition Action Healthletter*, 1875 Connecticut Ave., N.W., Suite 300, Washington DC 20009-5728. $24 for 10 issues.)

Index

E

F

G

H

I

J

K

S

T

U

V

W

X

Z